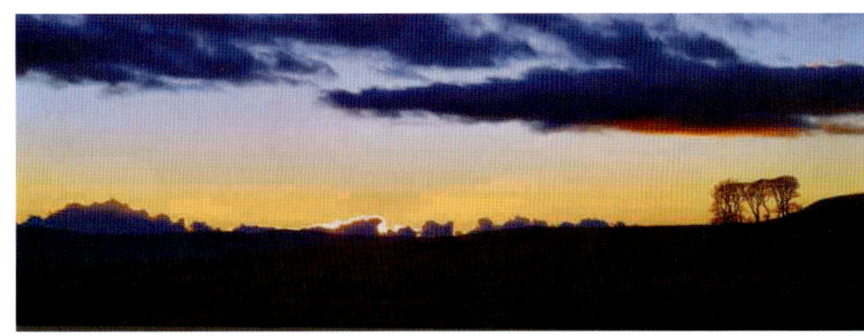

# COMPOSITION
# IN THE LANDSCAPE

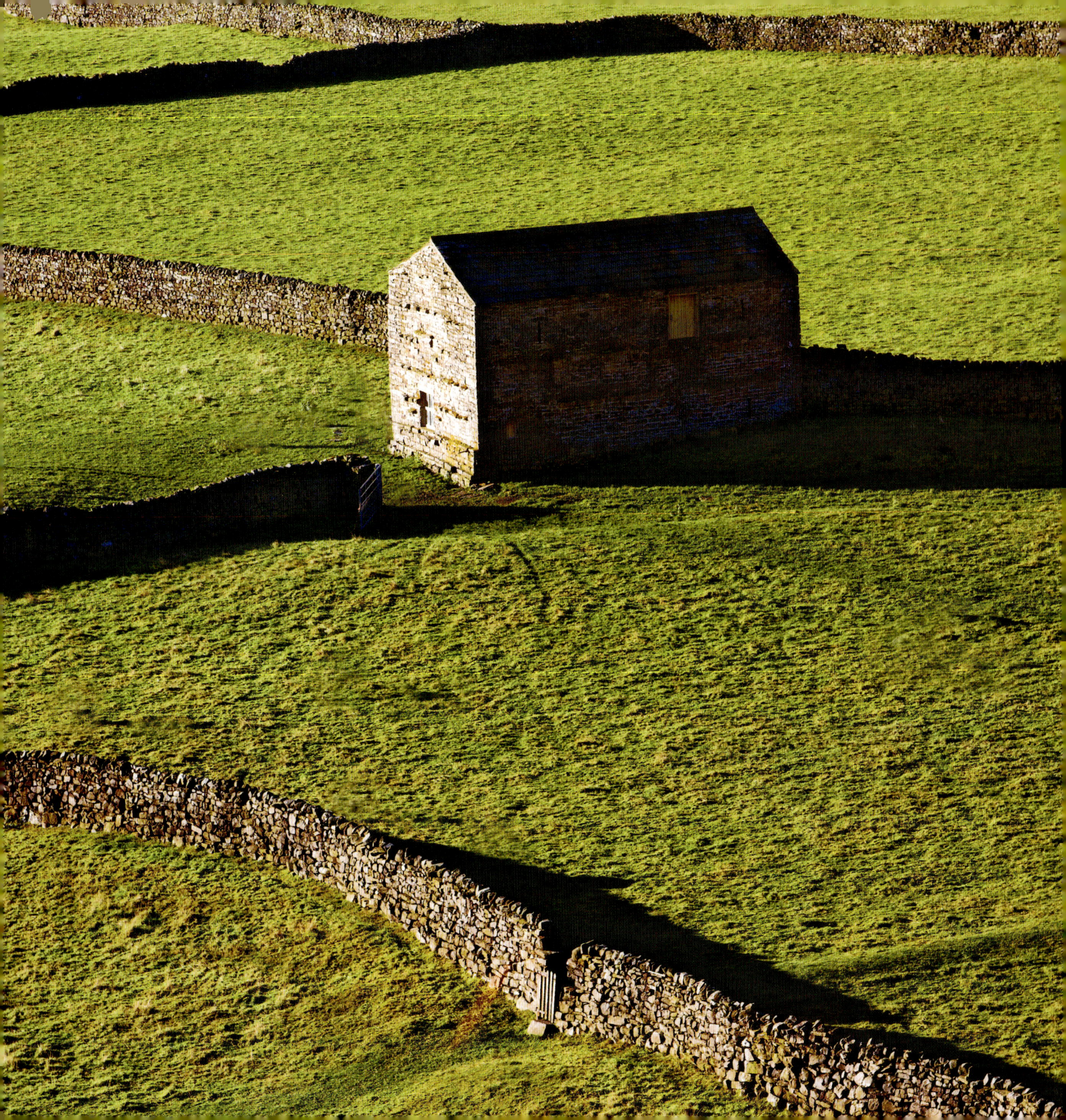

# COMPOSITION

## AN INSPIRATIONAL AND TECHNICAL GUIDE FOR PHOTOGRAPHERS

# IN THE LANDSCAPE

**PETER WATSON**

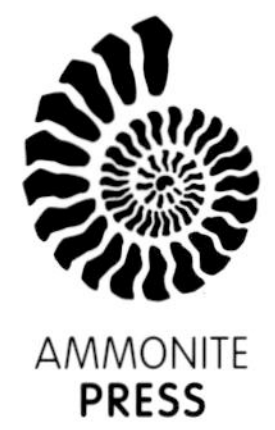

AMMONITE
PRESS

First published 2014 by
Ammonite Press
An imprint of AE Publications Ltd
166 High Street,
Lewes, East Sussex, BN7 1XU, UK



ISBN 978-1-78145-055-0



Publisher: Jonathan Bailey
Production Manager: Jim Bulley
Managing Editor: Gerrie Purcell
Senior Project Editor: Wendy McAngus
Editor: Sara Harper
Managing Art Editor: Gilda Pacitti
Designer: Robin Shields

Set in Syntax
Colour origination by GMC Reprographics
Printed and bound in China

PAGE 1

**Askrigg Common, The Yorkshire
Dales, England**

**Camera:** Mamiya 645 AFDII with Mamiya
digital back
**Lens:** Mamiya 150mm (telephoto)
**Filter:** 2-stop ND graduated
**Exposure:** 1/8sec at f/18, ISO 100
**Waiting for the light:** 30 minutes
**Post-processing:** Curves adjustment,
colour balance adjustment (warming)

PAGE 2

**Gunnerside, The Yorkshire Dales,
England**

**Camera:** Mamiya 645 AFDII with Mamiya
digital back
**Lens:** Mamiya 150mm (telephoto)
**Filter:** Polarizer (fully polarized)
**Exposure:** 1/15sec at f/16, ISO 100
**Waiting for the light:** 50 minutes
**Post-processing:** Curves adjustment

RIGHT

**Near Nenthead, Cumbria, England**

**Camera:** Mamiya 645 AFDII with Mamiya
digital back
**Lens:** Mamiya 35mm (wide-angle)
**Filter:** None
**Exposure:** 1/2sec at f/22, ISO 100
**Waiting for the light:** Immediate
**Post-processing:** Colour balance
adjustment (warming)

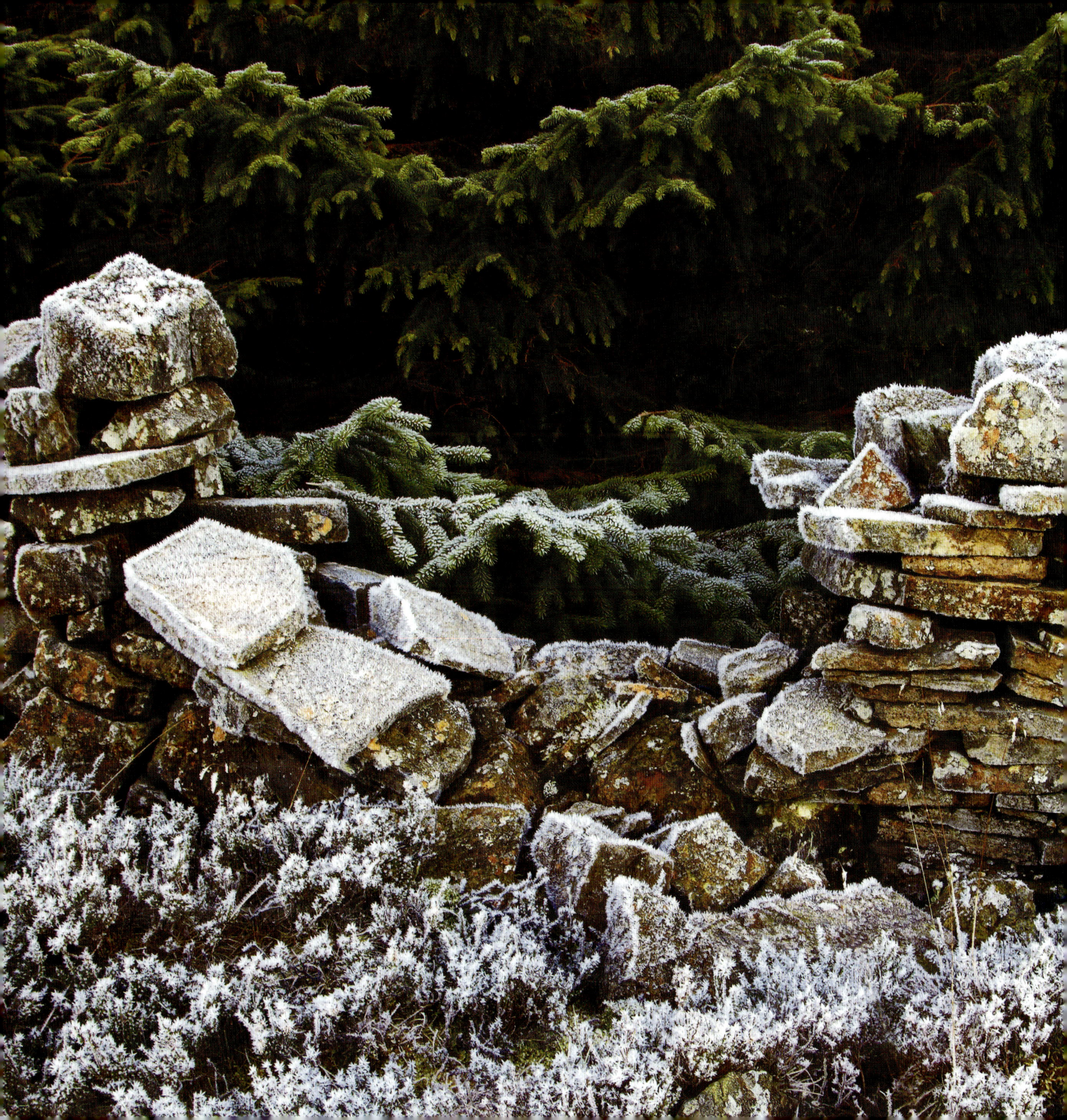

# CONTENTS

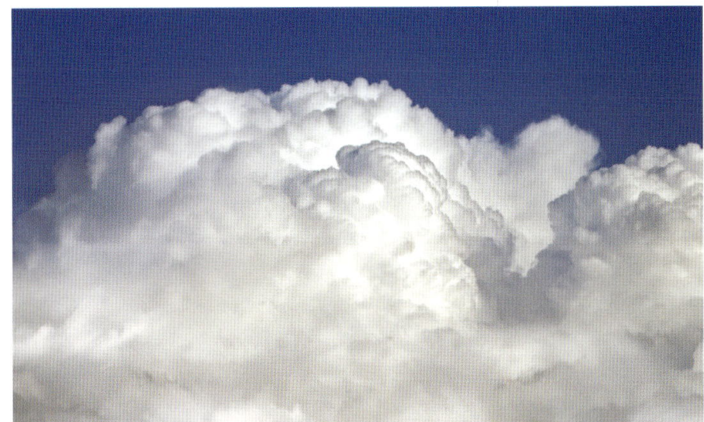

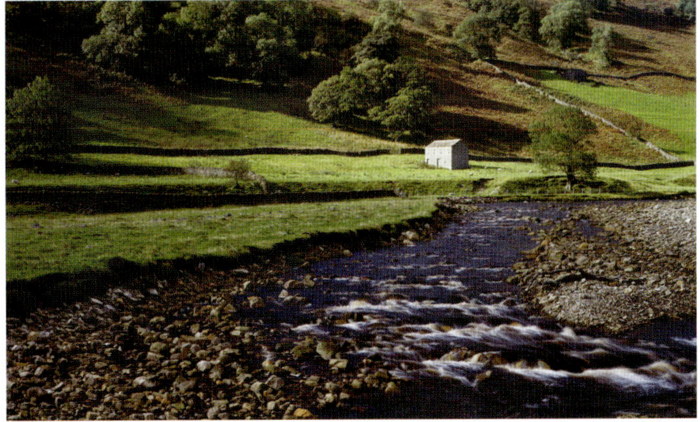





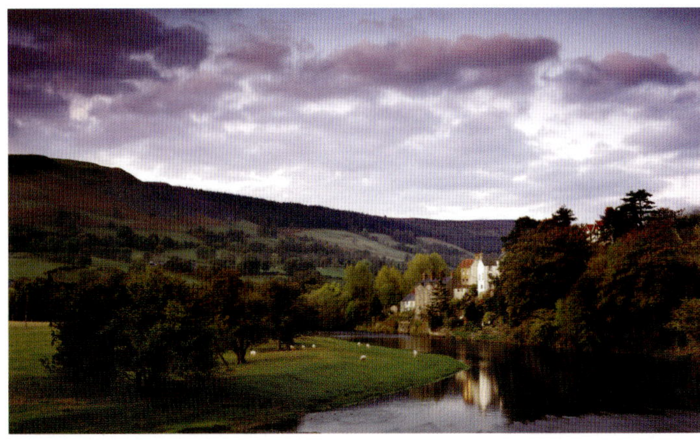

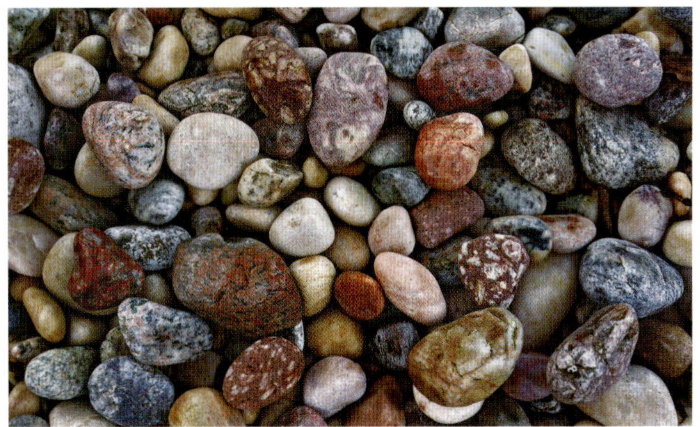

# > INTRODUCTION

Give three photographers an assignment to capture and depict the characteristics of
a specific location, and you will be presented with three sets of quite different images.
The place, the light and even the equipment used might all be identical, but as soon
as that crucial variable element – the photographer's vision – is introduced, results will
suddenly become diverse. Each photographer's approach will become the decisive factor,
and ultimately it will be their style and use of composition that determines the success or
otherwise of the assignment. The link between the right creative approach and success
is immutable – and it applies to every single picture we capture. How we view the
landscape, interpret its features and compose the photograph is, in this burgeoning era
of automated digital image-making, now more important than ever. The photographer's
input is of paramount importance and the development of a recognizable and creative
style is therefore a big step forward along the route to success.

Throughout this book we will consider every aspect of viewing the landscape and
composing images in such a way that they engage with the viewer and make a
lasting impression. We will also look at using light and colour to strengthen a picture's
composition, as well as covering the technical aspects of focusing, exposure and selecting
the right aperture and shutter speed. All the photographs in this book are supported by
descriptive text that reveals the techniques and creative processes that lie behind each
picture. Background information, some of my personal observations and anecdotes
concerning the practicalities of capturing images in ever-changing conditions are also
included. The aim of this book is to inspire and equip you with the knowledge to help
you produce photographs that are creatively composed and visually distinctive. As you
put into practice the techniques discussed throughout the book and venture out to
capture the captivating beauty of the landscape you will, I hope, discover that it is truly
a photographer's landscape.

**Cotterdale, North Yorkshire,
England**

**Camera:** Mamiya 645 AFDII with Mamiya
digital back
**Lens:** Mamiya 35mm (wide-angle)
**Filter:** 2-stop ND graduated
**Exposure:** 1/4sec at f/22, ISO 100
**Waiting for the light:** 45 minutes
**Post-processing:** Curves adjustment

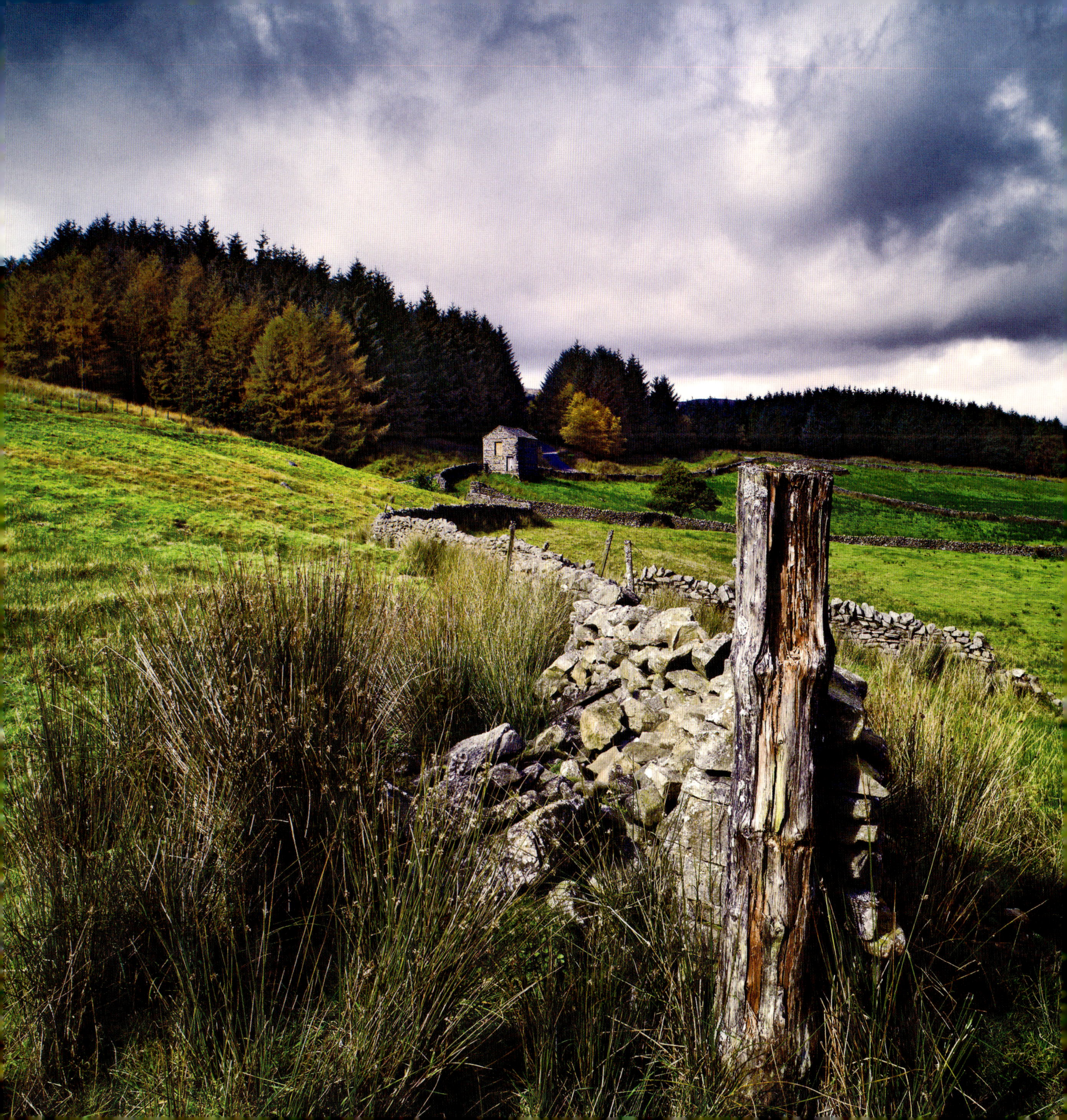

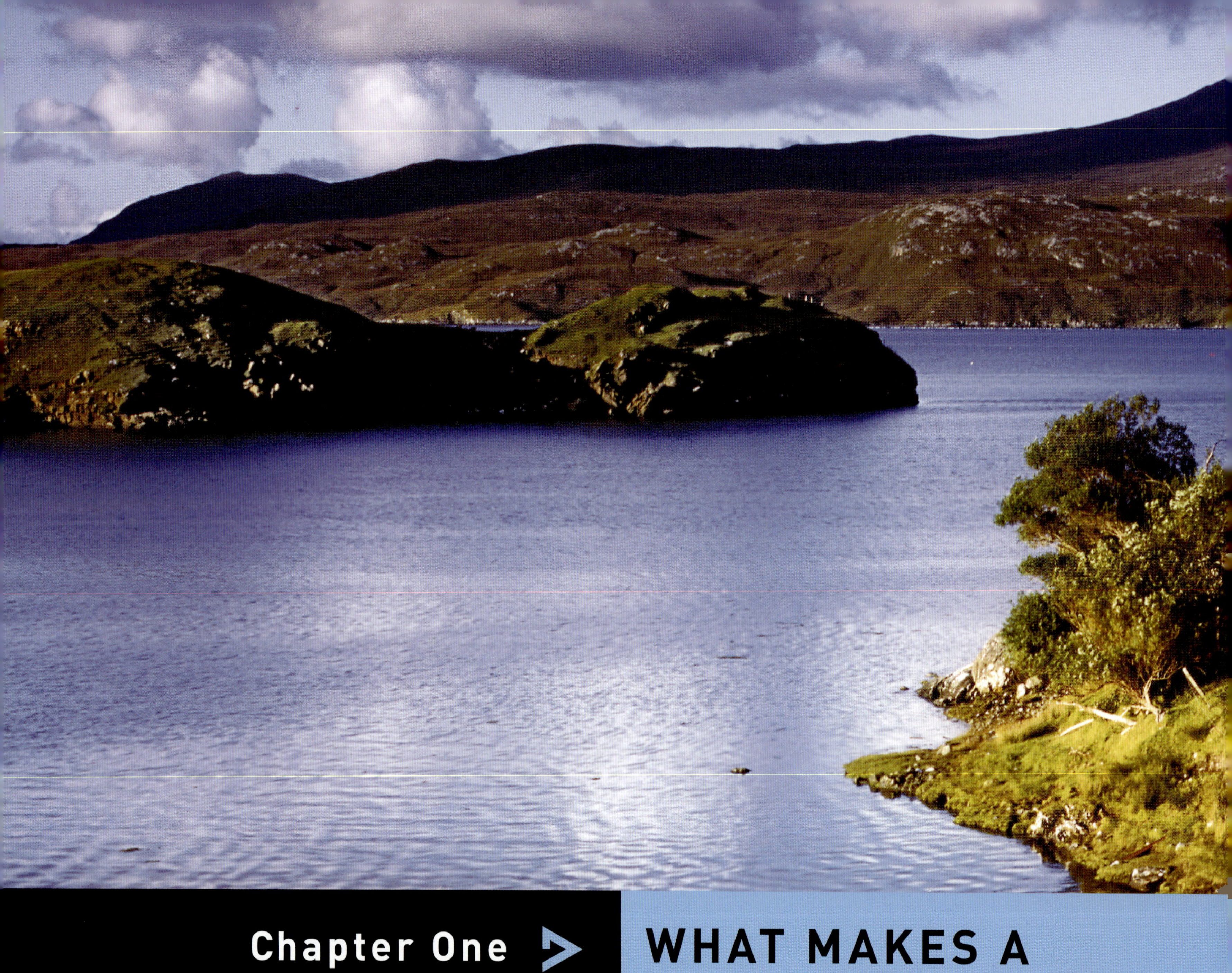

Chapter One ▶
WHAT MAKES A
GOOD LANDSCAPE?
The Isle of Harris, The Western Isles, Scotland

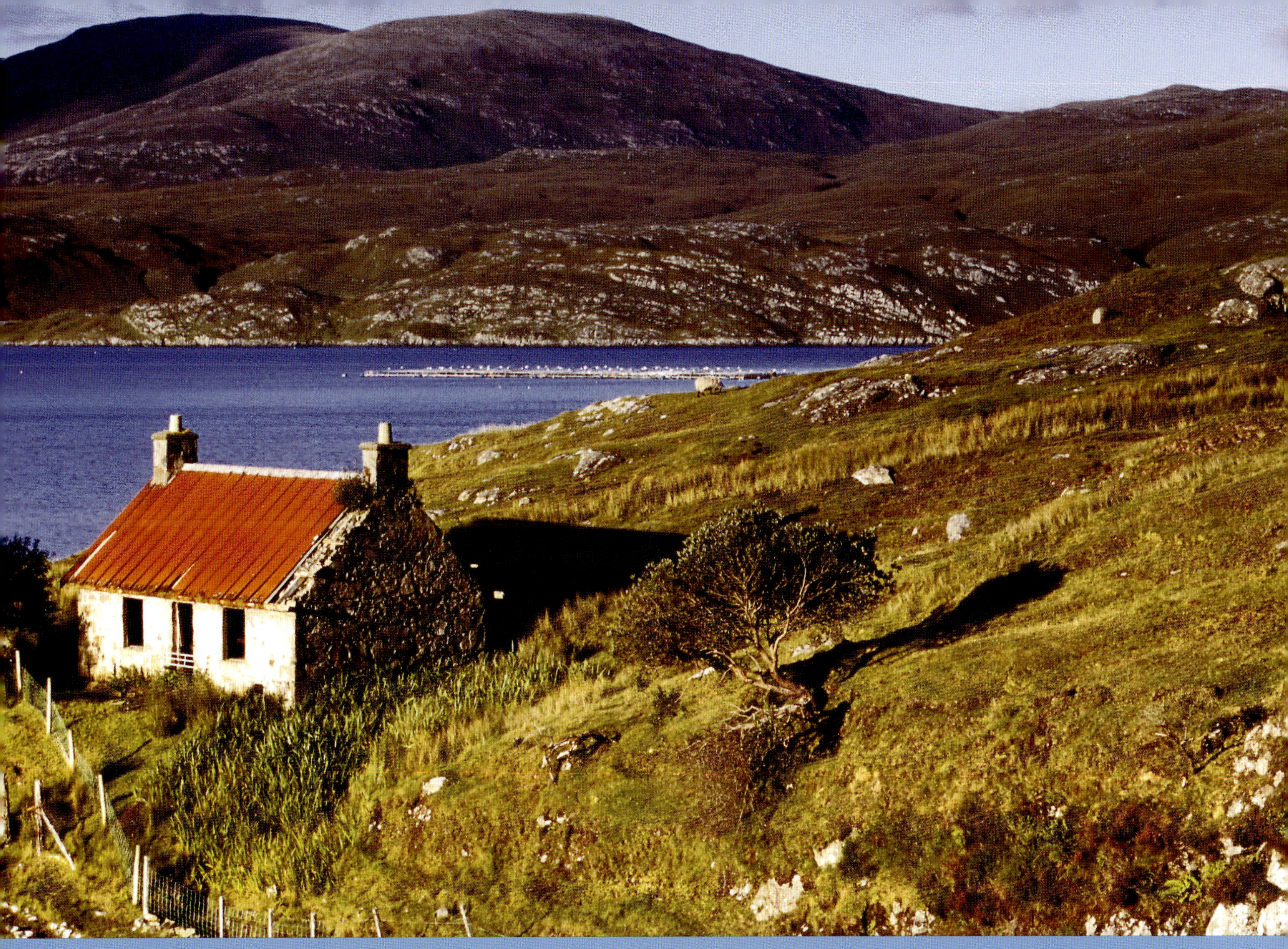

The landscape is not only endlessly varied, but also constantly changing, and this is what makes it such a fascinating and challenging photographic subject. Potential images exist everywhere, but the wide diversity of the natural world means that, inevitably, some places will be more productive than others. In this chapter I will explain the techniques that the top photographers employ to identify the most promising locations and spot the opportunities that exist in every type of landscape.

What, from a photographer's perspective, makes a good landscape? I must admit that it is a question that, on its own, had never really occurred to me, but it often arises during my seminars and workshops so I will attempt to address it here. However, before looking at the constituent parts of a photographer's landscape I must emphasize that every landscape – every field, river, tree, mountain, in fact any feature and any type of location – can, under the right conditions, be a worthy and rewarding subject. I have seen images of the most unlikely places that are quite stunning simply because the photographer was there at the right moment: the moment when the light and sky combined to transform a mundane image into a masterpiece. Having said that, there are certain features and qualities that, when present in a landscape, will increase your chances of making a successful picture, and these can be summarized as follows:

- **An interesting foreground** Look for features that lead the eye towards the distance and choose a viewpoint that gives you a clear, uninterrupted view of the horizon. Try to avoid including anything that obscures the view. You want to be able to 'travel' to the horizon without hitting any obstacles.

- **A balanced arrangement** Ideally, there should be an equal distribution of mass along the width of the image. The landscape is frequently anything but balanced, but you can often use cloud to compensate for this and prevent your photograph from looking one-sided. An example of using cloud in this way can be seen on page 129.

- **Focal points** The presence of a focal point, for example, a small building or a group of trees, will attract the eye and give a picture depth. Including a number of objects of diminishing size will also greatly enhance the impression of depth.

- **Simplicity** The landscape should not contain anything that is unattractive or irrelevant. Unwanted features should not be allowed to creep into the picture because, once photographed, they will become glaringly obvious and will spoil an image.

- **The landscape is balanced because of the matching pair of centrally positioned mountains. In the absence of such balance cloud can be used to prevent a picture looking one-sided.**

- **The foreground flows from the front to the back, encouraging the viewer to follow a winding pathway across the landscape to the distant mountain.**

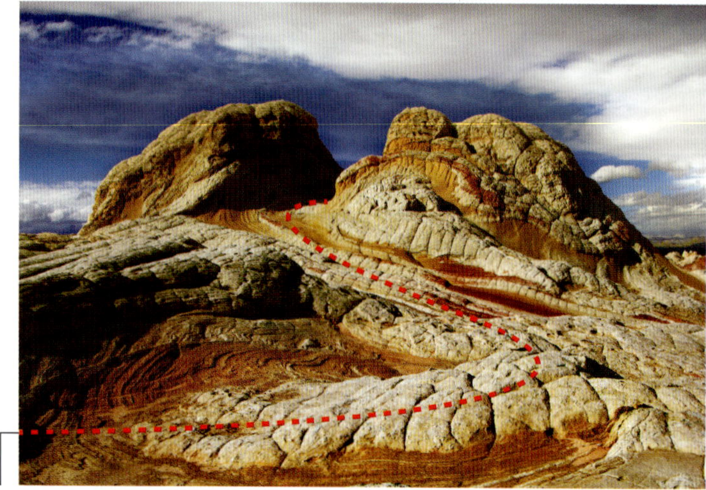

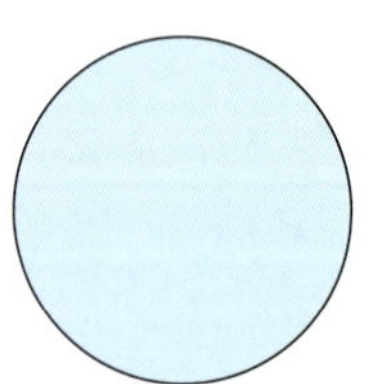

**Polarizer (fully polarized)**

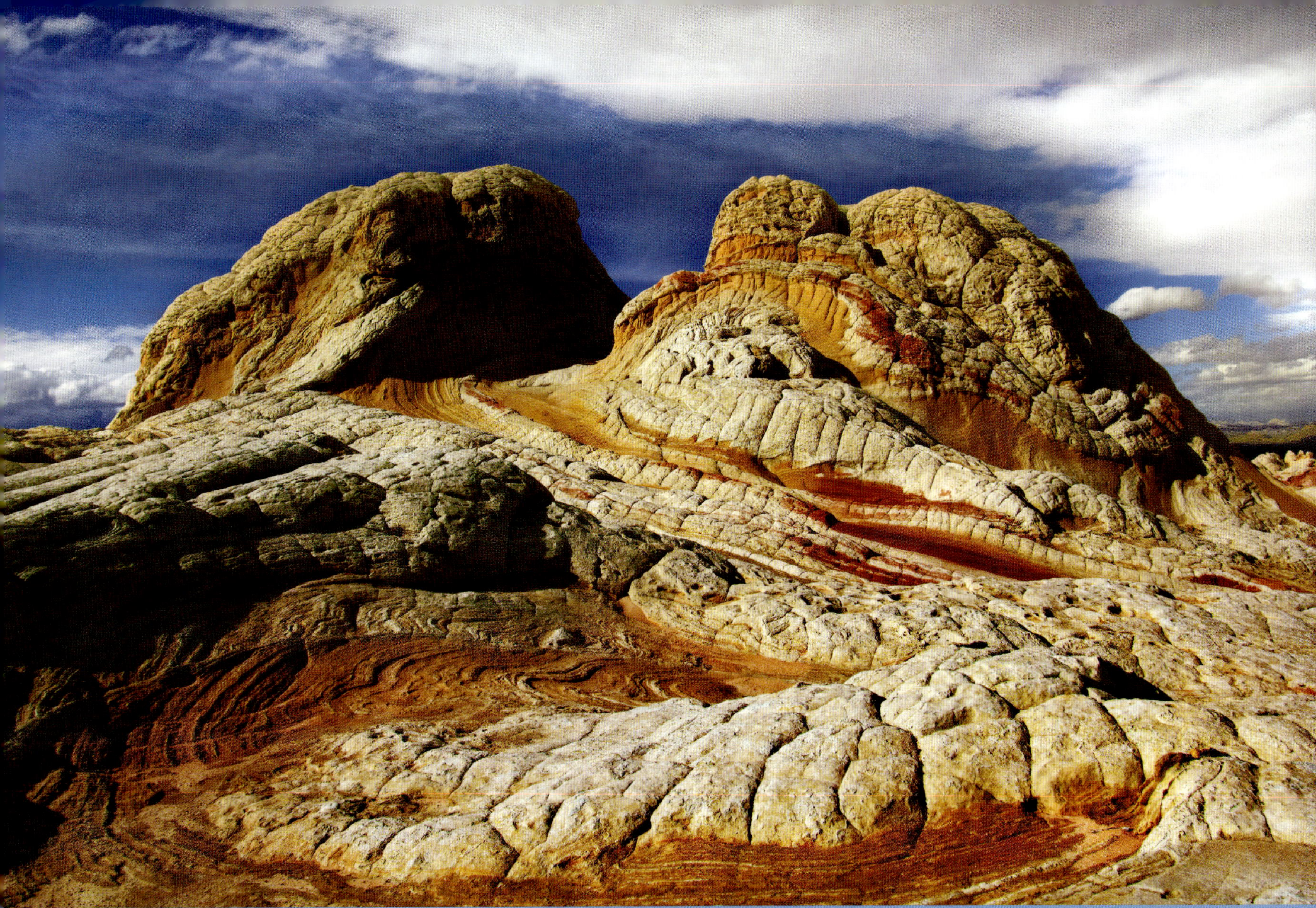

**White Pocket, Arizona, USA**

**Camera:** Mamiya 645 AFDII with Mamiya back
**Lens:** Mamiya 35mm (wide-angle)
**Filter:** Polarizer (fully polarized)
**Exposure:** 1/4sec at f/22, ISO 100
**Waiting for the light:** 90 minutes
**Post-processing:** Suppression of highlights

Some locations, because of their contours and lack of certain features, defy all attempts at creative or original composition. Sometimes you are restricted to a basic arrangement such as one-third foreground, one third middle/distant ground and one-third sky. This is not a hindrance to success because a simple approach often produces the best results but, when you use an undemanding composition, other qualities must be present if the picture is to have appeal. An interesting sky, for example, is always helpful, particularly if it mirrors features of the landscape beneath it. In the image opposite the mass of the sweeping cloud structure is similar to the mountain range it is hovering over, and this helps to give the upper portion of the photograph impact. However, the rest of the picture does not have the same visual interest because the foreground and middle ground are rather mundane. A small barn or a scattering of trees of receding size would have made a world of difference, as would a more elaborate foreground, but sadly there was a dearth of such features. The low sidelighting helps to a degree, but there is a limit to the improvement even the best-quality lighting can bring to a photograph if it is fundamentally flawed.

I was persuaded to make this picture because the mountain and sky were so well matched and also beautifully lit. I knew it wasn't perfect but I don't consider it to be a complete failure, because even with its deficiencies the photograph still portrays the character and grandeur of this spectacular part of America.

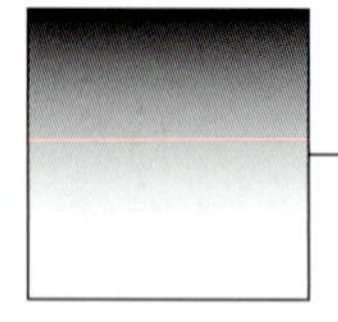

**2-stop (0.6) neutral density graduated filter**

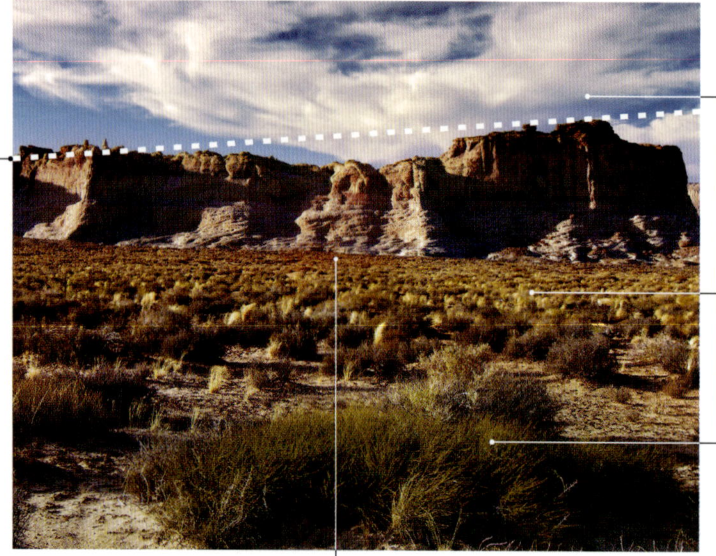

• **The angle of light is the most important feature as it gives shape to the mountain and helps to give the picture depth.  Without the shadows the image would have been a disappointing failure.**

• **The sky and cloud are a well-matched pair. They form a cohesive unit, but the photograph is diminished by the rather nondescript middle distance and foreground.**

• **Had trees or a small building been present, they would have attracted the eye to the middle ground and would have filled the void that is present in this area.**

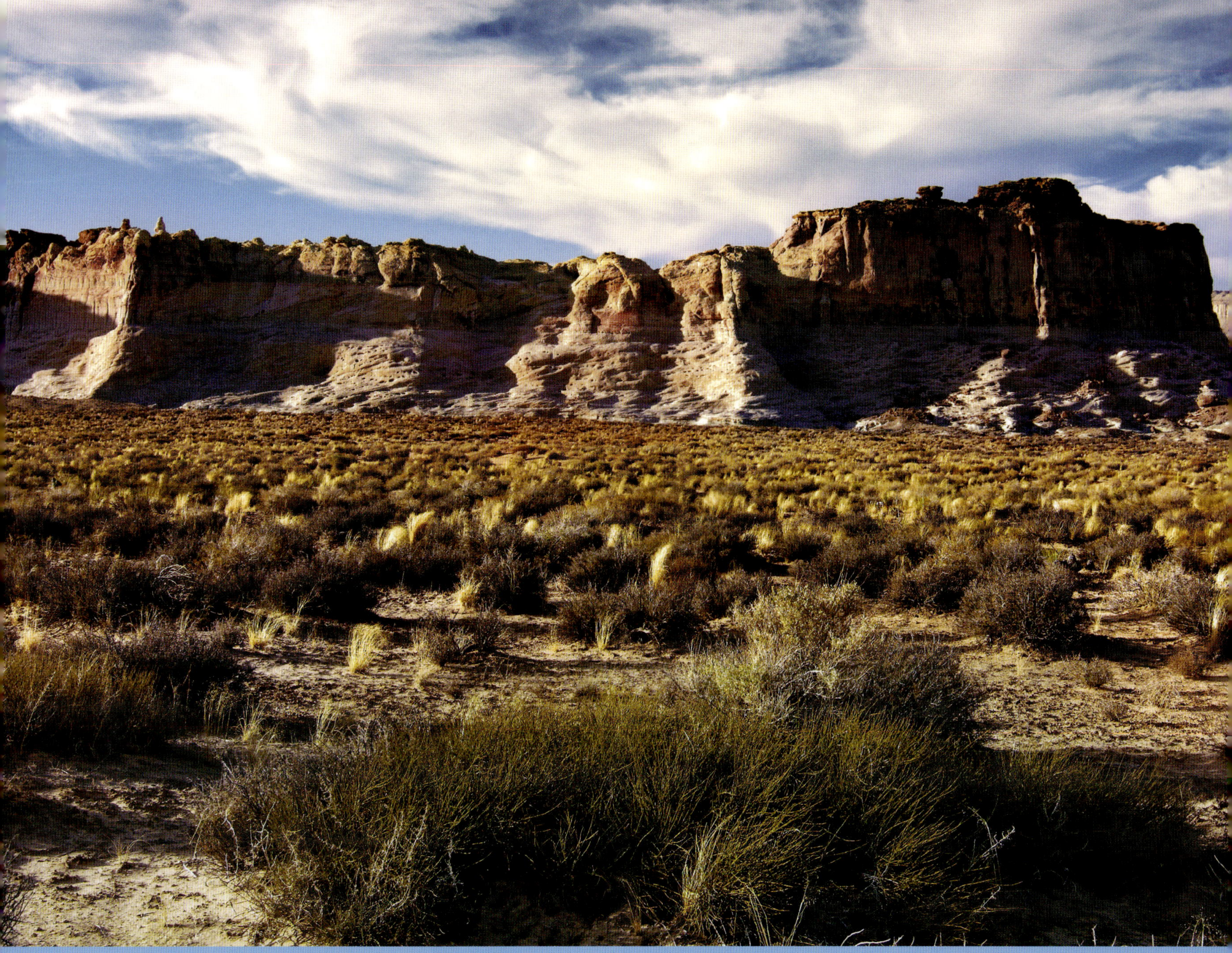

**Glen Canyon, Utah, USA**

**Camera:** Mamiya 645 AFDII with Phase One digital back
**Lens:** Mamiya 35mm (wide-angle)
**Filter:** 2-stop ND graduated
**Exposure:** 1/4sec at f/22, ISO 100
**Waiting for the light:** 30 minutes
**Post-processing:** Colour balance adjustment (warming)

The general opinion of those fortunate enough to have visited the Zion National Park is that it is a paradise for photographers. I had seen many images and they were all so compelling that I simply had to take a look for myself. After a great deal of research and planning, I thought I knew what to expect, but I was in for a big surprise. It was obvious from the moment of arrival that it was more – much more – than I could have dared to hope for. The park was simply magnificent and at first it was all a little overwhelming. A wonderland of towering mountains, expansive valleys, sprawling vistas, acres of trees and gushing rivers all competed for my attention, and I didn't know where to start. I was reluctant to spend time looking in detail at anything in case something better was around the corner. It was time to pause for a while and decide on a strategy.

I divided the park into eight sections and spent a day exploring and photographing each part. This allowed time to make return journeys to specific locations and view them in different lighting conditions. As always the light and sky were the main concern but, unlike most days back home in cloudy Britain, it was too much sunlight and too little cloud that had to be overcome. The only solution was to be patient and wait until favourable conditions developed. Fortunately clouds did, from time to time, make a brief appearance and I was able to pounce and capture the moment. Give a location sufficient time and eventually it will respond.

• A magnificent location still needs an attractive sky if it is to be photographed to its full potential. The presence of warm, sunlit cloud helps to maintain interest in the upper part of the picture.

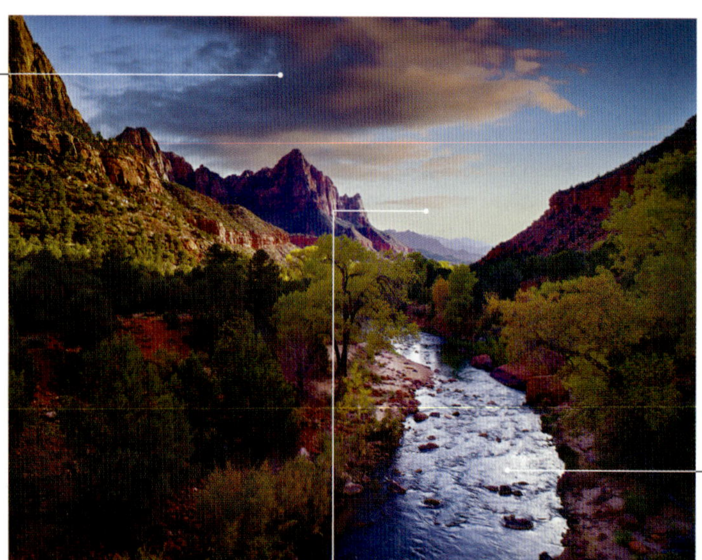

Polarizer (fully polarized)

• A polarizer was used to darken the blue in the sky and also to remove reflections from the surface of the river.

• Because of the shape of the mountains the use of a grey (neutral density) graduated filter was impractical. The brighter parts of the sky were therefore darkened in post-processing using the Curves and Shadows/ Highlights tools.

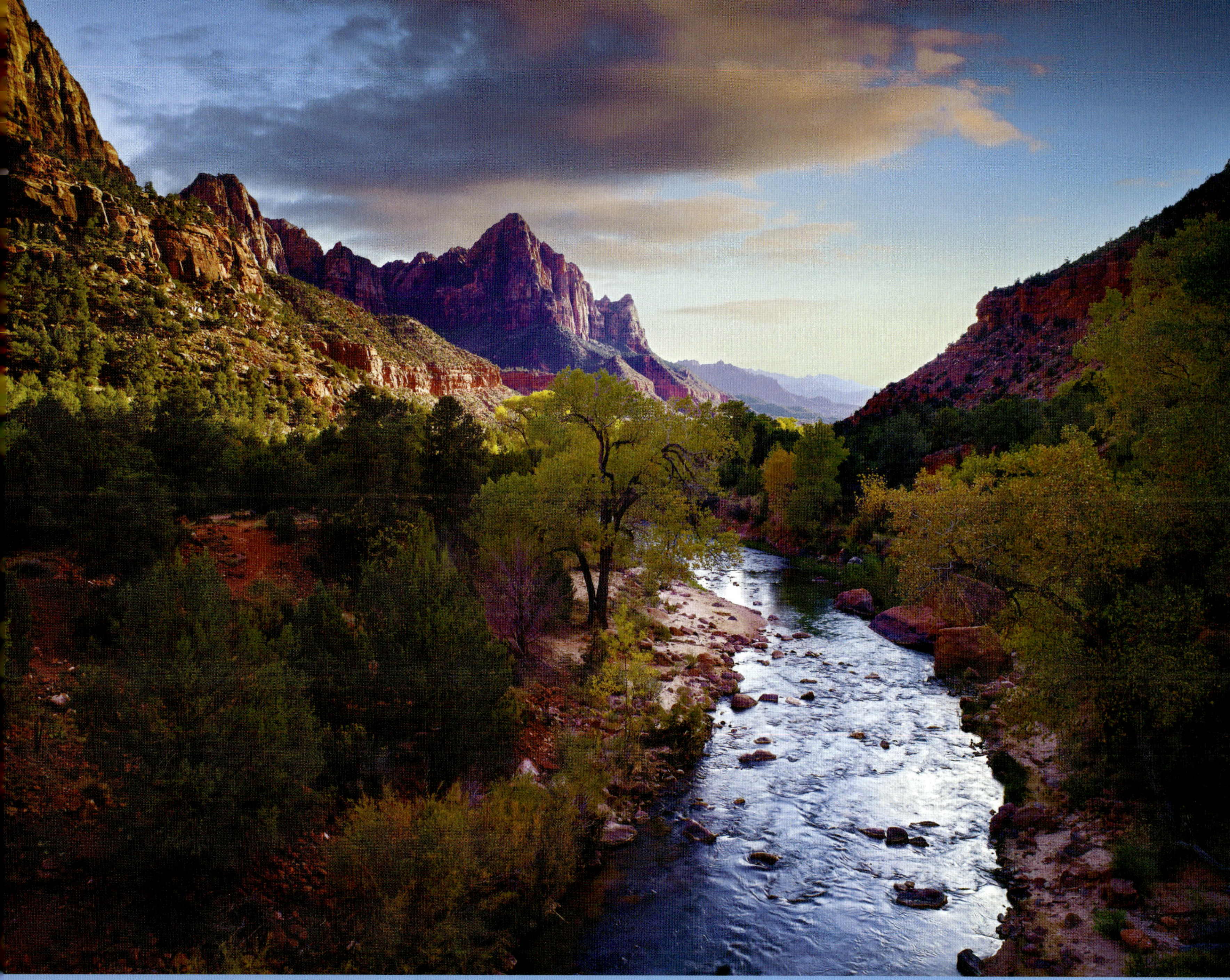

**Zion National Park, Utah, USA**

**Camera:** Mamiya 645 AFDII with Phase One digital back
**Lens:** Mamiya 35mm (wide-angle)
**Filter:** Polarizer (fully polarized)
**Exposure:** 1/8sec at f/16, ISO 100
**Waiting for the light:** 5 days
**Post-processing:** Darkening of sky with Curves and Shadows/Highlights tools

Along with the Zion National Park, the slot canyons of southwest America were one of the reasons I decided to make the 5,000-mile (8,000km) journey from the UK. Having seen pictures of the incredible rock formations, I felt an irresistible urge to visit them and personally experience their unique features. The photographs revealed dazzlingly intricate patterns of light and colour woven into time-smoothed curves and arches, and to say my appetite was whetted as plans were made for the trip is a huge understatement.

Often, when one's expectations have reached dizzying heights (as mine had) the reality of the occasion when it finally arrives is a disappointment. Despite being aware of this, my enthusiasm and optimism remained sky high, and it was with a great sense of anticipation that after months of waiting I entered Antelope Canyon. Parts of it resembled, appropriately, a cave, because it was an Aladdin's cave and much, much more than I could have imagined. Never before had I been surrounded by such incredible rock formations. There were picture-making opportunities everywhere and I spent an unforgettable two hours enjoying the unique experience and capturing images of a type that I had never before been able to make. The memories of that day will never fade and if you ever have the chance to visit the canyon, I urge you to do so. You will not be disappointed.

• Even though the sky was cloudy, high contrast still presented a challenge. A grey graduated filter is not appropriate in these situations because highlights can occur anywhere in the image. One solution is to choose a composition that avoids the brightest or darkest areas, which I have attempted to do here. Another option is to make two images of different exposures, one based on the highlights and the other of the shadows, then merge them during post-processing.

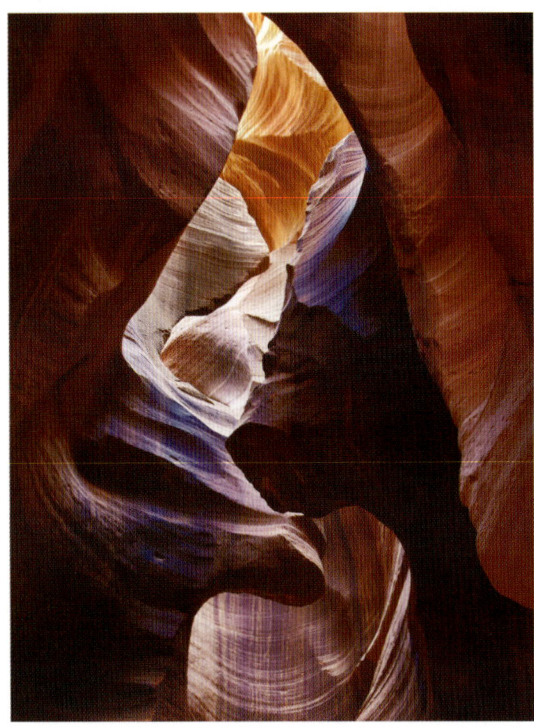

> **TIP:** Slot canyons can be very narrow and composition can be hindered by restricted access, particularly when using a tripod. A zoom lens is a great help in these situations as it will enable a number of different images to be captured with relatively small changes in camera position.

• There is no focal point, as such, in this photograph. The composition obviates the need for a visual anchor as it is, essentially, an abstract depiction of shape, colour and texture.

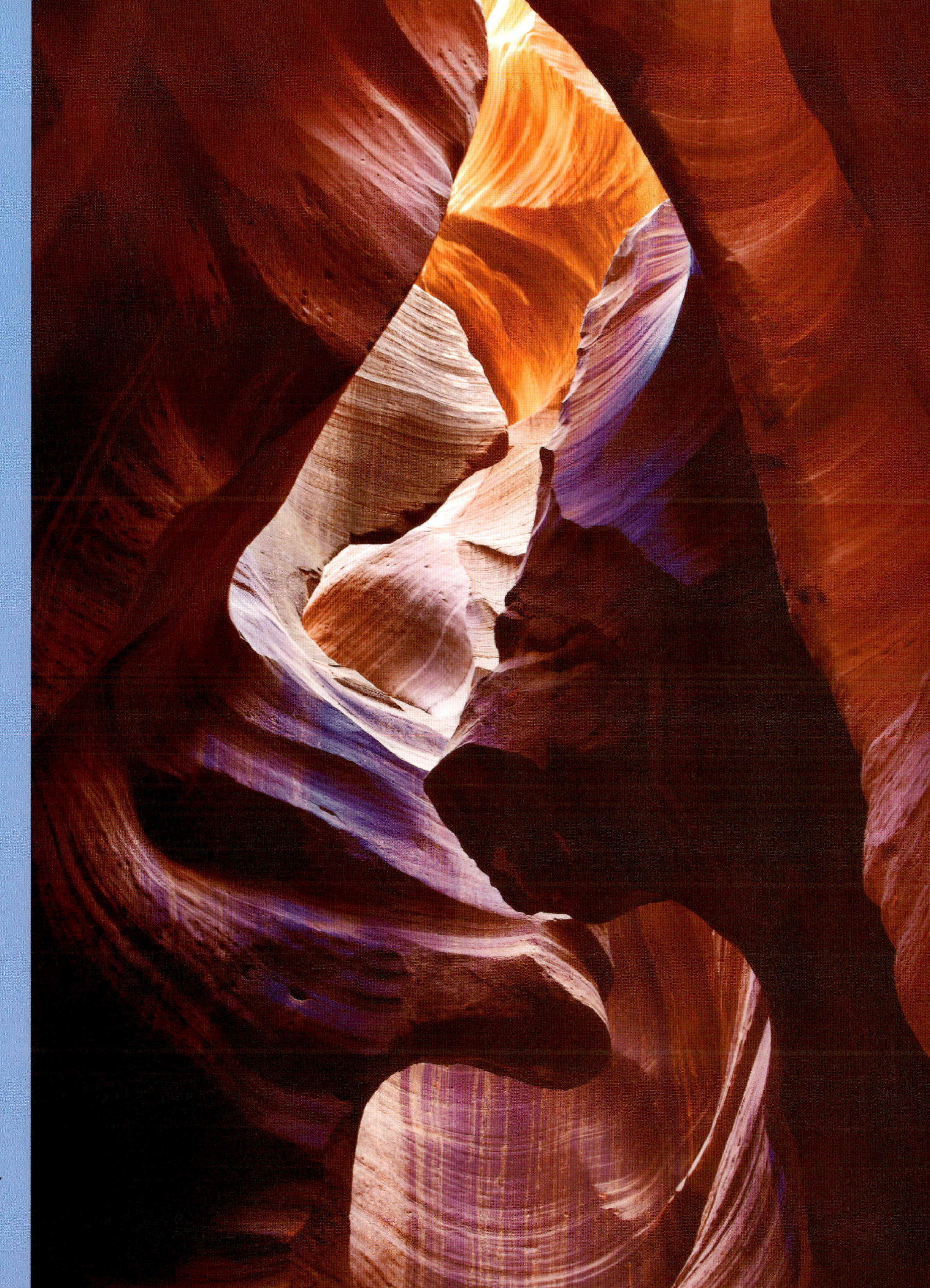

**Upper Antelope Canyon,
Arizona, USA**

**Camera:** Canon EOS 7D
**Lens:** Canon 24–105mm L IS
**Filter:** None
**Exposure:** 2sec at f/13, ISO 100
**Waiting for the light:** Immediate
**Post-processing:** Curves adjustment,
suppression of highlights

When looking for new locations I use, as an initial guide, topographic maps, which show land elevations. I tend to avoid flat areas and look for a rising and falling terrain. It can be either a softly undulating landscape or a towering mountain range: both have their attractions. Ideally there will be a combination of low hills and high mountains because, from a photographer's standpoint, variety is an important factor. The reason for this is simple. A varied location will produce a wide range of subjects, which in turn means that images can be captured in a variety of weather conditions. A rising and falling landscape will always yield more pictures than a flat terrain.

Having selected an area, use large-scale maps to take a closer look. You can never be absolutely certain of what you're going to find, but maps of 1:50,000 or 1:25,000 provide a lot of detailed information and are very helpful when searching for potential viewpoints and specific features. The picture opposite is a result of researching the area in advance, using an Ordnance Survey Landranger 1:50,000 map. The detail on the map provided important information; it was apparent that a winding road passed through a wide valley, the sides of which were covered by protruding limestone, pastureland and trees, and its aspect meant that it could be photographed under different angles of sidelighting throughout the day. On paper it appeared to be perfect and a quick search of online images confirmed its potential.

Two months later I made the journey and, after three days of waiting for the rain to stop, the picture was captured. The time spent waiting wasn't wasted, because it was possible to trek along both sides of the valley and identify a number of viewpoints. It was then a matter of waiting for the right light and sky and choosing the moment.

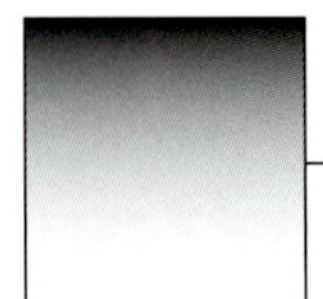

**2-stop (0.6) neutral density graduated filter**

- **A 2-stop ND graduated filter was used to prevent the sky from being overexposed.**

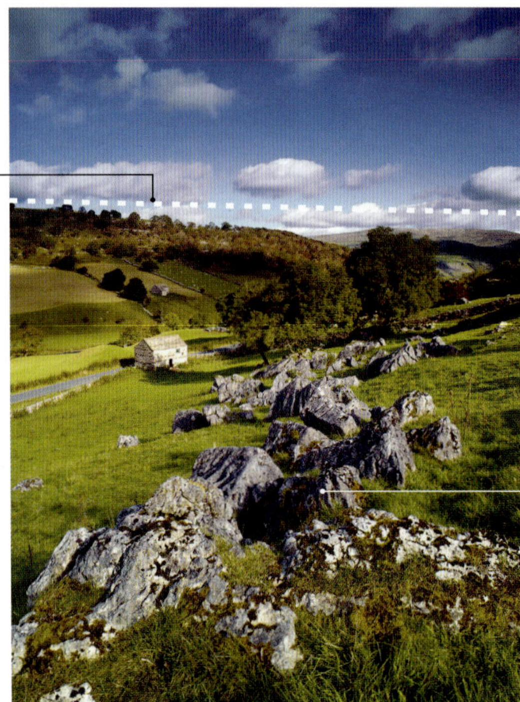

> **TIP:** Including trees and buildings in the mid and far distance will give an image depth and scale. They will also act as important focal points.

- **Soft but directional sunlight gives shape and depth to the receding line of limestone rocks.**

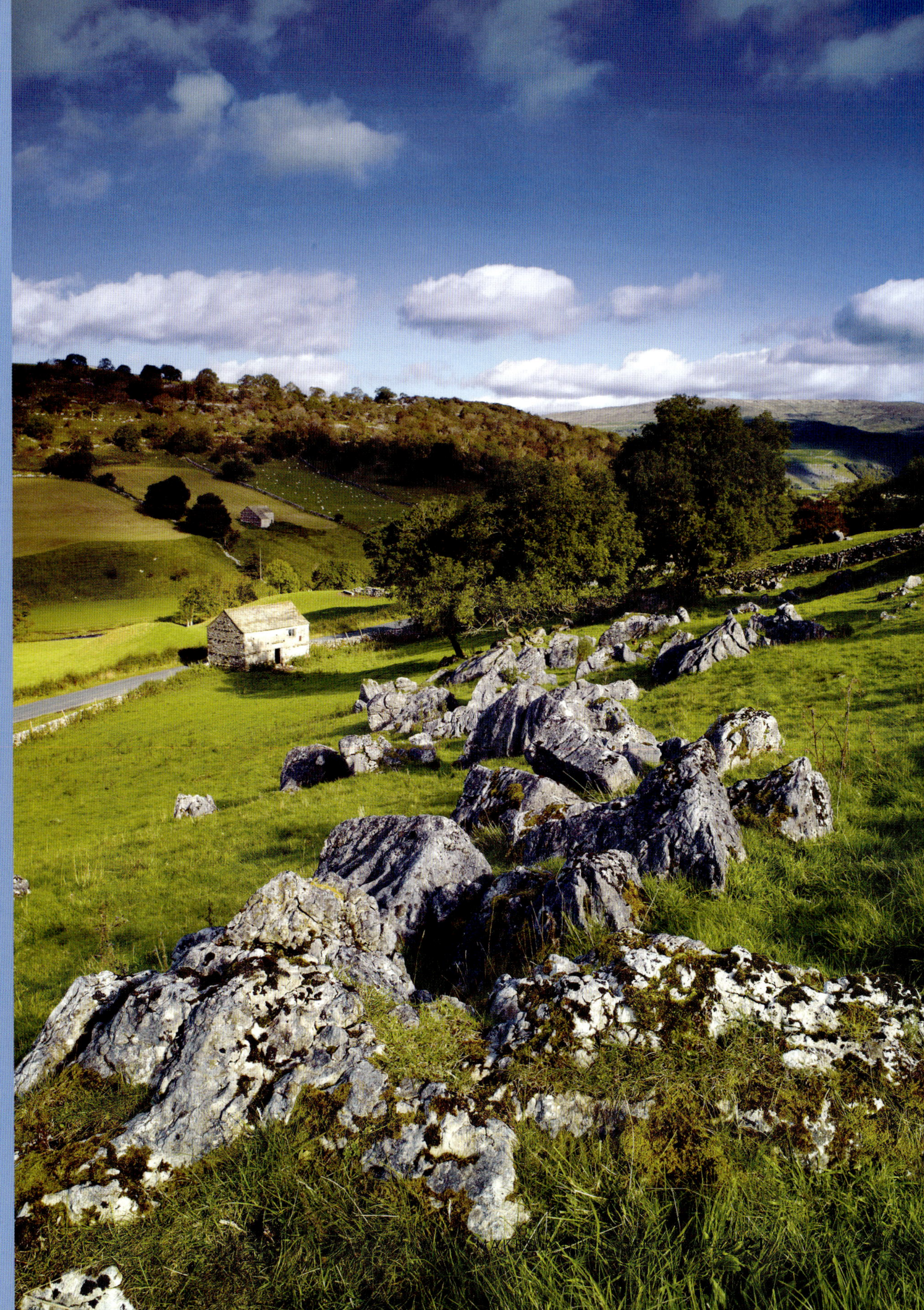

**Upper Wharfedale,
The Yorkshire Dales, England**

**Camera:** Mamiya 645 AFDII with
Mamiya digital back
**Lens:** Mamiya 35mm (wide-angle)
**Filter:** 2-stop ND graduated filter
**Exposure:** 1/8sec at f/22, ISO 100
**Waiting for the light:** 3 days
**Post-processing:** Curves adjustment,
colour balance adjustment

Gently rolling countryside doesn't have the overwhelming presence of more mountainous areas, but what it lacks in grandeur is more than compensated for by a serene and beguiling beauty of continually changing appearance. The seasonal nature of the rural landscape gives it variety, and during the spring and summer months changes can occur with remarkable speed. This means there is no shortage of subject matter; images are literally everywhere, and in many ways arable land in rural areas is as fertile for the photographer as it is for the farmer.

The building blocks of images – contours, patterns, curves and flowing lines – are in abundance, and if you look at the landscape in an abstract, analytical way photographs will begin to emerge.

Patterns and shapes will become apparent and you will be able to build your compositions around them. These subtle features can then be emphasized as the play of light sweeps across the land to reveal hidden contours and undulations. Flowing lines can be further enhanced by the variety of colours that erupt during the growing season as farmland is ploughed and crops become established. These are the photographic tools that nature provides and they can be the source of many fine images. Experiment with different compositions and with various focal lengths of lens. With practice your instincts will begin to tell you what the best combination of composition and focal length is and then you will be able to harvest many distinctive photographs from the bountiful rural landscape.

> **TIP:** Use elements such as trees and patches of colour to provide focal points and symmetrical patterns.

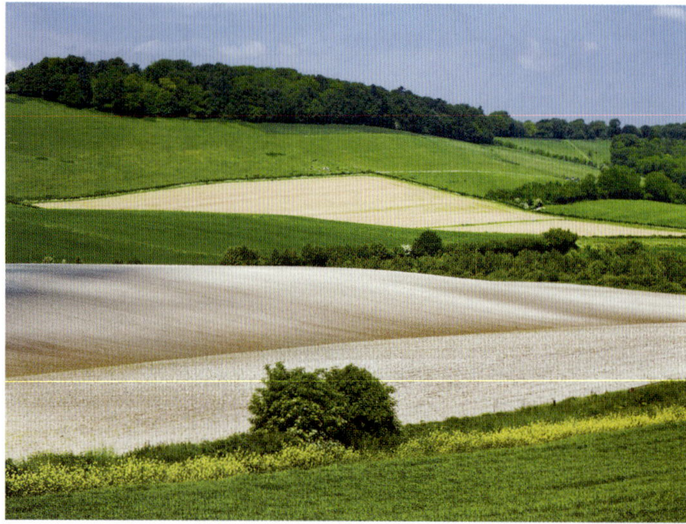

**Polarizer (fully polarized)**

• A polarizer was used to darken the sky and strengthen the colour of the ploughed fields.

> **TIP:** Use light and shadow to delineate the contours of a rolling landscape. Wait for the play of light to fall across specific features as you release the shutter.

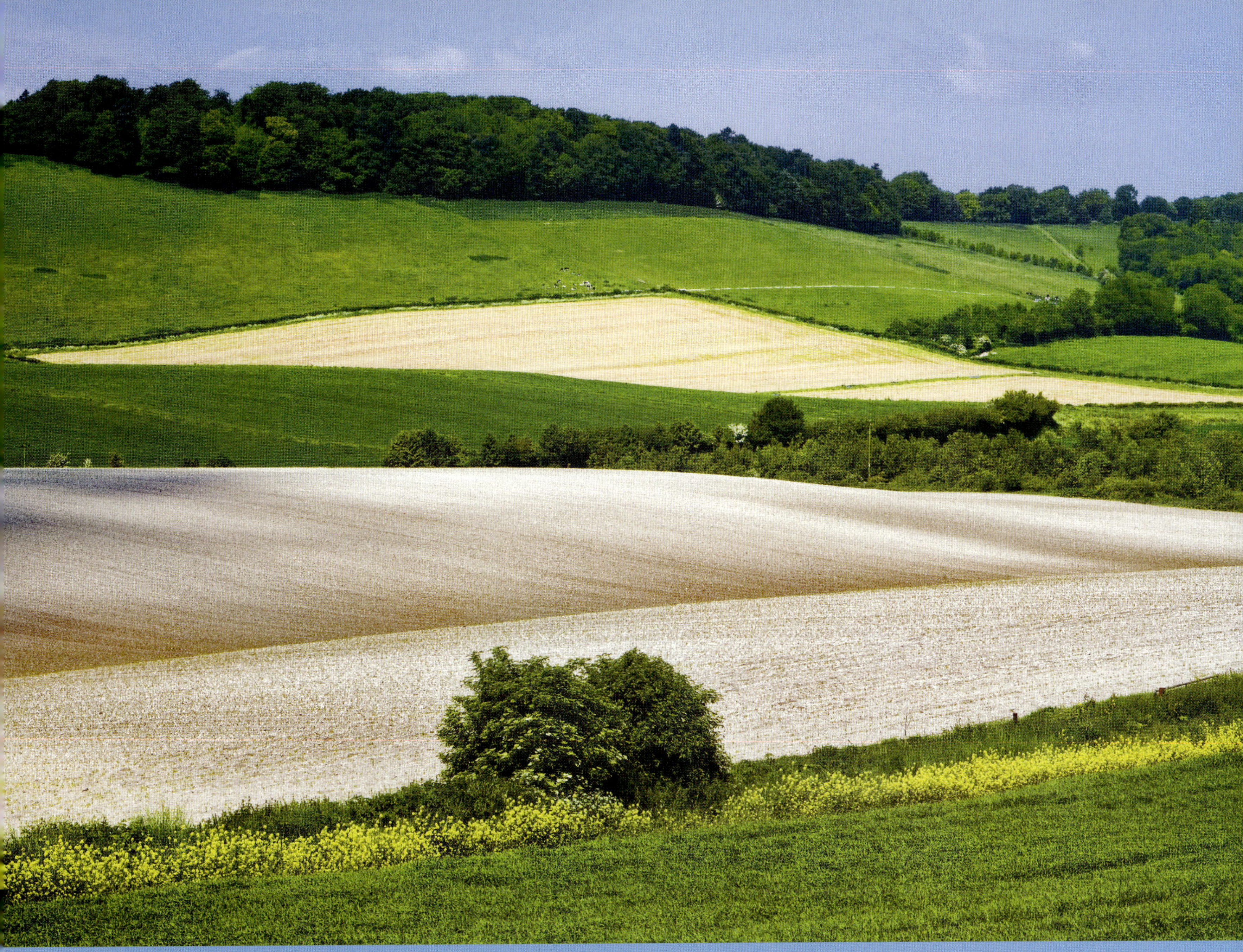

**Teglease Down, Hampshire, England**

**Camera:** Mamiya 645 AFDII with Mamiya digital back
**Lens:** Mamiya 150mm (telephoto)
**Filter:** Polarizer (fully polarized)
**Exposure:** 1/15sec at f/16, ISO 100
**Waiting for the light:** 50 minutes
**Post-processing:** Curves adjustment

Imagine a treeless world; it's not a pleasant thought, is it? Trees are one of the wonders of nature. Essential to life itself, they are also vital ingredients in many landscape images. As an adornment to an open view they act as focal points, create depth and space and give balance to a picture. On their own they are also rewarding subjects for the camera. Visit a deciduous forest in autumn and you will find yourself surrounded by image-making opportunities. There is possibly no finer sight than a group of trees radiating with glowing colour during those precious, short-lived days when their leaves gradually succumb to the onset of winter.

Timing is important during the autumn season because the peak moment can suddenly arrive and disappear just as quickly. Overnight frost and strong winds can be ruinous, so keep an eye on the weather and monitor your locations as autumn approaches. Weather conditions are not a major concern because colourful trees can be successfully photographed in the flat light of an overcast sky. Alternatively, if sunlight prevails, choose a viewpoint that enables you to point your camera towards the sun so that the trees are backlit. This type of lighting can be quite exquisite and will bring an added dimension to an autumn forest.

> **TIP:** To focus attention on the main subject, keep the composition tight. It is also usually preferable to exclude the sky from woodland scenes.

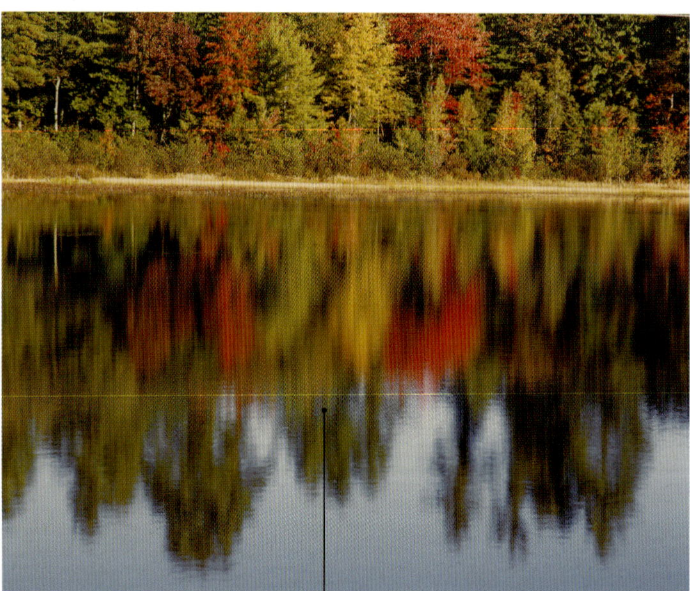

**Polarizer (fully polarized)**

> **TIP:** Use a polarizing filter to strengthen reflections on the surface of a lake. This will also improve the colour and clarity of autumn foliage.

• The reflections are as important as the trees themselves. I had to wait for an hour and a half for the wind to drop but there was no alternative, because the success of the picture depended upon the stillness of the water.

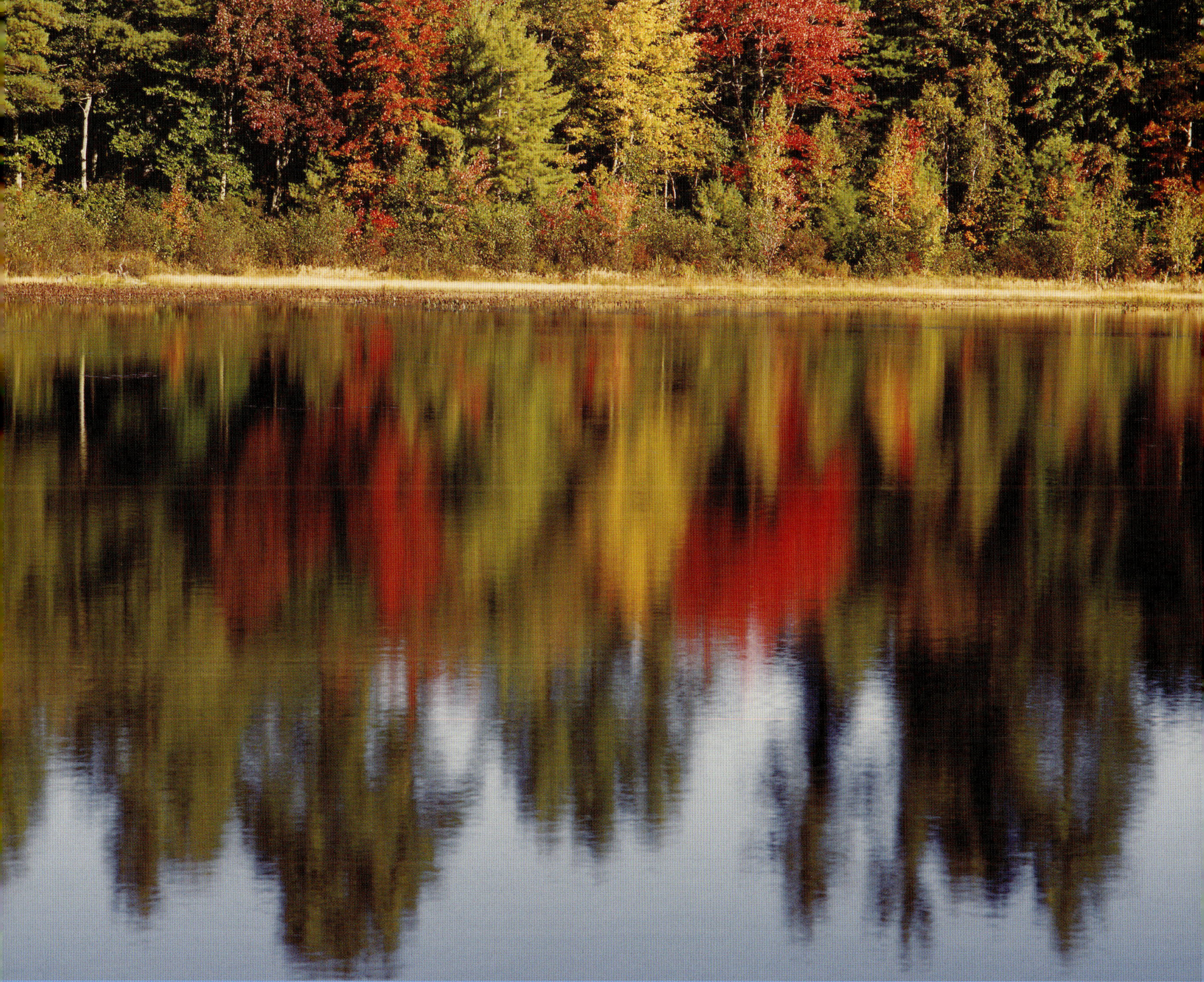

**Near Windham, Maine, USA**

**Camera:** Mamiya RB67 with film back
**Lens:** Mamiya 250mm (telephoto)
**Filter:** Polarizer (fully polarized)
**Exposure:** 1/15sec at f/16, ISO 100
**Waiting for the light:** 90 minutes (waiting for the breeze to drop)
**Post-processing:** None

Waterfalls and fast-flowing rivers and streams can be a haven of opportunity for the observant photographer. A thorough approach has to be taken, however, because the strongest compositions can take some time to find. They are often hidden away, buried deep within the splashing waters, and you will need to look hard to find the right combination of elements. These elements are time, movement and stillness, and waterfalls, more than any other landscape feature, offer a marvellous opportunity to use them to stunning effect. To successfully combine these ingredients in a photograph, look for a balanced arrangement that excludes areas that lack tonal range. Try to avoid expanses of either bright, washed-out highlights or dark, colourless rocks. There should be subtle tonal variations across all parts of the image and this requires the pairing of the right quantity of water and rocks. Too much of either one is likely to lead to a loss of visual impact, because the photograph will contain too many bland, featureless areas. This is why it is important to search and scrutinize to find the winning combination. Often the most attractive parts of a river can be found some distance away from the main waterfall. Look for images on a smaller scale as they usually offer more potential than the more obvious viewpoints, and they also offer more scope for creativity.

• **The viewpoint chosen for this image was not the most obvious. It took some finding (and involved a soaking!) but it enabled the composition to be built around the jagged rocks with four streams of cascading waters of a varied tonal range falling from above. Every part of the image makes a contribution – movement and time have, I like to think, been effectively depicted.**

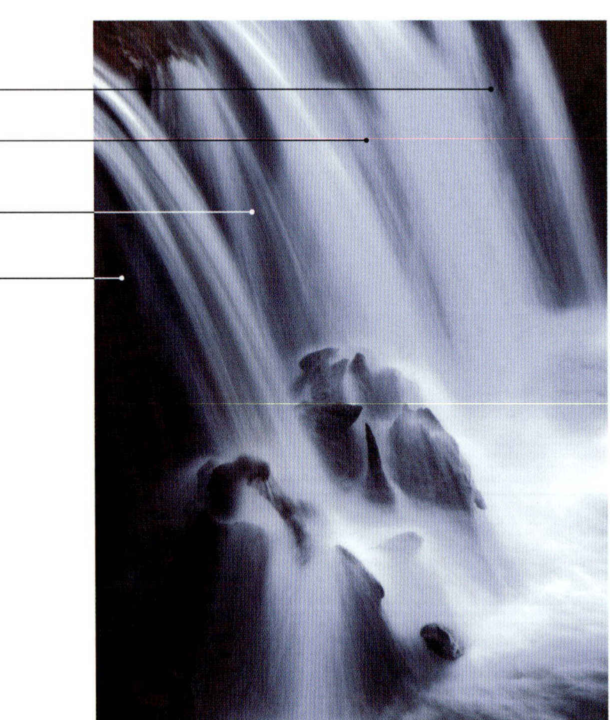

> **TIP:** If a river or waterfall looks unimpressive it might be the volume of water that's the problem. River levels can quickly rise and fall so return on another day and your search might be more successful.

> **TIP:** If required, use the Shadows/Highlights tool in post-processing to reduce the intensity of the strongest highlights.

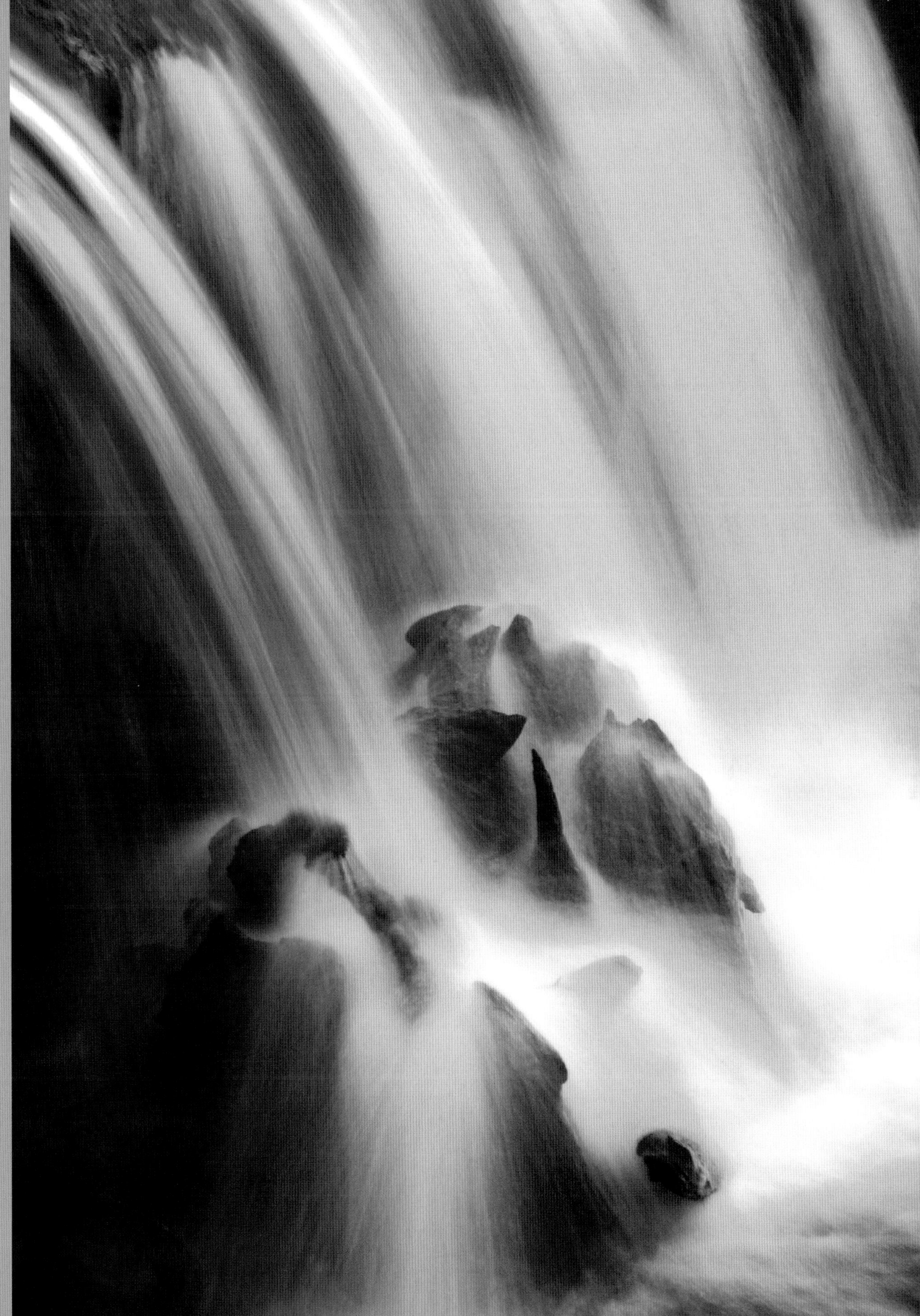

**Cenarth Falls,
Ceredigion, Wales**

**Camera:** Mamiya 645 AFDII
with Phase One digital back
**Lens:** Mamiya 80mm (standard)
**Filter:** None
**Exposure:** 1sec at f/22, ISO 100
**Waiting for the light:** Immediate
**Post-processing:** Reduction of
highlights with the Shadows/
Highlights tool

Normally I prefer to photograph water under flat light, because bright spots can conflict with highlights in the river and subtlety of tonal variation can be lost. There are always exceptions and this was the case as I contemplated the view of the lengthy Wain Wath waterfall high up along the River Swale. Because of its location it is open to the sky and, lacking the shelter normally found around waterfalls, the quality of light is of particular concern. Also of critical importance is the level and speed of the flowing water. I realized this during a return visit to the location the day after this picture was taken. The level had fallen overnight (it really is remarkable how quickly the appearance of waterfalls can change) and the cascading water you see here had been reduced to little more than a trickle. It was most fortunate then that the waterfall was captured during my first visit. It wasn't just the level of the river

that was perfect; the warm light from a setting sun was also ideal, giving the water a subtle glow that enhanced, rather than interfered with, the splashing waters. The other components in the picture – the rocks and background trees – have also benefited from the soft, directional evening light and, of course, the time of year suited the location. All things considered, it is unlikely that the photograph could have been better timed, but it was simply the result of sheer good luck. There had been no prior monitoring or investigation; I just happened to arrive at the right time. Missed opportunities are a common occurrence in the life of a landscape photographer, but occasionally fortune smiles on us and we should grab the opportunity with open arms. It might, after all, be some time before it returns.

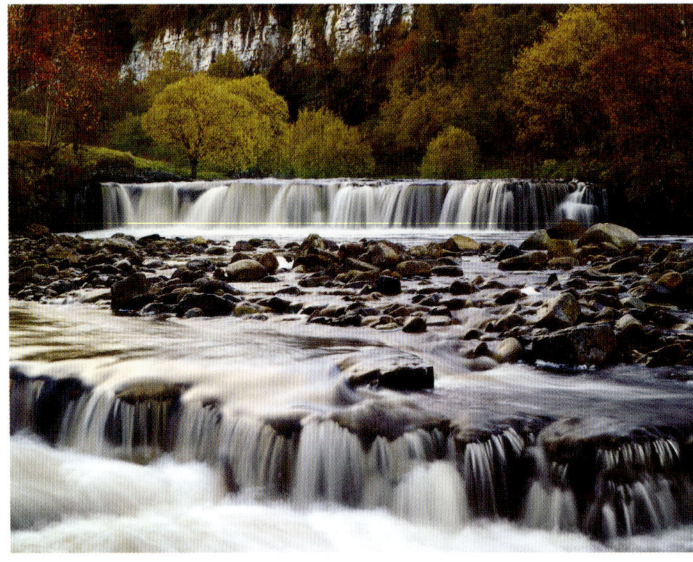

- I considered using a polarizer because it often improves the appearance of water, but on this occasion the warm reflections in the foreground brought a luminosity to the river that I didn't want to suppress. The image was therefore left unpolarized.

- A camera height of 3ft (1m) was used, which was low enough to capture the foreground but also gave an unimpeded view of the middle section of the river.

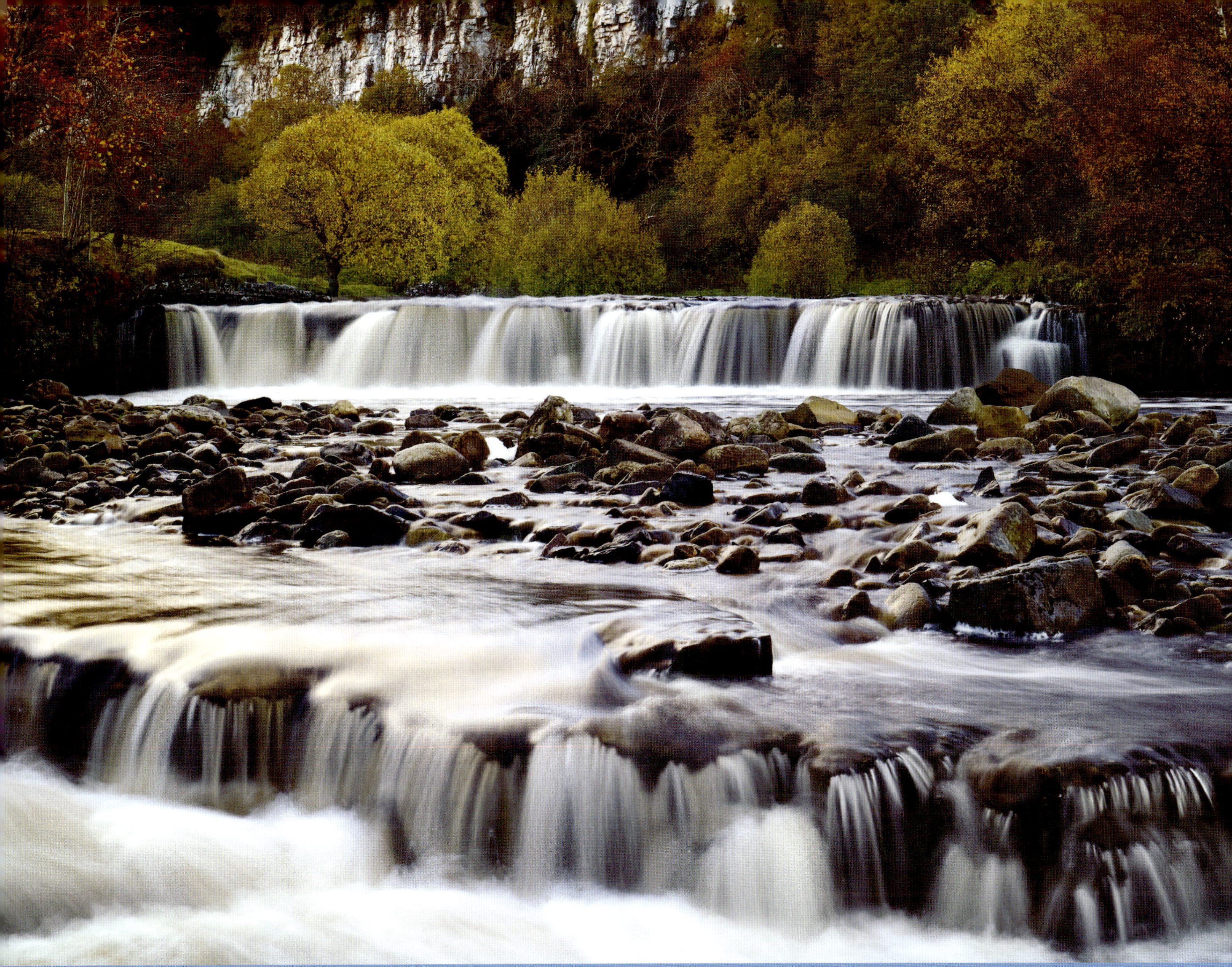

**Wain Wath Force, The Yorkshire Dales, England**

**Camera:** Mamiya 645 AFDII with Mamiya digital back
**Lens:** Mamiya 35mm (wide-angle)
**Filter:** None
**Exposure:** 1sec at f/22, ISO 100
**Waiting for the light:** Immediate
**Post-processing:** Colour balance adjustment (warming)

A walk along the coast can be a refreshing, invigorating experience. The sounds of the sea, the screeching of seagulls, the ozone-rich air and the wind in your hair all contribute to the appeal of the shoreline but, pleasant as these attractions are, there are other qualities to be found. Look around as you stroll along; if you look carefully you will see that there is more than just a distant view because coastal locations are a rich tapestry of patterns, colours and textures. This is fertile hunting ground because the shoreline is a unique type of landscape and provides unrivalled opportunities for creative image-making.

Strong visual elements (the building blocks of landscape photographs) are in abundance. They are so powerful that with the right composition you can make eye-catching pictures in virtually any type of light. Look for rock pools or water channels with colourful stones that lead the eye to the middle ground. Graphic lines and curves are common along the coast, so use them to create depth and impact. Even if the sky is grey and the lighting flat, strong images can still be made. Include elements of varying texture and colour, move in close to the foreground and shoot from a low position. This will accentuate the graphic nature of a landscape and is a perfect subject for an overcast sky.

The key to success is finding the right viewpoint and the right combination of features. Look hard and you can discover some intriguing and potentially very successful photographs.

2-stop (0.6) neutral density graduated filter

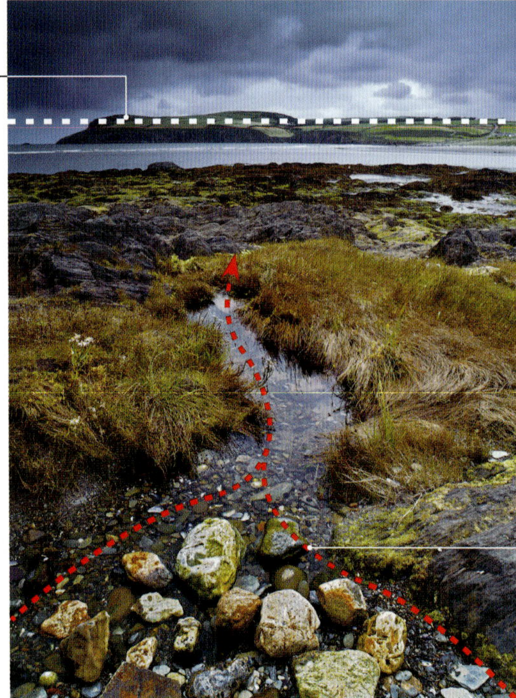

> **TIP:** A variegated and colourful landscape can be successfully photographed in low-contrast soft light from an overcast sky.

- A 2-stop ND graduated filter was used to reduce the brightness of the sky and prevent it from being overexposed. This enabled the structure and depth of the cloud formation to be depicted.

- Lines curving into the distance take the viewer on a journey across the landscape towards the horizon. These converging lines create depth and visual interest.

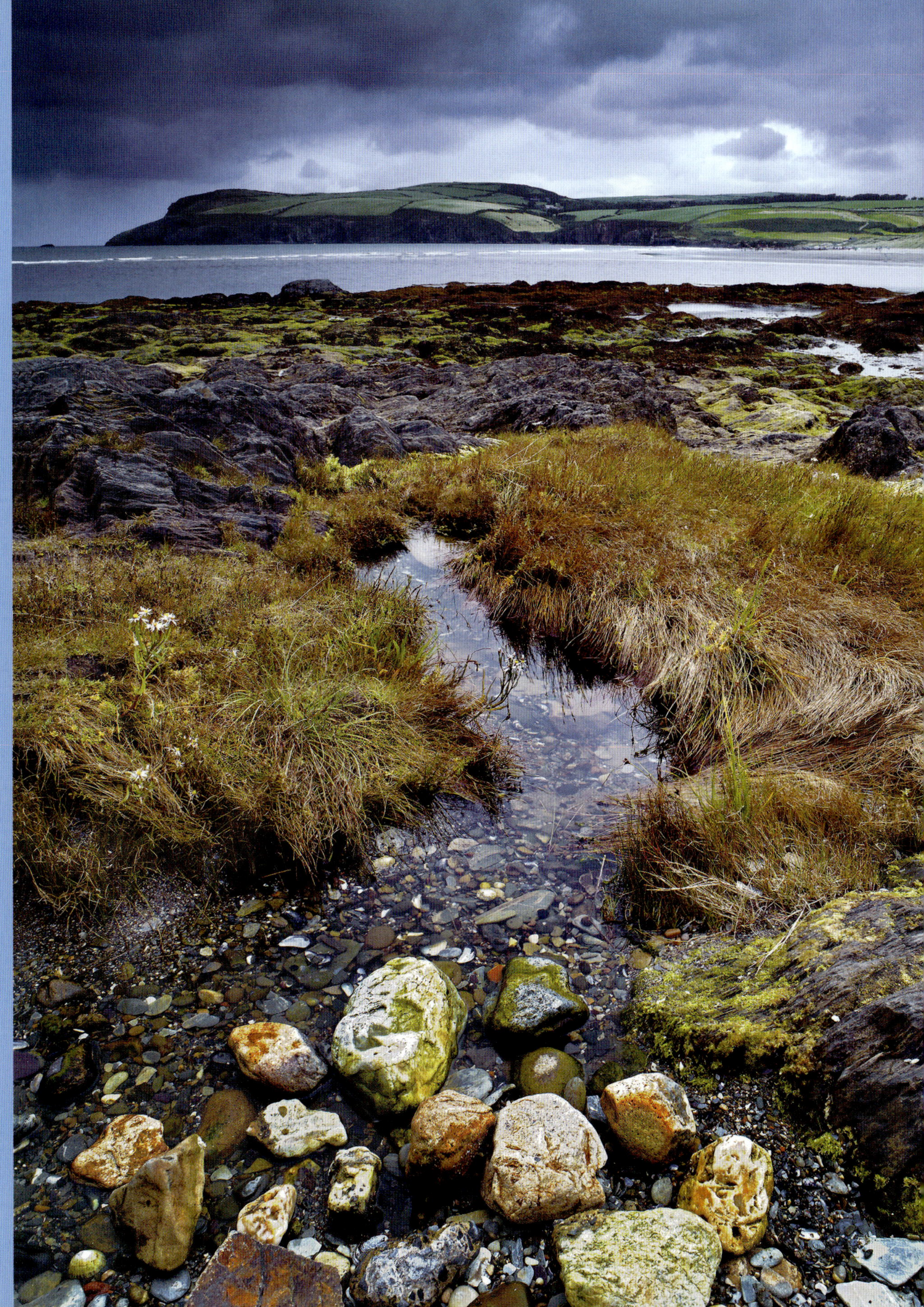

**Newport Bay,
Pembrokeshire, Wales**

**Camera:** Mamiya 645 AFDII
with Mamiya digital back
**Lens:** Mamiya 35mm (wide-angle)
**Filter:** 2-stop ND graduated
**Exposure:** 1/2sec at f/22, ISO 100
**Waiting for the light:** Immediate
**Post-processing:** None

In addition to its landscape, one of the most striking features of the coast is the light. Uninhibited by land, the light skims across the water and penetrates deep into every crack and crevice to bring a sparkle to your photographs. During the first and last hours of daylight the quality of light is such that it can transform even the most unremarkable stretch of shoreline into a dazzling display of coastal magnificence. This light, together with the wealth and variety of material to be found, makes the coast one of the most rewarding locations for the observant photographer.

To make the most of the light, visit your chosen viewpoints in advance to determine the position of the sun at dawn and dusk. Maps can of course help in this respect, but it is always useful to familiarize yourself with a place and pre-plan your composition. This can save valuable time, because lighting conditions change quickly at the beginning and end of the day and there is a risk of missing the best light if you are not prepared and poised and ready to release the shutter at the optimum moment. Time spent researching a location is always time well spent and will prevent many missed opportunities.

When planning your composition, combining a shaded foreground and brightly lit middle/far ground will help to provide the image with depth. Flat light on the foreground will also enable any subtle tonal variations, for example sea-weathered boulders, to be successfully depicted.

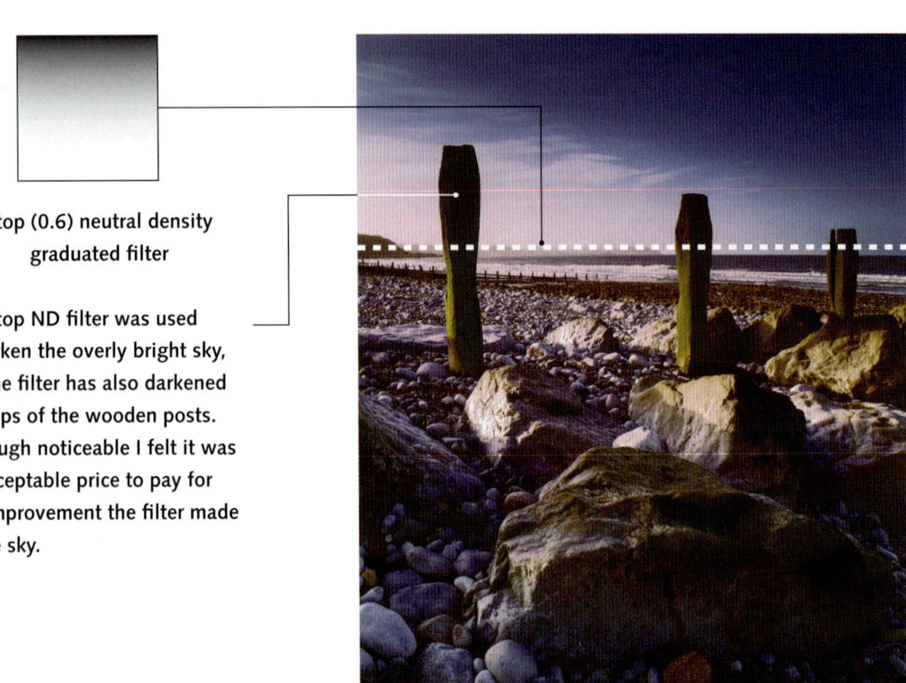

2-stop (0.6) neutral density
graduated filter

- A 2-stop ND filter was used to darken the overly bright sky, but the filter has also darkened the tops of the wooden posts. Although noticeable I felt it was an acceptable price to pay for the improvement the filter made to the sky.

> **TIP:** Use hazy sunlight to capture detail in both highlights and shadows, particularly when using backlighting.

> **TIP:** Use shadow to depict colour and texture in foreground objects. When combined with bright sunlight in the mid and far distance it will also help to create depth.

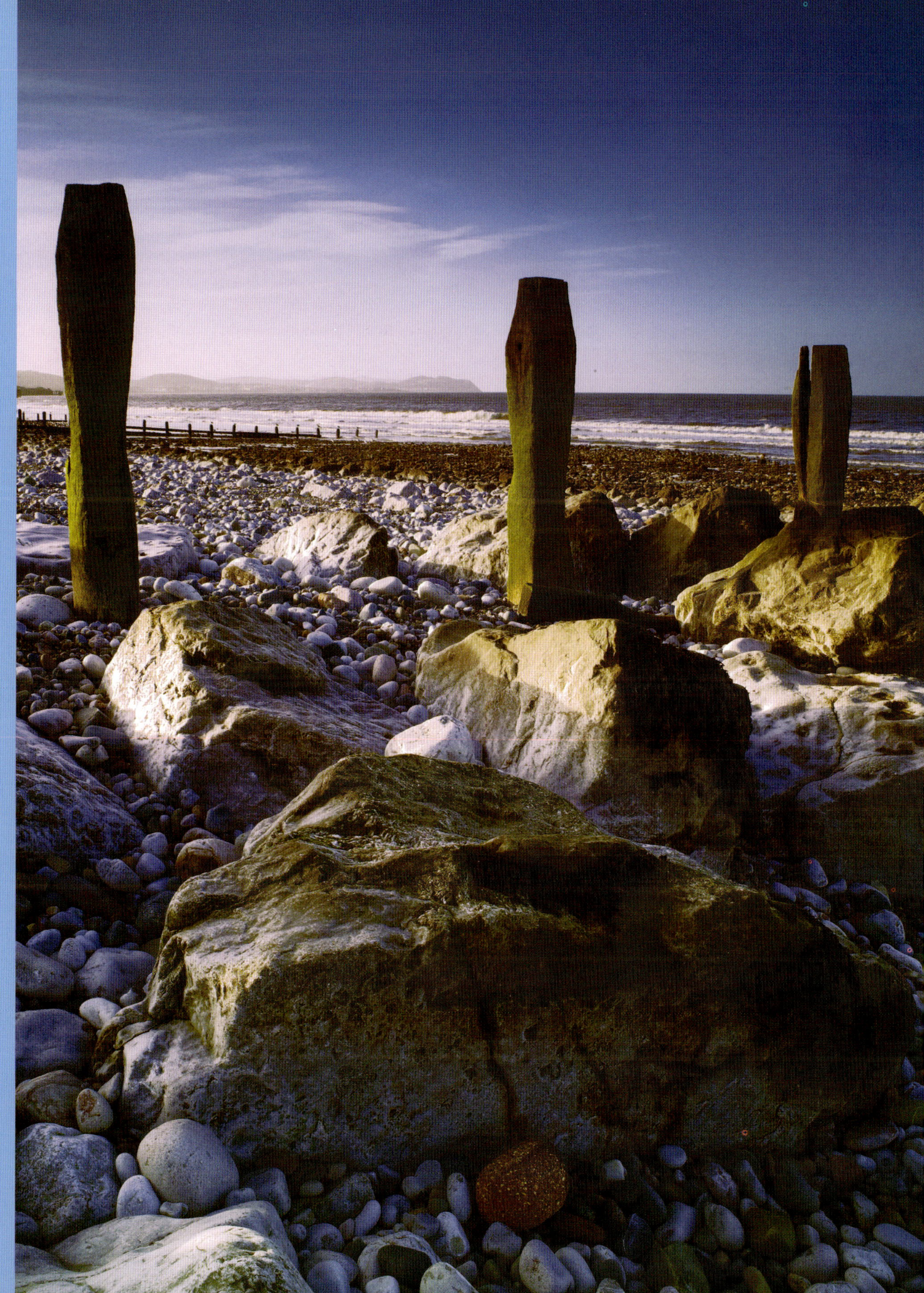

**Llandulas, Clwyd, Wales**

**Camera:** Mamiya 645 AFDII
with Mamiya digital back
**Lens:** Mamiya 35mm (wide-angle)
**Filter:** 2-stop ND graduated
**Exposure:** 1/8sec at f/22, ISO 100
**Waiting for the light:** 60 minutes
**Post-processing:** Suppression
of highlights

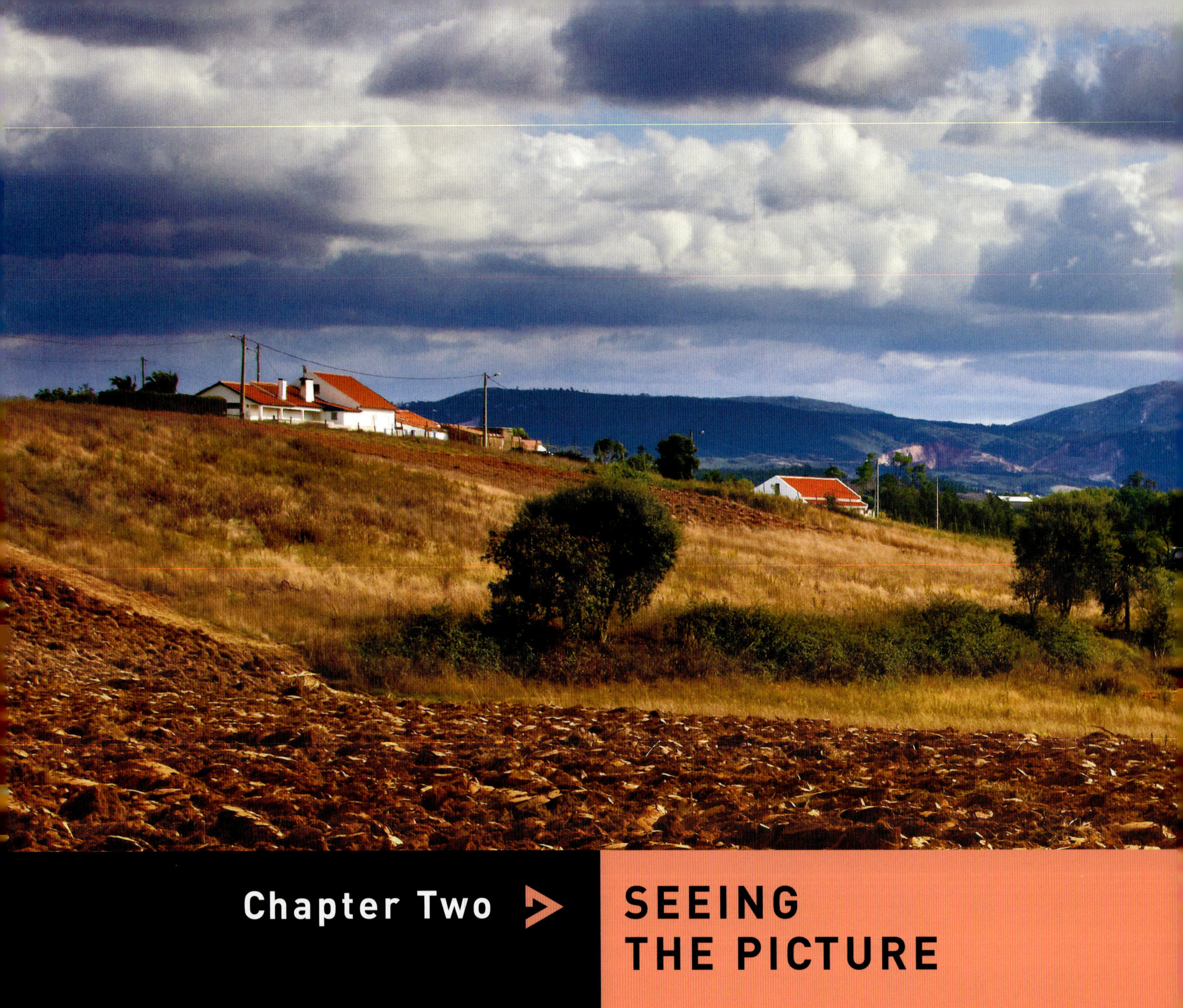
Chapter Two
SEEING
THE PICTURE
Near Rio Maior, Portugal

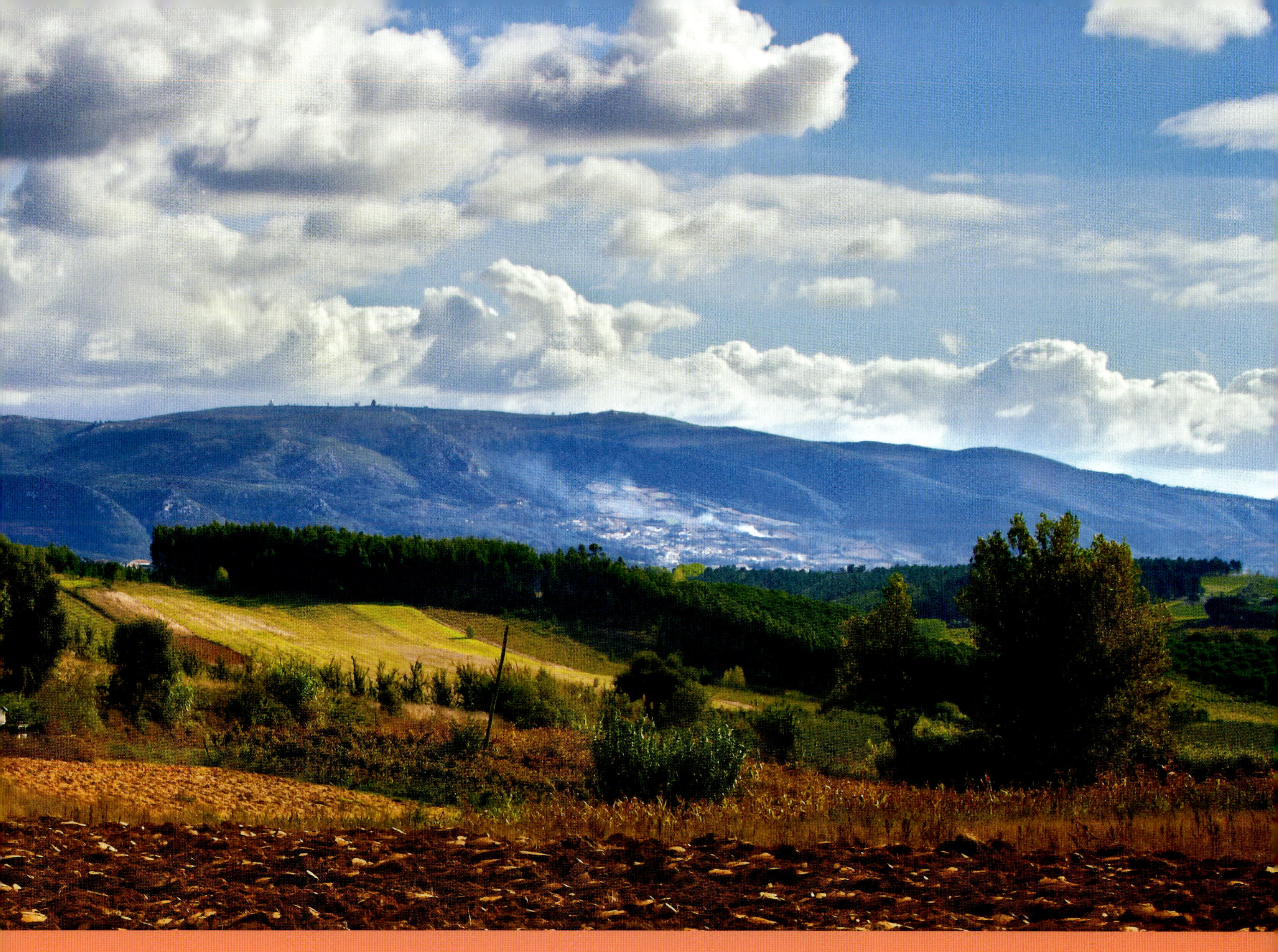

There is no shortage of pictures in the landscape. From an intricate close-up to a sweeping, majestic vista, images of every description are out there waiting to be captured, but before they can be taken they have to be seen. And it is the seeing that is the crucial factor; it is, quite simply, the difference between success and failure. To succeed, certain techniques have to be adopted to ensure that the landscape is carefully observed and opportunities discovered. These techniques are outlined and discussed in the following chapter.

Everything in the world has a shape. This might seem like a pointless statement because everything has to have some kind of shape in order for it to exist, but I state the obvious because an object's shape often goes unseen. We might look and observe, but outlines and contours don't always register, and from a photographer's perspective this is an incomplete view of the world. When seeking to make images it is a weakness, because a lack of awareness and appreciation of shape and form will lead to missed opportunities and inferior compositions. If there is one thought to carry with you as you venture into the landscape, it should be to look at the world as a series of shapes. When searching for pictures I find it useful to take a step back from reality and attempt to view the landscape in abstract form, so that what registers is the appearance and outlines of objects, rather than what they actually are.

Creative composition also requires an awareness of the effect of combinations of different shapes. Soft, curved lines tend to be relaxing, while straight lines, sharp edges and diagonals create tension. If you combine them, as has been done in the picture opposite, where a single circle is depicted against a series of squares and rectangles, it makes a strong visual impact. Suddenly shapes become apparent and the image, while realistic, has a graphic, abstract quality. Combinations of this type exist all around us, both in the man-made and natural world; they just need to be observed and then put together in a photograph. It is a relatively simple technique to master and a very useful creative tool.

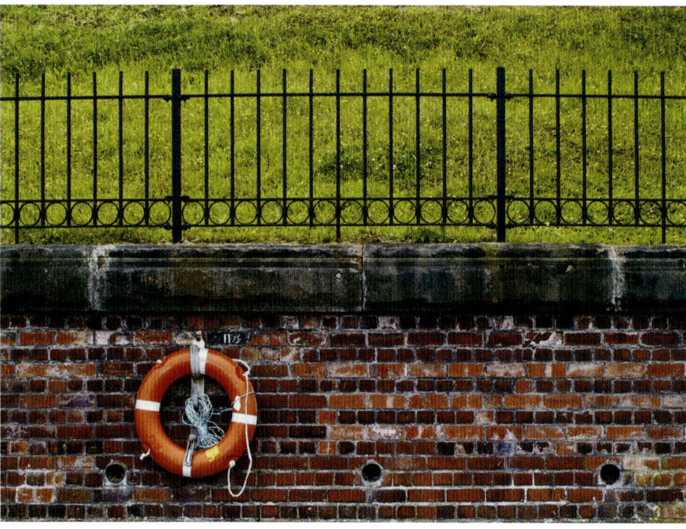

> **TIP:**  Look at the landscape as a collection of shapes and patterns. Use combinations of contrasting shapes to give a picture impact.

> **TIP:**  When shape and pattern are the theme of an image use a restricted range of colours. Clearly defined blocks of colour will help to convey the outline of the component parts.

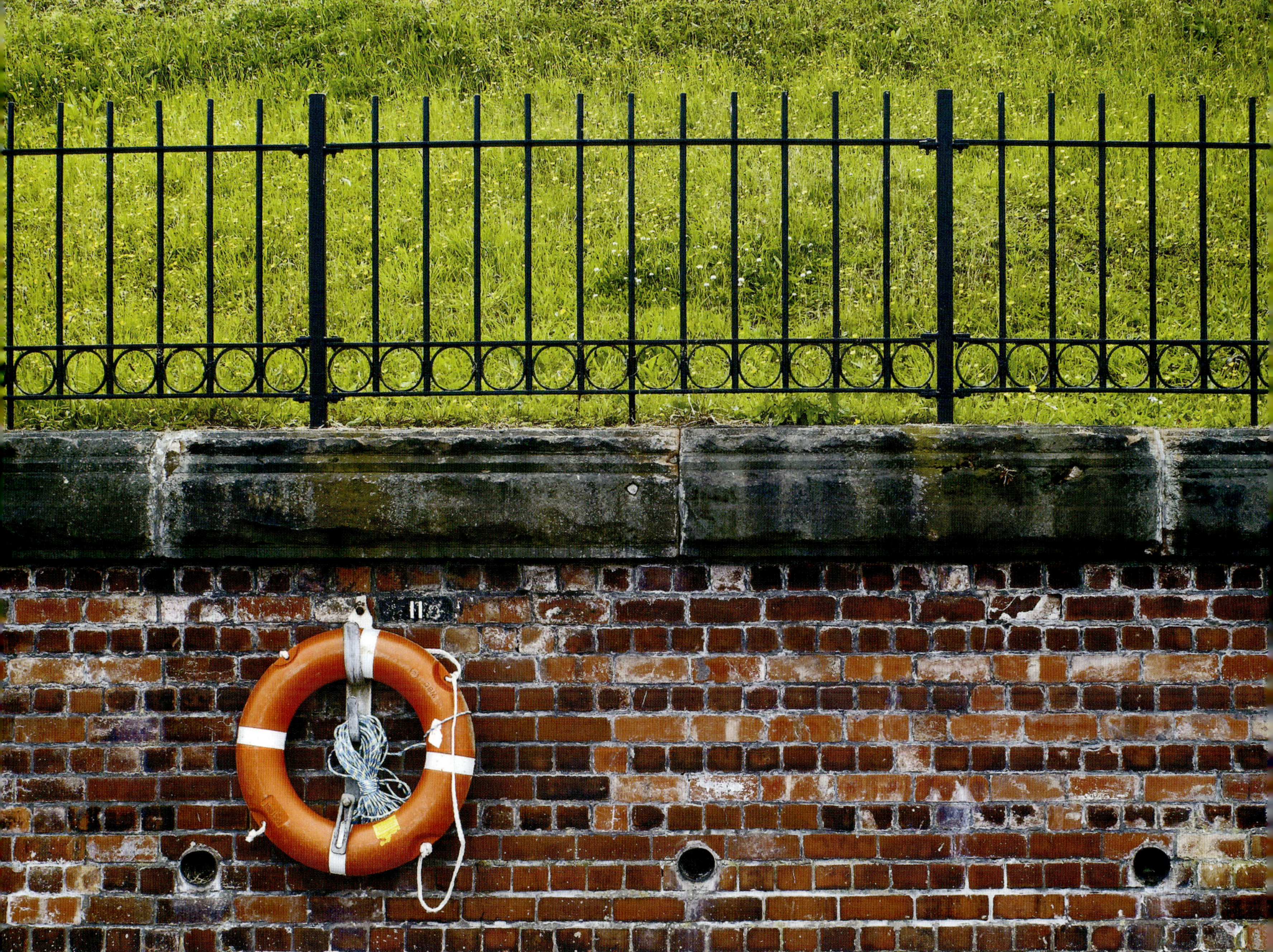

**Egremont, Wirral, England**

**Camera:** Mamiya 645 AFDII with Mamiya digital back
**Lens:** Mamiya 150mm (telephoto)
**Filter:** None
**Exposure:** 1/10sec at f/20, ISO 100
**Waiting for the light:** Immediate
**Post-processing:** None

Look carefully at a leafy landscape and you will realize that there is more to it than meets the eye. What initially might appear to be a jumbled, discordant wilderness will, under scrutiny, reveal an underlying structure. Rather than just a disorganized mass of flora, a patterned display of colours and textures will often begin to appear. It may not be apparent to the casual observer, but study this type of subject carefully and images will begin to emerge.

Your success as a photographer to a certain extent can be determined by your ability to find attractive compositions buried within the fabric of the landscape. To discover them, examine the landscape at a deeper level so you begin to see its component parts. By this I mean the shapes, patterns, contours, textures and tones. You can ignore reality.

It doesn't matter what the subject is; it is what it actually looks like when observed through the lens of the camera that is most important. The remote and anonymous corner of the Vermilion Cliffs Wilderness pictured here is by no means spectacular. Being surrounded by more renowned attractions it could easily be overlooked, but the combination of the delicately varied tonal range and the repetition of both similar and contrasting shapes makes this, in my view, an interesting image. Pictures like this can work on two levels: they can be viewed as a realistic portrayal of a subject or as an abstract arrangement. How they are perceived is subjective and different people see these images in different ways. When displayed as large prints they do, however, have a strong visual impact and can look striking when framed and hung.

- **A viewpoint was chosen that enabled the composition to include a band of dark bushes across the top of the image. This helps to frame the picture and give it depth.**

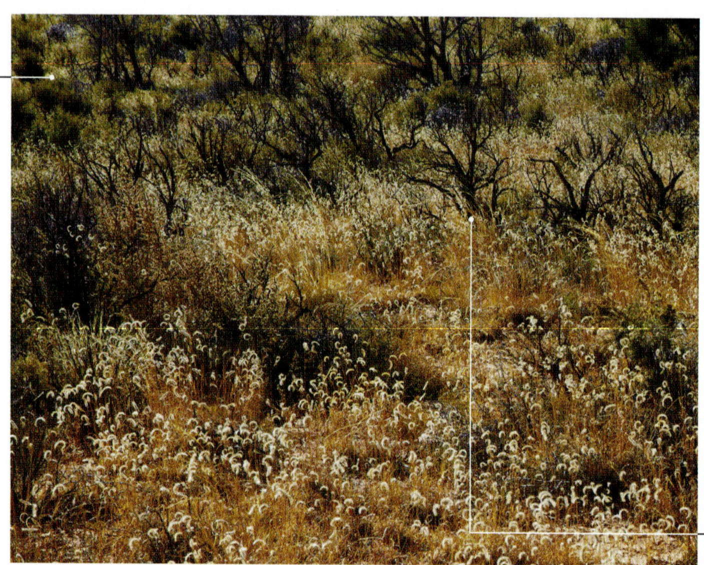

Polarizer (fully polarized)

- **Even when dry, shiny surfaces of flora can create bright reflections. A polarizer was therefore used to suppress highlights and give the image additional impact.**

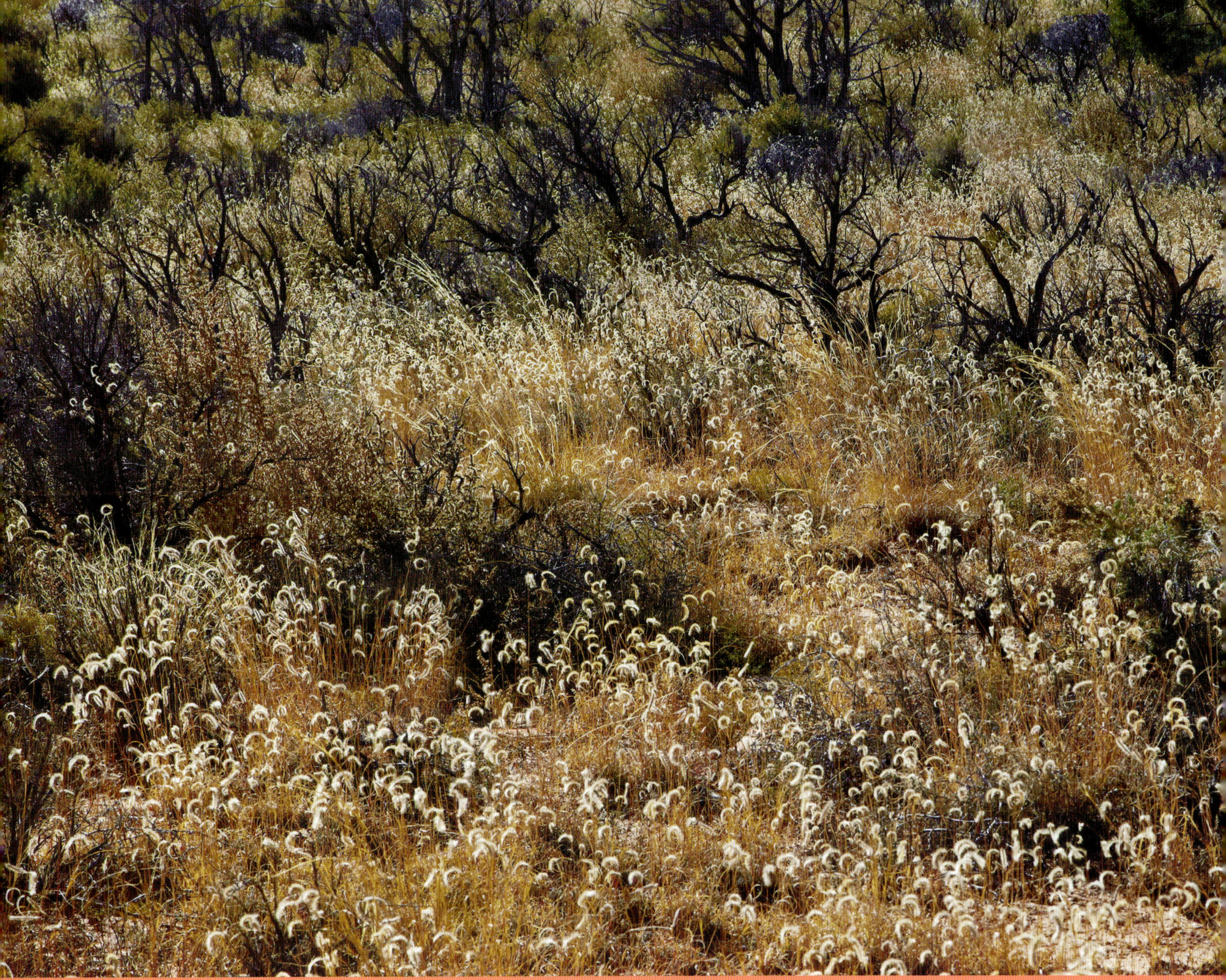

**Vermilion Cliffs Wilderness, Arizona, USA**

**Camera:** Mamiya 645 AFDII with Phase One digital back
**Lens:** Mamiya 80mm (standard)
**Filter:** Polarizer (fully polarized)
**Exposure:** 1/30sec at f/22, ISO 100
**Waiting for the light:** Immediate
**Post-processing:** None

Intricately patterned rocks are the type of subject where a close-up composition can be the most successful approach, because they often lose impact when viewed from a distance. There are exceptions, though, and I gradually came to this conclusion as I tried and failed to find a small area of rock along the rugged patchwork of cliffs along St Brides Bay that did justice to the whole.

Perhaps I didn't look hard enough, but other than abseiling down the cliff face there was little more that I could have done to widen the search for the perfect arrangement. The only option was a slightly wider view, one that took in a portion of the pebble-covered beach and extended to a height of approximately 7ft (2.1m). I then spent the best part of an hour pacing forwards and backwards along the length of the bay with the incoming tide lapping at my feet. There were many possibilities and after much deliberation I eventually settled on a composition that seemed to encapsulate the character of the cliffs. There is a dynamic, rugged quality to the picture that is emphasized by the contrasting colour combination. The tension in the image is then eased slightly by the narrow strip of pebbles that helps to place the craggy rock face in its environment and prevents the picture from becoming a total abstract. Photograph taken, and being mindful of the fact that saltwater and delicate electronics are best kept apart, I quickly packed away my equipment and waded back to higher ground. The pebbled beach gradually disappeared under the relentless splashing and foaming of the incoming waves as rain clouds gathered. The day was over, but thankfully it had been productive.

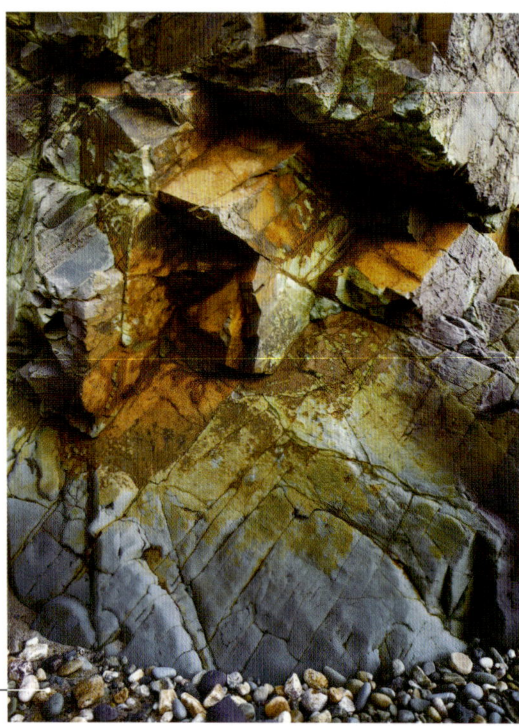

• The inclusion of the pebbles gives the image scale and allows it to be viewed as a realistic portrayal of a subject instead of an abstract arrangement.

> **TIP:** Stripping down an image to its basic elements can often be an effective way of depicting the character of a subject, but there are occasions when omitting features – by using a tight, close-up composition, for example – can be the wrong approach. Sometimes, because of the nature of the subject, a looser, more inclusive arrangement is better.

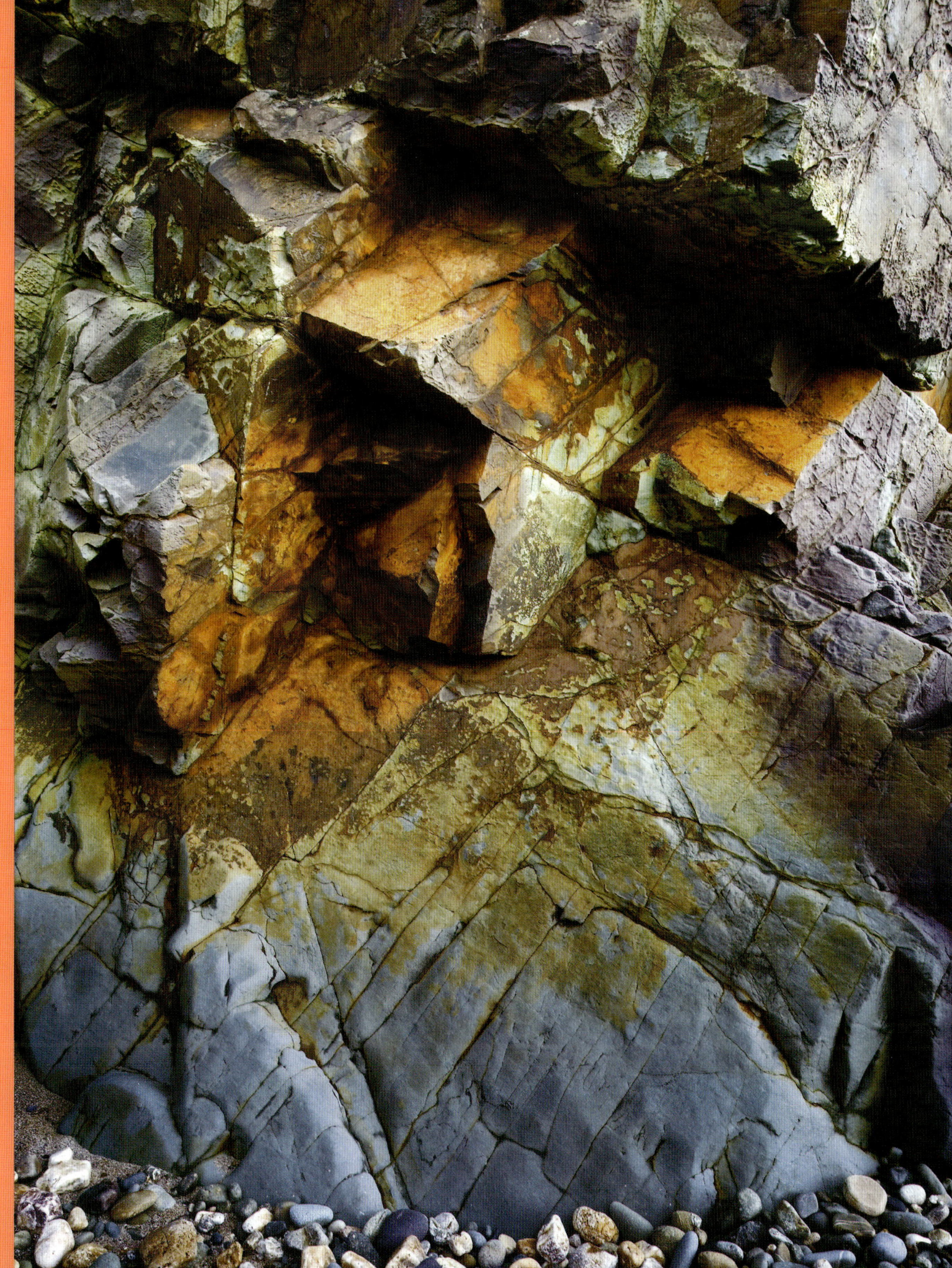


**St Brides Bay,
Pembrokeshire, Wales**

**Camera:** Mamiya 645 AFDII
with Mamiya digital back
**Lens:** Mamiya 35mm
(wide-angle)
**Filter:** None
**Exposure:** 1/5sec at f/18,
ISO 100
**Waiting for the light:**
Immediate
**Post-processing:** Curves
and colour balance
adjustment

Ensconced in the middle of the mountains and valleys of Snowdonia during the depths of winter, the thought of capturing an urban landscape hadn't crossed my mind. I had no plans to visit any towns, but of course man-made structures, of one description or another, are scattered across the rural landscape. One that caught my attention was the house I happened to be staying in. Specifically it was the tiled roof, because the consistently falling snow had settled on its sloping surface in a repeated pattern that accentuated the roof's regimented uniformity. It was apparent that there was potential for a photograph, but timing was going to be important.

It wasn't just a matter of seconds, minutes or even hours, as is normally the case. I monitored the roof for a total of four days and it was interesting to observe how its appearance changed according to the depth of the fallen snow. Too much obscured the colour of the tiles, while too little weakened the underlying pattern. Finally, as the novelty of roof-watching was beginning to lose its appeal, there seemed to be the right combination of tiles and snow and the image was at last captured. It was taken through an open window and, as I recall, was the first landscape picture I ever took from indoors. It wasn't what I was expecting from a week in Snowdonia, but photographs can emerge from the unlikeliest sources and the nature of the subject is unimportant. If a picture appeals to you, then capture it.

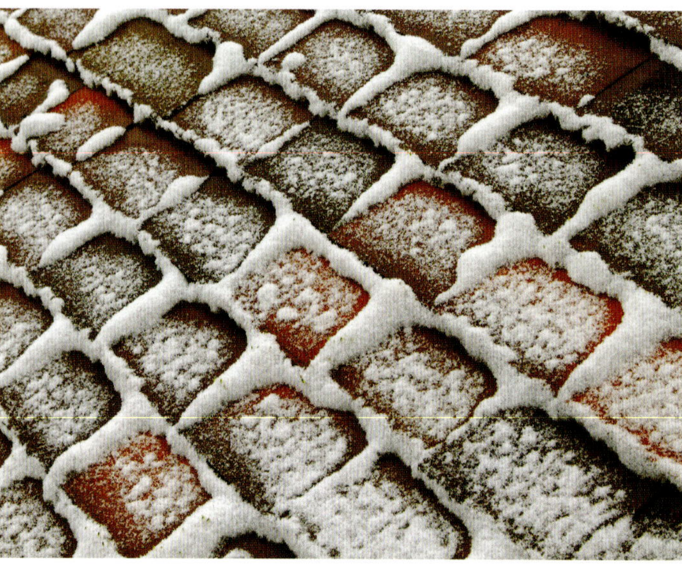

• **Repeating blocks of colour are the theme of this image. Their arrangement as a series of diagonal, rather than horizontal and vertical, lines gives the picture a more dynamic quality.**

**>** **TIP:** Man-made structures can be a rich source of pattern, texture and repetition. Use close-up compositions to isolate specific features and the result will often be eye-catching abstract or semi-abstract photographs.

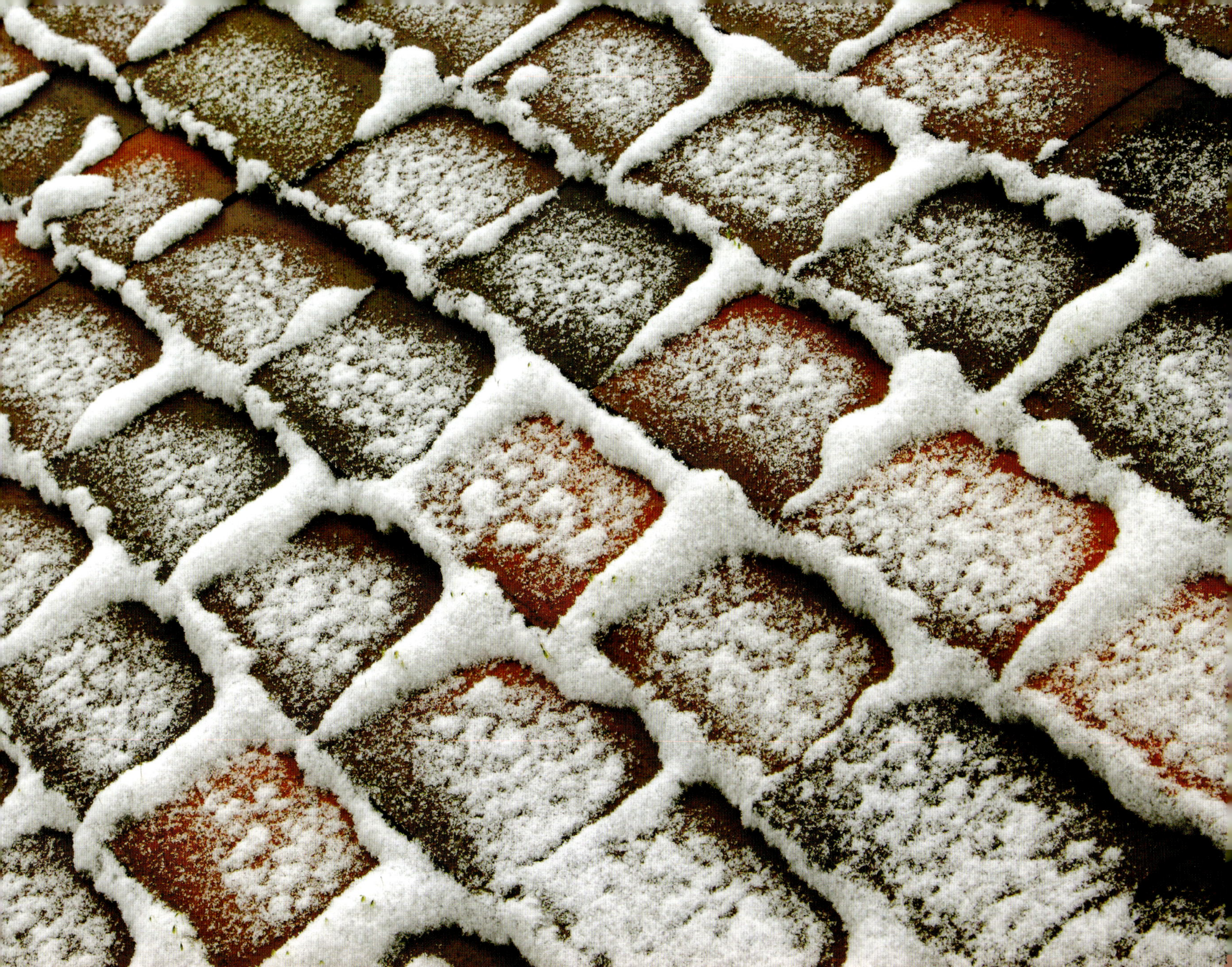

**Bala, Snowdonia, Wales**

**Camera:** Mamiya 645 AFDII with Mamiya digital back
**Lens:** Mamiya 80mm (standard)
**Filter:** None
**Exposure:** 1/8sec at f/22, ISO 100
**Waiting for the light:** 4 days (waiting for the snow)
**Post-processing:** Suppression of highlights, colour balance adjustment (warming)

A bright splash of colour is a powerful element when present in a photograph. It has a magnetic quality and a vividly coloured object – even one of moderate proportions – can act as the cornerstone around which an image is constructed. For maximum impact, using a limited tonal range of just two contrasting colours can be very effective, particularly when the composition consists of repetitive, easily perceived shapes. Solid blocks, rather than a scattered kaleidoscope, of colour are normally the best arrangement.

I wasn't thinking specifically about colour as I strolled through the narrow alleys and passageways of the medieval French town of Souillac – the ancient buildings were of greater interest. However, as soon as I caught a glimpse of the bright red geraniums hanging in glorious isolation against a muted, rather neutral background the possibility of making a picture suddenly arose. The tonal contrast between the flowers and the alleyway was striking and there was also a satisfying combination of opposite shapes. The regimentation of the repeated vertical lines is the perfect foil for the softly contoured flowers and together they bring an added dimension to the image.

As a general guideline, when a block of a single colour is the main feature there should be no other areas of the same colour, and for that reason I removed a handful of fallen petals. Looking at the photograph now I'm not sure if it was the right thing to do. Perhaps the loose petals would have added a touch of reality. Although I didn't think so at the time, the image seems a little sterile. It is now obvious that the scene should have been captured both with and without the petals and then the results could have been compared. It didn't occur to me at the time, which was a mistake, because when the opportunity arises to produce two versions of the same photograph it should always be taken.

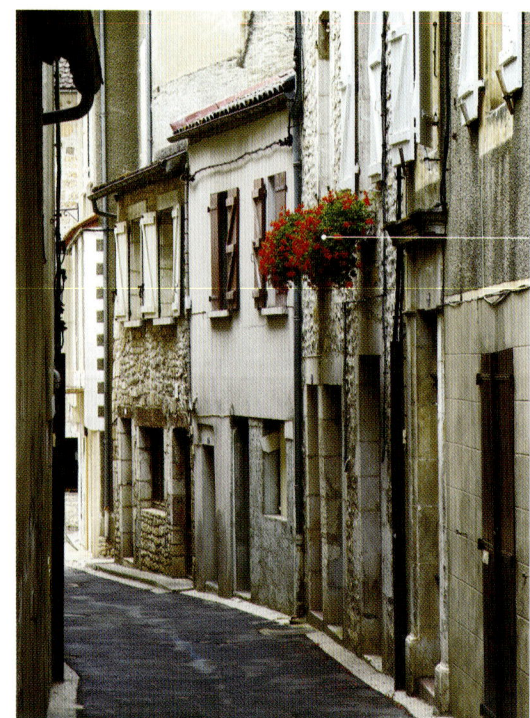

**The restricted colour range draws attention to the bright red flowers. Had there been other expanses of a similar colour present the picture would have suffered as a result. The exception is possibly a few fallen petals below the basket. Would they have been a positive or negative addition? My failure to capture them prior to their removal means that the question must, regrettably, remain unanswered.**

**The round shape of the flowers acts as a softening device against the angular background.**

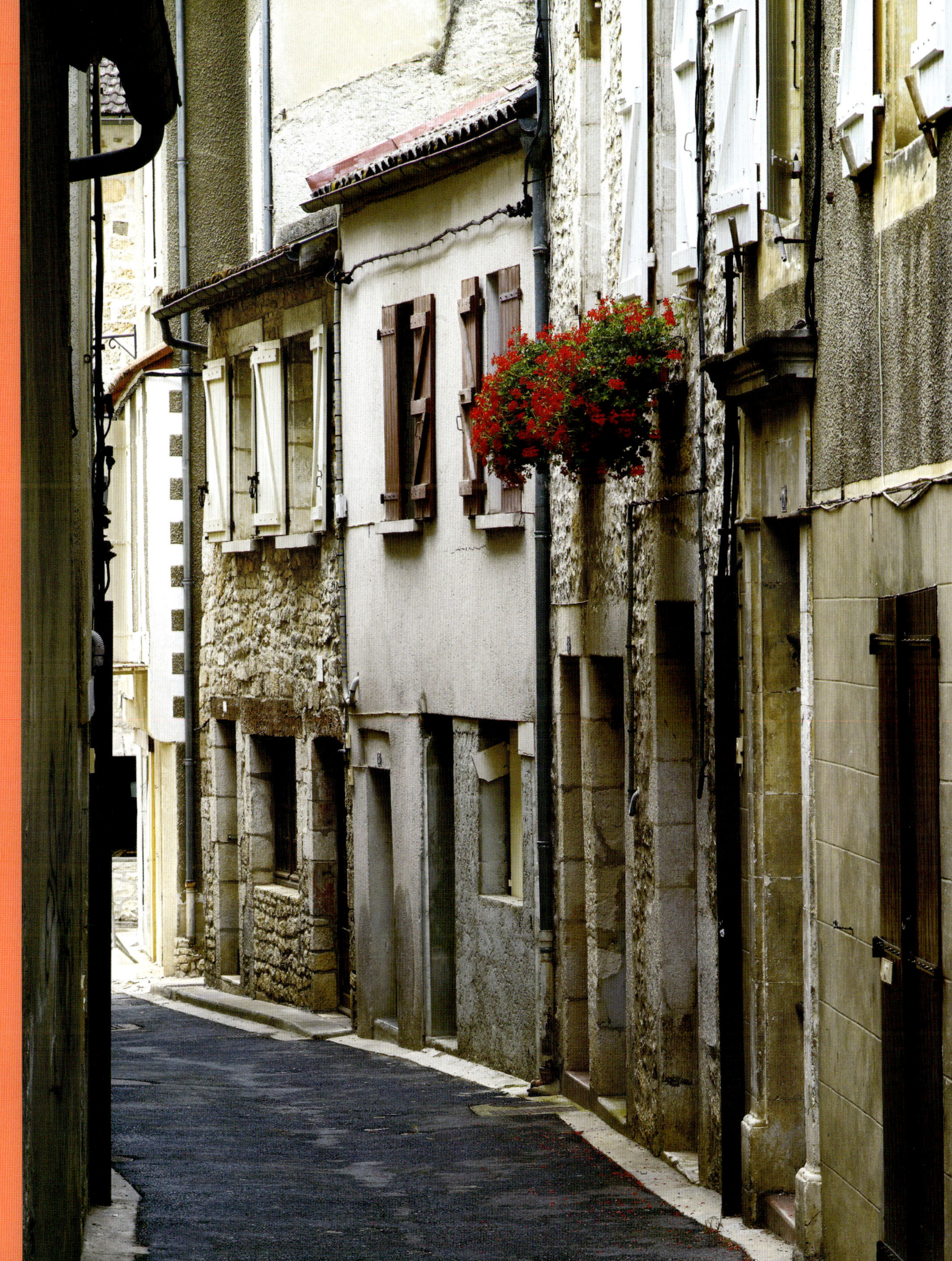

**Souillac,**
**The Dordogne, France**

**Camera:** Mamiya 645 AFDII
with Mamiya digital back
**Lens:** Mamiya 35mm
(wide-angle)
**Filter:** None
**Exposure:** 1/2sec at f/22,
ISO 100
**Waiting for the light:**
Immediate
**Post-processing:** Curves
and colour balance
adjustment

Colour and pattern are the core elements of this semi-abstract image. Although you know what it is you're looking at, the reality of the subject is of secondary importance; design and appearance are what matter. This type of picture, where the object is recognizable, but the portrayal of it is highly stylized, is perfect for the photographic medium. Unlike a landscape view, the creation of such images is entirely the product of the photographer's observational skill and creative interpretation. Such pictures are conceived and assembled solely in the photographer's mind. This is, of course, what 'seeing the picture' means. To capture an image you have to see it first and, while some people might have a natural eye for design, this is a skill that I believe everyone can develop. As discussed elsewhere in this book, the most effective way to look at the world is through the eyes of a photographer. So, when you are seeking images – and indeed even when you're not – look at your surroundings in an abstract way. Ignore reality and learn to observe patterns, shapes, colours and contours. Train your eye and mind to perceive the world in this way (well, perhaps not all the time – not when you're driving, for example!) and you will begin to see pictures in the most unlikely subjects. Your heightened visual perception will then become apparent in the images you make.

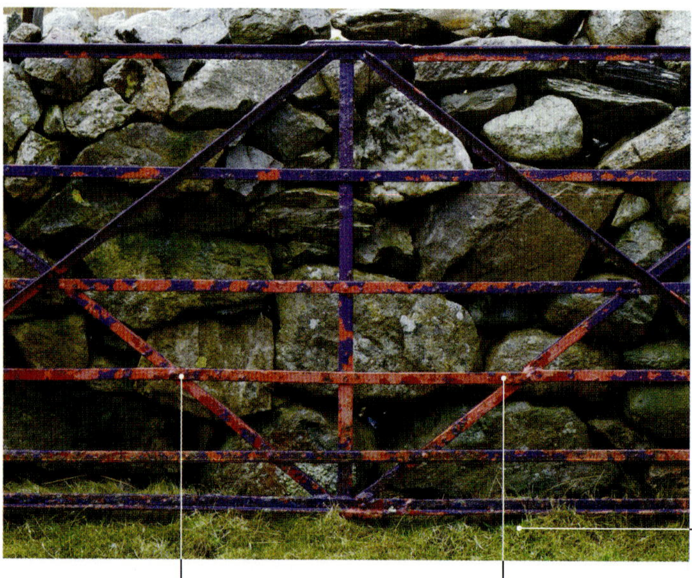

- It was the distinctive colour of the painted metal gate that caught my attention here. I am not usually that keen on metal, preferring instead old, wooden structures, but the glorious, weathered colours of the peeling paint were irresistible. When it became apparent that there was an opportunity to introduce a symmetrical, patterned arrangement, I set up my camera without hesitation.

- The grey tonal range of the dry-stone wall is a perfect background for the distinctively coloured gate. The strip of grass, while it introduces another colour that isn't really necessary, acts as a base upon which the rest of the picture stands.

- Symmetry is an important feature of this image and it was most fortunate that the design of the gate enabled the picture to be arranged as a left and right mirror image. An asymmetrical composition would have weakened the image, possibly to the point of failure.

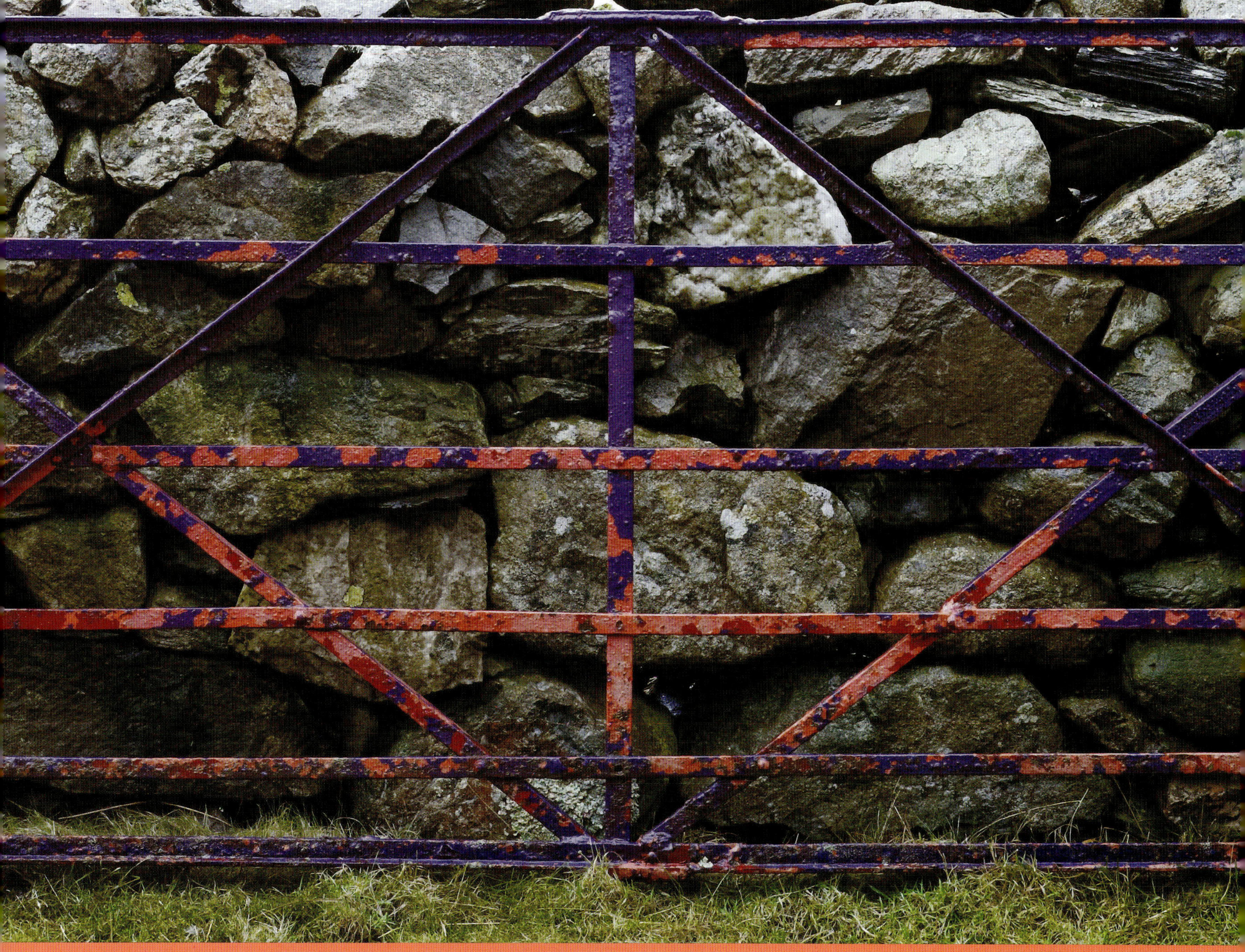

**Nant Ffrancon, Snowdonia, Wales**

**Camera:** Mamiya 645 AFDII with Mamiya digital back
**Lens:** Mamiya 35mm (wide-angle)
**Filter:** None
**Exposure:** 1/5sec at f/18, ISO 100
**Waiting for the light:** Immediate
**Post-processing:** None

This picture consists almost entirely of rectangles. Remove the foliage and you are left with a collection of right-angled, four-sided shapes. It is very distinctive because every block of colour, from the green wall to the white window frame, is an individual rectangle. There are no other shapes or random objects to interfere with the symmetry. This is also emphasized by the simplicity of the combination of four plain, but striking, colours (or five if you include the weathered strip along the foot of the image, which, fortunately, is also a rectangle). On their own the shapes make an interesting composition but not, perhaps, a complete picture. They need another element, not only to soften the rigid symmetry of the straight lines, but also to counterbalance the rather one-sided, bottom-heavy arrangement. How marvellous then that, as if conjured up out of thin air to order, the perfect foil was positioned in exactly the right place. The foliage in the top right corner was also the right size, shape (i.e. no particular shape as such) and colour. I was almost jumping for joy as I stood and gazed upon this ready-made image. My role as the photographer was simply to point the camera straight and level at the wall, focus and release the shutter.

It was hardly a demanding task, but all the work had been done in the search for the picture. The day had been spent travelling from village to village trawling through passages and alleys looking for that special arrangement, that snippet of rural Portugal that could be successfully captured. Images like this are few and far between, and perseverance and keen observation are required if they are to be discovered. Once seen the creative input is virtually done, the actual taking of the photograph being little more than the satisfying conclusion of your vision and patient groundwork.

> **TIP:** If there is a window in your picture, take care to avoid capturing your reflection in the glass. If possible use a camera position that is not directly opposite the window. A polarizer can also help to reduce reflections.

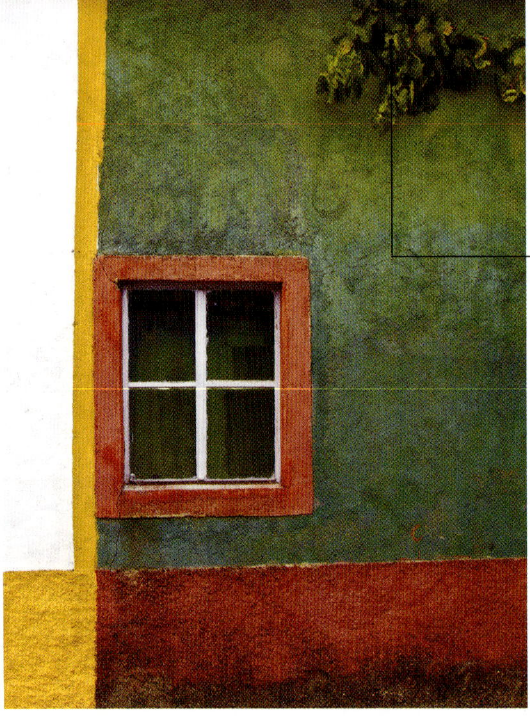

• The clearly defined blocks of colour help to portray the symmetry. It was therefore fortunate that the foliage did not introduce another distinctive colour. A clash of contrasting hues would have weakened the arrangement.

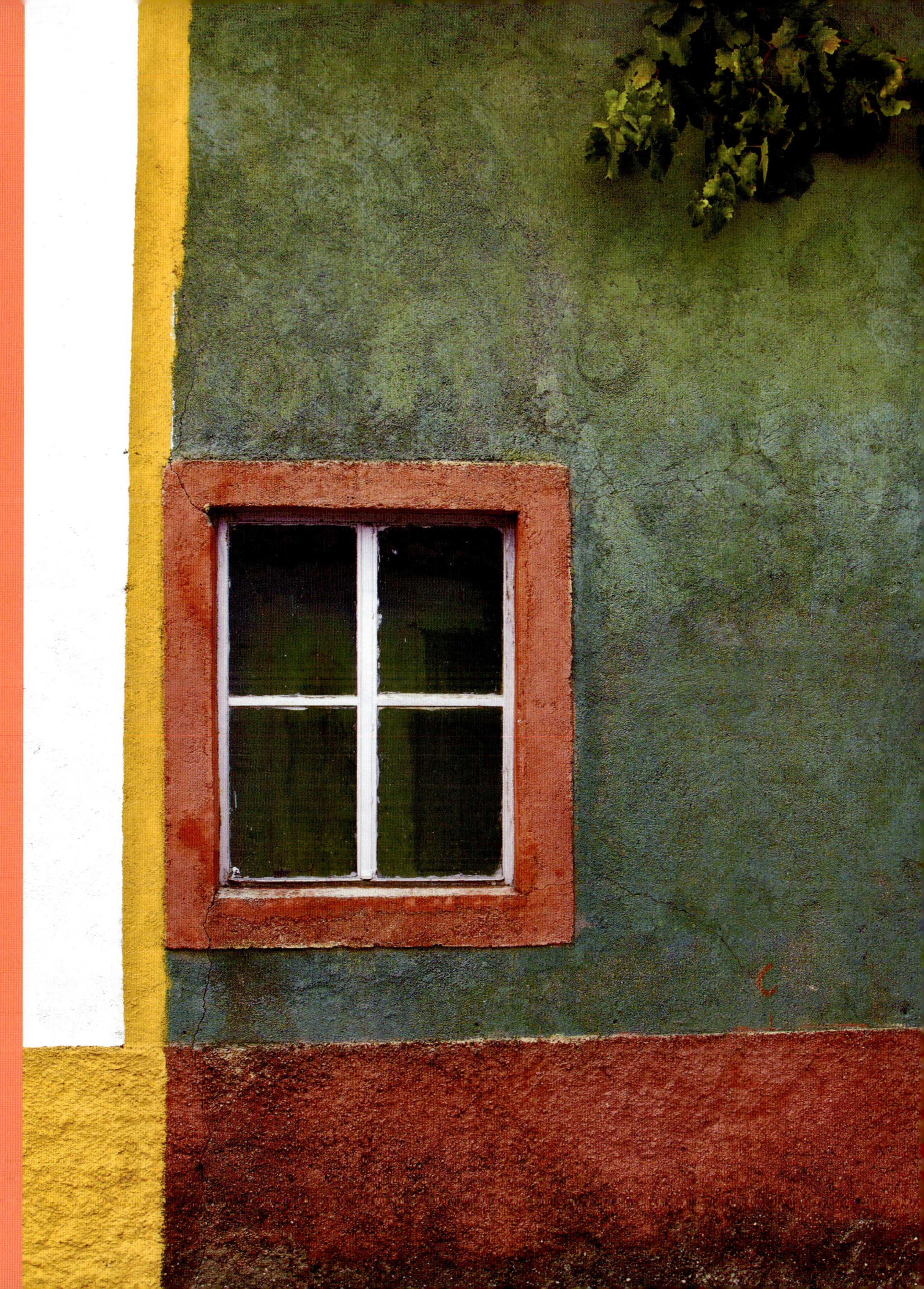

**Arneiro, Portugal**

**Camera:** Mamiya 645 AFDII with
Mamiya digital back
**Lens:** Mamiya 150mm (telephoto)
**Filter:** None
**Exposure:** 1/20sec at f/16, ISO 100
**Waiting for the light:** Immediate
**Post-processing:** None

Most people who look at this photograph for the first time don't quite know what to make of it. It is usually perceived as an unusual rock formation, which indeed it is, but beyond that it becomes a little vague. This is often the case with abstract images when they are viewed in isolation and in the absence of any descriptive information. The confusion is a result of scale, or rather a lack of it. Is the picture a close-up or even a macro representation of the subject or is it, perhaps, a more distant view?

There are many images of the Coyote Buttes and other similar locations where, in order to avoid confusion, the photographer has deliberately included people. It is an effective approach and your perception of the scale of the subject is immediately transformed, but personally I prefer to leave people out of pictures. The reason for this is simple: human beings are the most powerful focal points on earth. If your image includes people the eye will be immediately drawn to them and at that point the landscape begins to suffer. It is no longer a landscape image; it becomes a travel picture or in extreme cases a portrait. There is nothing wrong with this, of course. I have many photographs of family and friends in splendid locations, but I don't consider them intrinsically to be landscape images.

So, that brings us back to the question of scale. Is its absence in a picture a negative factor? There is of course no definitive answer because there are no rules that can be applied. It is a matter of opinion, but personally I am quite happy for my images to contain an element of mystery. Viewers make their own assessments and judge pictures on their visual merits, not on matters of scale or size. If the origin of the subject is a little vague it can bring an added dimension to an image and prompt thought and discussion, and if a photograph does that then I believe it has achieved something.

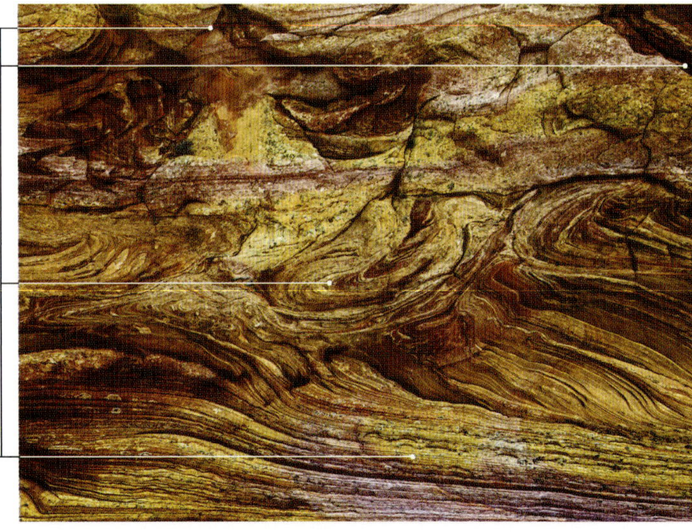

• Composition was based around the central band of curls, supported by the horizontally flowing lines of rock underneath. The rock formation along the top acts as an upper frame, particularly where diagonal lines bisect the two corners and help to direct attention towards the centre of the image. Overall the pattern makes a cohesive, self-contained picture and this was the main reason the image was captured.

• In case you're wondering, the dimensions of the rock face are approximately 8 x 6ft (2.4 x 1.6m).

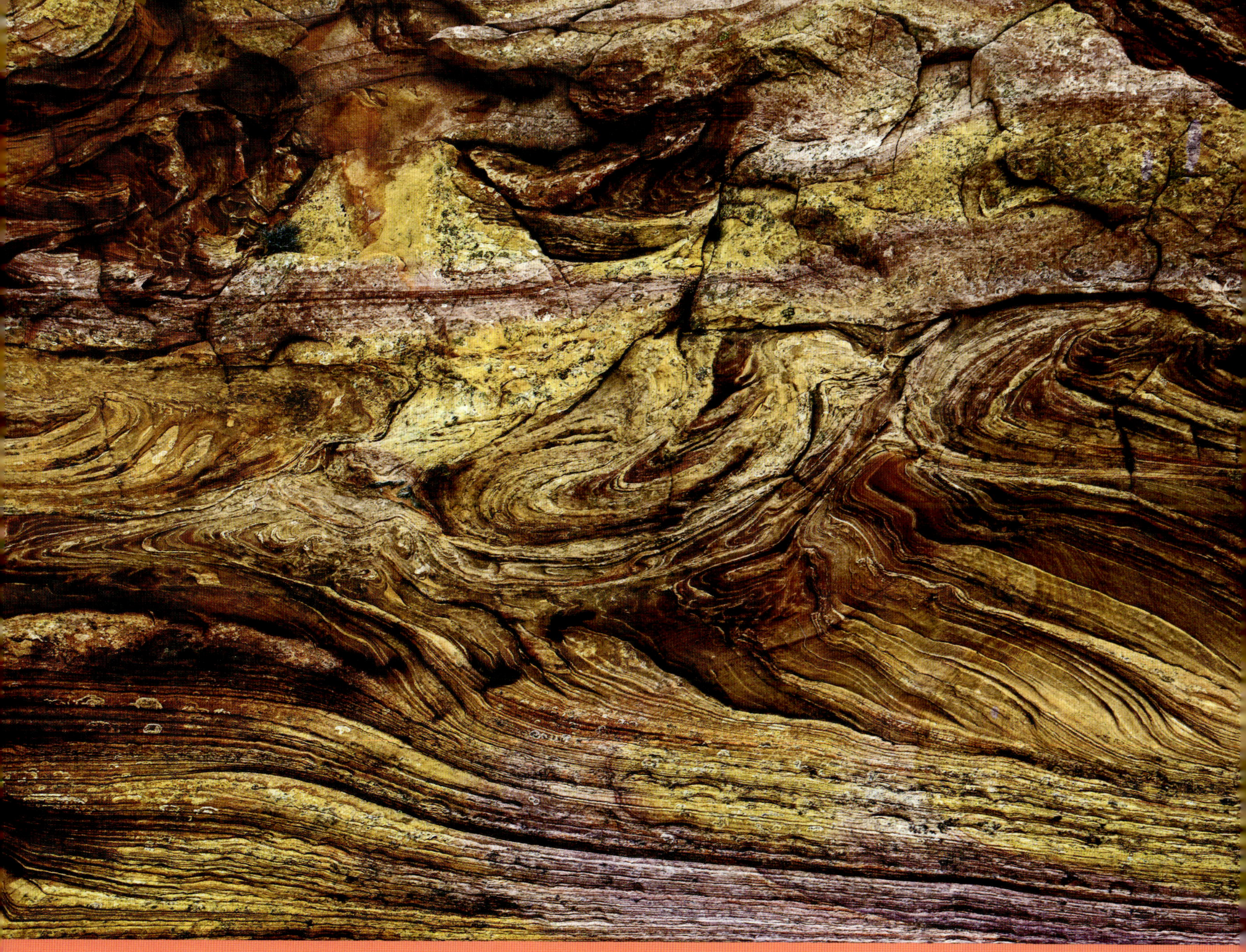

**South Coyote Buttes, Arizona, USA**

**Camera:** Mamiya 645 AFDII with Phase One digital back
**Lens:** Mamiya 80mm (standard)
**Filter:** None
**Exposure:** 1/8sec at f/20, ISO 100
**Waiting for the light:** Immediate
**Post-processing:** Curves adjustment

Old, decaying buildings can be fascinating because they are often a treasure trove of intriguing images, and the historic township of Paria was therefore at the top of my list of Utah locations. Unfortunately my 'infallible' research was, I am embarrassed to admit, seriously flawed, because as I arrived at the destination the town was conspicuous by its absence. It had apparently been destroyed by fire several years earlier. Although its sad demise was a disappointment, the day still held promise because the site of the former town was surrounded by what are undoubtedly the most colourful and distinctive mountains imaginable. The area was so spectacular and so unusual it could have been on a different planet. Thoughts of the old town were forgotten as, lost in another world, I gazed in awe at the unique landscape. It was a totally absorbing, breathtaking experience, but eventually I managed to suppress my wonderment and gather my thoughts. It was time for a reality check; time to think about the best way to depict the location and convey its unique appearance.

After an hour or more of experimenting with different viewpoints I finally settled on the picture opposite. There were a number of options but this image, more than any other, seemed to encapsulate the beauty and character of the mountains. Although the field of view is restricted, it reveals more about the subject than would have been the case had a wider, more distant composition been used. The narrow angle of coverage is a result of the long focal length of the lens. The other effect is that distance has been compressed and the result of the flattened perspective is that greater emphasis has been placed on the distinctive patterns and colours, which many would say are the most important features of these mountains.

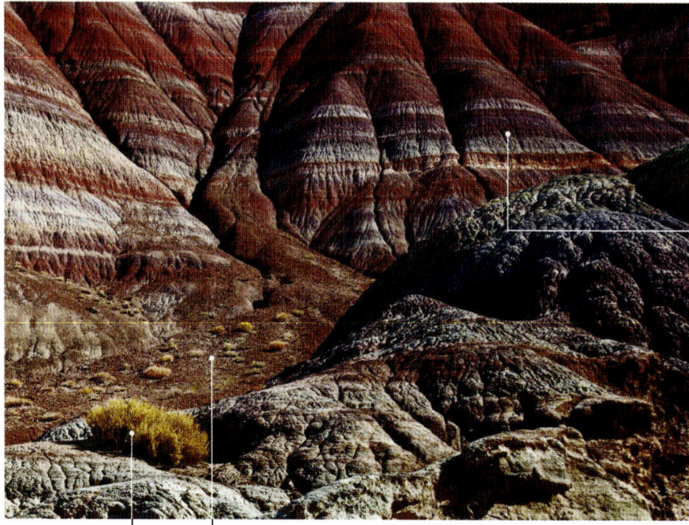

• **The background mountains were more distant than they appear. They therefore have an enhanced presence, which helps to depict their colourful, flowing contours. This is a result of using a telephoto lens.**

• **The image was composed around the small shrub in the foreground, which acts as an important focal point. Despite the compression of the long lens it gives the picture a degree of depth, because the smaller, more distant shrubs create a sense of scale.**

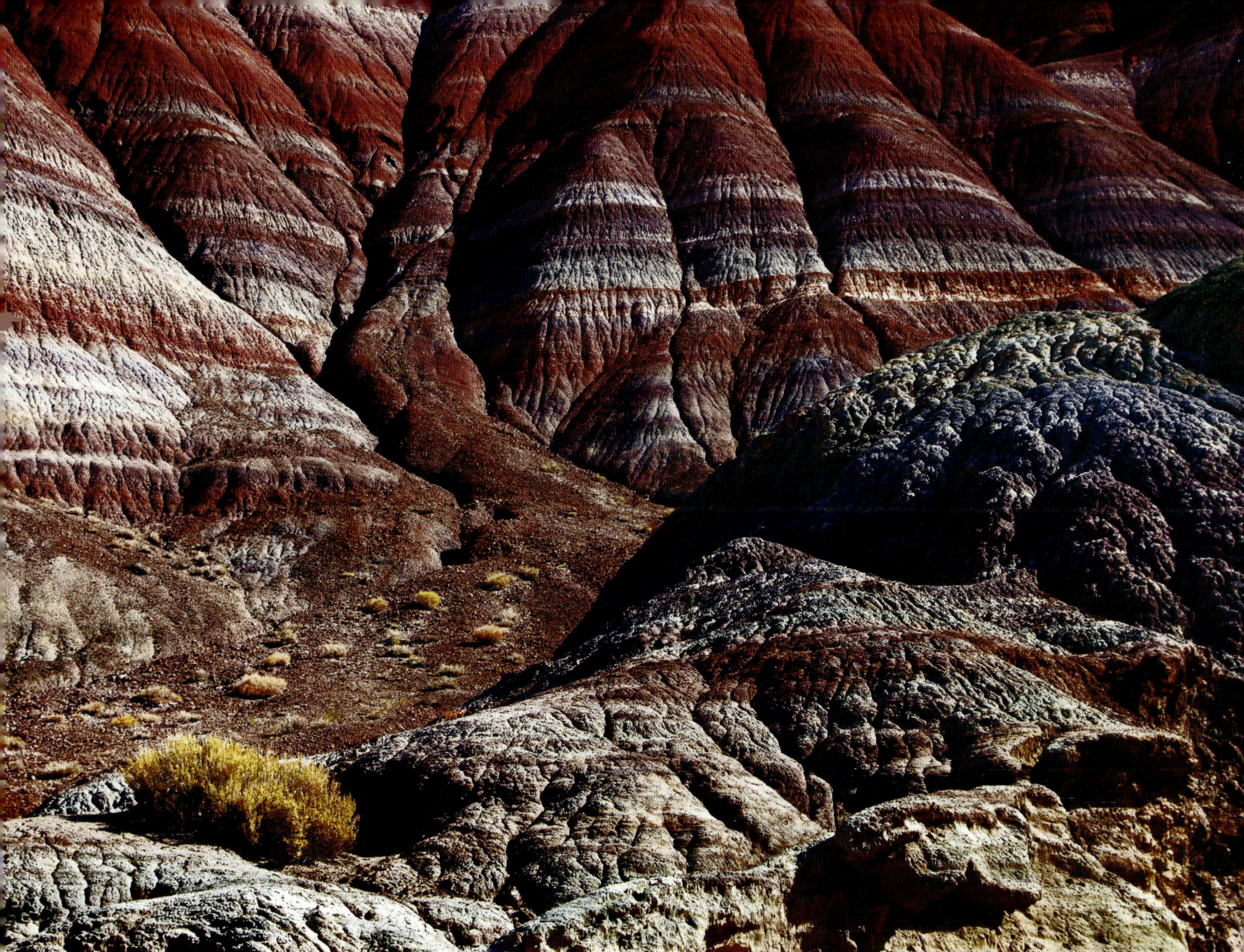

**Paria Canyon, Utah, USA**

**Camera:** Mamiya 645 AFDII with Phase One digital back
**Lens:** Mamiya 150mm (telephoto)
**Filter:** None
**Exposure:** 1/20sec at f/22, ISO 100
**Waiting for the light:** 90 minutes
**Post-processing:** None

At first glance it might appear that minimalist photography produces an unrealistic portrayal of the landscape. This is understandable because the landscape is, by nature, anything but minimal; indeed, it could be described as the exact opposite. However, this isn't always the case and often the minimal image is overlooked simply because we don't see it. From a photographer's perspective we can sometimes see too much; we don't filter out unwanted elements unless we consciously make the effort to do so. The result is that opportunities for making minimalist pictures often go unnoticed.

When the landscape is covered by a blanket of snow it becomes easier, because much of the unwanted detail is obscured. Everything is reduced to the extent that scenic views often consist of just a few stark features. Minimalist images become the default option in these conditions, which is to be welcomed because they can be very rewarding to capture.

Clear skies, normally the downfall of many pictures, add to the minimalist theme and in these circumstances can usually be included as an integral part of the composition. Less is certainly more in this type of photograph, as the inclusion of a wide expanse of empty space punctuated by a small number of distinct features is likely to be the most successful arrangement. Look out for opportunities to represent the landscape in this way. Think in terms of less, not more, and you are likely to make some interesting and distinctive images.

**• Without the snow this picture would not have been worth taking – it would have been no more than an unremarkable rural view. However, obscured by a thick white blanket, the landscape has gained a minimalist quality.**

**• The pale sky has contributed to the minimalism. For this reason no ND graduated filter was used to reduce its brightness.**

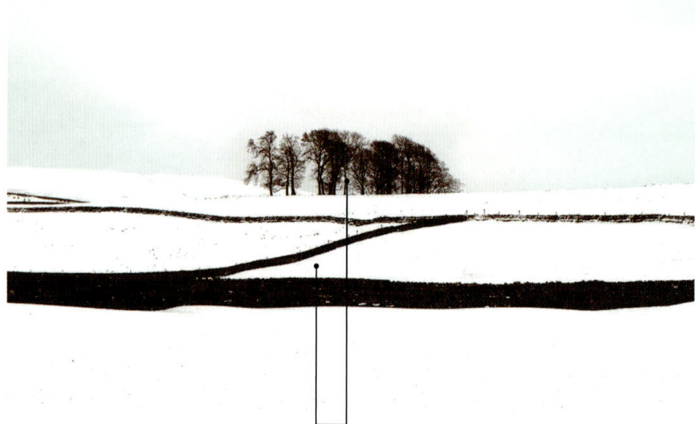

**• The central position of the trees and the diagonal line of the wall give the picture a degree of symmetry. The empty space created by this composition also helps to accentuate the minimalism.**

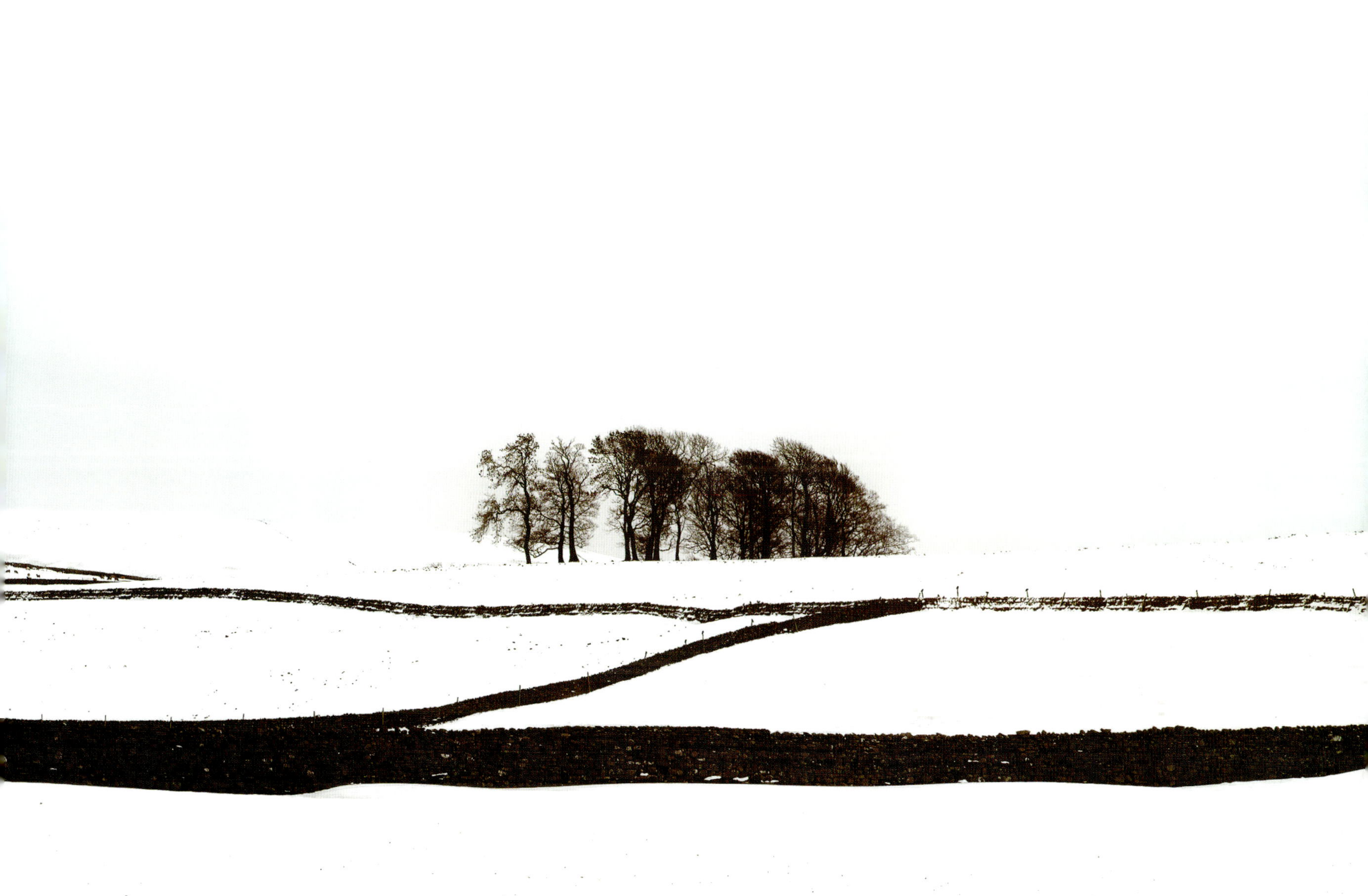

**Thornton Rust, The Yorkshire Dales, England**

**Camera:** Mamiya 645 AFDII with Mamiya digital back
**Lens:** Mamiya 80mm (standard)
**Filter:** None
**Exposure:** 1/5sec at f/16, ISO 100
**Waiting for the light:** 1 hour
**Post-processing:** Suppression of highlights

Graphic simplicity exists in the landscape in many forms. Although by its nature it is likely to be unspectacular, a graphic landscape is very photogenic and can look impressive as a piece of visual art. There is often a minimalist quality in subjects of this type and this can be exploited to strong effect as the image is being composed. Repetition of lines and curves and symmetrical patterns can be used to strengthen impact, and when these elements are present they should, if possible, be emphasized.

Fields of crops display strong graphic qualities and can be a source of distinctive and original photographs. Timing is important because the appearance of fertile arable farmland can change very quickly during the growing season. Regular monitoring of locations is therefore likely to be required to ensure that the peak moment is not missed.

The sky is not always an integral part of these images; including it is a decision that can only be made at the time the image is being composed. Omitting the sky will strengthen a picture's abstract qualities, while including it will convey reality. Its presence is likely to dilute a graphic theme so careful thought needs to be given to this as you consider your composition. If in doubt my advice would be to include the sky, because it can always be removed by cropping, or you could of course simply take two different images and decide later. Capturing these photographs is relatively straightforward, but before they can be taken they must of course be seen. A keen eye is necessary because the lack of spectacular features in this type of landscape makes them easy to overlook. Think creatively in terms of pattern, lines, repetition and colour and you will find these pictures. They are out there – you just need to look carefully!

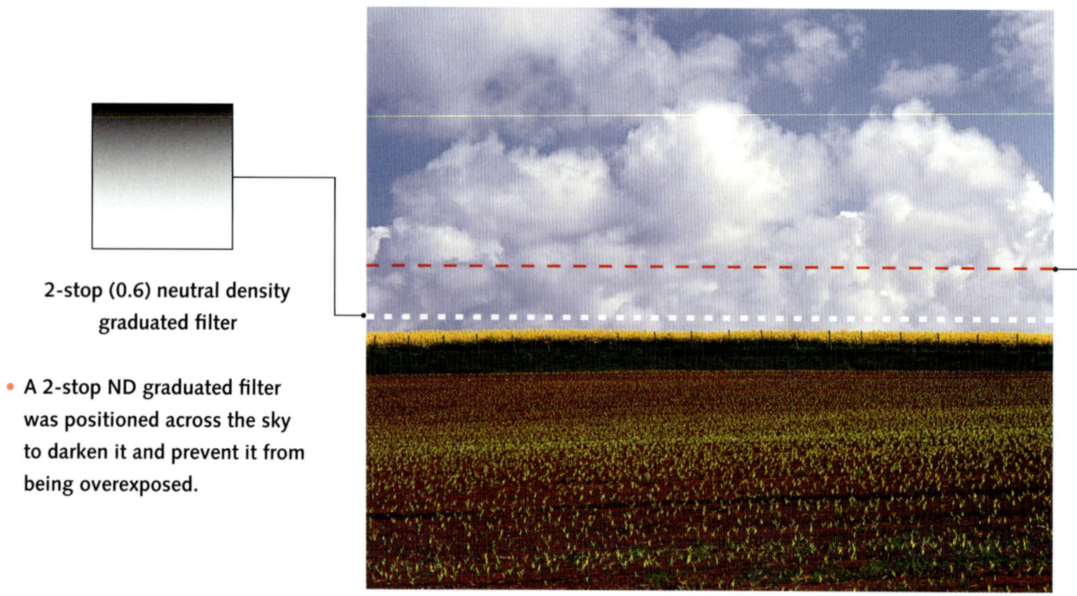

**2-stop (0.6) neutral density graduated filter**

• A 2-stop ND graduated filter was positioned across the sky to darken it and prevent it from being overexposed.

• A portion of sky had to be included, but I was undecided as to how much. One option would have been (and still is) to show only a thin strip as indicated by the red crop line. Had the sky been cloudless I would have done this, but I liked the cloud structure and chose to include a broad expanse. It is not ideal, however, because the sky is now bigger than the landscape.

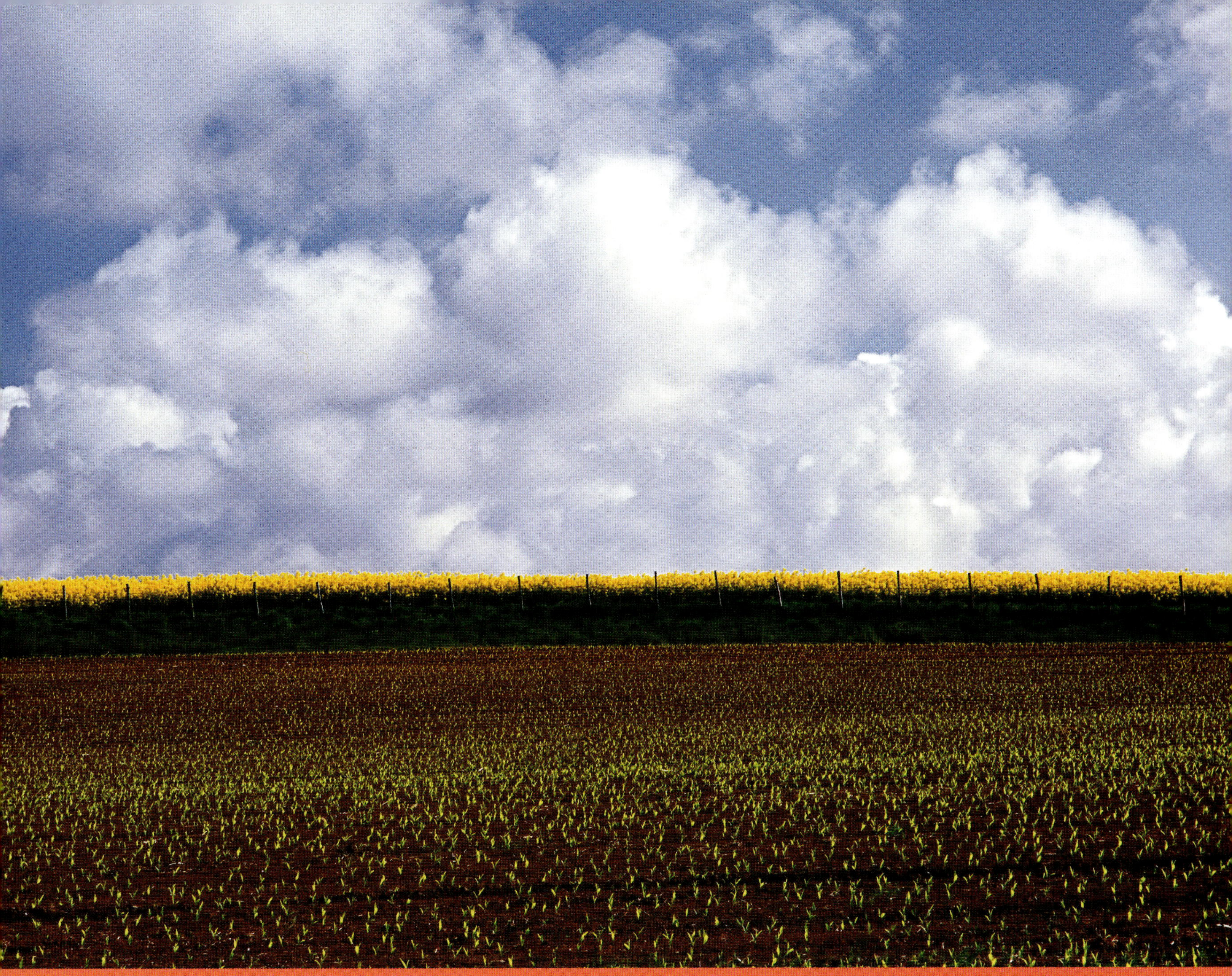

**Thurstaston, The Wirral Peninsula, England**

**Camera:** Mamiya 645 AFDII with Mamiya digital back
**Lens:** Mamiya 80mm (standard)
**Filter:** 2-stop ND graduated
**Exposure:** 1/5sec at f/18, ISO 100
**Waiting for the light:** 20 minutes
**Post-processing:** Suppression of highlights, colour saturation

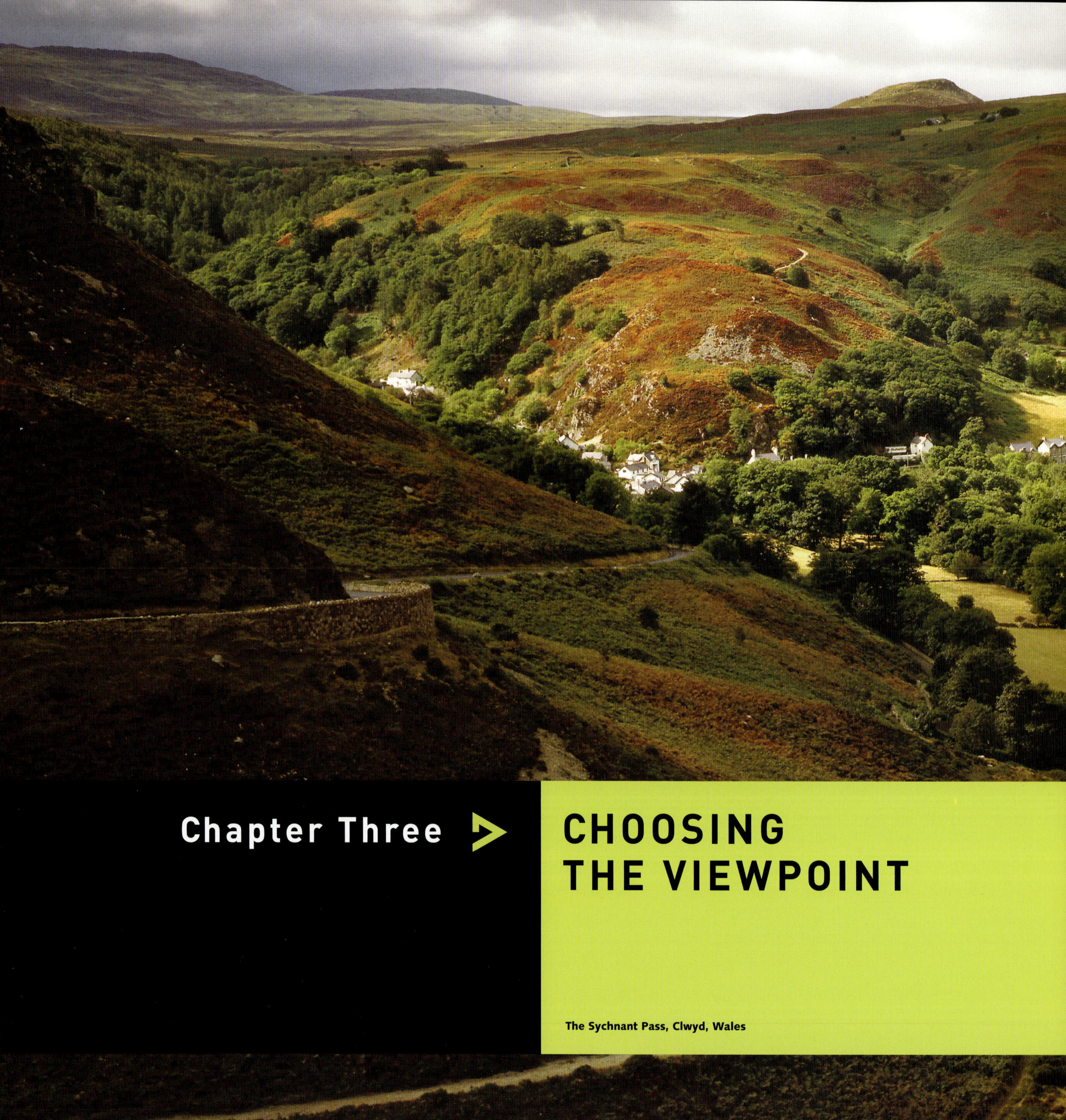


Chapter Three  >
CHOOSING
THE VIEWPOINT
The Sychnant Pass, Clwyd, Wales

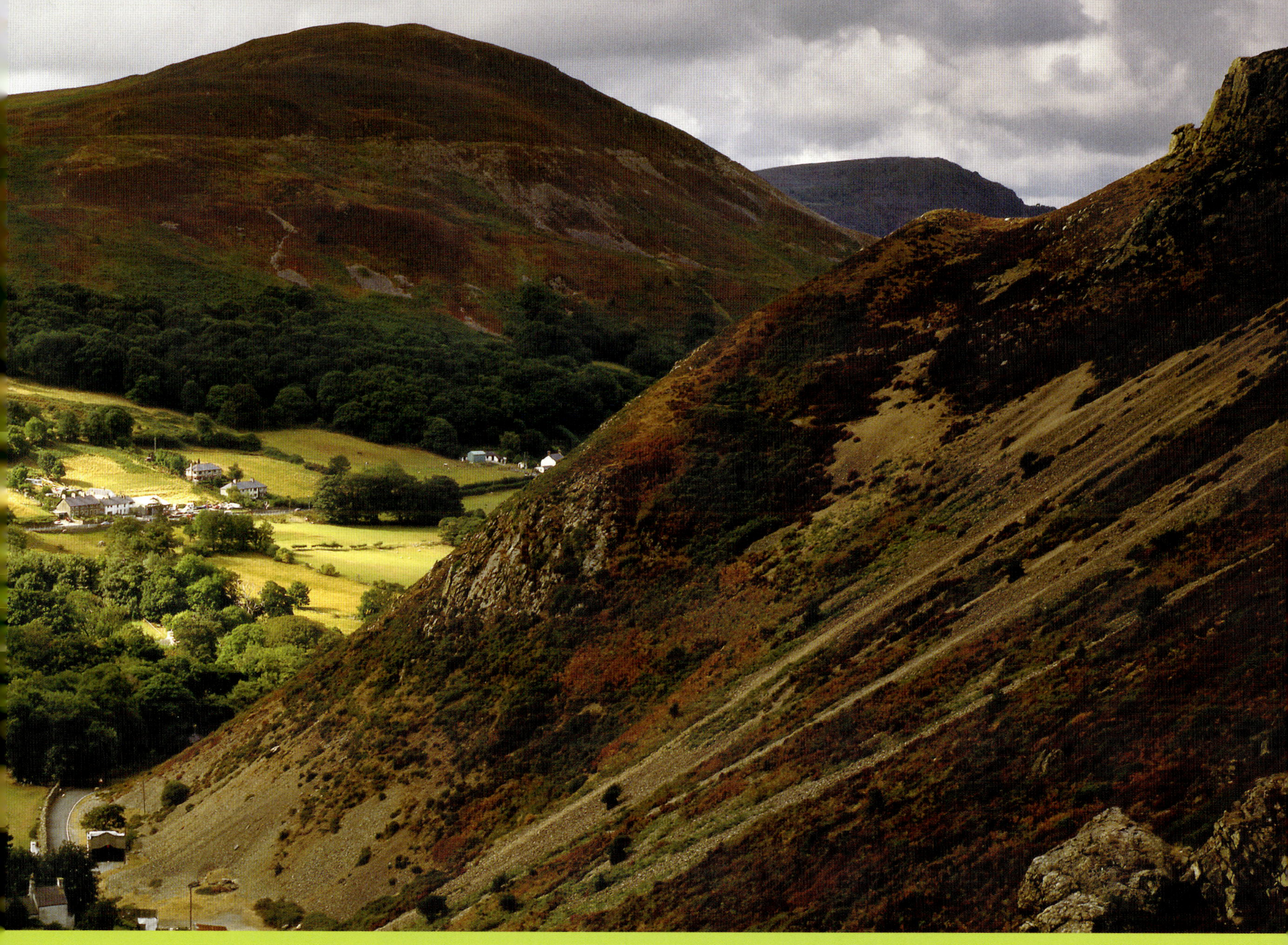

If you ask five photographers to capture one image of the same location you are likely to receive five quite different pictures. The subject will be identical but the images will, in all probability, have been taken from different viewpoints. Some photographs will be more successful than others simply because some vantage points will have been better than others. Composition starts with choosing the best viewpoint, and with your camera in the right place you will be one step closer to making a successful image.

A rural view can be a challenging subject; in order for it to be successfully photographed it must be composed in such a way that there is something for the viewer to latch onto across all areas of the image. Dead spaces should therefore be avoided, as should a weak sky, and the composition should be balanced, both vertically and horizontally. The distribution of light and shadow can, to a large extent, be used to create this equilibrium, as can a number of strategically placed trees, particularly in a view of undulating countryside.

Finding the right balance begins with the choice of viewpoint. Look for an elevated position that provides an uninterrupted view of the horizon with, if possible, all parts of the landscape visible. There should be no major blind spots that obscure the view as they will interfere with the visual journey across the picture. A frequent drawback of a high vantage point is an absence of foreground, but in a large-scale view this can be overcome by placing one or more brightly lit focal points in a prominent position. This will draw the eye and establish scale and depth, which will be enhanced if similar points of interest are present at receding intervals all the way to the horizon.

Focal points can also be used to create lateral balance, and trees or small buildings are very useful in this respect. Positioning similar objects, such as groups of trees, along both sides of an image will create a frame and this will keep attention focused on the picture. They will also add visual interest and, in an undulating landscape, will help to portray the rise and fall of the terrain. By choosing your viewpoint carefully and by using a combination of focal points and a scattering of light and shadow you should be able to produce a successful photograph that captures the beauty and character of an expansive location.

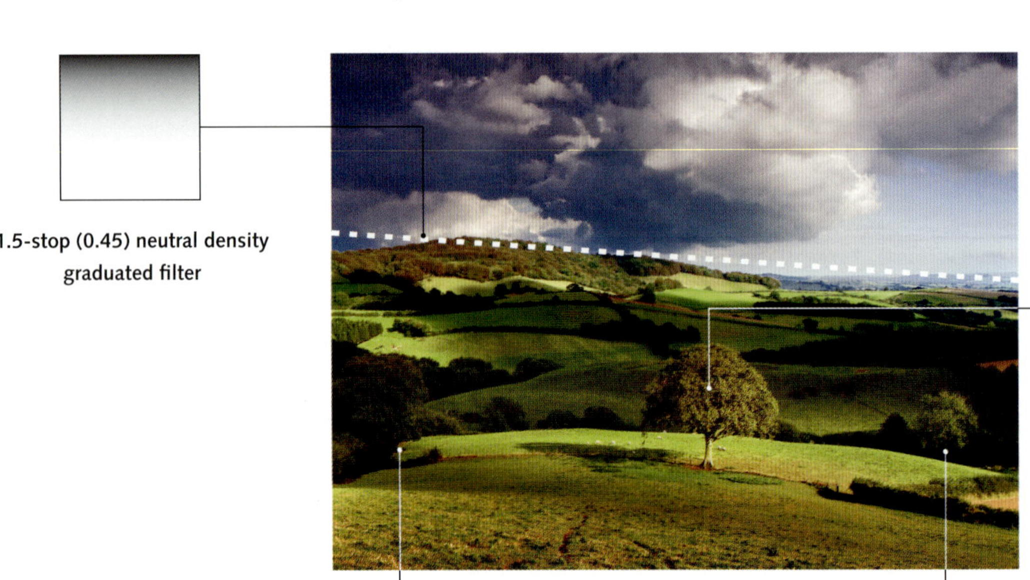

1.5-stop (0.45) neutral density graduated filter

• The centrally placed tree is a strong focal point and compensates for the lack of foreground.

> **TIP:** A combination of sunlight and shadow can be used to depict contours. Watch as the play of light moves across the landscape and choose the moment when the undulations become apparent.

• The groups of trees at the edges help to frame and balance the picture.

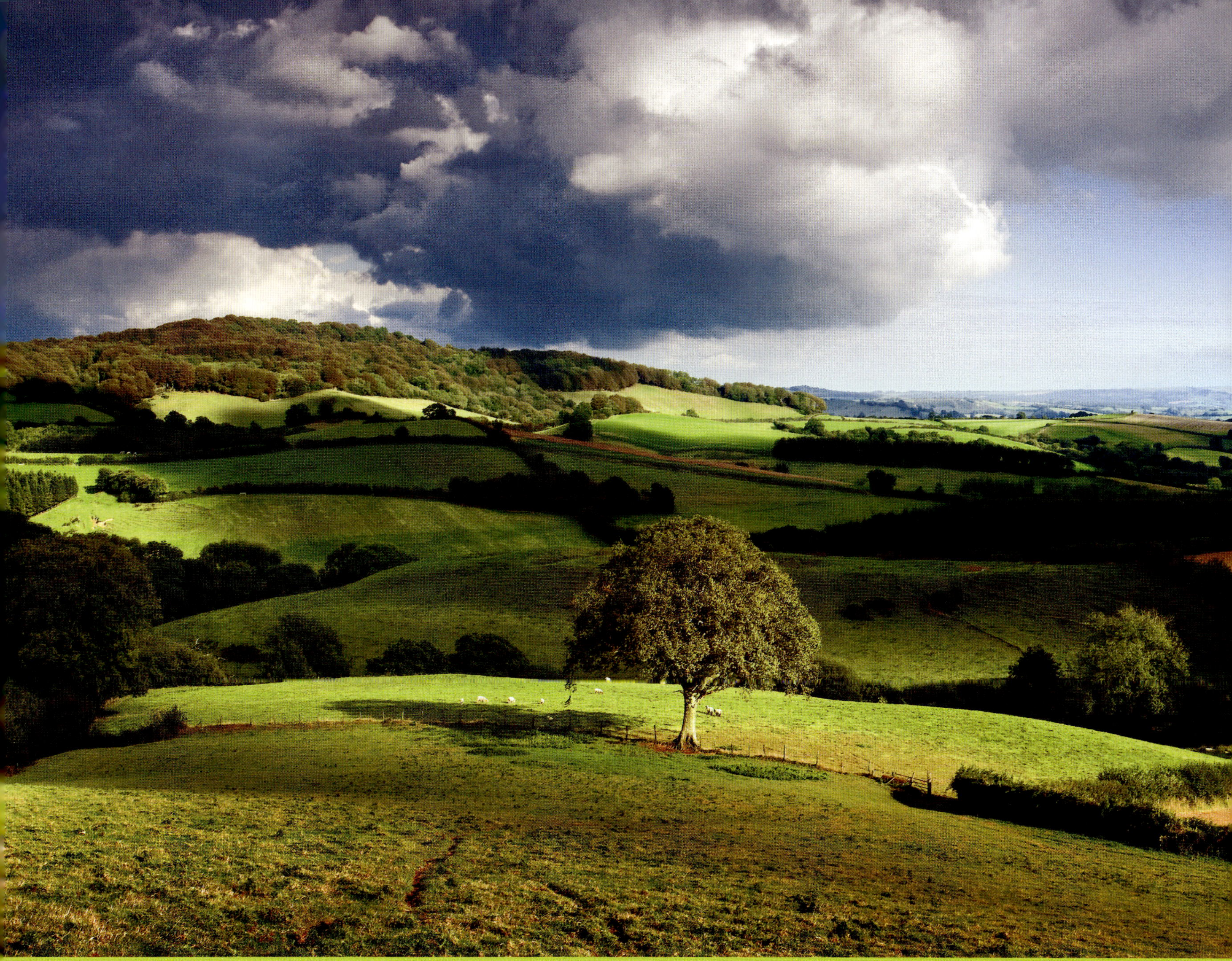

**Near Beaminster, Dorset, England**

**Camera:** Mamiya 645 AFDII with Mamiya digital back
**Lens:** Mamiya 35mm (wide-angle)
**Filter:** 1.5-stop ND graduated
**Exposure:** 1/15sec at f/16, ISO 100
**Waiting for the light:** 90 minutes
**Post-processing:** Curves adjustment

Magnificence can, as mentioned earlier in the book, sometimes be overwhelming. A truly spectacular location may offer the photographer so much choice and opportunity that it can be a little daunting to know where to begin. The temptation might be to make the most of the opportunity and photograph as much as possible, but rarely is this approach successful. Invariably, if quantity is the objective then quality will suffer. A small number of well-researched, thoughtfully composed images will, ultimately, prove to be more rewarding and will portray the character and grandeur of a place more effectively than any number of postcard-type snapshots. Often a close-up or semi close-up of a small part of a subject can be more revealing than a distant view. Another advantage of this approach is that close-up compositions require you to look carefully at your subject and, under scrutiny, creative opportunities are likely to emerge. This was the case as I walked through a steep-sided valley and, ignoring the towering peaks above me, concentrated on attractions closer to the ground. There were many options, but after much deliberation I chose a viewpoint that took in a rugged section of mountain and part of the valley floor. When composing images of this type I prefer to include a portion of ground – particularly if it is carpeted with a layer of colourful leaves – as it acts as a base and support for the rest of the picture. It also enables the subject to be seen in its environment, which adds an additional element of interest.

**1-stop (0.3) neutral density graduated filter**

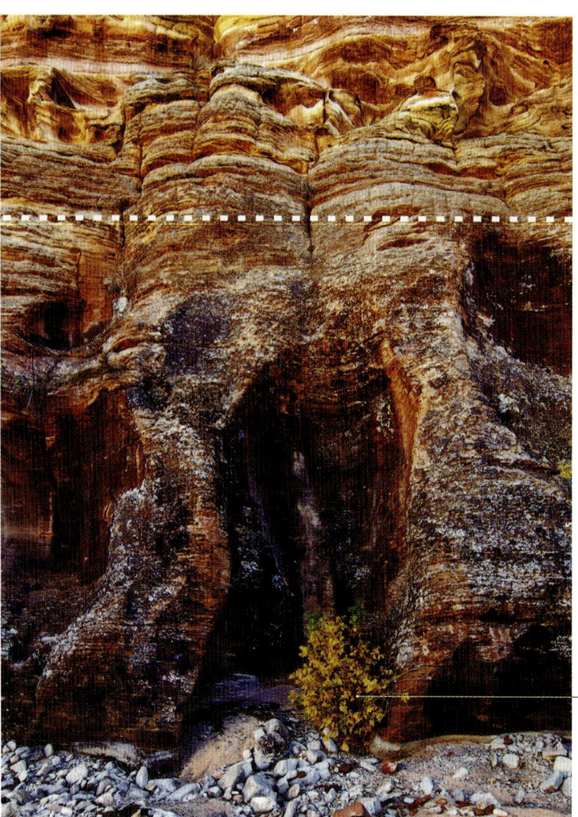

- Sunlight was falling across the upper part of the mountain face. To enable the entire image to be correctly exposed, a 1-stop ND graduated filter was used to darken this part of the image.

- The position of the viewpoint was determined by the shape of the rock face and also by the small, autumn-coloured bush. It was placed slightly off-centre, just above a narrow strip of ground. The low position helps to emphasize the height and mass of the rock face. It also gives scale to the picture.

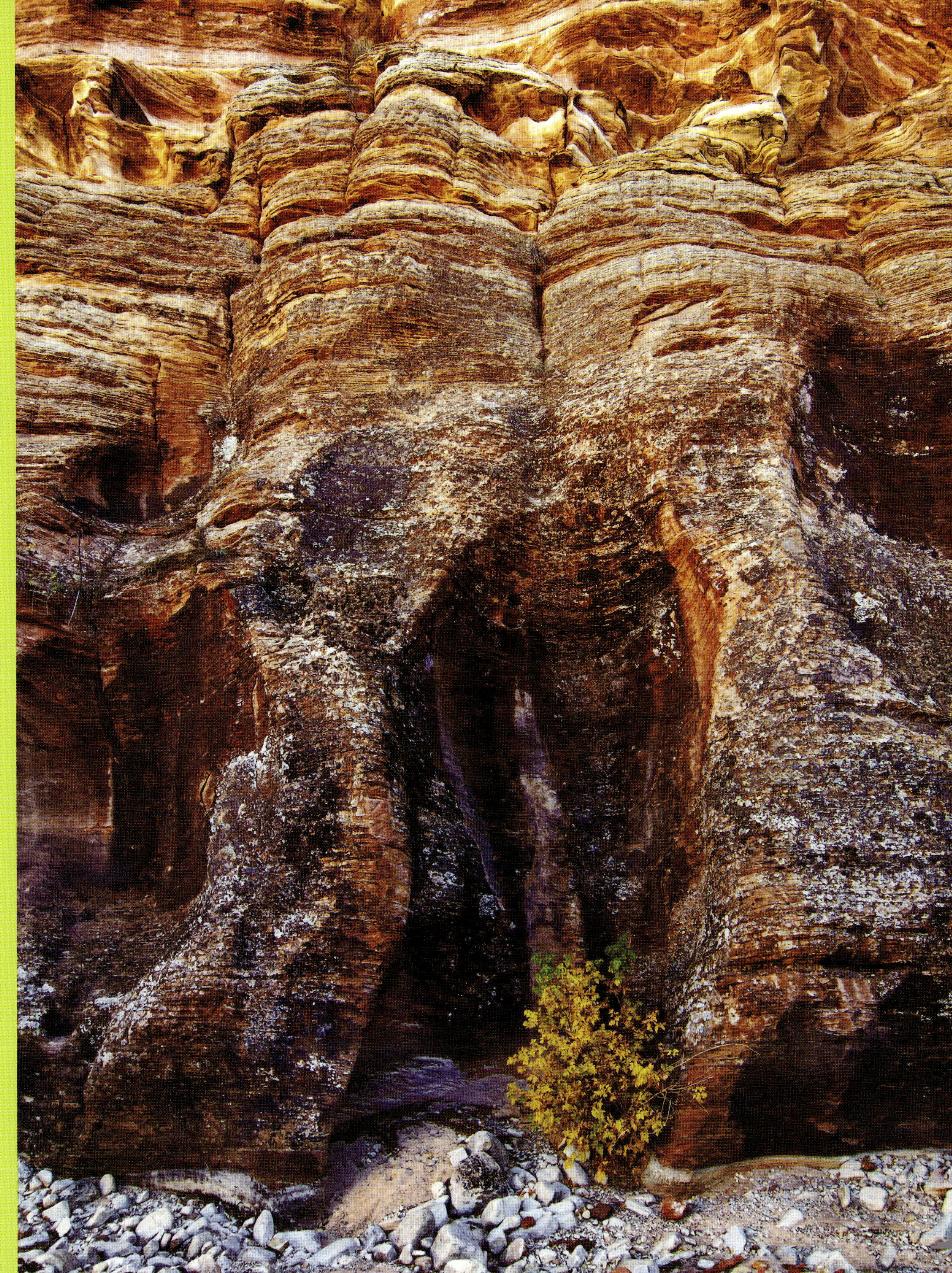

**Zion National Park,
Utah, USA**

**Camera:** Mamiya 645 AFDII
with Phase One digital back
**Lens:** Mamiya 150mm
(telephoto)
**Filter:** 1-stop ND graduated
**Exposure:** 1/8sec at f/14,
ISO 100
**Waiting for the light:**
30 minutes
**Post-processing:** Curves
adjustment, colour balance
adjustment (warming)

Occasionally a piece of landscape is so perfectly arranged that it composes itself. Apart from setting up camera and tripod, in what is likely to be a fairly obvious position, there might be little more to be done. The only variable elements might therefore be the light and sky and, in a photograph that has an undemanding composition, these must be chosen and used with the utmost care.

Other than place my tripod in front of the gloriously isolated tree there was little more to be done to capture this striking part of Hadrian's Wall. The contour of the hills provided natural balance and, picture composed, my thoughts turned to the sky and light. Sunlight falling onto the tree against a dramatic sky was the preferred option. It was a breezy day and clouds drifted by at a steady pace, but there was no

formation that was really appealing. The sky was important because the landscape itself was a little threadbare and I therefore felt it was preferable to give the sky prominence. In the end I settled for the picture you see here. Although by no means perfect, the dark band of cloud across the top of the image does at least counterbalance the strip of land beneath the tree, and this gives the upper and lower portions of the photograph equal weight.

I like to think that the image is reasonably successful, but this location is still a work in progress. This type of subject, where the sky plays a dominant role, could be captured at any time of day or year and no two pictures would be identical. There is, therefore, scope for improvement. I hope to verify this on my next visit.

2-stop (0.6) neutral density graduated filter

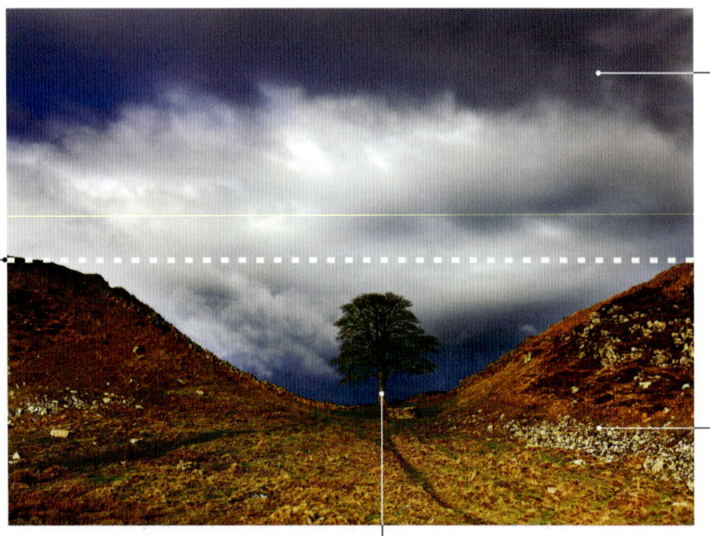

• The band of dark cloud is of similar mass to the strip of land beneath the tree. This gives balance to the upper and lower portions of the picture.

• An off-centre position is usually preferable for single, isolated objects. As a rule I prefer a placement to the right, rather than left, of centre.

**>** **TIP:** The success of images that consist of a simple structure will, to a large extent, depend upon the quality of the supporting elements. In most cases this means having the right sky and light.

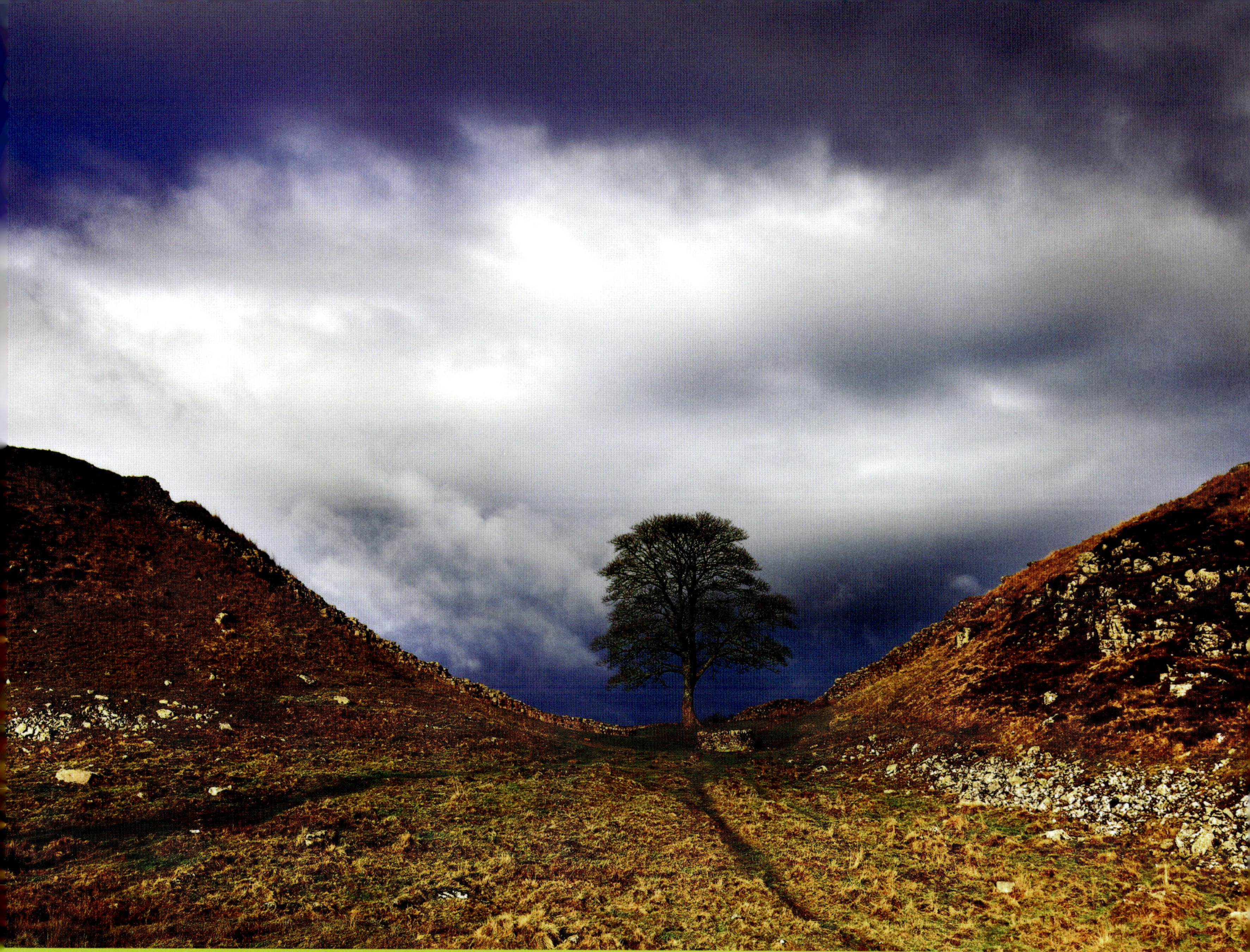

**Hadrian's Wall, Northumberland, England**

**Camera:** Mamiya 645 AFDII with Mamiya digital back

**Lens:** Mamiya 35mm (wide-angle)

**Filter:** 2-stop ND graduated

**Exposure:** 1/8sec at f/18, ISO 100

**Waiting for the light:** 60 minutes

**Post-processing:** Curves adjustment, colour balance adjustment (warming)

I caught a glimpse of this glorious conglomeration of wild, unfettered nature and rustic dilapidation as I passed a bend in a remote road in the Yorkshire Dales. A glimpse was enough, though, to bring me to a halt to take a closer look. Often this type of building fails to live up to expectations when subjected to close scrutiny, but on this occasion everything, from the fading colour of the door and windows to the rampant greenery, was, from a photographer's point of view, flawless. Rain was threatening, so I wasted no time in setting up my camera and taking an image. My initial thought was to include part of an attractive dry-stone wall that was protruding through the overgrown grass to the right of the picture you see here. This meant capturing the building at an angle but this always creates sloping diagonal lines, which I try to avoid. I was unsure about the composition and, as the first drops of rain began to fall, quickly changed position and adopted a viewpoint that produced a more balanced arrangement, with the building appearing above a softly curving green base and either side of a burgeoning leafy column. This created an evenly proportioned composition, with the building and greenery making equal contributions and both reinforcing the theme of ruin and decay. Visually they are a well-matched pair and together they produce an eye-catching image that is both symmetrical and chaotic.

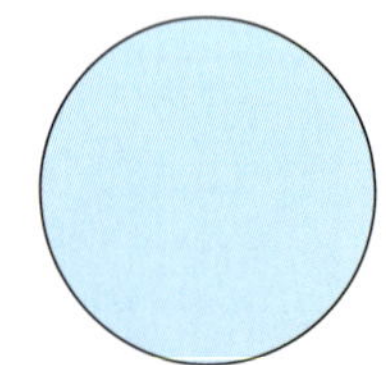

**Polarizer (fully polarized)**

> **TIP:** Use a polarizer to darken window panes and prevent the introduction of distracting highlights.

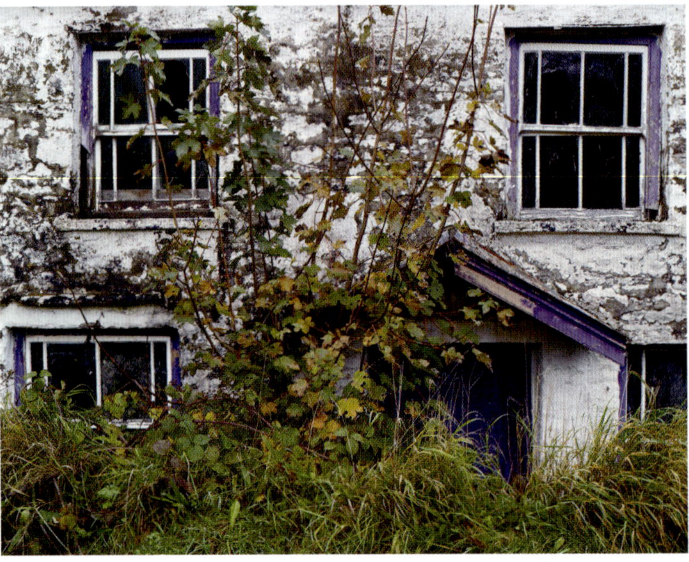

> **TIP:** Combining straight lines and hard-edged angles with soft, irregular shapes will produce an arresting, dynamic image. To prevent the picture from becoming a confusion of too much visual information, use a restricted range of colours and a balanced composition.

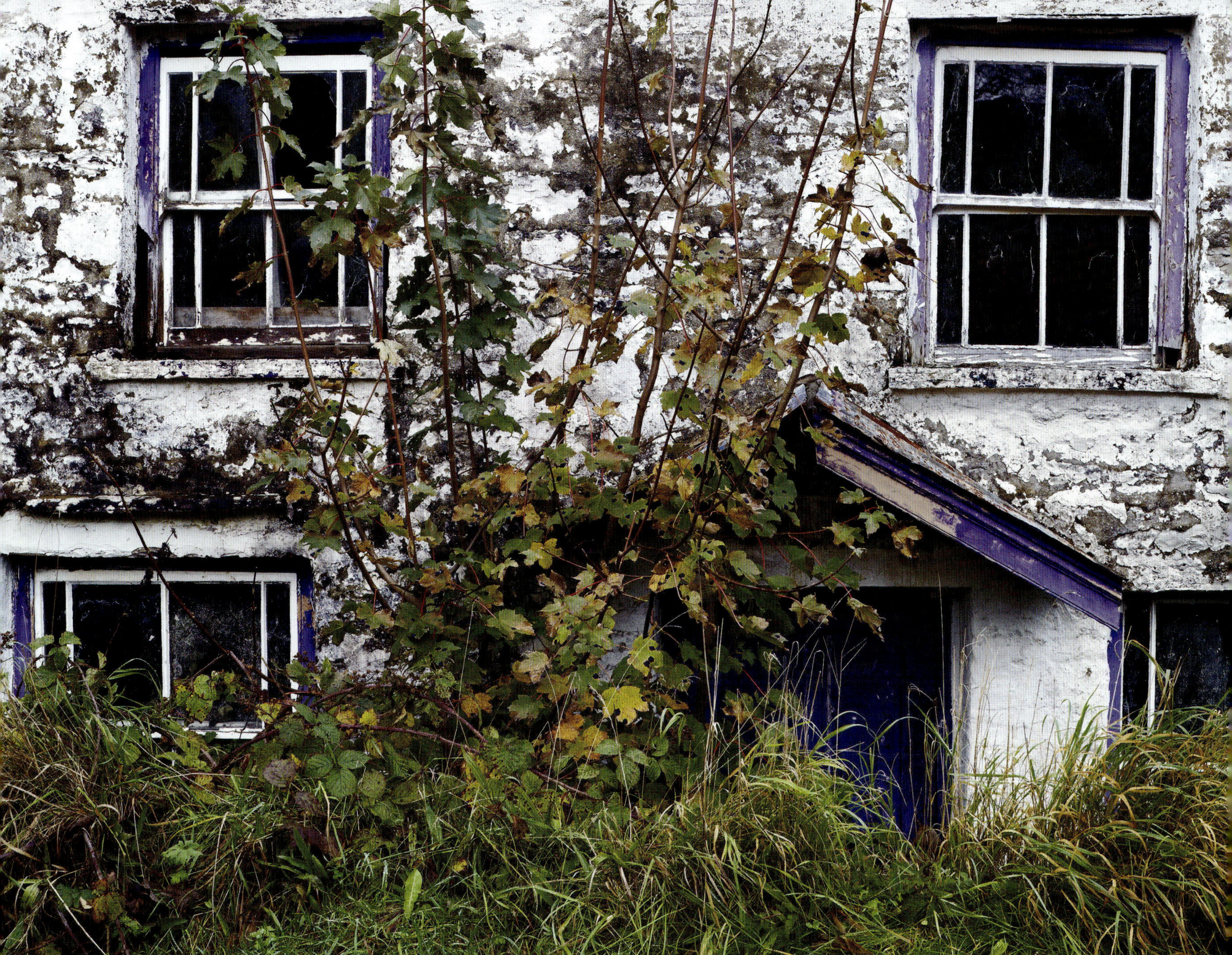

**Near Hawes, The Yorkshire Dales, England**

**Camera:** Mamiya 645 AFDII with Mamiya digital back
**Lens:** Mamiya 35mm (wide-angle)
**Filter:** Polarizer (fully polarized)
**Exposure:** 1/8sec at f/20, ISO 100
**Waiting for the light:** 60 minutes
**Post-processing:** Suppression of highlights

Big, open views can look flat once they have been captured. The scale of a distant vista is so dramatically reduced when seen as a photograph it is inevitable that depth will, to a greater or lesser degree, be lost. The presence of a strong foreground will help to minimize the loss, but there are many situations where the inclusion of foreground elements is impossible. All is not lost, though, because a lack of foreground in your viewpoint need not be an obstacle to depicting depth and distance (this is also discussed on page 60). By choosing a camera position that includes prominent features in the near and middle ground and by using the right combination of light and shadow, it is possible to give images a strong three-dimensional appearance. A prominent feature, brightly lit, will draw the eye and if it is placed at or near the front of your composition it can act as your foreground. An elevated vantage point that looks beyond the feature will then create the impression of distance. This will be further enhanced if light and shadow are scattered across the landscape, particularly if the furthest point is strongly lit. Select your viewpoint carefully, use scattered light to give shape to the terrain, and you will have the makings of a successful image.

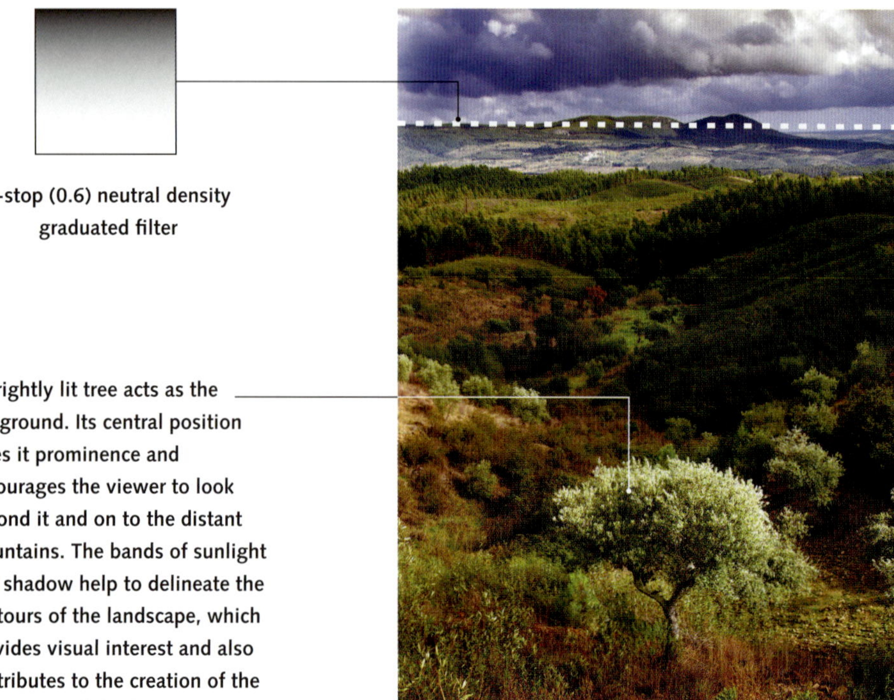

**2-stop (0.6) neutral density graduated filter**

• A brightly lit tree acts as the foreground. Its central position gives it prominence and encourages the viewer to look beyond it and on to the distant mountains. The bands of sunlight and shadow help to delineate the contours of the landscape, which provides visual interest and also contributes to the creation of the impression of depth.

**> TIP:** In an open view it is possible to give the landscape a three-dimensional quality by using sunlight to highlight distant features. This will encourage the eye to travel towards the horizon and will help to give the image depth.

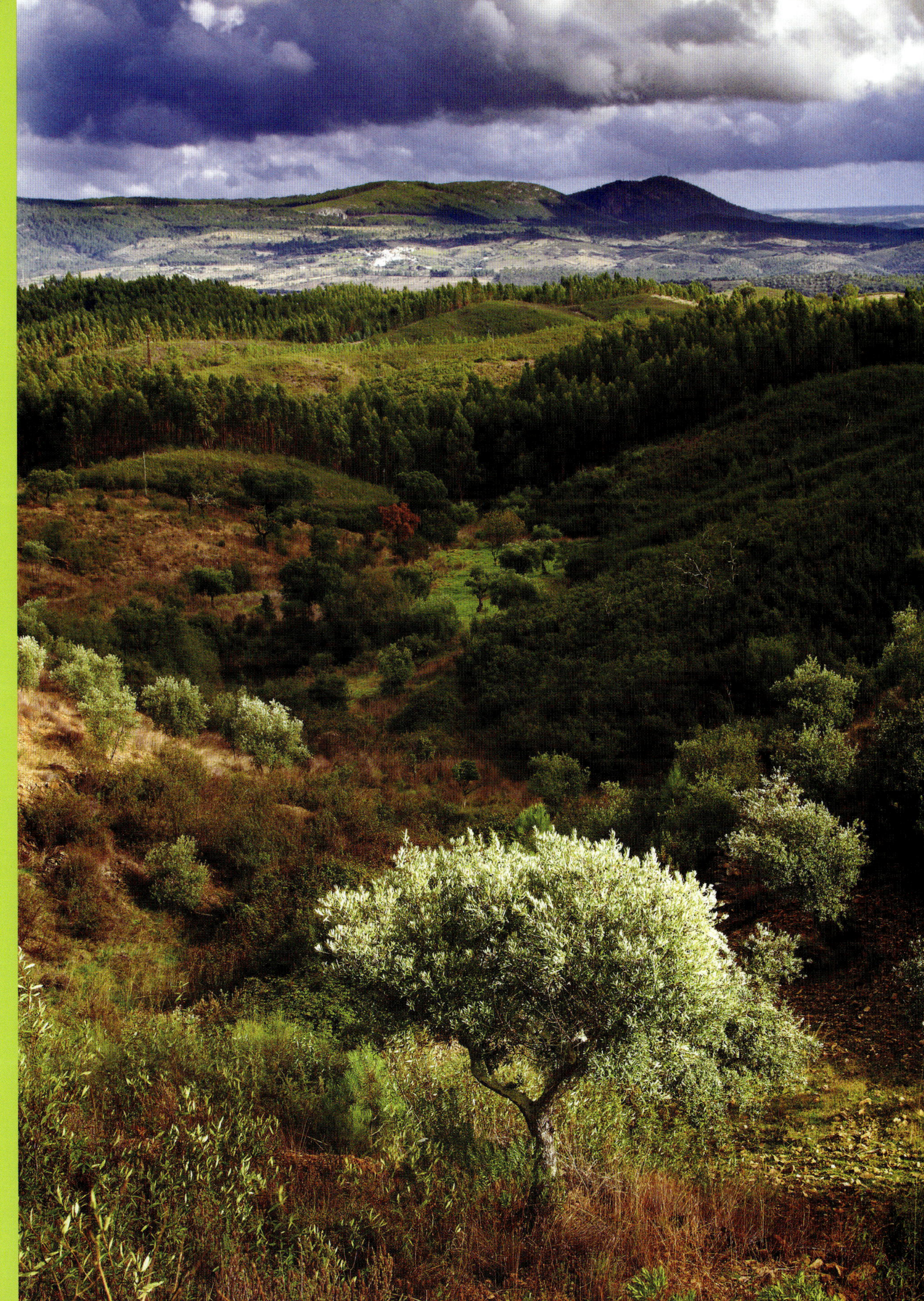

**Near Fratel, Portugal**

**Camera:** Mamiya 645 AFDII
with Mamiya digital back
**Lens:** Mamiya 80mm (standard)
**Filter:** 2-stop ND graduated
**Exposure:** 1/30sec at f/16, ISO 100
**Waiting for the light:** Immediate
**Post-processing:** Curves
adjustment

The choice of viewpoint is often determined by the foreground. A change in position of a few paces might have little effect on the aspect of a distant view, but it can have a dramatic effect on foreground. This can be useful, because taking just a few steps to the left or right can give you a completely new foreground and, effectively, a new photograph. I adopted this approach during a visit to a breathtakingly magnificent but remote part of Arizona known as White Pocket. It was unlikely that I would ever return to the area and as the sky had, for the first time in several days, a favourable cloud formation I wanted to make the most of the occasion. Impressive as the landscape was, it was also challenging because the viewpoints and therefore the composition were going to be dictated by the position of the sun. Because of the rugged nature of the terrain, it was important to have it lit by an oblique angle of light and this reduced the number of options. But give a location time and the light will of course change. The picture opposite was captured some four hours after it was first seen and composed. As the sun travelled through its arc, shadows gradually emerged across the rocky ground and, with the sun at virtually a right-angle to the camera, I made the first exposure. Having taken one image it was then possible to move the camera to several new positions and make similarly lit, but quite different, photographs. So, four hours of waiting: six pictures. That, I think, is time very well spent.

1-stop (0.3) neutral density
graduated filter

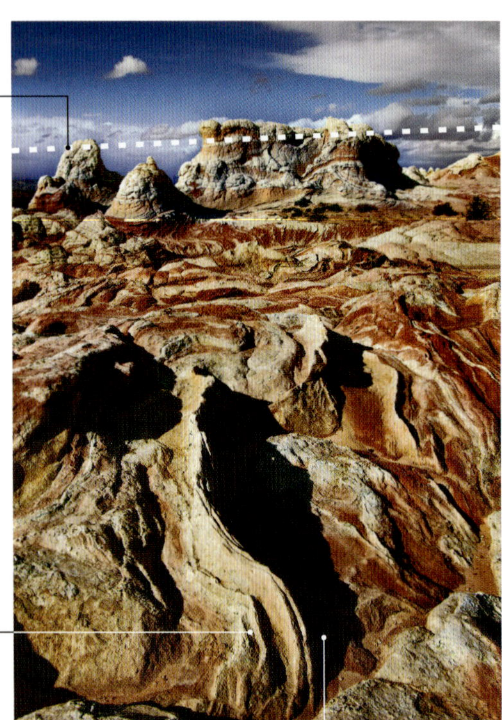

• Composition was based around a section of rugged, flowing rock. This creates visual interest in the lower half of the picture and provides foreground/ background balance.

• The right-angled light has created shadow along a visual pathway that draws the eye into the picture.

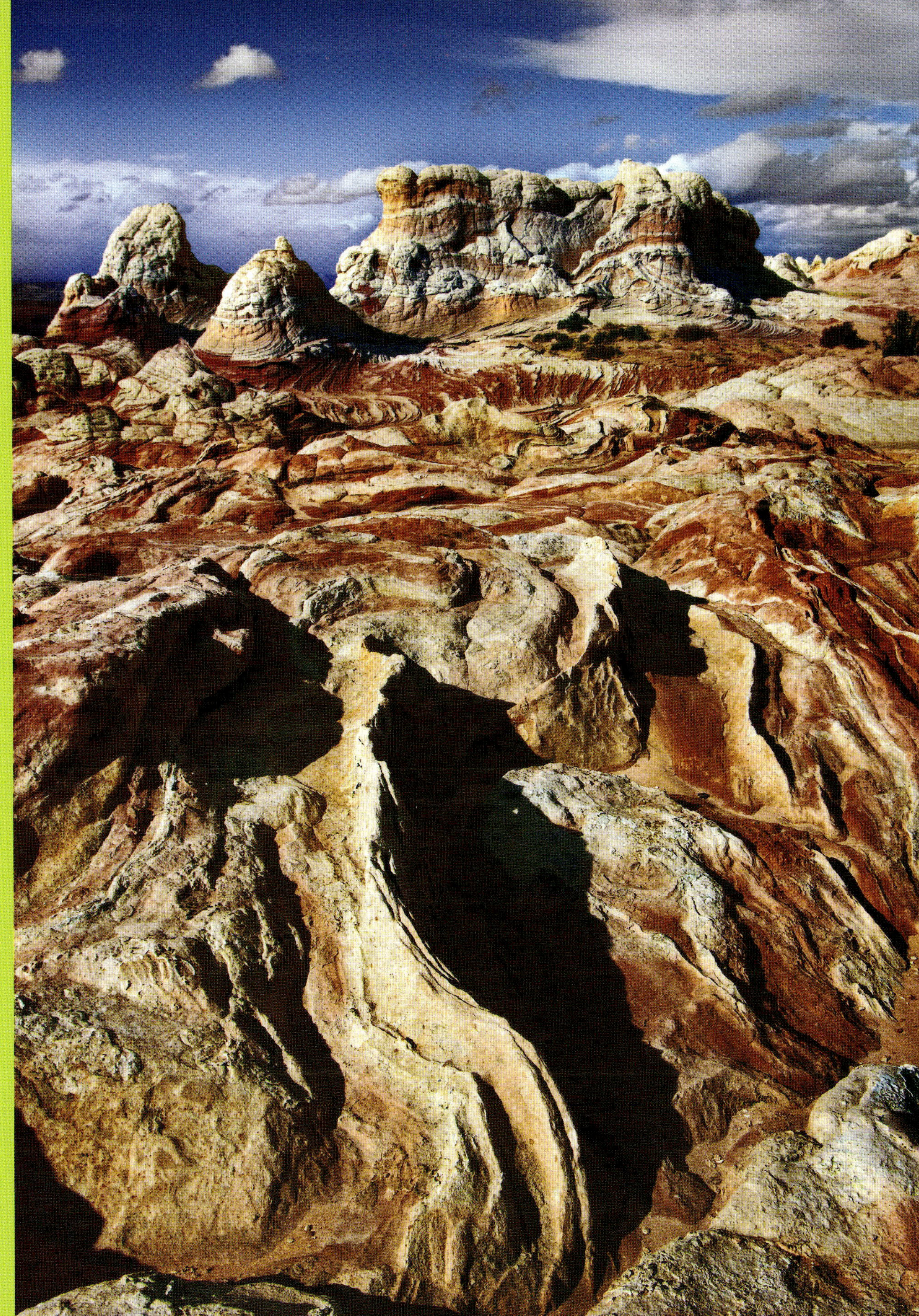

**White Pocket, Arizona, USA**

**Camera:** Mamiya 645 AFDII with
Mamiya back
**Lens:** Mamiya 35mm (wide-angle)
**Filter:** 1-stop ND graduated filter
**Exposure:** 1/15sec at f/22, ISO 100
**Waiting for the light:** 4 hours
**Post-processing:** Suppression
of highlights

Long telephoto lenses are used relatively infrequently by many landscape photographers. Although indispensable when photographing wildlife, because of their restricted angle of view and the shortening effect they have on distance they are not so widely used when capturing scenic views. The compressed appearance they produce is clearly demonstrated if you capture the same view from a fixed position using both wide-angle and telephoto lenses because you will have two completely different images. In most cases the wide-angle version will be the better photograph, but there are exceptions and sometimes a long focal lens becomes an essential piece of equipment. The landscape will need to be compressed if it has underlying graphic qualities that you want to bring to prominence. The magnifying effect

of a long focal length will, by reducing apparent distance, flatten a view and this will then link together elements from foreground to background. The result of this is that subtle features such as textures and contour lines will suddenly take centre stage and become the most noticeable part of the picture. Depth will be lost but the depiction of distance isn't necessary in this type of composition. Photographs created this way will have a semi-abstract quality and a flat, two-dimensional appearance can often enhance this.

An example of a similar image captured in a different location can be found on page 138.

> **TIP:** When creating a graphic theme in an image, frame it tightly and exclude the sky. This is easily done due to the restricted angle of view provided by a telephoto lens.

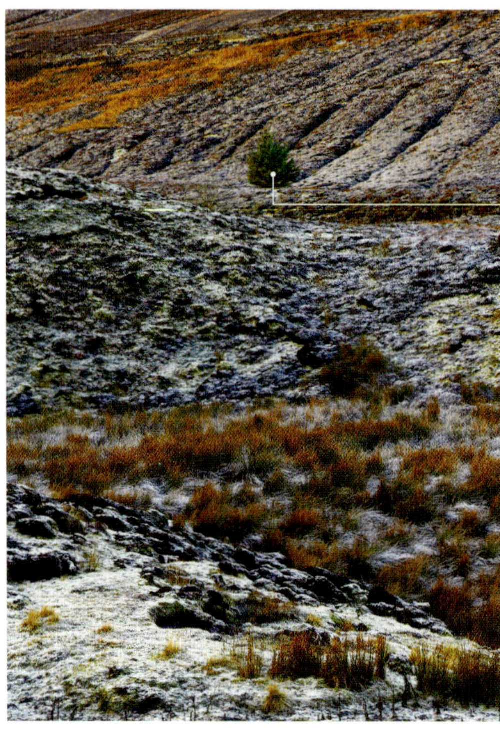

- The small tree has benefited from the use of a long focal length. A wide-angle lens would have reduced its size to such an extent that it would have been lost in the background.

- The flattening effect on this landscape is a result of using a telephoto lens. It doesn't suit all subjects but on occasion this type of compression can be employed to create interesting, original images.

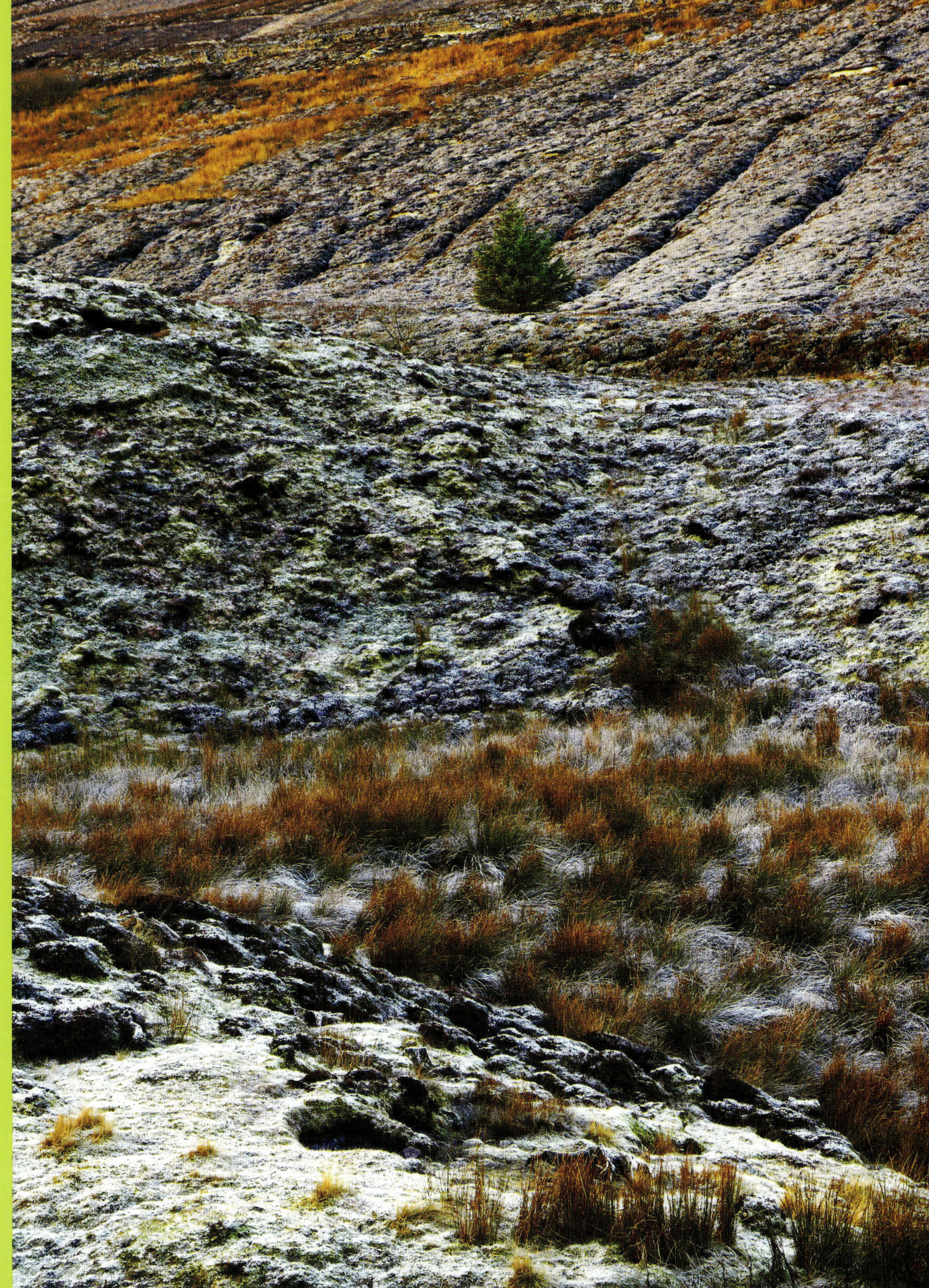

**Near Hexham,
Northumberland, England**

**Camera:** Canon EOS 7D
**Lens:** Canon 24–105mm L IS
**Filter:** None
**Exposure:** 1/20sec at f/13,
ISO 100
**Waiting for the light:** Immediate
**Post-processing:** Suppression
of highlights, colour balance
adjustment (warming)

Medieval towns can be the source of many fine images, but capturing them can often be an arduous procedure, because the ancient paths and alleyways are sometimes so narrow that setting up a tripod can be a spatial challenge. Until recently a tripod was essential for this type of photograph, because the buildings are often in permanent deep shadow and exposure values are therefore relatively low. Now, however, we have image stabilization and I must say that in my experience this is one of the more useful developments in digital technology. Unfortunately at the time the picture opposite was taken the stabilization of camera movement was little more than a concept and there was no alternative to using a tripod. I was using a large-format camera and despite experimenting with various shooting angles involving a number of body-twisting contortions, it wasn't possible to squeeze the bulky camera and tripod into the confined space. Fortunately, all was not lost because I had with me a more moderately proportioned digital camera with a very wide-angle lens. The problem was immediately solved because the extreme angle of view produced by the short focal length of the lens enabled the photograph to be captured at a very short distance. It was still a tight fit, but it was just possible to position the camera without it being compromised by restricted movement. This was important because in order to avoid converging parallels, the camera had to be both horizontally level and vertically parallel with the facing walls and door. I was fortunate on this occasion, but there is no doubt that image stabilization will in the future simplify the capture of this type of picture.

> **TIP:** Flat light is preferable for this type of image because there is no requirement for highlights and shadows and they can, in fact, be a distraction. Weathered colour and texture are also depicted more effectively by soft light.

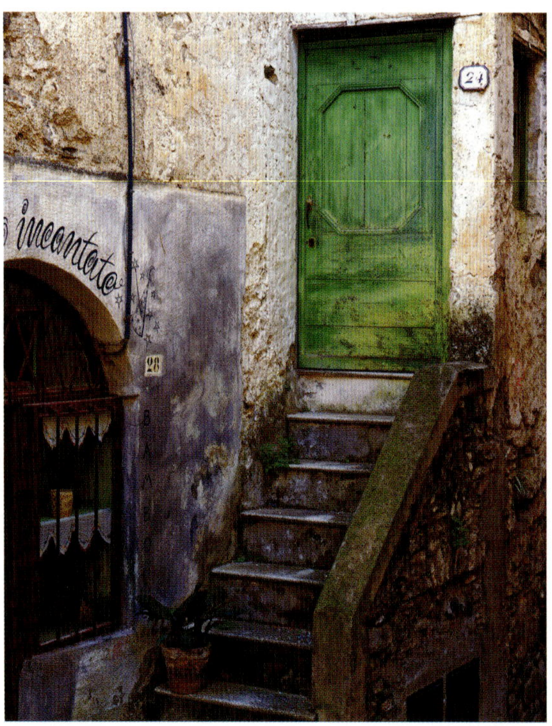

> **TIP:** To avoid converging parallel lines, use a spirit level to check the camera is both vertically and horizontally parallel with your subject.

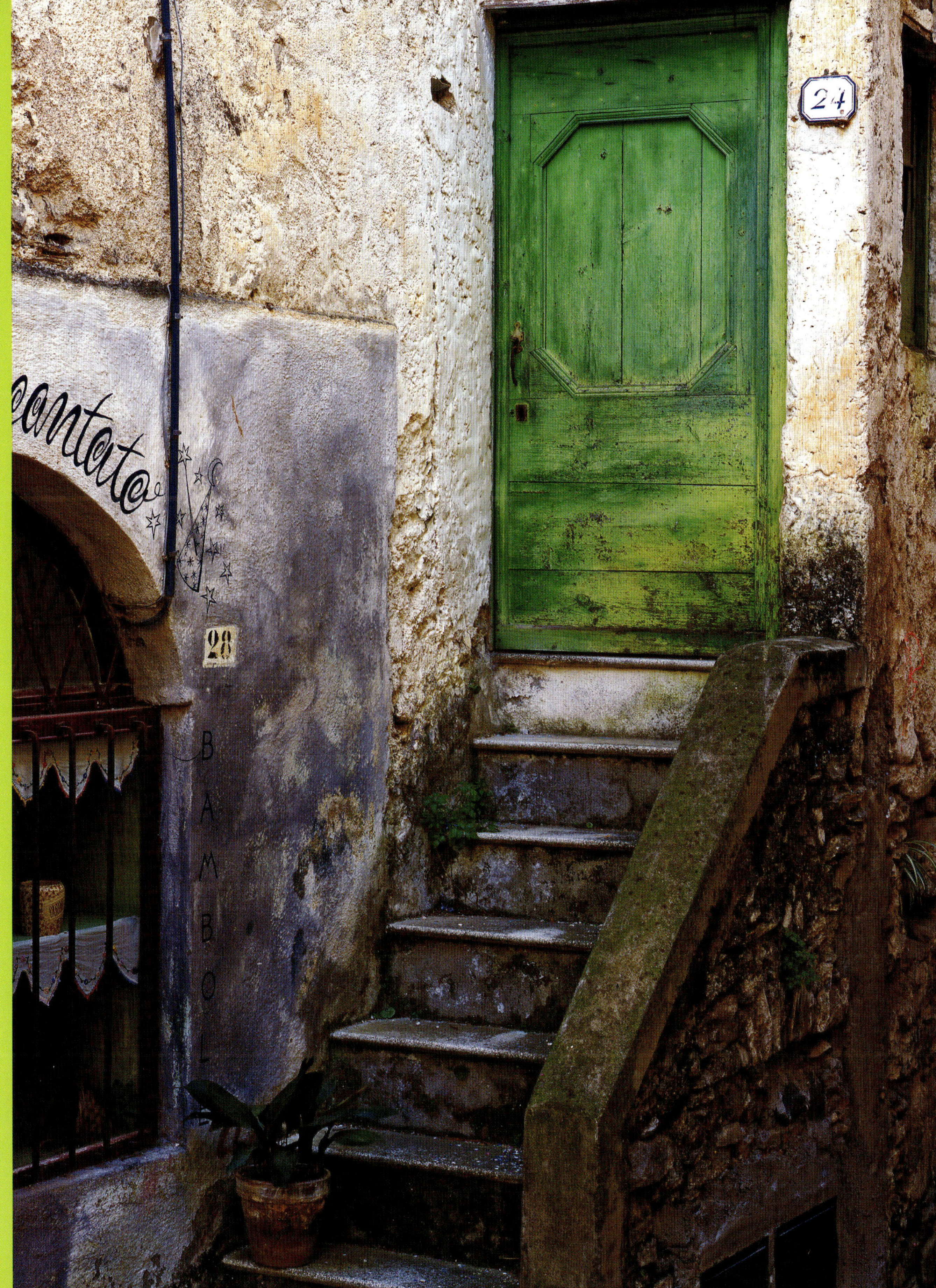

**San Biagio, Imperia, Italy**

**Camera:** Mamiya 645 AFDII
with Mamiya digital back
**Lens:** Mamiya 35mm
(wide-angle)
**Filter:** None
**Exposure:** 1/2sec at f/22,
ISO 100
**Waiting for the light:**
Immediate
**Post-processing:** None

There is a fundamental guideline in composition that is based on the theory that the human eye is drawn to specific parts of a picture. These are the intersection points of imaginary lines placed across the picture in thirds, both horizontally and vertically. The red lines on the photograph below indicate these points. The theory states that following this guideline will give a photograph a balanced, easy on the eye appearance, and it is therefore a useful starting point when you are deciding on a composition.

A result of this 'rule' is that the horizon is often placed one-third from the top of the picture, giving a composition of one-third sky/ two-thirds landscape. Again this is only a starting point and the precise arrangement should be determined by a number of factors, such as the quality of the sky and the type of landscape. For example, in this image of the Cumbrian fells the portion of sky has been reduced and the distant line of trees has instead been placed along the upper one-third position. This gives a degree of emphasis to the trees and the picture is to an extent built around them; the eye is drawn to them and they act as the visual anchor that gives the photograph depth and scale.

There is also a secondary element that plays an important role. It is the steep undulation of the fells in the foreground that acts as an avenue that encourages the eye to travel across the landscape towards the distant trees. Its position approximately one-third from the left accentuates its presence and this strengthens the lower part of the image. The result is that the picture has a balanced composition that rests comfortably with the viewer.

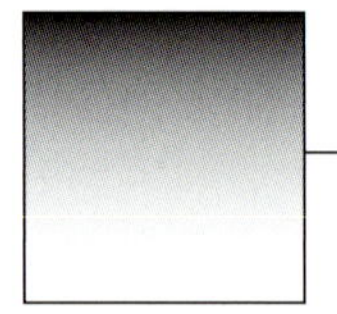

2-stop (0.6) neutral density graduated filter

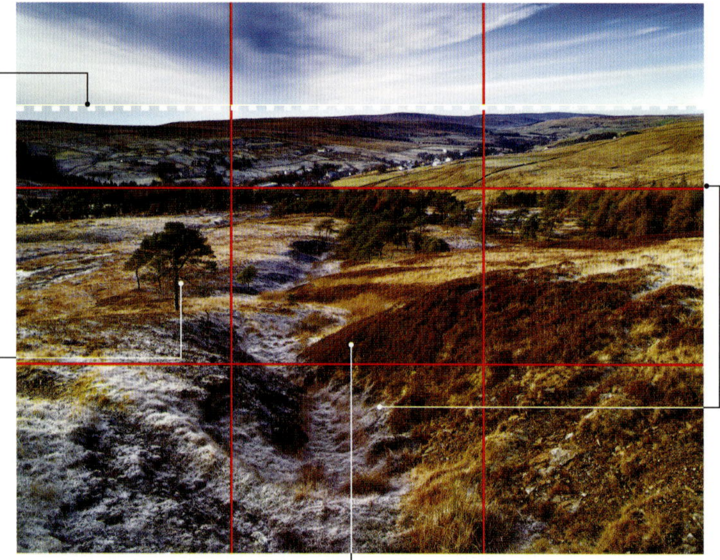

**The positions of the two key elements in this image, the line of trees and the foreground undulation, roughly follow the rule of thirds. This gives them prominence and strengthens the picture's composition.**

**The tree in the middle distance also makes a contribution. It balances the left side of the image and adds interest to the middle ground.**

**The angled slope of the terrain helps to keep the eye focused on the pathway leading towards the trees and horizon.**

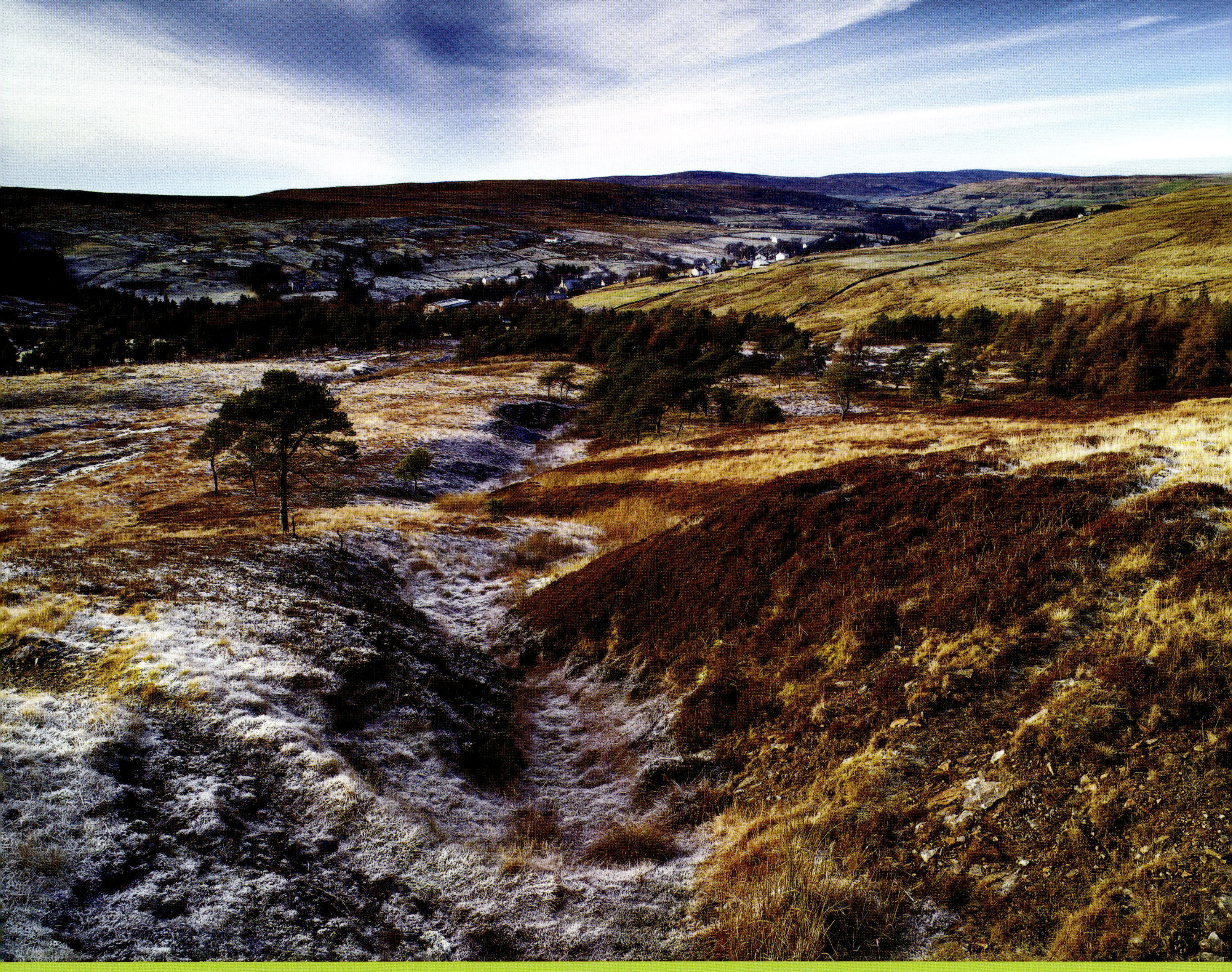

**Nenthead, Cumbria, England**

**Camera:** Mamiya 645 AFDII with Mamiya digital back
**Lens:** Mamiya 80mm (standard)
**Filter:** 2-stop ND graduated
**Exposure:** 1/5sec at f/20, ISO 100
**Waiting for the light:** 2 days
**Post-processing:** Colour balance adjustment (warming)

As I began the process of capturing this view of the Peak District moorland everything seemed to fall into place quite naturally. The picture basically composed itself and instead of the landscape my thoughts were mainly occupied with the quality of the light and sky. I wasn't particularly aware of it at the time but when I now look at the photograph it is apparent that its composition conforms strongly to the rule of thirds. The foreground rocks engage the viewer because they follow two vertical paths spaced at one-third intervals. This explains the ease with which the image was composed, but what is particularly interesting is the position of the tiny village in the distant hills. It covers the top left intersection of two lines, which is a very strong part of the photograph that automatically draws the eye.

Despite its diminutive size the hamlet has a presence and it makes an important contribution to the picture. This is largely due to the visual effect of the rule of thirds.

In an open view of this type, composition alone will not make a successful photograph. The right quality of light is also essential and in this image the low, fairly soft, sidelighting gives depth and texture to the moors and fells. It reveals the shape of the rocks and gives the landscape a subtly varied tonal quality. The result is that the viewer is encouraged to make the journey from the close foreground to the distant horizon. It is always the combination of light and composition that determines the success of a photograph of a large-scale view.

**2-stop (0.6) neutral density graduated filter**

• **A 2-stop ND graduated filter was used to darken the sky and allow the cloud detail to be portrayed.**

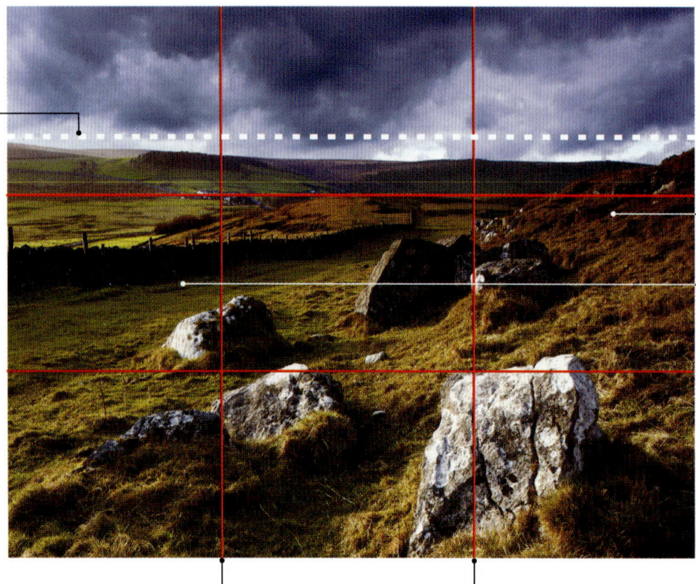

• **The sloping hillside and stone wall also make a contribution by balancing both sides of the image. They also help to give the picture depth and scale.**

• **The key elements in the picture – the foreground rocks and the distant village – occupy positions that conform to the rule of thirds. This strengthens their presence and draws the viewer into the scene.**

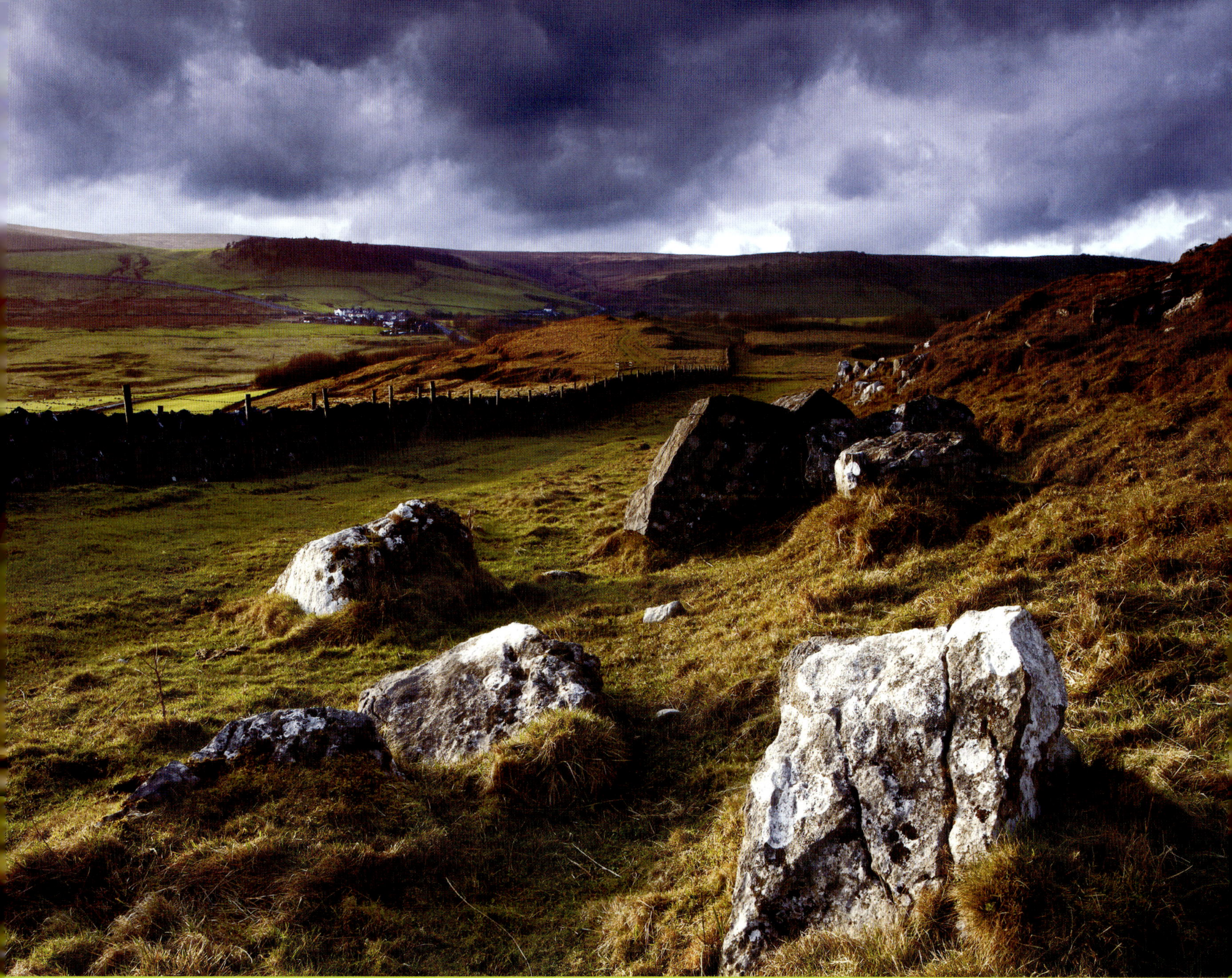

**Near Buxton, Derbyshire, England**

**Camera:** Mamiya 645 AFDII with Mamiya digital back
**Lens:** Mamiya 35mm (wide-angle)
**Filter:** 2-stop ND graduated
**Exposure:** 1/4sec at f/22, ISO 100
**Waiting for the light:** 3 hours
**Post-processing:** Curves adjustment, colour balance adjustment (warming)

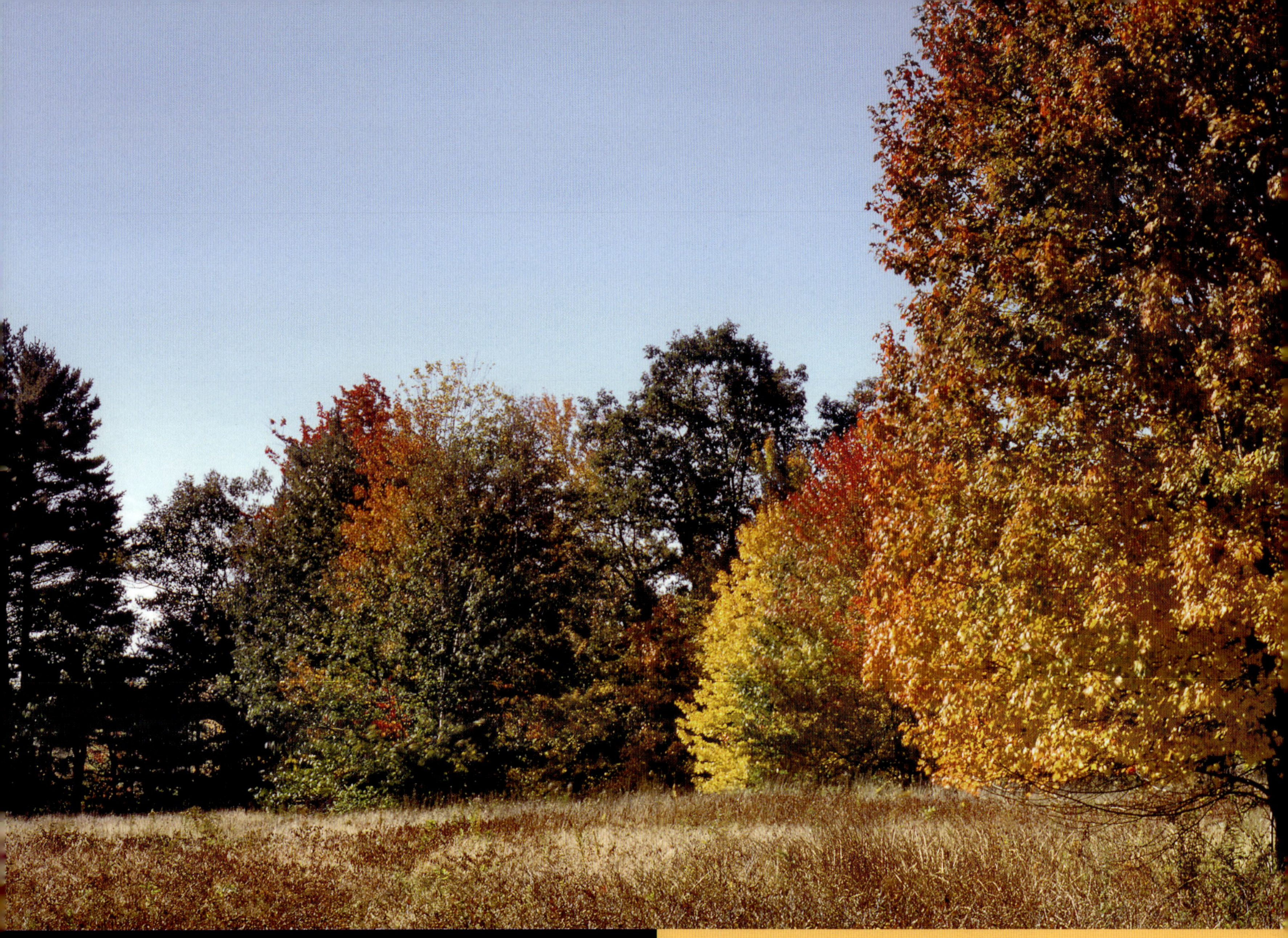

Chapter Four > **USING LIGHT AND SHADOW**

Near South Windham, Maine, USA

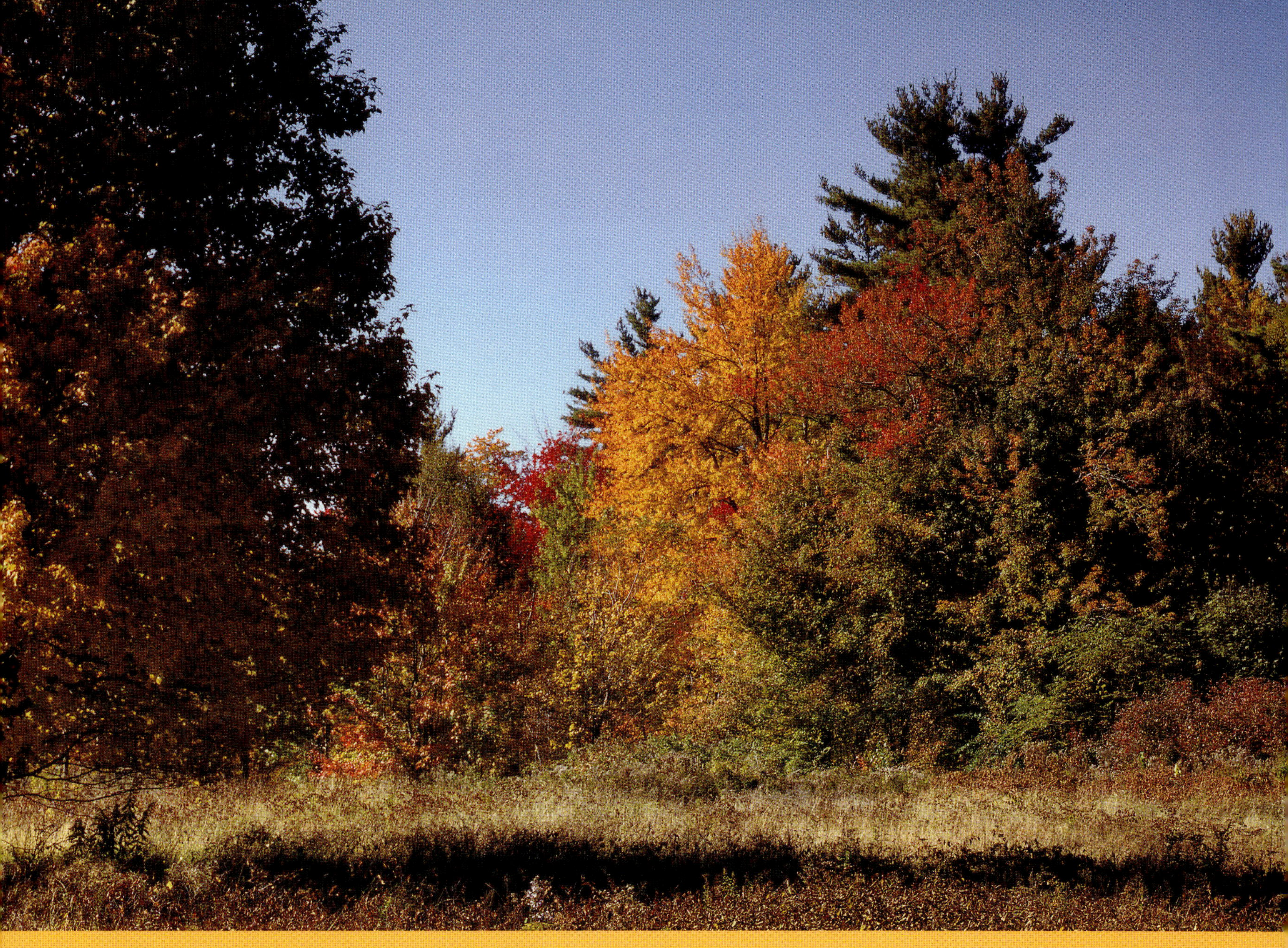

There is more to composition than just the arrangement of visual elements. Light also has to be considered, because the distribution of highlights and shadows will have a fundamental affect on the appearance and quality of your image. Composition, light and shadow and also the position of the sun must all be considered together as a single entity if maximum impact and success are to be achieved. The right approach to using light and shadow in composition is discussed and explained in the following pages.

If you have ever been inside a photographic studio you will have seen a bespoke workplace filled with an array of lights that enable the photographer to use several sources of illumination of precisely controlled, and totally variable, intensity. Highlights and shadows can be intricately adjusted and moved at will, as can virtually every other aspect of lighting the subject. And it is all controlled by the flick of a switch or the click of a mouse. This is the world of the studio photographer.

The landscape photographer's 'studio' has a rather more primitive lighting system. It's been around for a long time – I believe somewhere in the region of 4.5 billion years – but, showing no signs of age, it still serves its purpose perfectly well. Although unpredictable, unreliable and frustratingly difficult to control, it is, it must be said,

rather beautiful and with practice and experience we often use it to astonishing effect. Our single light source bears little resemblance to the artificial illumination found in purpose-built studios; they are, literally, worlds apart. Instead of snoots, strobes and spots we have a much simpler system; we have the sun. This is the world of the landscape photographer and to succeed in it we must be vigilant, observe at all times what is happening and grab any opportunities the split second they occur.

Above everything else it is the quality of light that matters. Carry that thought with you every time you venture out into the landscape and you will be one very large step closer to achieving that much sought-after success.

2-stop (0.6) neutral density
graduated filter

• A 2-stop ND graduated filter was used to darken the sky and allow detail to be recorded across all parts of the image.

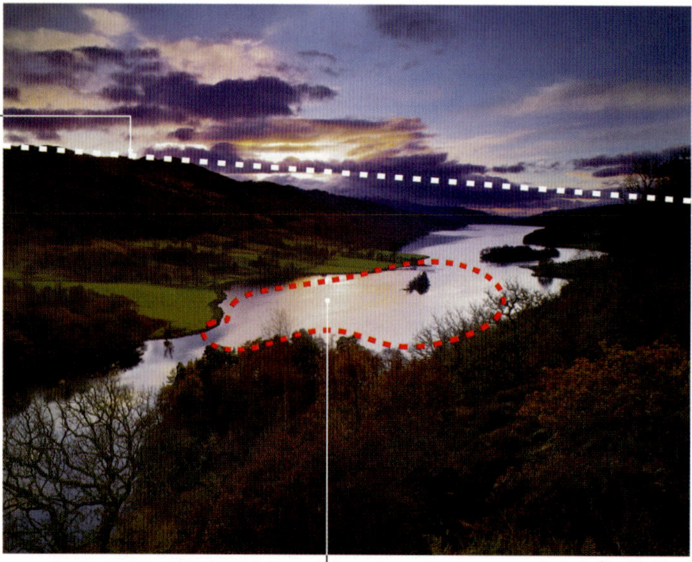

• Strong highlights on the water were reduced by selecting part of the lake with the Lasso tool and darkening the brightest parts with the Shadows/Highlights tool.

> **TIP:** To avoid lens flare, wait for the sun to be obscured by a thin layer of cloud. This will also help to reduce bright, overexposed areas in the sky.

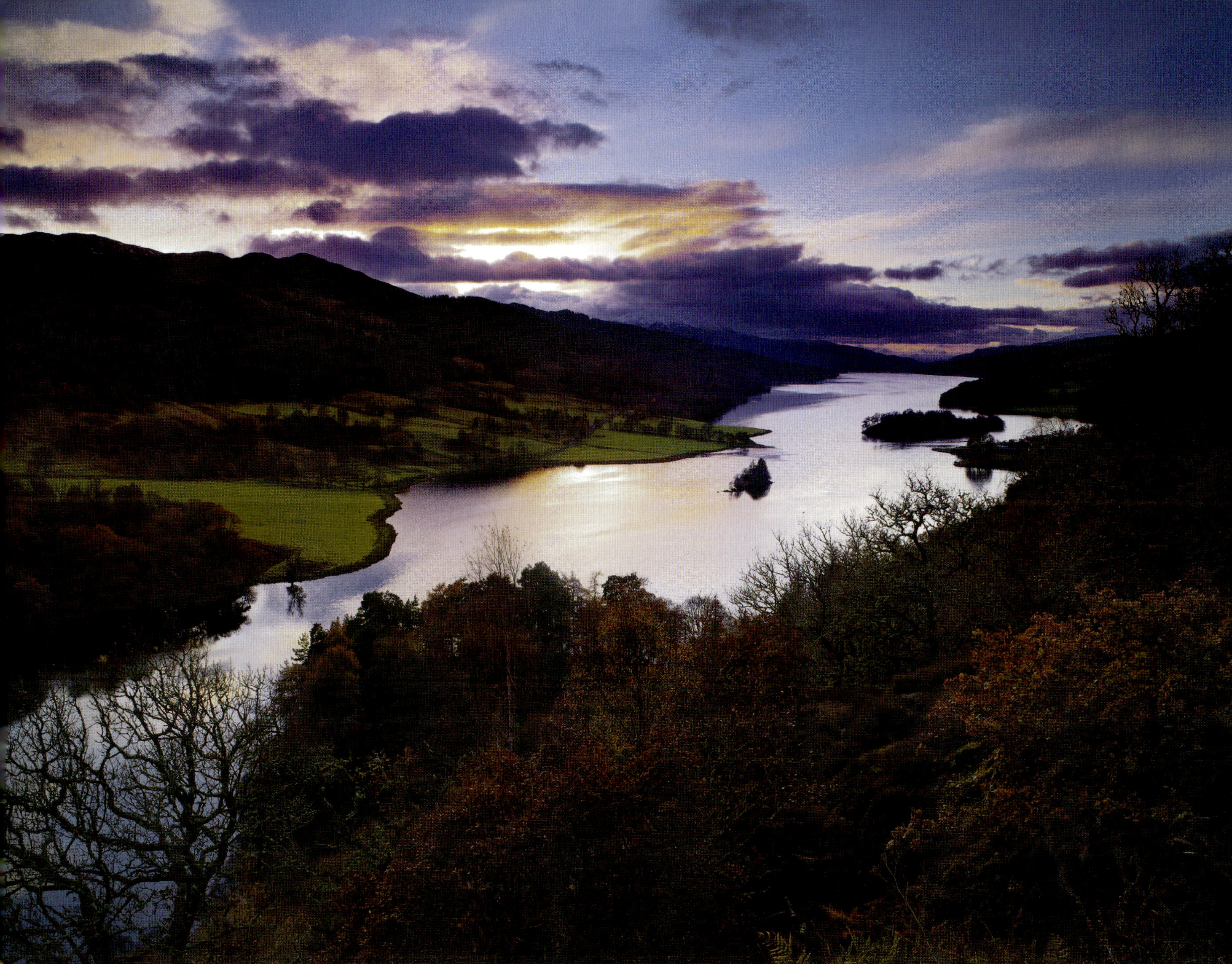

**Loch Rannoch, Perthshire, Scotland**

**Camera:** Mamiya 645 AFDII with Mamiya digital back

**Lens:** Mamiya 35mm (wide-angle)

**Filter:** 2-stop ND graduated

**Exposure:** 1sec at f/14, ISO 100

**Waiting for the light:** 60 minutes

**Post-processing:** Selective suppression of highlights, colour balance adjustment (warming)

Magnificent as they are, mountainous areas can be troublesome to photograph, the main challenge being to capture their size and scale. To a large extent this can be achieved by including the right type of foreground and focal points in the composition, but this can sometimes be difficult because you might be restricted in your choice of viewpoint. Unless you are a trained and highly skilled mountaineer you might have to settle for photographing from the roadside or, if there are no other options, a designated viewpoint. There is nothing wrong with joining the crowds and using these viewing areas, but it will be difficult to find an original composition. Having said that, I would guess that at least 90 per cent of the images captured from these places have been taken at the wrong time and in the wrong light, so your picture can stand out from the rest by simply giving a little thought to the photograph you want to create and its timing.

Consider carefully the light, the sky and the time of day. This can be a critical factor because when you are surrounded by high peaks a small change in the position of the sun can make a big difference to the pattern of light and shadow falling across your subject, particularly when you are restricted to a single vantage point. The absence of positional options means you cannot move so you must therefore wait for the sun to make the movement for you. Watch carefully as the sun travels through its arc (or return at regular intervals) and observe the gradually changing appearance of the view. Visual impact and the depiction of depth and distance will be determined by the play of light across the landscape, so choose the moment when the scattering of light and shadow illuminates your subject to maximum effect.

This image of the Kolob Mountains was taken from a viewing area long after the crowds had disappeared. It was captured during the last hour of daylight as alternating bands of light and shadow extended across the entire depth of the landscape including, importantly, the distant ridge along the horizon. Lighting the scene in this way emphasizes distance and gives the photograph scale, even without the presence of foreground.

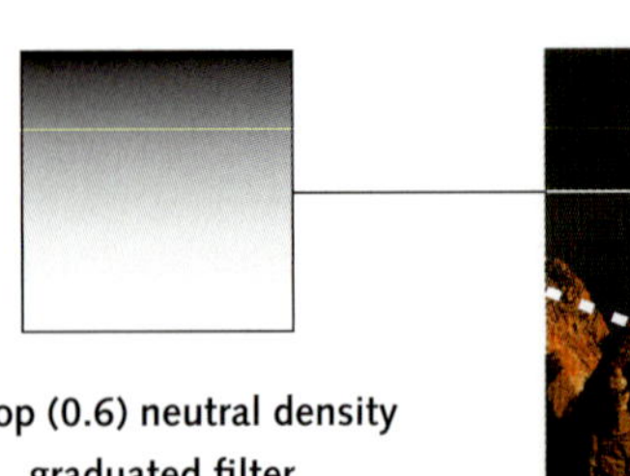

2-stop (0.6) neutral density
graduated filter

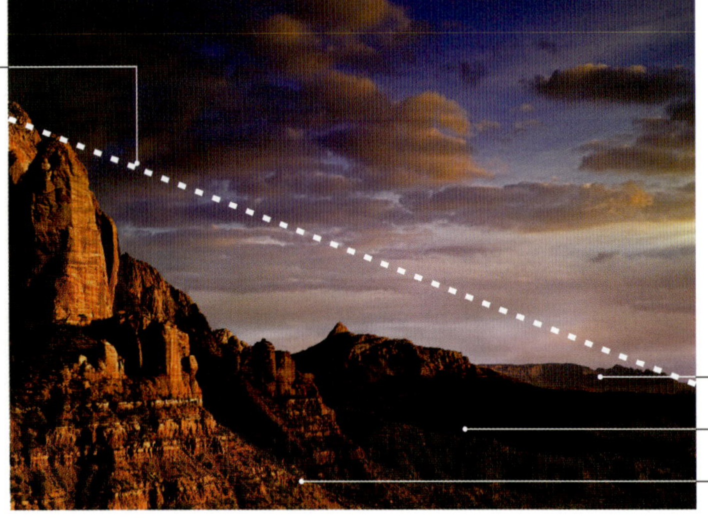

• In the absence of foreground the interplay of light and shadow becomes critically important. The angle of sunlight and the alternating bands of light and shadow give this photograph depth, distance and scale.

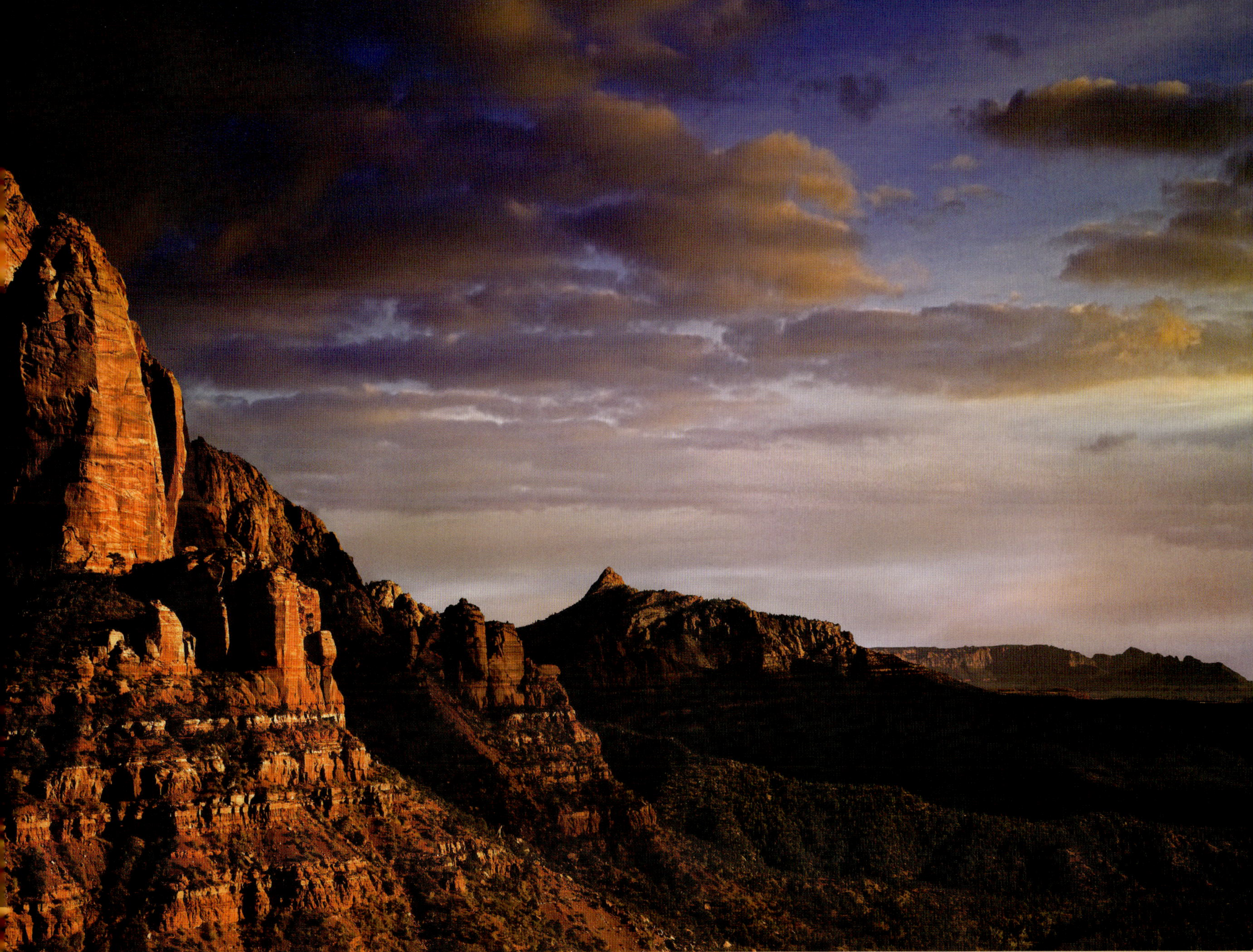

**Kolob Mountains, Utah, USA**

**Camera:** Mamiya 645 AFDII with Phase One digital back

**Lens:** Mamiya 35mm (wide-angle)

**Filter:** 2-stop ND graduated

**Exposure:** 1/60sec at f/16, ISO 100

**Waiting for the light:** 3 days

**Post-processing:** Colour balance adjustment (warming) and reduction of highlights

Appealing as the area is, I had a slight reservation about photographing the outstanding landscape of Arizona and Utah. Its reputation acts as a magnet to photographers throughout the world and I was concerned that it would be impossible to find virgin, unphotographed territory. It is always more rewarding to make original images and search out the unseen to create something different, but places like the Zion National Park have been heavily photographed since the days of the pinhole camera. It was therefore going to be a challenge to find interesting locations that had been spared the attentions of insatiably zealous landscape photographers (people like me, in other words!) and capture new pictures.

Red Cliffs Reserve is a wilderness area hidden away in a corner of Utah and, overshadowed by its more renowned neighbours, it receives relatively few visitors. It would be pleasing to say that it was discovered through painstaking research, but the truth is that by sheer good fortune my cabin was situated opposite it. Prior to booking the accommodation I had no idea the wilderness was there, but it couldn't be missed because it was on the doorstep. As if that wasn't enough, the aspect of the view was tailor-made for low, evening sunlight. All that had to be done was to wait for good light and a strong sky to materialize.

Cloud can be a rare commodity in this part of America but, after a week of hoping and praying, perfect conditions arrived and I gratefully made several exposures as the sun sank and shadows lengthened across the undulating landscape. At no point during many visits to the area did I see another soul, and there is every chance that I have captured a small number of images without following in the footsteps of other photographers. Original pictures have, hopefully, been made.

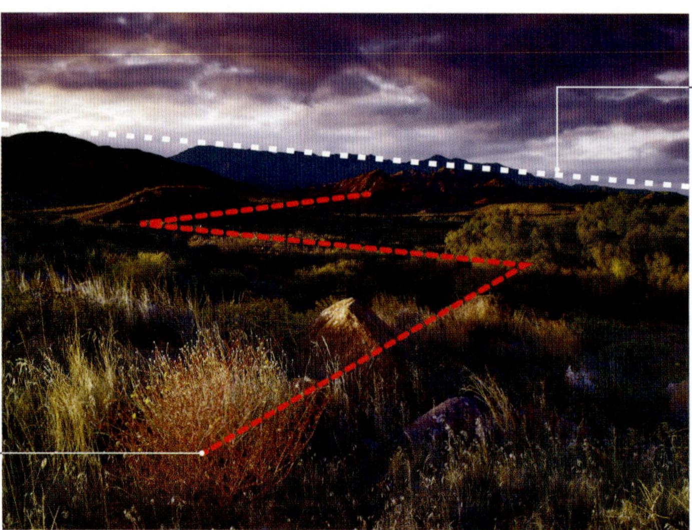

• The composition is built around the light. The four brightly lit areas lead the eye from the foreground bush onto the trees, across to the hillside and then onto the distant mountains. Visual interest is then maintained beyond the horizon by the colourful sky. All areas of the photograph, from left to right and top to bottom, have been visited as the viewer travels across the landscape. This is due solely to the distribution of the light.

2-stop (0.6) neutral density graduated filter

• A 2-stop ND graduated filter was used to darken the sky and prevent it from being overexposed.

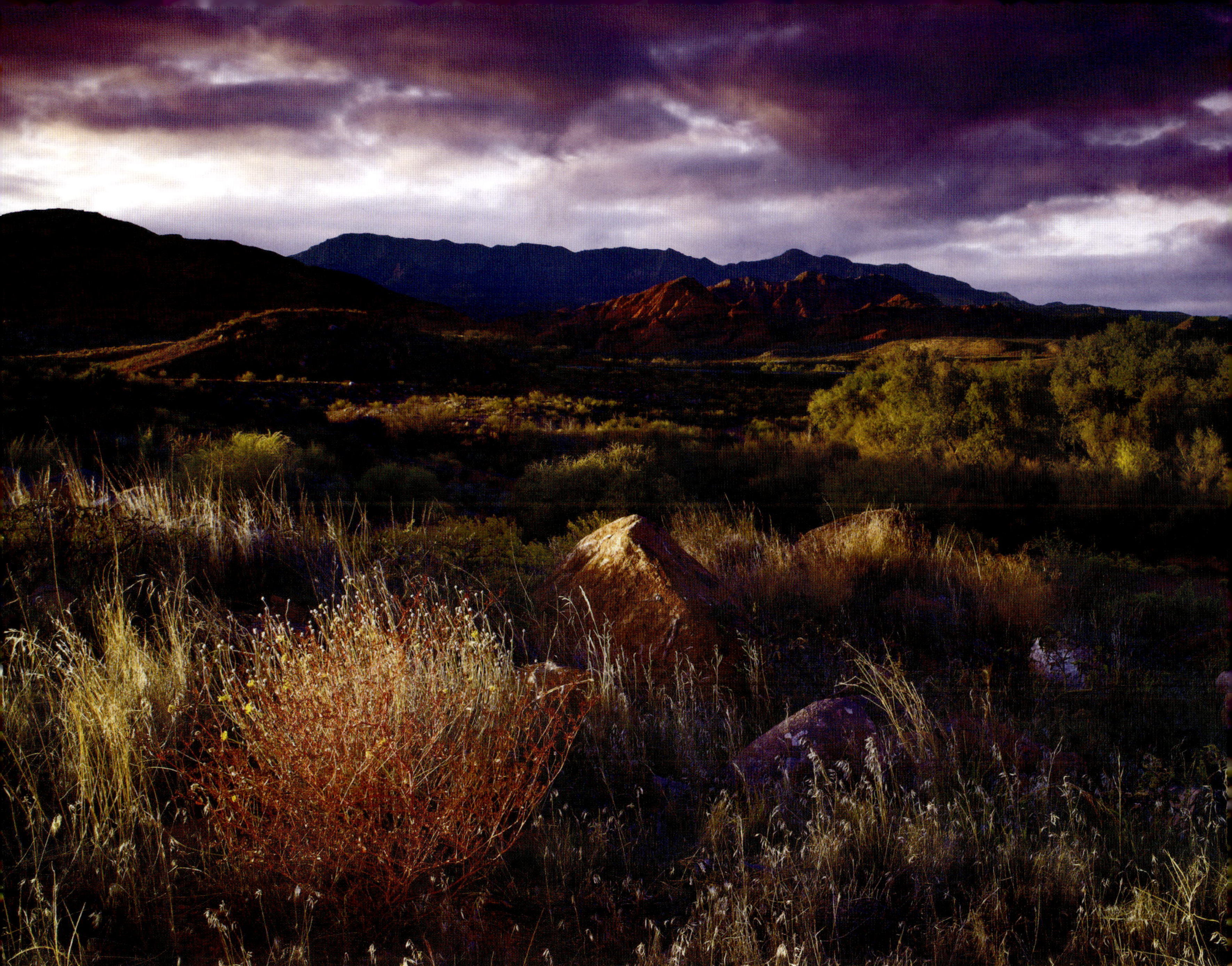

**Red Cliffs, Utah, USA**

**Camera:** Mamiya 645 AFDII with Phase One digital back

**Lens:** Mamiya 35mm (wide-angle)

**Filter:** 2-stop ND graduated

**Exposure:** 1/2sec at f/22, ISO 100

**Waiting for the light:** 5 days

**Post-processing:** Colour balance adjustment (warming)

A sharply undulating landscape provides the perfect opportunity to employ light to its maximum effect. Locations of this type are profoundly satisfying to photograph. Even doing no more than watching as the play of light dips in and out of the hills and valleys is an enthralling experience, and the sense of involvement you feel when capturing these light-dappled vistas is, I believe, unsurpassed by any other subject.

To find these places careful research is important. The Ordnance Survey Landranger maps (scale 1:50,000) are very useful because they show contour lines, landmarks and many other interesting features. So, before visiting the part of Dent Dale in the picture opposite, I was able to ascertain that there was in all probability an elevated viewpoint that was side/backlit during the morning, which included a viaduct that spanned a valley and was surrounded by a hilly landscape partly covered with deciduous trees. This type of detailed information is invaluable. Although you never know exactly what you will find when you arrive, the maps do at least show you the areas with the greatest potential and save a lot of time when searching for images.

Having found a location and suitable vantage point it is then a matter of waiting for the right conditions. The appropriate distribution of sunlight and shadow falling across the landscape is of course the critical factor. To make the most of a hilly terrain, the pattern of light should delineate its contours and introduce impact. The sky can also help in this respect, so watch and wait for an attractive cloud formation. Return visits might be necessary but your patience and perseverance should, with any luck, be well rewarded.

2-stop (0.6) neutral density graduated filter

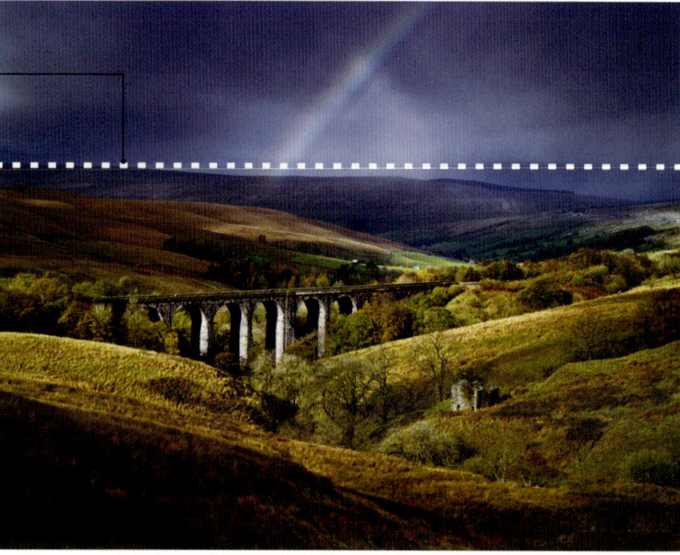

- Rainbows can never be predicted and are always a surprise bonus. They are frustratingly short-lived and should be captured as soon as they appear. Unless you are set up and ready to make your exposure, or can react very, very quickly, the likelihood is that they will vanish before being captured. I have lost count of the number I have missed by seconds. This example was a rare, and very fortunate, exception.

> **TIP:** Use a pattern of light and shadow to give shape and depth to a hilly landscape. Splashes of sunlight should be used to highlight contours and specific features.

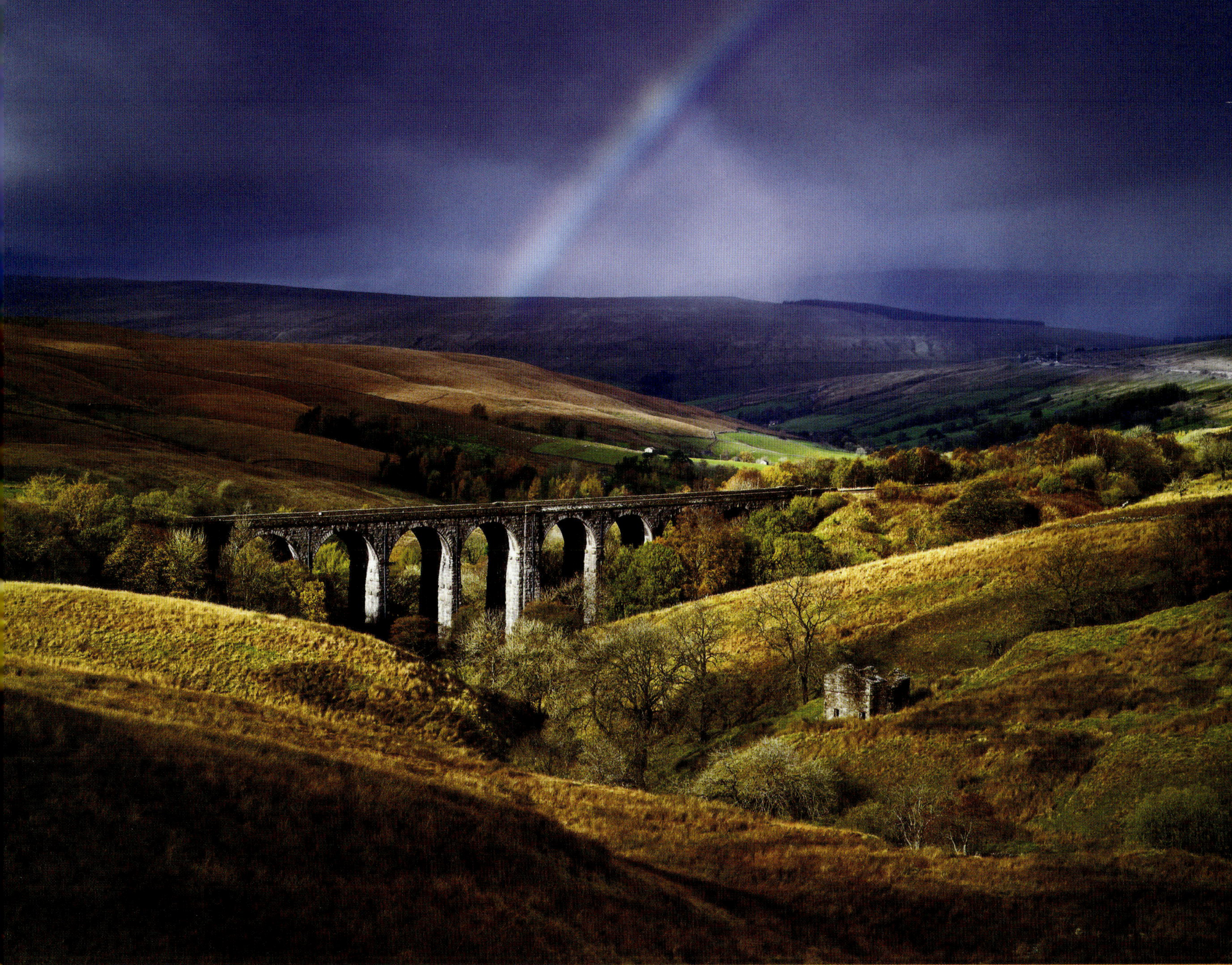

**Dent Dale, The Yorkshire Dales, England**

**Camera:** Mamiya 645 AFDII with Mamiya digital back
**Lens:** Mamiya 35mm (wide-angle)
**Filter:** 2-stop ND graduated
**Exposure:** 1/10sec at f/18, ISO 100
**Waiting for the light:** 2 hours
**Post-processing:** Curves adjustment, colour balance adjustment (warming)

Spotlighting a specific feature is one of the most effective methods of drawing attention to a small part of an image. A spotlit object will shine like a beacon when photographed against a subdued background, and this was certainly the case as I gazed upon a shimmering tree hidden in the depths of a valley in the Zion National Park. It grabbed my attention and had me reaching for my camera the second it came into view. Its glowing radiance was in stark contrast to the towering mountain behind it; the imposing background of the mountain face accentuated the tree's vibrant appearance and the picture was therefore composed in a way that enabled both elements to make a contribution. Placing the tree in the lower part of the image reveals more about its environment. It allows the tree to be seen in the context of its surroundings and the broad expanse of dark background helps to strengthen the spotlit effect of the light.

The picture was taken within minutes of arrival, which was fortunate because sunlight was beginning to clip the mountain face as I packed away my equipment. Imagine this photograph with patches of bright illumination scattered across the background – it would have been a dismal failure. Spotlighting means exactly what its name implies: a light shining specifically on one small part of an image. There must be no other highlights; everything else must be subdued. Timing is therefore important because in all probability you will have only a brief opportunity in which to make this type of photograph. Watch as the sun travels through its arc and be in position, poised and ready to make your exposure at exactly the right moment.

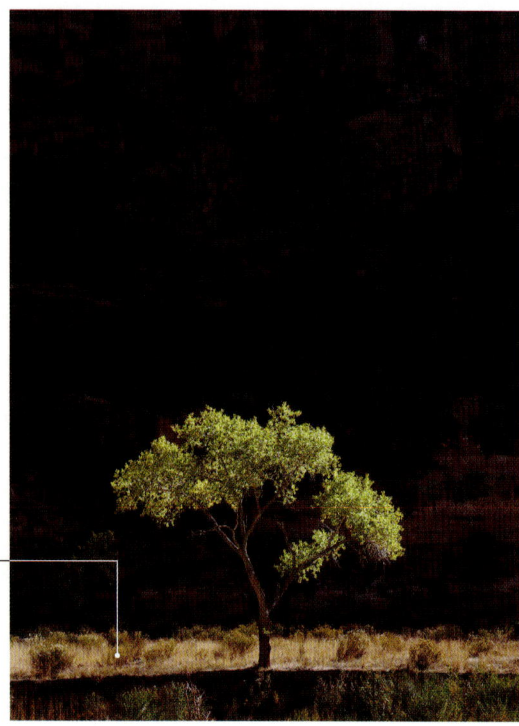

Ideally the foliage and strip of grass behind the tree should be in shadow. Fortunately, because they are in the foreground and connected to the tree, they are not too intrusive.

> **TIP:** When viewing a photograph the eye is automatically drawn to brightly lit features. This can be a useful aid to composition but it can also be a hindrance and can interfere with subtle elements in a photograph. It is therefore important to scrutinize every part of your subject before you release the shutter. Once captured, light won't disappear – it will, when seen in a photograph, become the dominant feature – so ensure that your subject is lit in precisely the way you require.

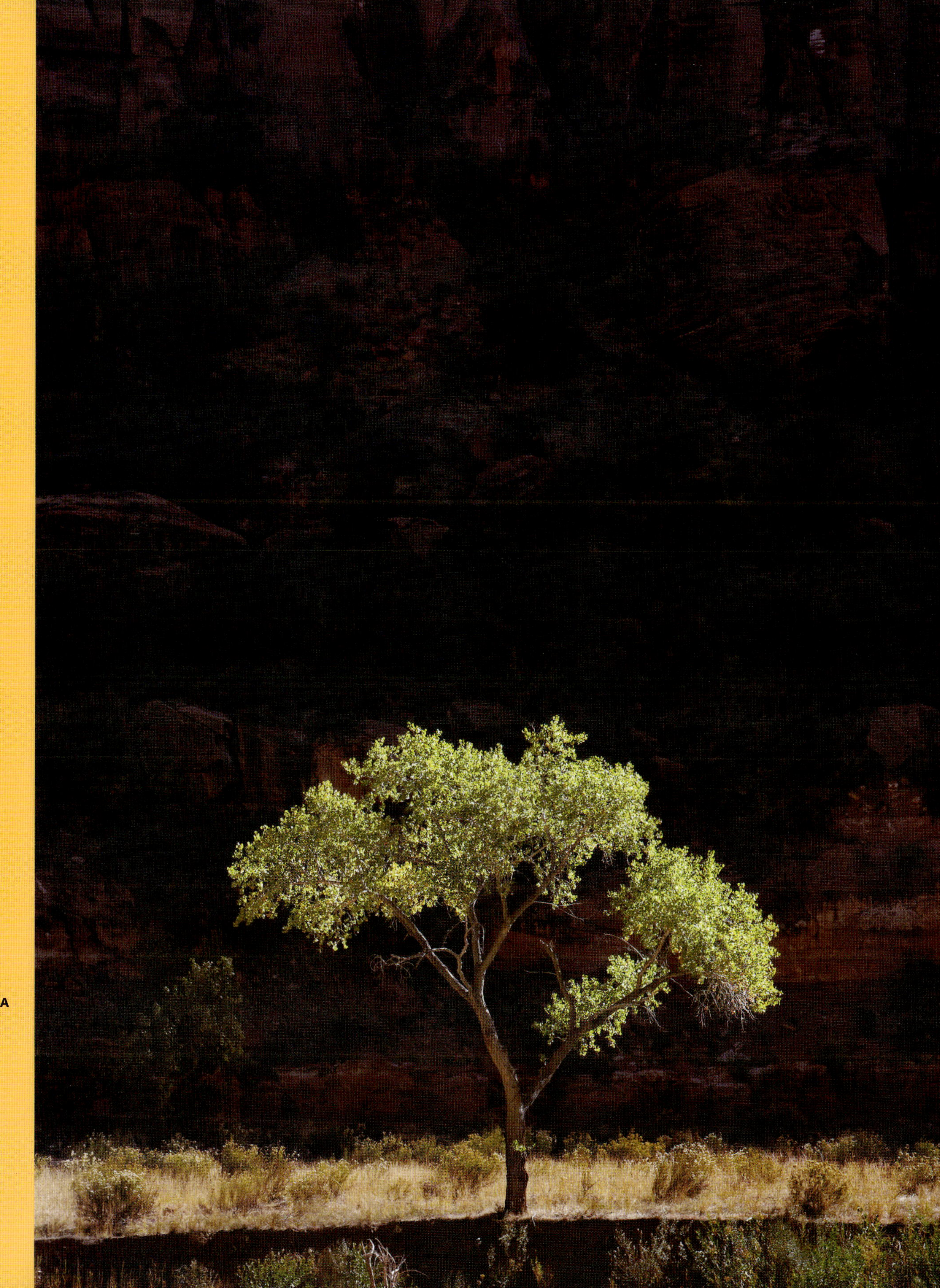

**Zion National Park, Utah, USA**

**Camera:** Canon EOS 7D
**Lens:** Canon 24–105mm L IS
**Filter:** None
**Exposure:** 1/60sec at f/10,
ISO 100
**Waiting for the light:** Immediate
**Post-processing:** Suppression of
highlights

In the making of this photograph of mountains overlooking Lake Powell the light and shadow were as important as the subject itself, and hopefully you can see why.

Without the sidelighting and the specific way the mountains are lit, the picture would not have been worth taking. There was virtually no cloud in the sky and the entire landscape was bathed in sunlight, the shadows in the image being solely the result of the direction and low angle of the light. It was the essential ingredient and the photograph's composition was therefore determined by the play of the warm evening sunlight and shadow across the mountain range.

The spotlit mountain face has been placed centrally as the main focal point (brightly lit features will always act as a strong attraction, so be careful to avoid sunlight falling on part of your picture that you would prefer not to emphasize) and the image was then cropped to reduce the expanse of sky and foreground. A squarer format would have weakened the photograph because the most attractive feature is undoubtedly the mountain range. Cropping is a useful compositional aid and before you dismiss a picture-making opportunity the effect of reducing it to a panoramic format during post-processing should be considered. It can transform an image, particularly when there is a weak foreground or an uninteresting sky.

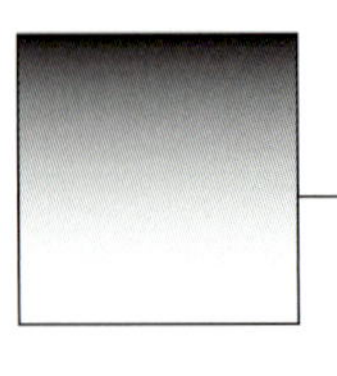

2-stop (0.6) neutral density graduated filter

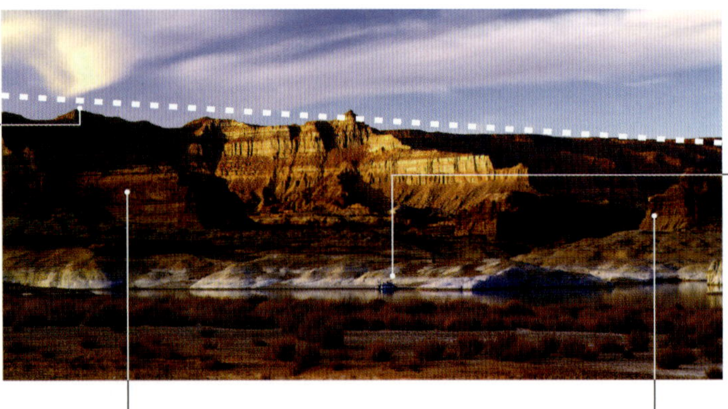

• The presence, and position, of the boat is a small but important feature. It helps to draw the eye into the picture and also brings a sense of scale to the image.

• The softly lit mountains on either side help to frame the main subject. The quality of light was important because, while these small mountains are in sunlight, they are not as brightly lit as the section in the middle. The light therefore allows them to make a noticeable contribution to the photograph without distracting from the central feature.

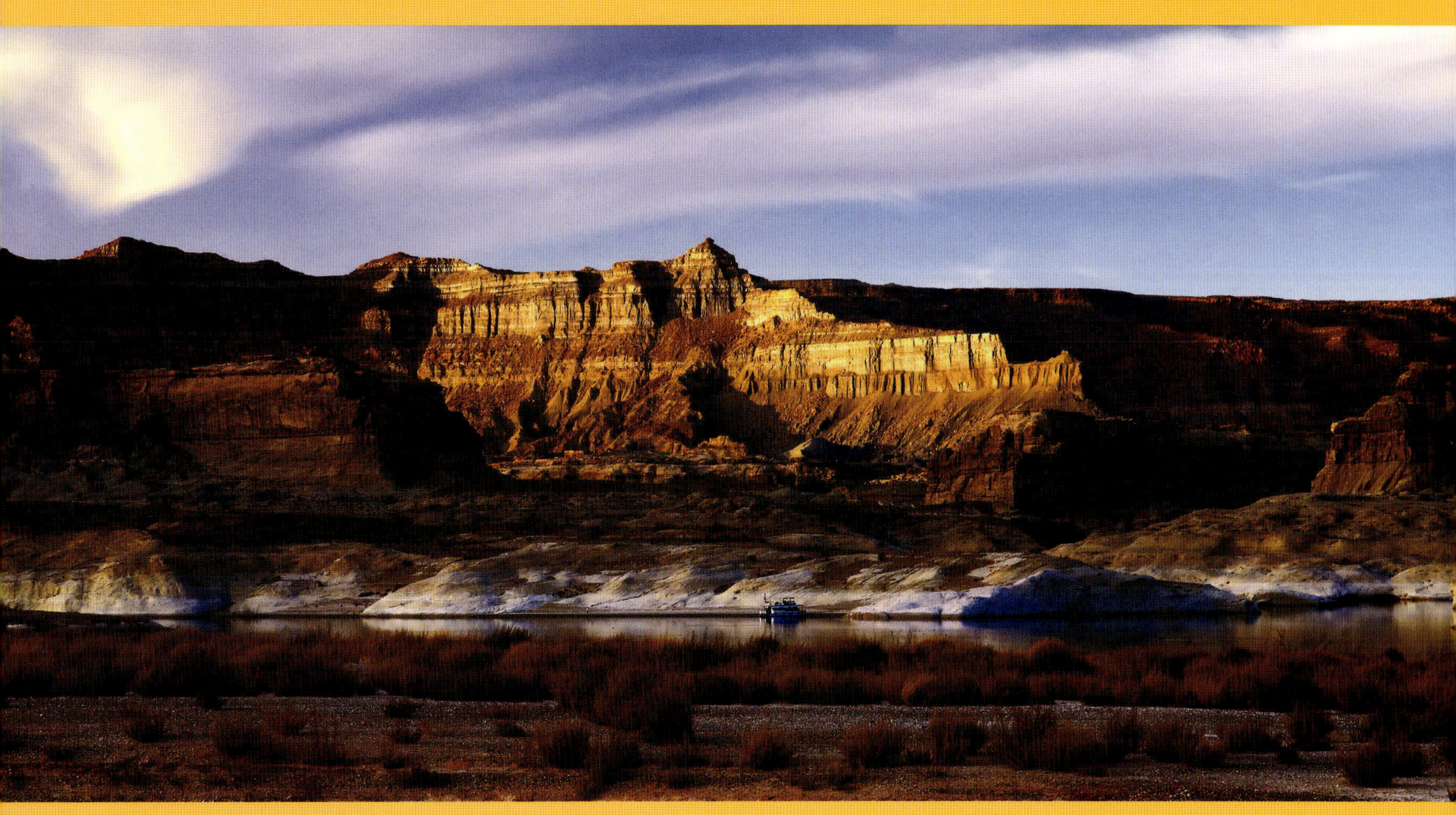

**Lake Powell, Arizona, USA**

**Camera:** Mamiya 645 AFDII with Phase One digital back
**Lens:** Mamiya 80mm (standard)
**Filter:** 2-stop ND graduated
**Exposure:** 1/4sec at f/22, ISO 100
**Waiting for the light:** 45 minutes
**Post-processing:** Colour balance adjustment (warming)

When composing an image it is important to consider the position of the sun. The choice of viewpoint will be affected by it and the time of capture will be determined by it. There is always a right time to make a photograph, and the angle of light and the distribution of highlights and shadows will dictate this time.

For an open view to be successfully captured it must display distance and shape. This is particularly noticeable in a woodland terrain because trees will not reveal their rounded shape unless a specific angle of light is used. To convey them as solid, three-dimensional objects they should be partly backlit, i.e. the sun should be slightly in front of the camera.

This will create shadows on both the front and one side of the trees and this combination of back and sidelighting is a very effective means of depicting depth. Any open view is likely to be improved by this type of light and for this type of picture it is my preferred lighting.

Contrast can be high in a backlit scene, so to avoid harsh shadows and overexposed highlights hazy sunshine is preferable. This will allow detail to be retained across all parts of the image and will also reduce the possibility of lens flare, which can easily occur when pointing your camera towards the sun.

• **The sky has been excluded because it has no role to play in this type of image.**

> **TIP:** When photographing a backlit scene use an umbrella to shield the camera lens from direct sunlight. Take care, particularly when using a wide-angle lens, that it does not protrude into the corner of the picture frame.

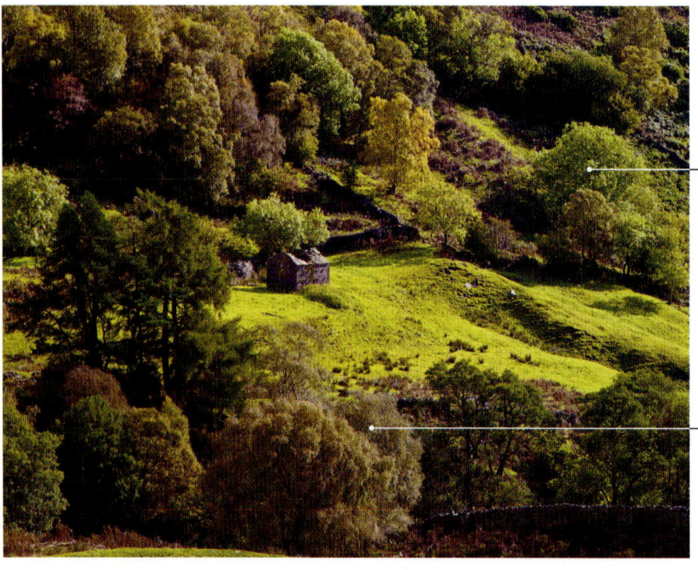

• **The position of the sun – slightly in front of the camera – has created a combination of side and backlighting. This has given the trees a solid, three-dimensional appearance.**

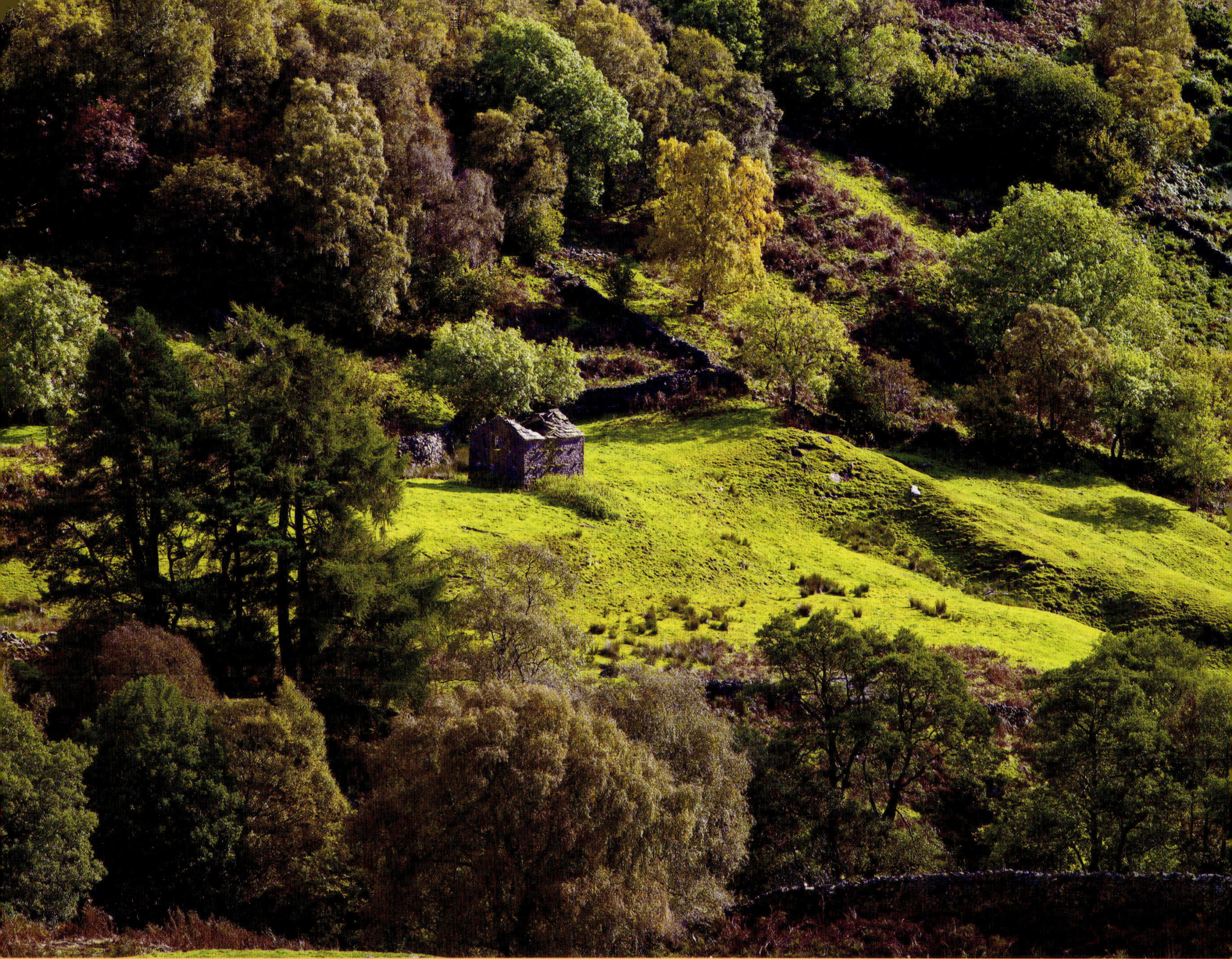

**Near Keld, The Yorkshire Dales, England**

**Camera:** Mamiya 645 AFDII with Mamiya digital back
**Lens:** Mamiya 80mm (standard)
**Filter:** None
**Exposure**: 1/10sec at f/18, ISO 100
**Waiting for the light:** 45 minutes
**Post-processing:** Curves adjustment, colour balance adjustment (warming)

Take care when capturing a backlit scene. The sky is likely to be a lot brighter than the landscape – four or more stops is not uncommon – and filtration will be necessary if detail is to be retained in the highlights. A pale overexposed sky is the kiss of death to an image; to prevent this a neutral density graduated filter of a density of at least two stops will be needed. Stronger filters can further improve the appearance of the brightest areas but have to be used with care because they can over darken other parts of the sky. I prefer to use a 2-stop filter and then undertake additional darkening, as necessary, to specific areas in post-processing, using either the Curves or Shadows/Highlights tool (or a combination of both). In the image opposite the sun was to the right, just outside the frame of the picture, and as a result the right side of the sky was very bright. This area was selected in post-processing using the Lasso tool and darkened with the Shadows/Highlights tool. (More information concerning the use of neutral density graduated filters can be found on page 100.)

I had visited this location several times and had seen it when it was more frontally lit. Its appearance always suffered as a result of the light because the farmhouse and surrounding trees were largely indistinguishable from the background. Once backlit, however, the shadows cast on the far hills created a dark backdrop and this immediately introduced depth and distance and allowed the small building and trees to become much more prominent. The backlighting has also improved the foreground, giving the field of crops a rich texture, which adds visual interest to this part of the picture and also helps to create foreground/background balance.

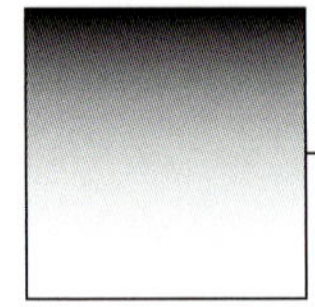

**2-stop (0.6) neutral density graduated filter**

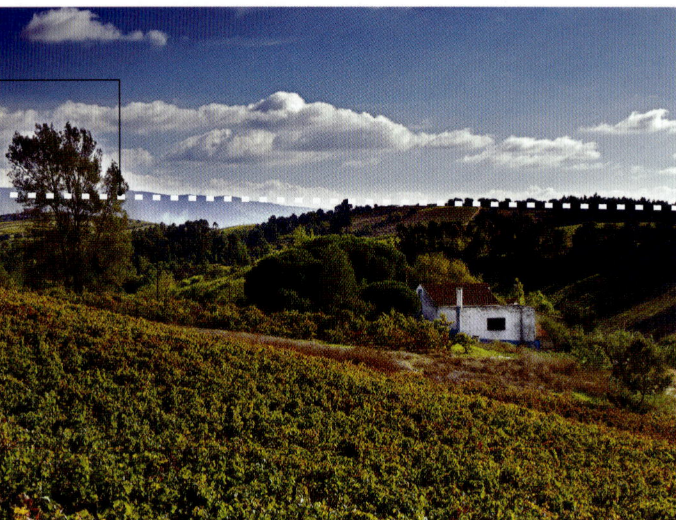

> **TIP:** To strengthen the appearance of a specific feature use shadows created by backlighting to distinguish it from the background. This will also enhance the impression of depth.

> **TIP:** Use backlighting to give a field of crops shape and a pronounced three-dimensional quality.

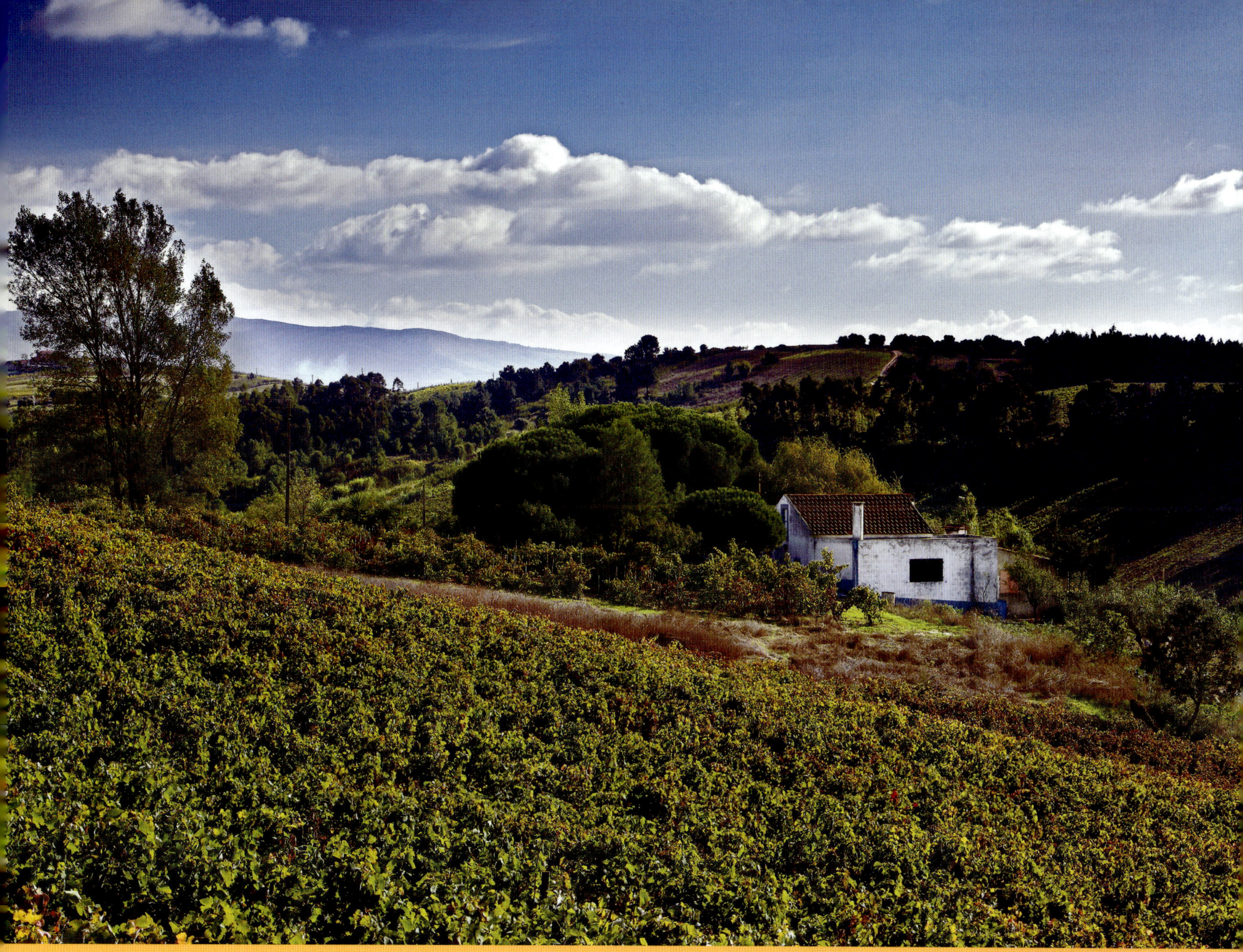

**Near Obidos, Portugal**

**Camera:** Mamiya 645 AFDII with Mamiya digital back
**Lens:** Mamiya 80mm (standard)
**Filter:** 2-stop ND graduated
**Exposure:** 1/10sec at f/22, ISO 100
**Waiting for the light:** 3 hours
**Post-processing:** Suppression of highlights in the sky

The benefit of backlighting can be seen in the picture opposite. The rows of vines have a three-dimensional appearance and this is solely due to the position of the sun. The small shadows created at the front and side of each vine give them shape, depth and prominence. Had this scene been lit from the front, the shaded trees in the foreground, which so effectively frame the main subject, would have been brightly illuminated and then the sloping vineyard would have been lost in the background. At that point the picture would have been a complete failure. Remember that in every landscape view, the subject is only as good as the light falling on it; I hope that fact is demonstrated clearly by this photograph.

Backlit scenes that contain no sky are not technically difficult to photograph. Exposure can be calculated by taking exposure readings of both the highlights and shadows then using an average of both readings. Hazy sunlight is still preferable as it will prevent the occurrence of extreme contrast ratios and allow detail to be captured across the entire tonal range. Lens flare is, depending upon the position of the sun, still a potential problem and you should avoid sunlight falling directly onto the camera lens. When there is no sky, ND graduated filters or a polarizer are usually unnecessary (polarizers are, in any case, depending upon the position of the sun, either ineffective or inclined to cause uneven darkening when using backlighting).

• **The use of a distant viewpoint and a telephoto lens has compressed the image and enabled the vineyard to be framed by the foreground trees. This arrangement, together with the ploughed field along the base of the picture, allows the vineyard to be seen in its environment without being dominated by it.**

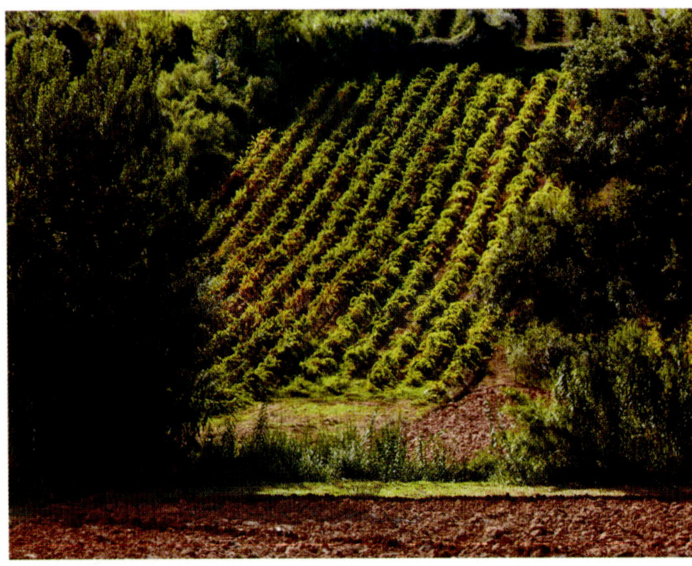

> **TIP:** Contrast was relatively high. I therefore lightened the shadows in the trees using the Shadows/Highlights tool in post-processing. This is an effective means of controlling contrast when the use of filters is impractical.

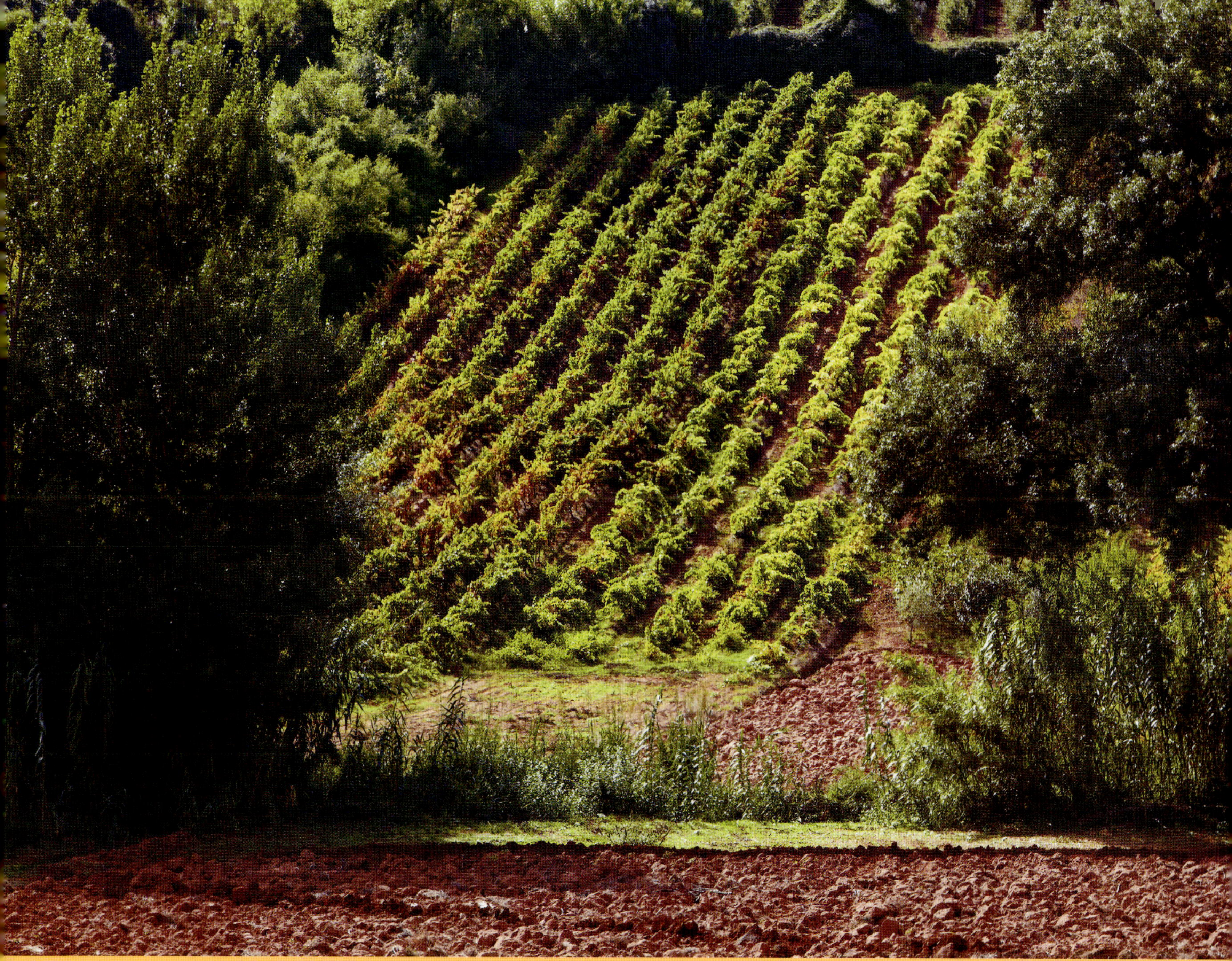

**Near Rio Maior, Portugal**

**Camera:** Mamiya 645 AFDII with Mamiya digital back
**Lens:** Mamiya 150mm (telephoto)
**Filter:** None
**Exposure:** 1/10sec at f/22, ISO 100
**Waiting for the light:** 1 hour
**Post-processing:** Lightening of shadows

One of the most important aspects of capturing landscape images is the correct exposure of all parts of the scene. Overexposed areas will lack detail and look pale and colourless and, as previously explained, this is particularly the case with the sky. Invariably the sky is always brighter than the land beneath it, even one that is heavily clouded. It therefore has to be darkened and the easiest way to do this is to use a neutral-density graduated filter. The sole purpose of this filter is to absorb light and this is achieved by positioning the dark portion over the sky so that it will reduce its brightness and enable both sky and landscape to be correctly exposed.

These filters are available in various strengths, from 0.1 (1/3 f/stop) up to 0.9 (3 f/stops) or more. Using the appropriate filter is of course important and the best way to achieve this is to take separate exposure readings of the sky and landscape. I use a handheld meter, but a camera's built-in meter is also perfectly suitable. If it has a spot-reading capability then you will be able to take accurate readings across all parts of the image and gather detailed information of both exposure and contrast across the entire tonal range. This can be very useful (and also educational), but as you gain experience you should find it relatively easy to assess the brightness of sky and choose the appropriate filter without the need to take meter readings. More often than not I use a 0.6 (2 f/stops) filter as I find that in most cases it gives very satisfactory results.

In addition to filters there is now, thanks to digital imaging, an alternative method of achieving the same result. Two photographs of different exposures can be captured in quick succession and merged together. This will enable highlights and shadows to be correctly exposed and detail will, as a result, be retained across the complete tonal range. Personally I prefer to use filters but post-processing adjustment is now a viable option.

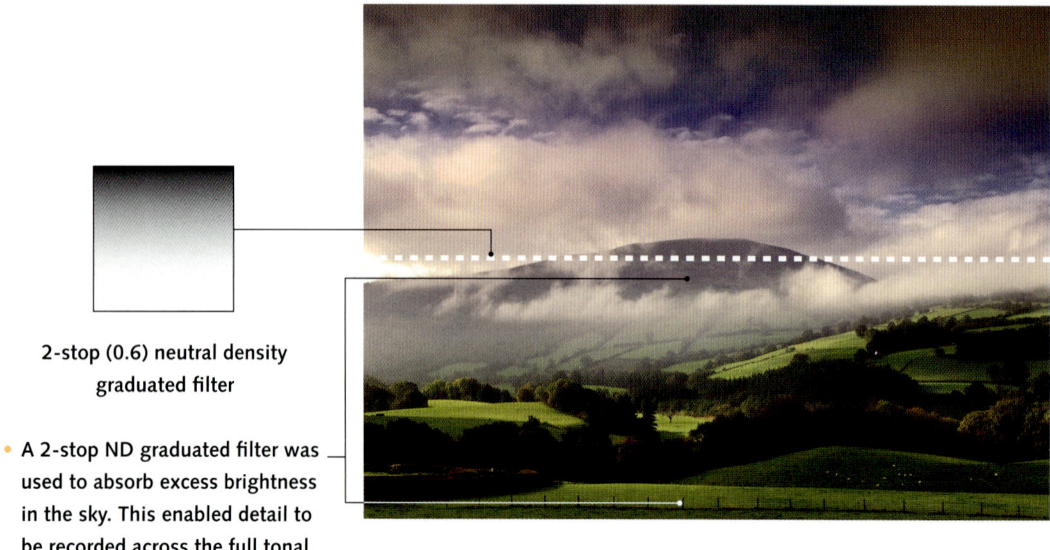

**2-stop (0.6) neutral density graduated filter**

• **A 2-stop ND graduated filter was used to absorb excess brightness in the sky. This enabled detail to be recorded across the full tonal range of the image.**

> **TIP:** If, as an alternative to using a ND graduated filter, you merge two images together, ensure that you use a rigid tripod. The position of the camera must be identical for both exposures.

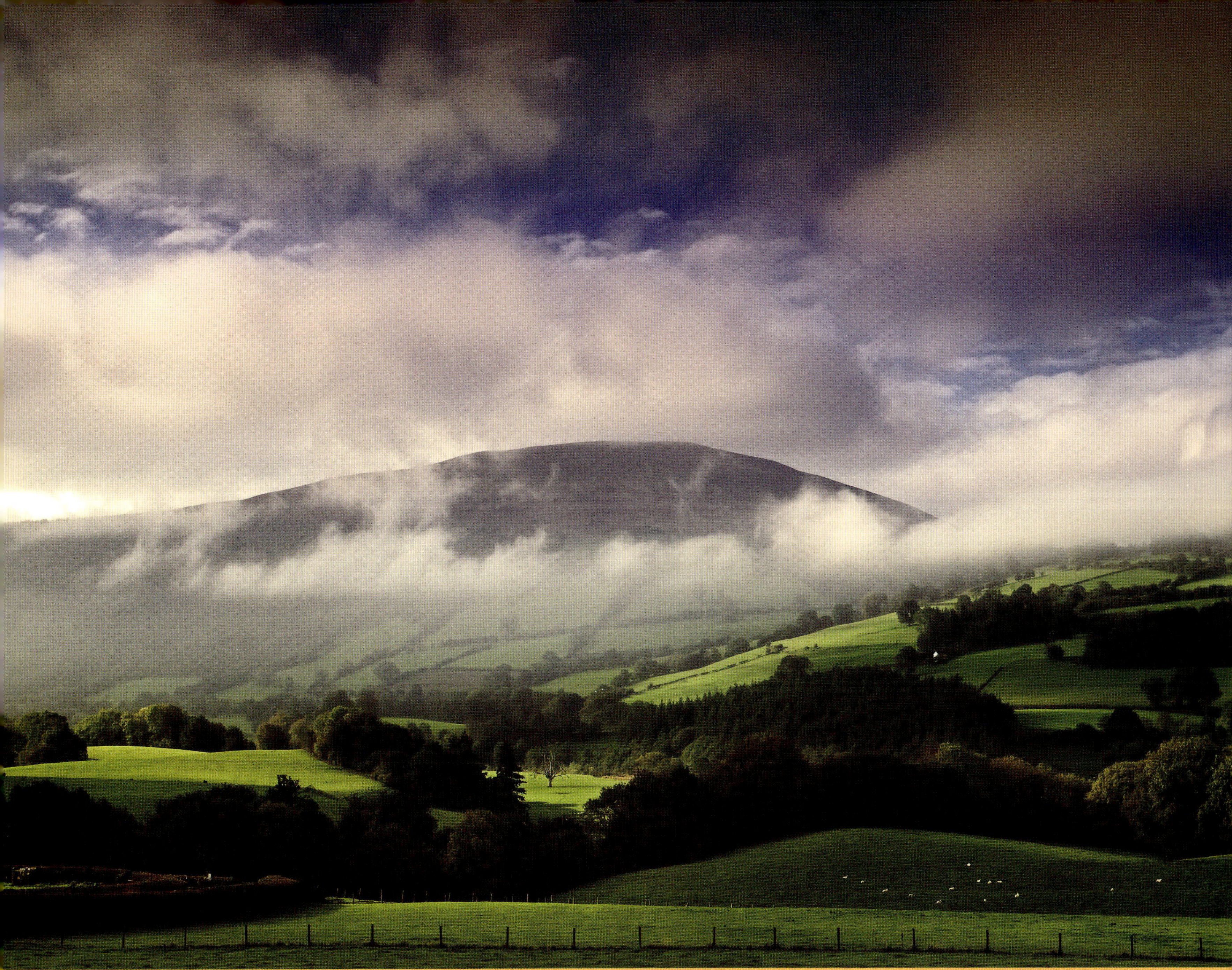

**Near Llangynidr, The Brecon Beacons, Wales**

**Camera:** Mamiya 645 AFDII with Mamiya digital back
**Lens:** Mamiya 35mm (wide-angle)
**Filter:** 2-stop ND graduated
**Exposure:** 1/15sec at f/18, ISO 100
**Waiting for the light:** 60 minutes
**Post-processing:** Curves adjustment

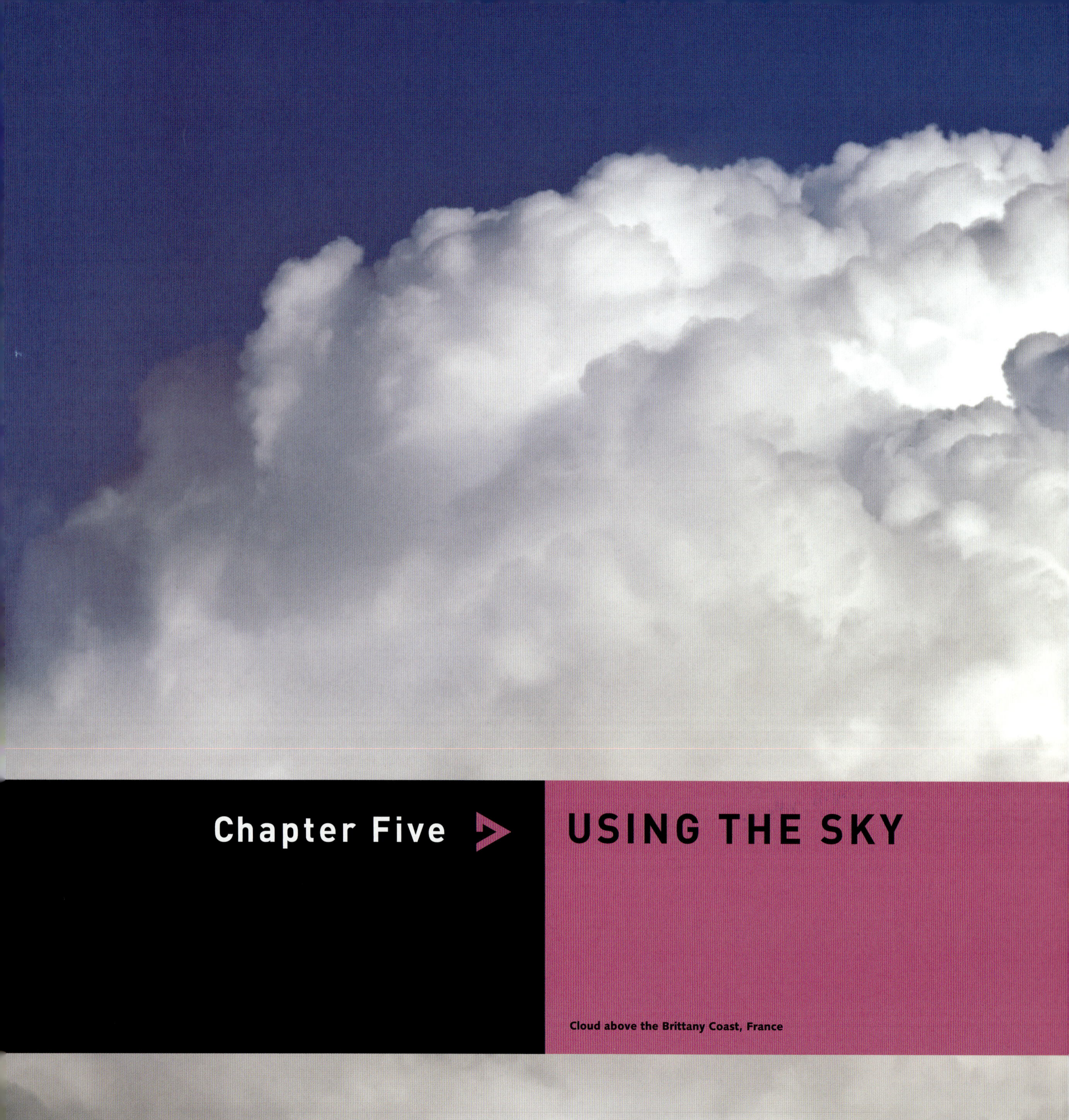

Chapter Five ▶ USING THE SKY

Cloud above the Brittany Coast, France

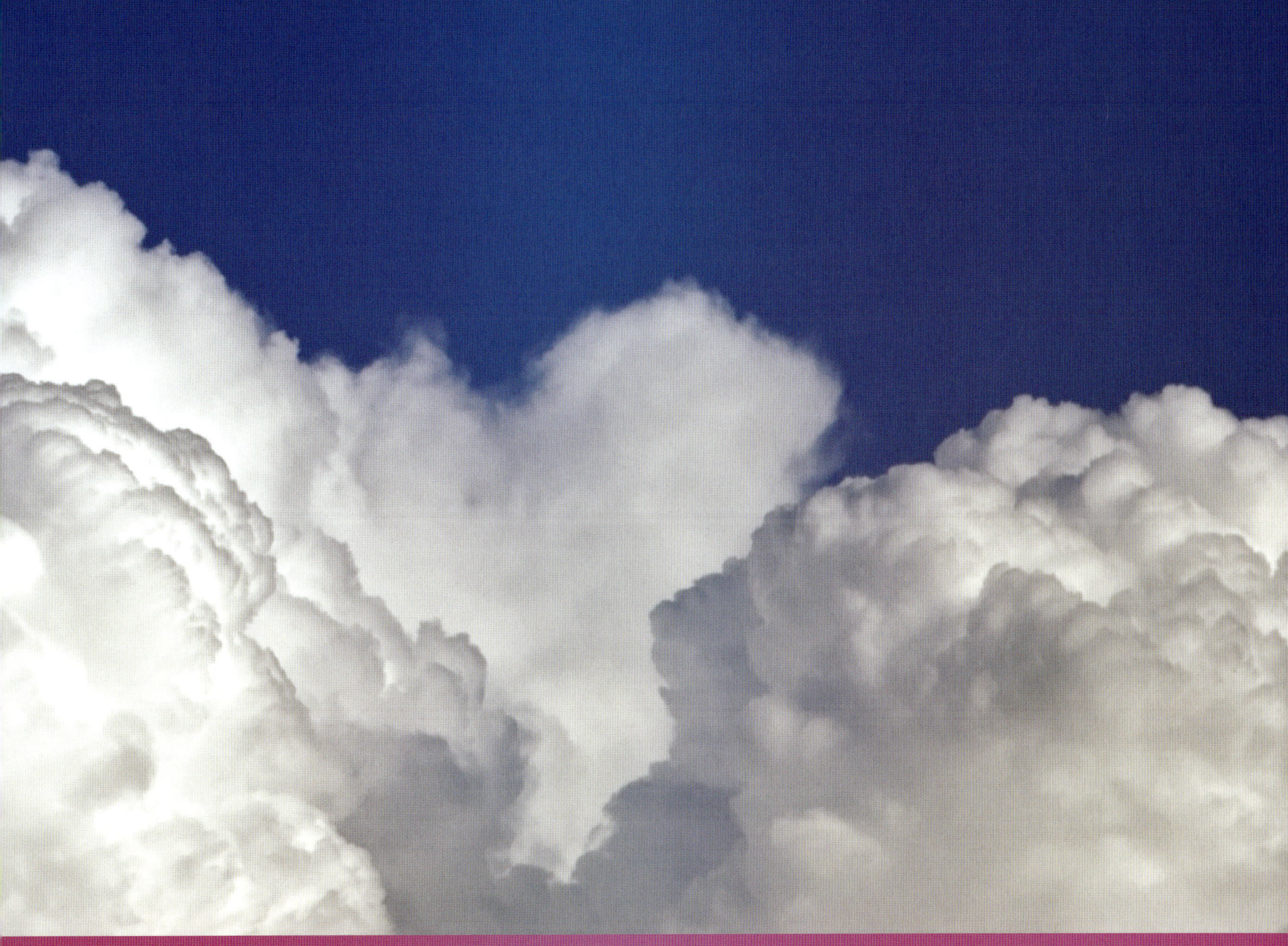

The sky can be a powerful presence in a landscape image. It is as important as the land itself and the effect it can have on a photograph should not be underestimated. An expanse of sky can contribute mood, drama and symmetry to a picture, as well as success or failure. This chapter shows how to employ the sky as a creative tool, and how the appropriate pairing of landscape and the right type of sky can elevate and even transform a photograph into something really spectacular.

If I were asked to pass on just one piece of advice, my answer would be short and simple; it would be to pay attention to the sky. Seasoned photographers have learned (quite possibly the way I did – through painful experiences and many failures!) that the sky matters. It is a crucial element and its importance in a landscape image should not be underestimated. From acting as a supporting device to taking centre stage as the main subject, the sky, when it is part of the composition, always has a role to play. Dismiss its importance and the risk of your photographs failing will increase dramatically. Think sky at all times and that alone will elevate you to a position where you can capture images with confidence.

Successful photographs often consist of a sky and landscape that share similar characteristics. As a guideline a dramatic, stormy sky will often suit a dramatic, rugged terrain while a lighter, less threatening cloud structure is likely to be a good match for a softer landscape. But this is no hard and fast rule and sometimes the opposite approach can be a winning combination, with a dramatic sky being paired with a smooth landscape and vice versa.

What matters most of all is that you, as the photographer, consider your options and decide on the combination of sky and landscape that best suits the mood and theme of the image you are creating.

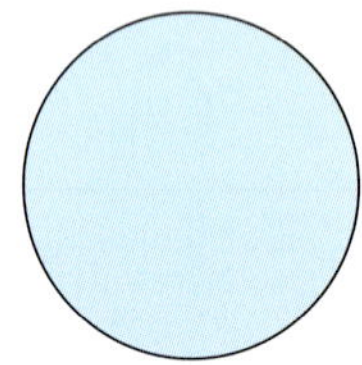

**Polarizer (fully polarized)**

• This picture is both a skyscape and a landscape. While the sky, because of its distinctive cloud formation, is the more prominent feature, the landscape is still important. The tree, in particular, is essential because it draws the viewer's eye to the horizon and acts as a connecting link between the two elements.

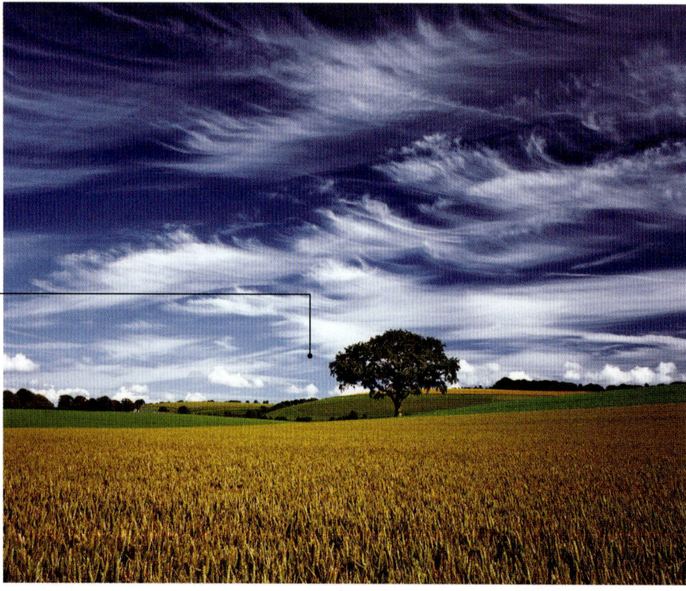

• This is a perfect sky for polarizing. The polarizer has saturated the blue expanse, which has strengthened the presence of the wispy cloud and increased its impact.

**>** **TIP:** The importance of the sky cannot be overstated. Assess the sky with a critical eye every time you include it in an image and don't accept second best. This alone will ensure that the quality of your photographs will rise and the number of disappointments fall.

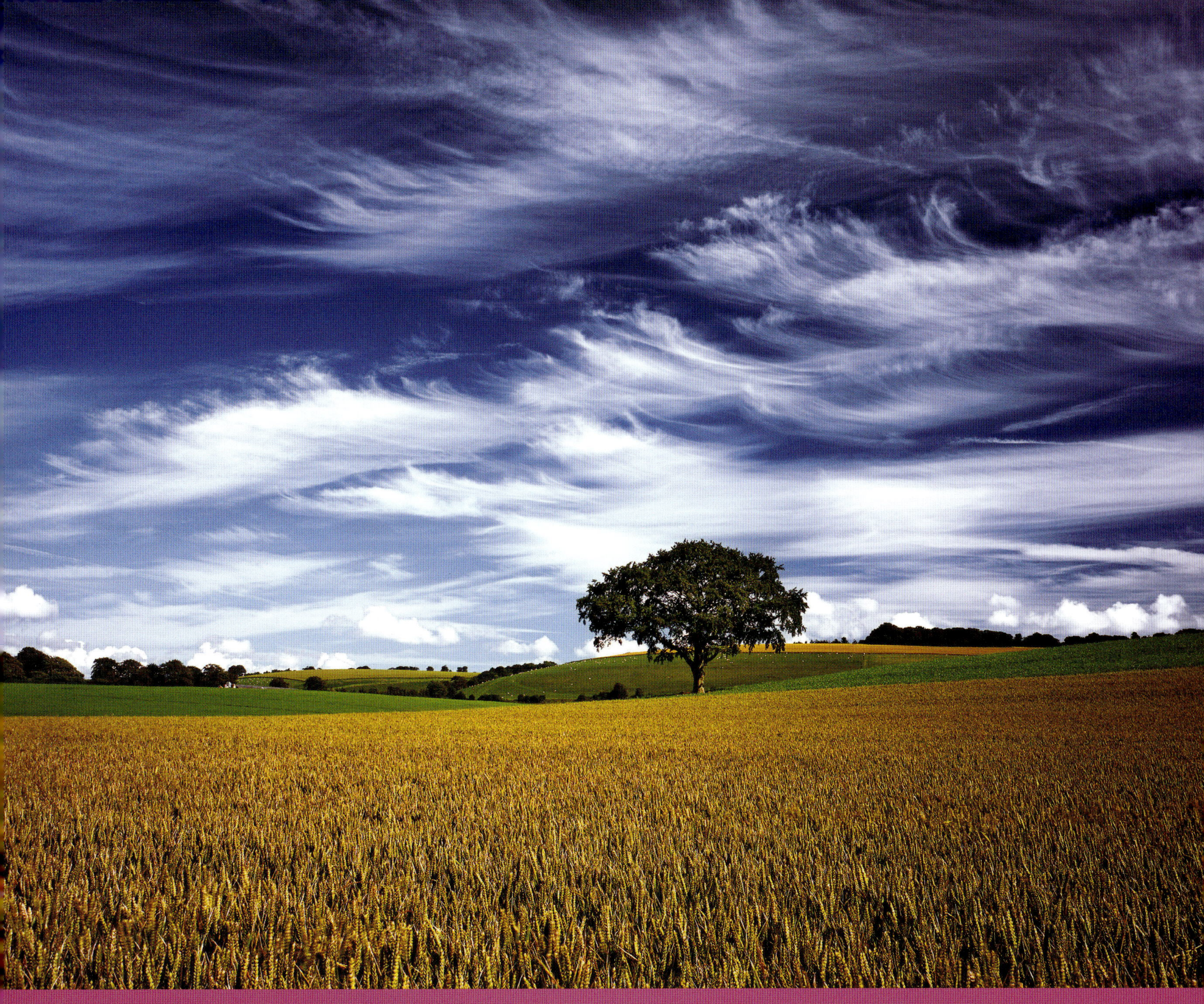


**Near Petersfield, Hampshire, England**

**Camera:** Mamiya 645 AFDII with Mamiya digital back
**Lens:** Mamiya 35mm (wide-angle)
**Filter:** Polarizer (fully polarized)
**Exposure:** 1/5sec at f/22, ISO 100
**Waiting for the light:** 20 minutes
**Post-processing:** Curves adjustment

My heart leapt as I caught a glimpse of an isolated cloud protruding above a sun-drenched poppy field in the depths of the Hampshire countryside. Apart from that single cloud the sky was completely clear and picture-making opportunities were therefore scarce. But that cloud gave me hope. I knew my fortunes were about to change and it was with a mixture of relief and excitement that I parked my car opposite the field and quickly set up my camera.

Time was of the essence because clouds can be deceptive. They can appear to be motionless but they seem to possess an uncanny ability to change shape and lose definition with unnerving ease, as you watch in horror while the photograph you were contemplating melts away in front of you. Mindful of this, I quickly composed the image by placing the cloud in a central position, attached a polarizer and

made three exposures. It was all over in two or three minutes. I then gazed contentedly at the sky as the cloud drifted away and gradually disappeared beneath the horizon.

This image is as much a skyscape as it is a landscape. On their own neither element would really be worth photographing but together they make a complete picture. The sky here is as essential as the field of poppies because it brings an added dimension to the image. This is an important role of the sky because, photographically speaking, it often forms a symbiotic relationship with the land beneath it. Both elements benefit from the presence of the other and this creates many opportunities for the observant photographer. Remain vigilant and view the sky and landscape as a single entity, and you will find pictures.

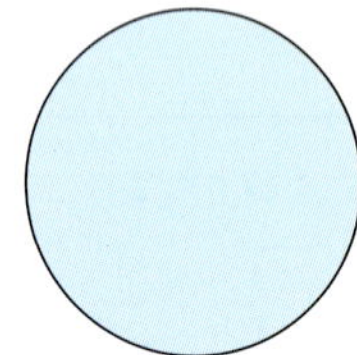

**Polarizer (fully polarized)**

• **The image consists of four distinctly coloured elements: blue sky, white cloud, red poppies and green wheat. The clearly defined blocks of colour strengthen the composition and visual impact.**

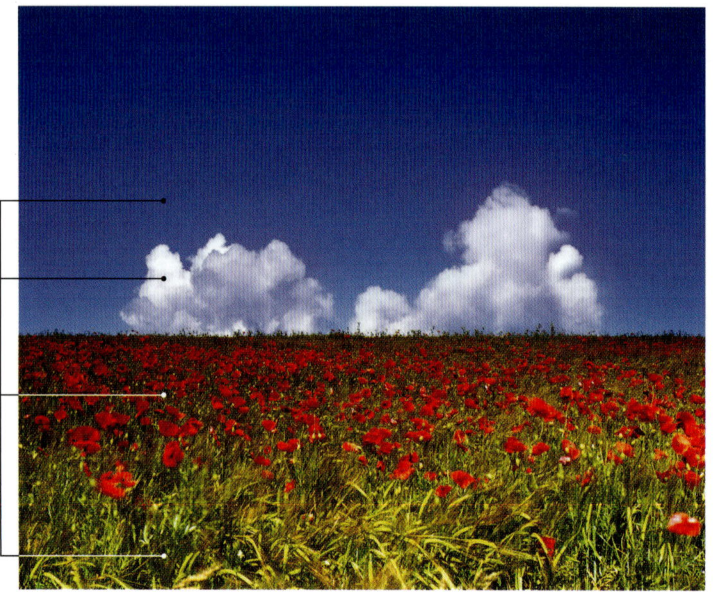

> **TIP:** Always be aware of the sky and remain vigilant for any opportunities it might create. React quickly when you discover a potential image because cloud formations can change quickly.

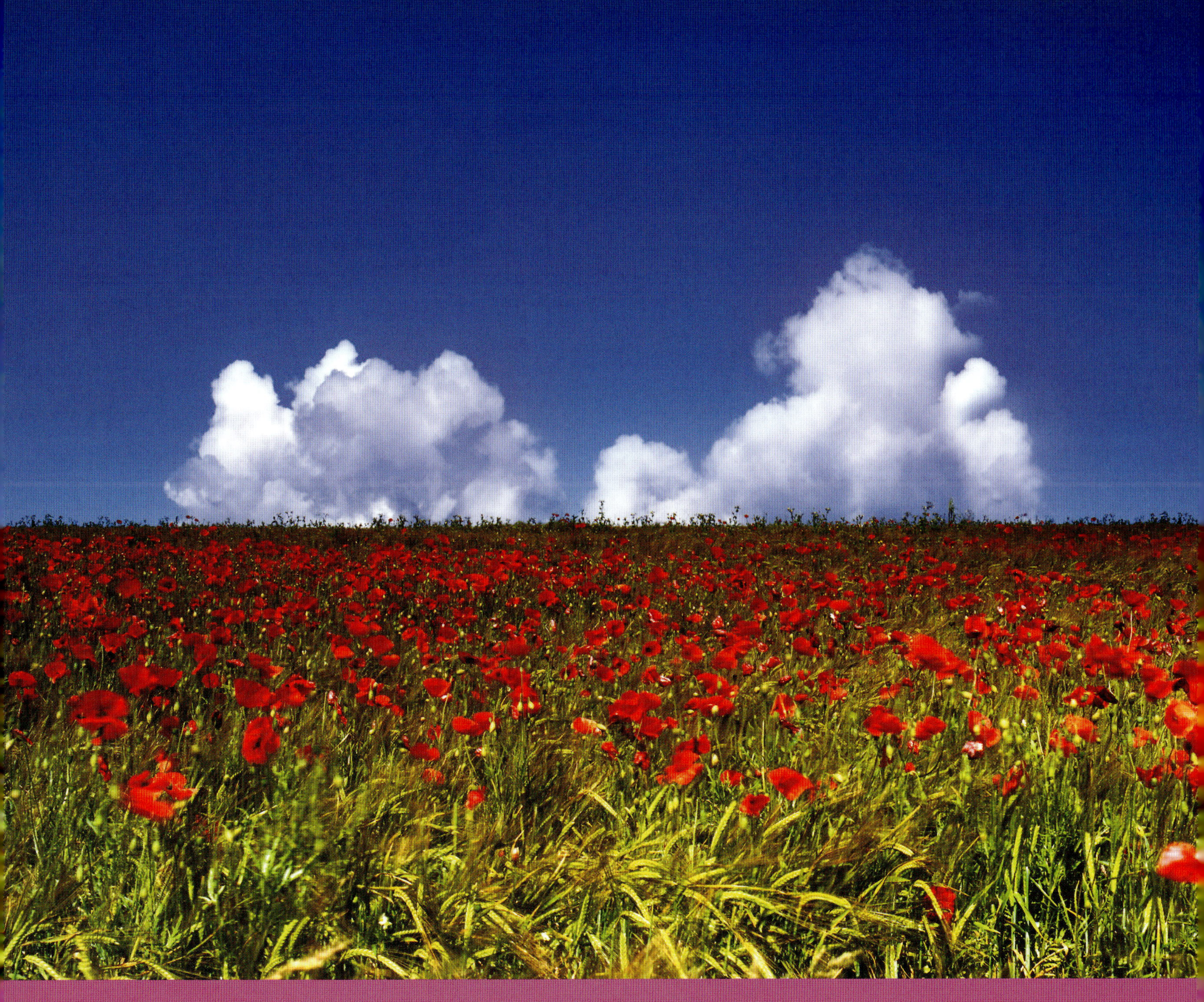

**Near East Meon, Hampshire, England**

**Camera:** Mamiya 645 AFDII with Mamiya digital back
**Lens:** Mamiya 35mm (wide-angle)
**Filter:** Polarizer (fully polarized)
**Exposure:** 1/8sec at f/22, ISO 100
**Waiting for the light:** Immediate
**Post-processing:** Curves adjustment, suppression of highlights

Things don't always go to plan. Frustrating as it is, this is to be expected from time to time, particularly when attempting to tie down uncontrollable forces and predict the appearance and prevailing conditions of a specific location at a specific time. This is a handicap shared by all outdoor photographers and, judging by one particular day I spent along the North Wales coast, it is apparently a handicap that is also shared by our weather forecasters. Their prediction for the day had promised a bright, sunny morning with rain clouds gathering late in the afternoon. In practice it was just the opposite; dawn broke under a grey sky and steady drizzle that showed no sign of clearing. It seemed that (yet another) unproductive day was in store when, late in the afternoon, the sky began to brighten. It looked promising but there was barely an hour of daylight left and the photograph that had been envisaged required morning light. It was time for plan B so I quickly chose a new location (one of the advantages of coastal photography is that new viewpoints are always relatively easy to find) and then waited anxiously to see what would materialize.

For a brief period a sunset seemed a possibility, but ultimately it wasn't to be. All was not lost, though, because the cloud continued to dissolve. Forty minutes later – this was now forty minutes after the sun had set – a crescent moon and a glowing horizon brought the day to an unexpected, but very memorable, end. The day had not gone as planned but that is all part of the outdoor experience. The weather forecasters are not to blame; 100 per cent accuracy cannot be guaranteed and most of the time their predictions, if taken one day at a time, are fairly reliable. In any case, just imagine if every day was completely predictable with no surprises and no unexpected moments of unmitigated joy; such days would quickly lose their sparkle. It is, after all, always the surprise gift that is the most memorable, and also the most appreciated.

> **TIP:** To retain some detail in the landscape use a ND graduated filter to darken an evening sky. This will prevent the land being depicted as a silhouette and will help to maintain visual interest in the lower portion of the image.

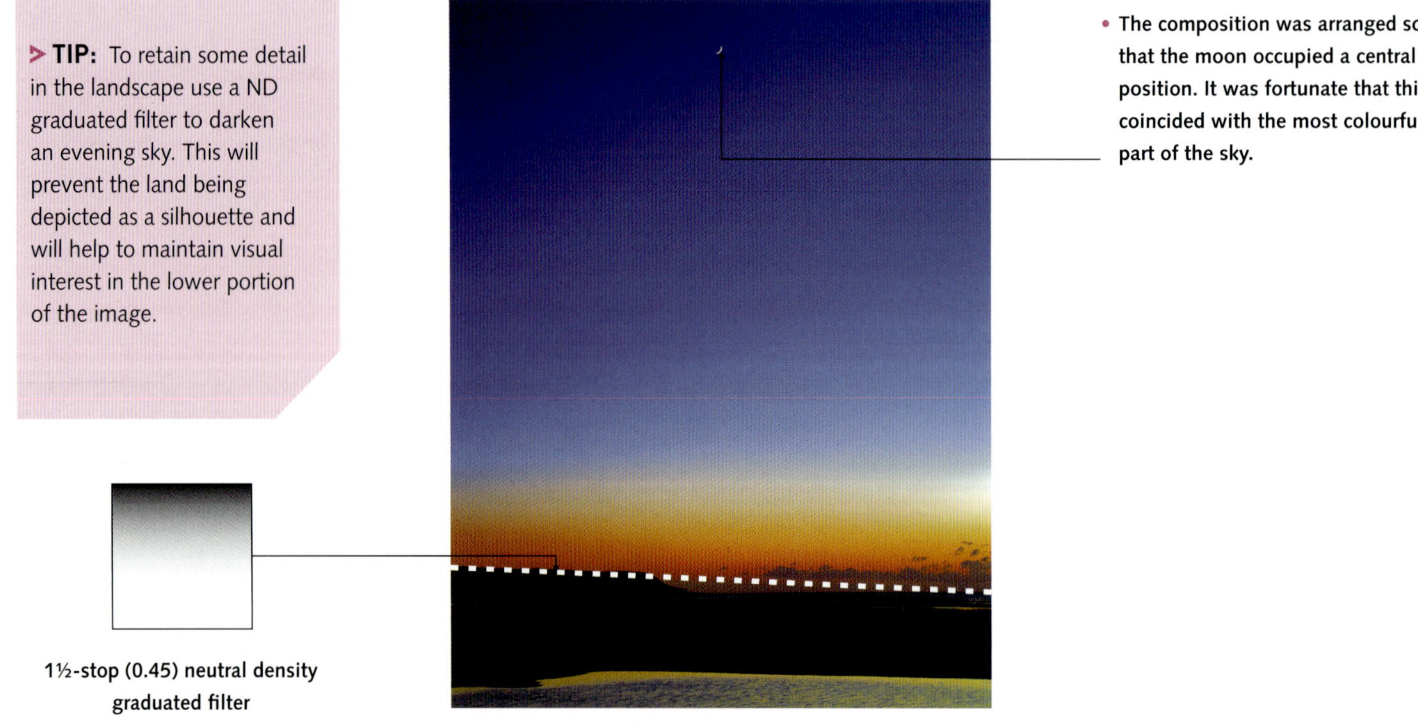

• The composition was arranged so that the moon occupied a central position. It was fortunate that this coincided with the most colourful part of the sky.

1½-stop (0.45) neutral density graduated filter

**Barmouth Bay, Gwynedd, Wales**

**Camera:** Mamiya 645 AFDII with
Mamiya digital back
**Lens:** Mamiya 80mm (standard)
**Filter:** 1.5-stop ND graduated
**Exposure:** 1/5sec at f/18, ISO 100
**Waiting for the light:** 40 minutes
**Post-processing:** Suppression
of highlights and colour balance
adjustment (warming)

There are times when the presence of cloud is essential, not only for the improvement of composition but, more fundamentally, for the creation of the picture itself. This is often the case in a rural landscape, particularly when the terrain is a little flat. In the absence of trees or mountains the sky is likely to have a prominent role to play and this was certainly the case on the perfect summer's day when this image of a Hampshire wheat field was captured. An isolated tree was visible above the horizon but there were no other features to build a composition around, apart from the sky. A layer of cloud spanned the width of the field and while this added another element of interest, in terms of making a photograph it would have been an incomplete picture.

There was too little to provide impact or visual interest and I was about to dismiss the scene when a small cloud began to drift slowly into view. It was lazily floating from right to left and, being fairly low in the sky, would, I hoped, soon be perfectly positioned to make a telling contribution to an image that was by now beginning to materialize in my mind. This was a classic example of a landscape that on its own warranted no further attention, but as soon as you add another element – and in this case the only option was the right type of sky – it would complete the composition and a picture could at that point be captured.

> **TIP:** Don't immediately dismiss a view because of a dearth of features. If you think a scene has potential consider using the sky to create additional interest. The right cloud formation can be as important as the landscape and together they can often make powerful images.

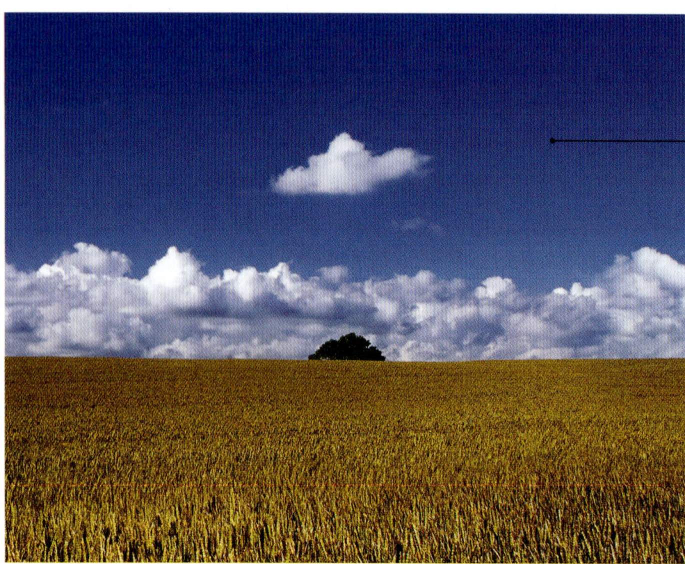

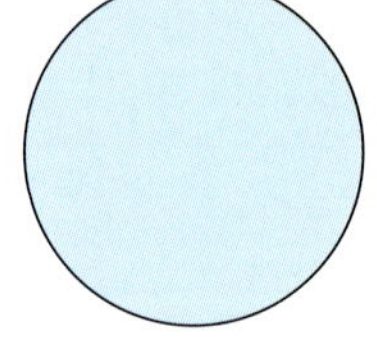

Polarizer (fully polarized)

- The polarizer has enriched the blue sky without affecting the appearance of the clouds.

- The cloud and tree were centrally positioned because there are no other similar features present. An off-centre arrangement would have looked a little unbalanced.

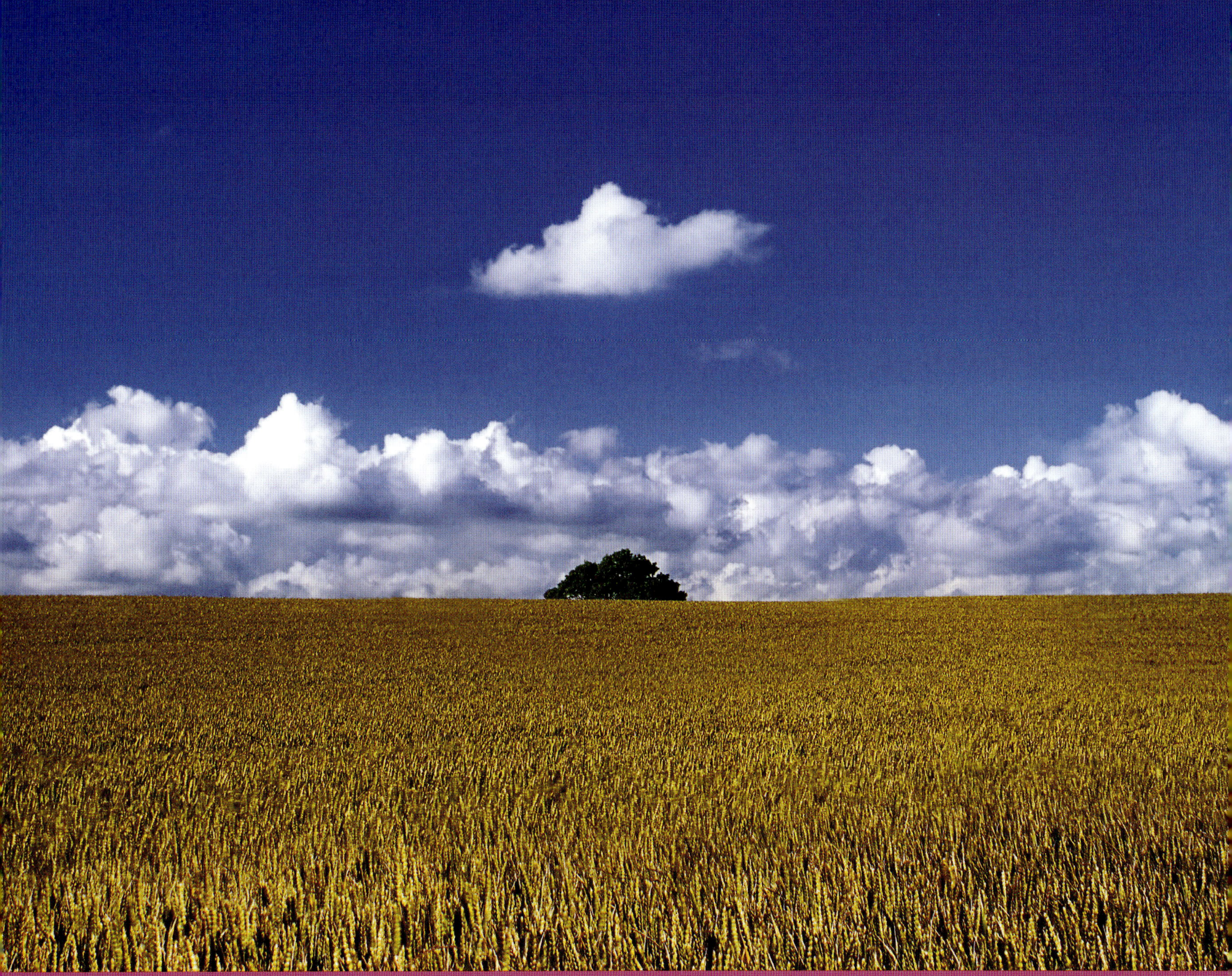

**Near Petersfield, Hampshire, England**

**Camera:** Mamiya 645 AFDII with Mamiya digital back
**Lens:** Mamiya 35mm (wide-angle)
**Filter:** Polarizer (fully polarized)
**Exposure:** 1/5sec at f/22, ISO 100
**Waiting for the light:** 30 minutes
**Post-processing:** Curves adjustment

Having succeeded in taking the image on page 87, I wasn't expecting to return to Red Cliffs, but fate and the weather conspired in a serendipitous way and culminated in the capture of this marvellous view as a memorable autumn evening drew to a close. Any plans for the day had been thrown into disarray by a damaged wheel, which was entirely my own fault (lesson learned: keep looking at the road ahead, not the spectacular landscape beyond the rock-strewn ditch!).

By the time the tyre had been replaced it was too late to visit any of the planned locations and, as the sky was cloudless, I decided to call it a day and head back to my cabin. The route passed through the Red Cliffs wilderness area and as it came into view a small but significant scattering of cloud could be seen hovering above the horizon. A thrill of anticipation ran through me. Was the day that had started so badly going to end, quite unexpectedly, on a momentous high note? Apart from the cloud above the mountain peaks the sky remained

clear so, without the benefit of cloud-assisted highlights and shadows, it was a matter of waiting for the light to soften and become more discriminating in its illumination of the landscape. The low, right-angled sunlight enabled an image to be built around a shaded rocky foreground and a brightly lit wooded area in the middle ground. Beyond that the directional light graphically depicted the rugged contours of the mountains, which prevented them from being lost in the background. As the end of daylight approached, I made four exposures and then watched as lengthening shadows gradually engulfed the sprawling wilderness.

Photographs taken, I packed away my equipment and continued on the short journey home, reflecting on the vagaries of life as a landscape photographer. Days that start disastrously – as this day had – can end on spectacularly, and it is occasions like this that make the capture of landscape images such a satisfying pursuit.

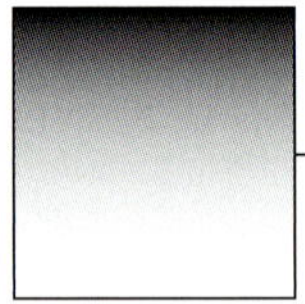

2-stop (0.6) neutral density
graduated filter

• **A 2-stop ND graduated filter
was used to reduce the brightness
of the sky and prevent it from
being overexposed.**

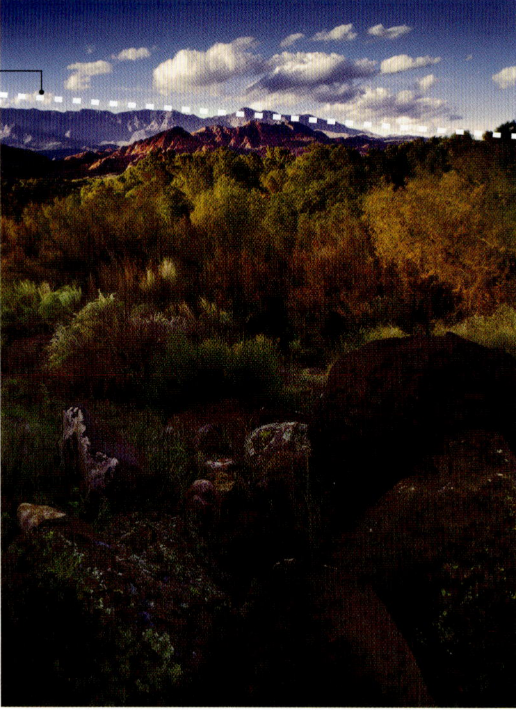

> **TIP:**  Don't give up on a day. Small changes in the light or sky can make a world of difference. Remain vigilant throughout all daylight hours.

> **TIP:**  Use subdued light to prevent a large expanse of foreground from becoming too dominant.

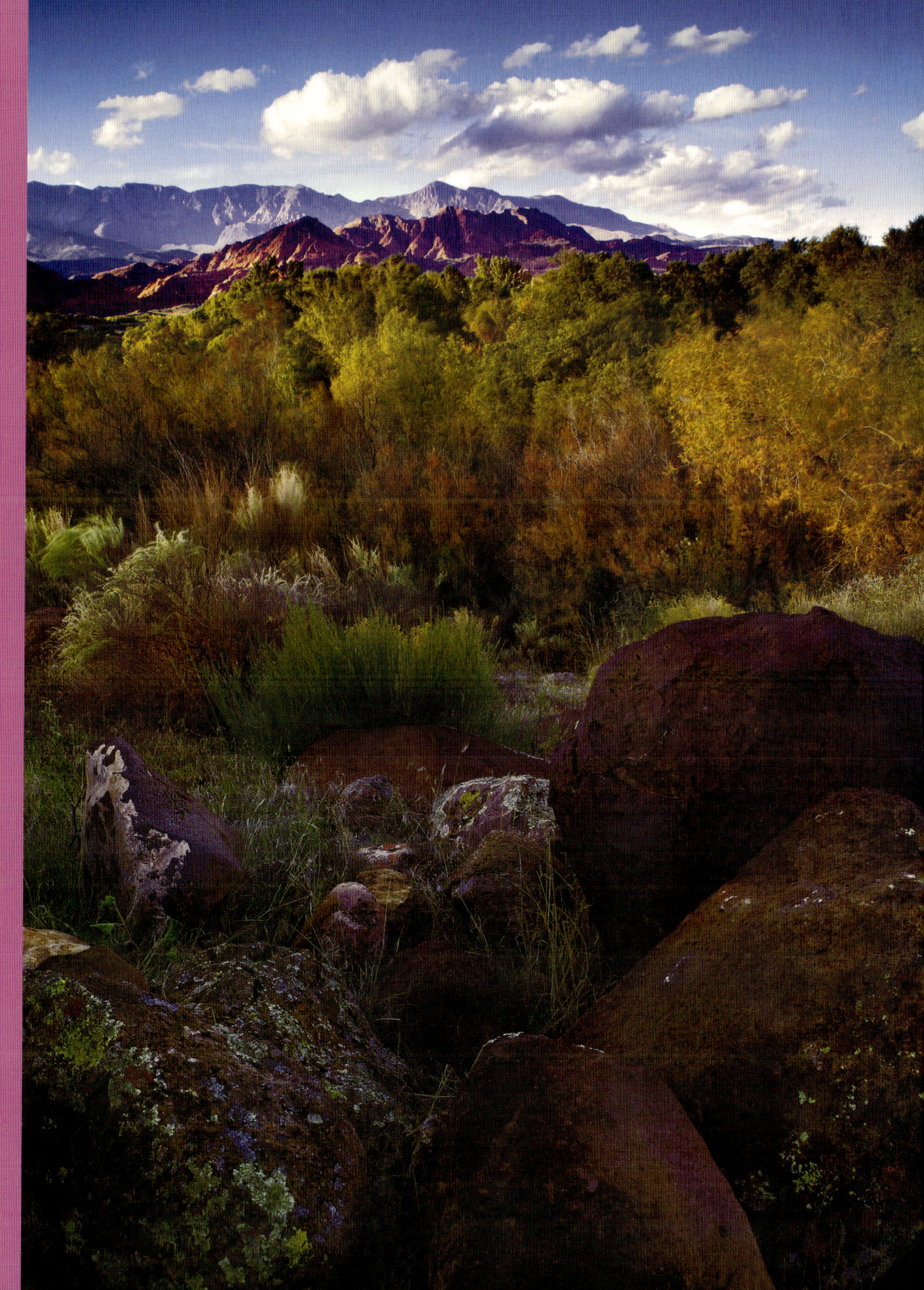

**Red Cliffs Reserve, Utah, USA**

**Camera:** Mamiya 645 AFDII with
Phase One digital back
**Lens:** Mamiya 35mm (wide-angle)
**Filter:** 2-stop ND graduated
**Exposure:** 1/2sec at f/22, ISO 100
**Waiting for the light:** 20 minutes
**Post-processing:** Colour balance
adjustment (warming)

The first time I saw this view the sky was completely clear; the second time the mountain was hidden by dense fog; but third time lucky, and I was able to choose the optimum moment as a canopy of the most perfect cloud formation drifted by. This was a sky to savour, and it was a heart-lifting occasion to be there at that time and be able to capture the glorious spectacle. If anything the sky was too good – no, I'm not complaining! – because it is bordering on being the dominant feature. Had it been a concern at the time there was an easy solution, because it would have been possible to have simply waited for the cloud to break up and lose some of its uniformity. That option didn't cross my mind but with hindsight it would have been useful, for comparison and discussion purposes, to have made a second image with a slightly weaker sky. I did return a few days later to make another picture but it was taken from a different viewpoint and the two photographs cannot be usefully compared.

This type of sky very effectively illustrates the benefit of using a polarizer. These filters come into their own when used to darken a blue sky with a scattering of cloud. They give a sky great impact by increasing colour saturation and boosting the blue/white contrast. The landscape also benefits because tonal values are enriched and the entire photograph therefore becomes more dynamic and vibrant. The filter will increase contrast slightly so it should be used with caution when there are large areas of shadow. In the picture opposite the shaded part of the mountain has been darkened as a result of polarization. On this occasion it has improved the photograph because it helps to delineate the shape and depth of the mountain.

**Polarizer (fully polarized)**

• The polarizer has enriched the blue sky without affecting the cloud. It has also increased contrast slightly, which has helped give the mountain shape.

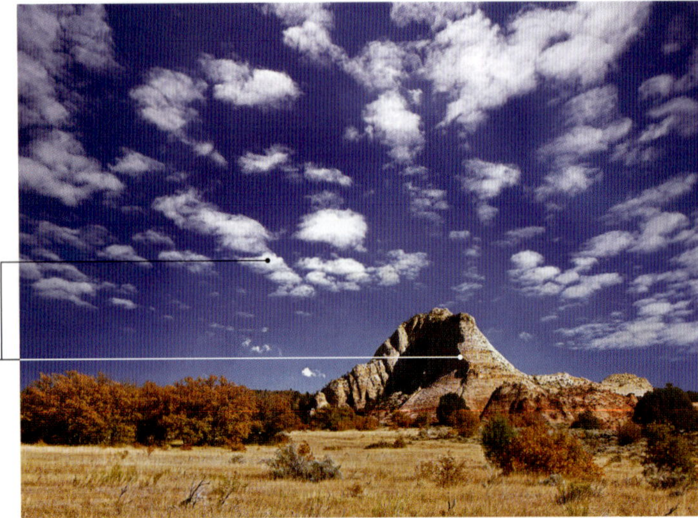

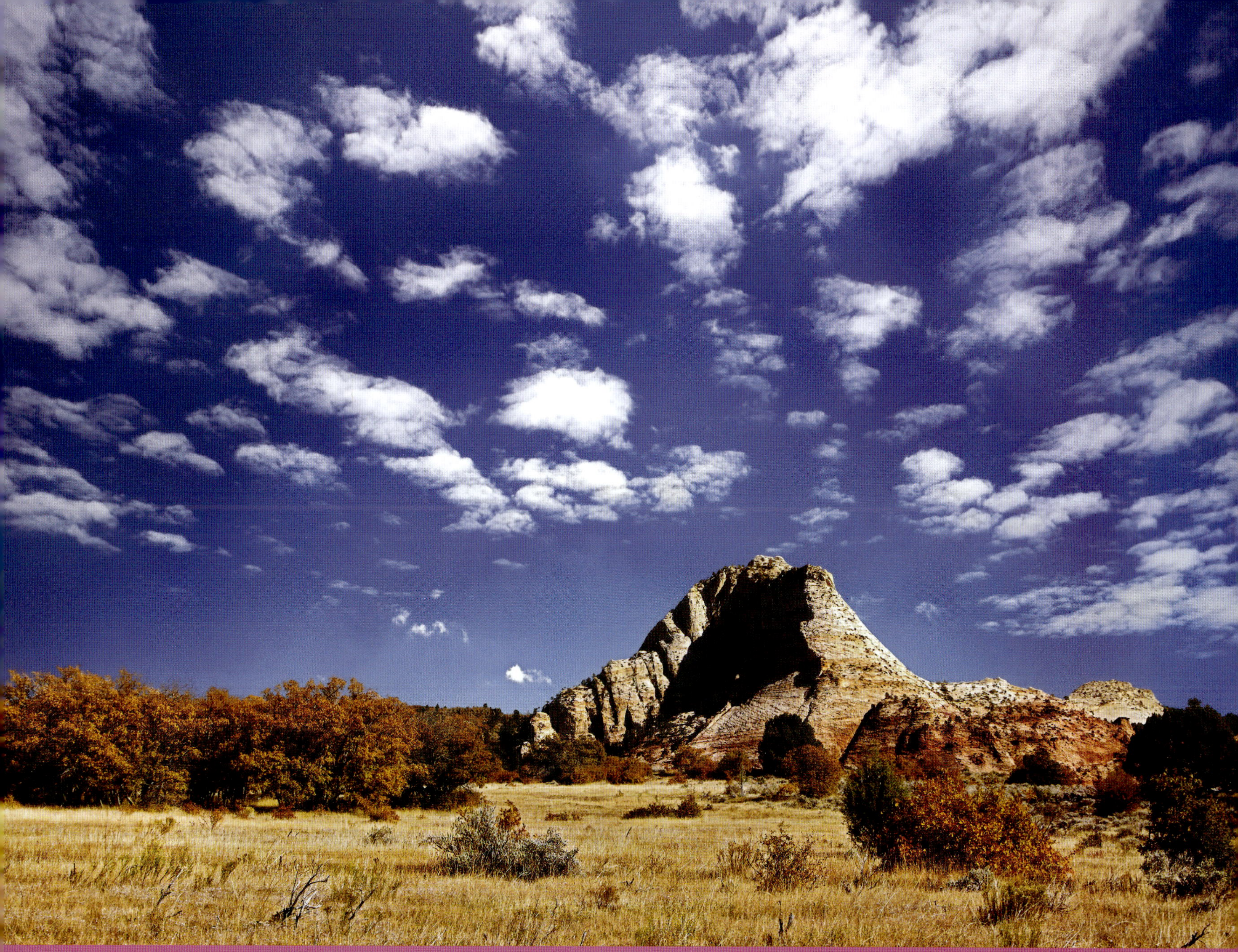

**Near Kolob, Utah, USA**

**Camera:** Mamiya 645 AFDII with Phase One digital back
**Lens:** Mamiya 35mm (wide-angle)
**Filter:** Polarizer (fully polarized)
**Exposure:** 1/8sec at f/16, ISO 100
**Waiting for the light:** 3 days
**Post-processing:** Reduction of highlights

There is something compelling about a sunset. As the day draws to a close and the sun gradually sinks towards the horizon, the sky, if conditions are right, will become the main attraction as it begins to glow with captivating promise. As daylight fades, warm colours will as if by magic start to develop with an ever-increasing intensity. They are an entrancing, irresistible sight and it's no surprise that they are a perennially popular subject throughout the world. I think part of the attraction is their unpredictability – you never know until the last few seconds what the sky will look like – and, of course, every sunset is unique. You can return to the same place time and time again and you will never replicate an earlier image.

The most important factor in a sunset is the cloud formation. Often a layer of cloud will lie stubbornly along the horizon, but this is undesirable because the strongest colours appear when this part of the sky is clear. A cloud-free horizon will enable rays from the setting sun to illuminate the sky above, and it is in these conditions that a fine sunset is most likely to develop. Often the spectacle can take several minutes to peak, so wait until you are absolutely certain that you have captured the optimum moment. Don't rush off too soon. I have seen many skies reach their climax long after the sun has disappeared from view.

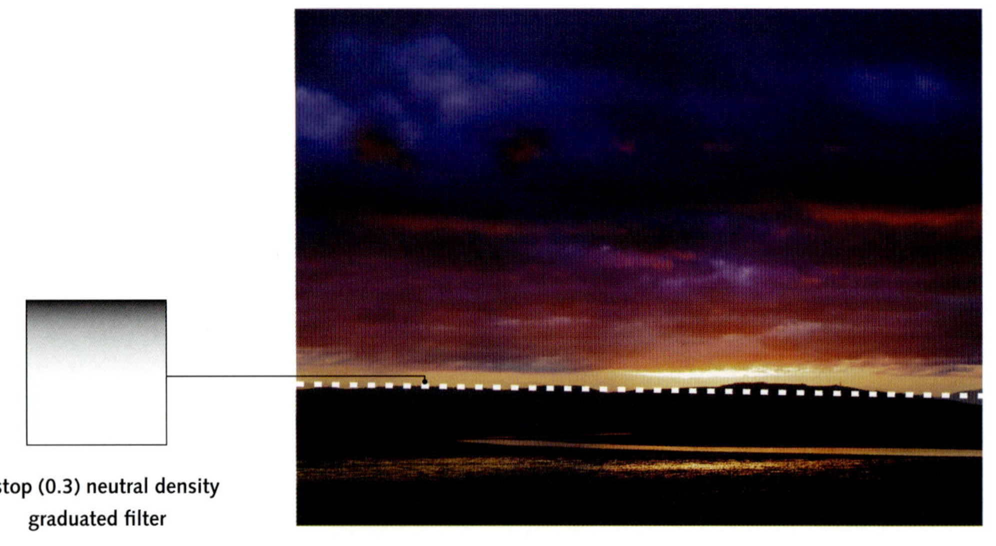

1-stop (0.3) neutral density
graduated filter

> **TIP:** The most spectacular sunsets appear when the area of sky immediately above the horizon is clear. This will enable the setting sun's rays to reach the higher clouds and warm colours will then begin to develop.

• A 1-stop ND graduated filter was used to reduce the exposure value of the sky to that of the water. This has enabled both sky and water to be captured without loss of detail.

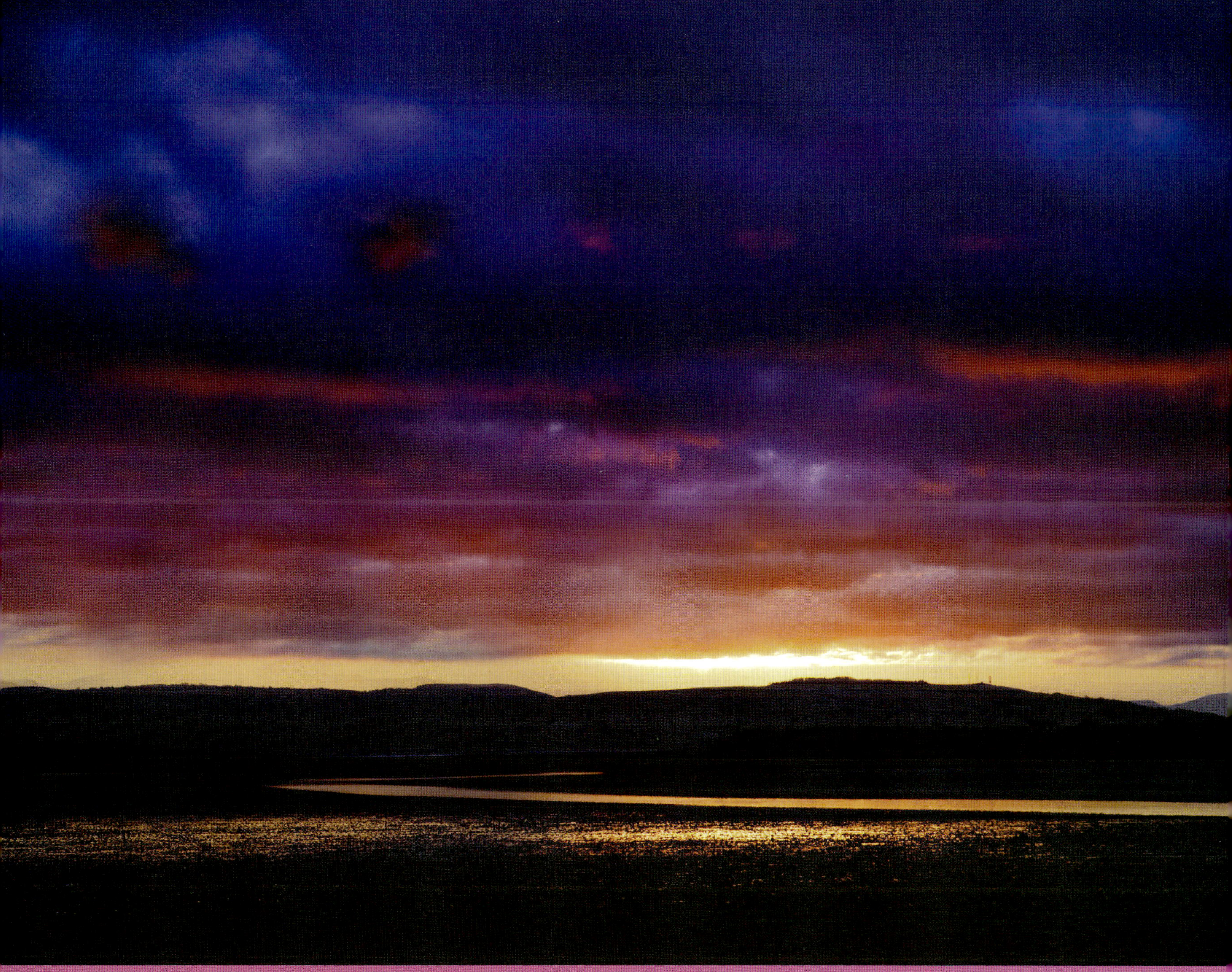

**The Dee Estuary, Clwyd, Wales**

**Camera:** Mamiya 645 AFDII with Mamiya digital back
**Lens:** Mamiya 80mm (standard)
**Filter:** 1-stop ND graduated
**Exposure:** 1/10sec at f/18, ISO 100
**Waiting for the light:** 30 minutes
**Post-processing:** Suppression of highlights and colour balance adjustment (warming)

Living in the north of England, I am accustomed to slow, lingering sunsets (when the sun deigns to appear!), which are then followed by a usable period of twilight of thirty minutes or more. Nearer the equator, while sunsets are more frequent, they are of a shorter duration and you have to be alert to what is happening if you want to capture the spectacle at the peak moment.

The equator is still over 2,000 miles (3,200km) away from the southern part of the United States, but Britain is twice that distance and it makes a noticeable difference at the end of the day as daylight fades with unexpected rapidity. This became evident during a visit to Arizona, when I was almost caught out by the rapidly changing sky as the sun disappeared with undue haste behind the Paria Mountains. Having spotted the opportunity, it was technology that enabled the image to

be taken. With no time to set up a tripod I used my smaller camera, which was fitted with an optically stabilized lens. The ISO speed of the sensor was increased to 200, an ND graduated filter attached and, with the sky beginning to lose its radiance, I used the roof of my car and an improvised bean bag for support, then quickly made three bracketed exposures. The moment quickly passed and it brought to mind previous occasions when a picture had been missed by seconds as a result of being restricted to shooting on sheet film with a large-format camera. I still use the camera and am very attached to it, but there is nothing worse than seeing a photograph slip tantalizingly away to be lost forever. There are times – and this fleeting display of celestial splendour was certainly one of them – when the benefits of digital imaging are there to be seen in those unexpected, split second photographs you manage to grab.

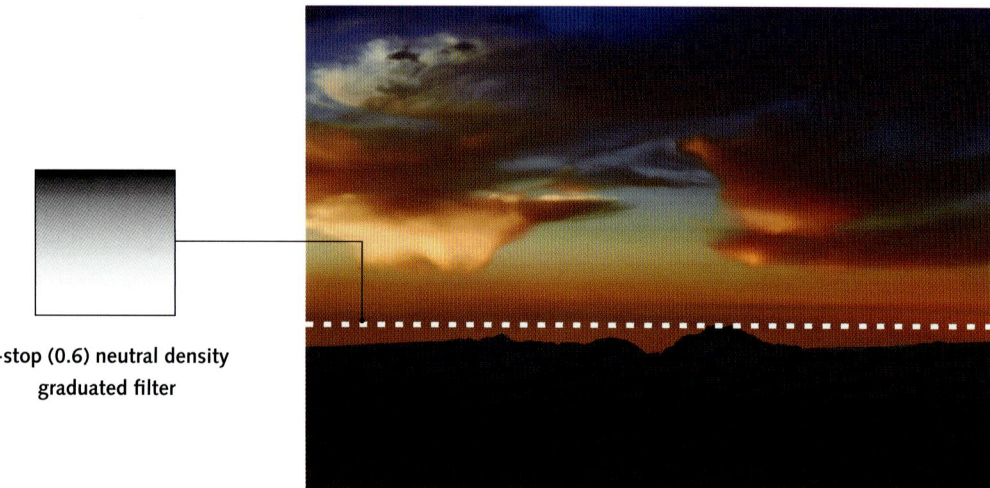

2-stop (0.6) neutral density graduated filter

> **TIP:** To prevent the landscape being recorded as a silhouette, use a 2-stop ND graduated filter. This will in most cases darken the sky sufficiently to enable some detail to be captured across the entire tonal range. Light levels can change so bracket your exposures in 1/2- or 1-stop steps.

> **TIP:** When shooting with film it can be beneficial to use a warming filter when capturing sunsets and sunrises. For digital imaging I prefer to use no filtration and adjust the colour balance in post-processing.

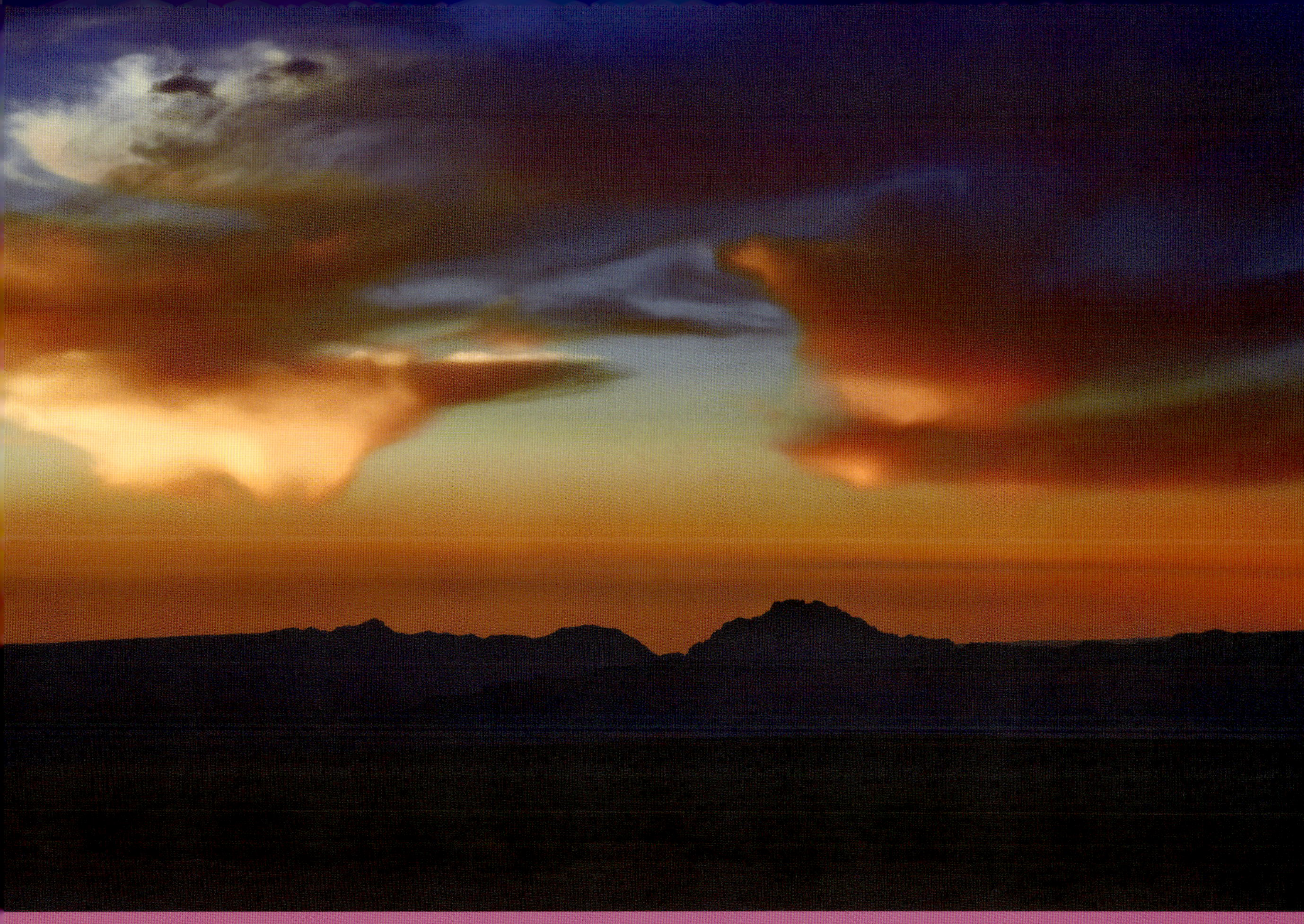

**Paria Mountains, Arizona, USA**

**Camera:** Canon EOS 7D
**Lens:** Canon 24–105mm L IS
**Filter:** 2-stop ND graduated
**Exposure:** 1/50sec at f/8, ISO 200
**Waiting for the light:** Immediate
**Post-processing:** Colour balance adjustment (warming)

Had there been no moon, this twilit scene would not have been captured. There is no sun and no attractive cloud, so without the moon you are left with a rather bland sky. I wanted to maximize its presence and therefore used a telephoto lens, which has a magnifying effect on distant objects. It has also increased the apparent size of the large rock, which is an important feature; but there was a price to be paid for this because the lens has also enlarged the island behind the rock. Its presence is, unfortunately, a distraction. In theory it should add depth and improve the composition, but in practice it merely draws attention away from more attractive parts of the image. It also has, because of its one-sided position, an unbalancing effect. Had it spanned the width of the photograph it would have been much easier on the eye, but as it is it's a little unsettling. Regrettably it wasn't possible to change the viewpoint so the arrangement had to stay. Fortunately the moon does at least redress the balance to a small degree.

The other consequence of using a long focal length is the loss of foreground. This is a dilemma that occurs from time to time; do you use a telephoto lens to emphasize distant features or a wide-angle to place the emphasis on the foreground? There is no rule or guideline; it is a decision that can only be made after a careful assessment of the respective qualities of each part of the view. A zoom lens will enable you to take both options and it can then be a useful part of the learning curve to compare the results and assess the merits of each of the different compositions.

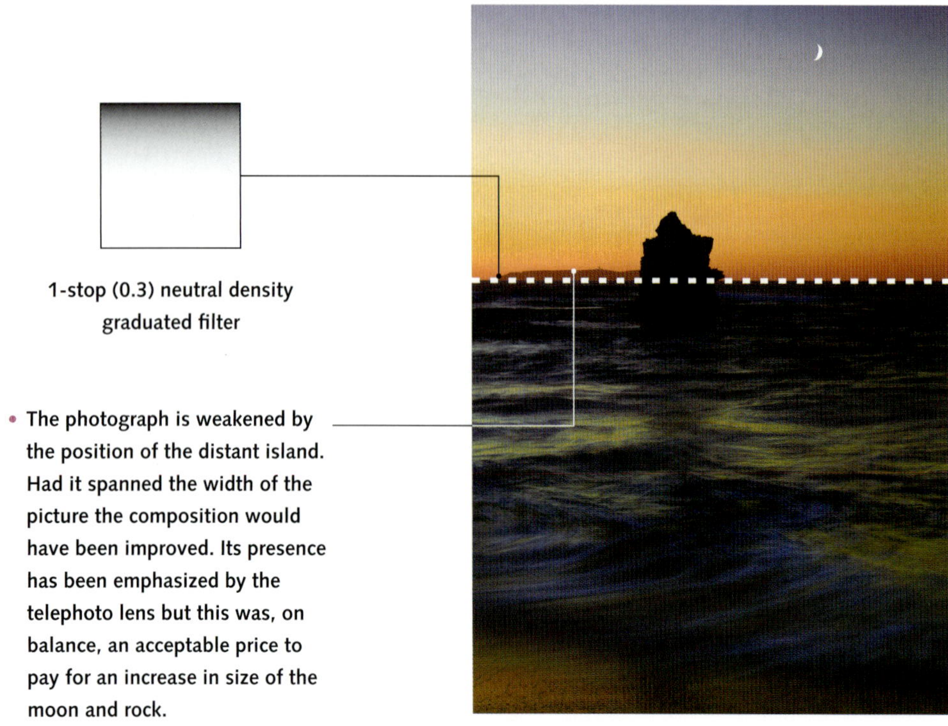

1-stop (0.3) neutral density
graduated filter

• The photograph is weakened by
the position of the distant island.
Had it spanned the width of the
picture the composition would
have been improved. Its presence
has been emphasized by the
telephoto lens but this was, on
balance, an acceptable price to
pay for an increase in size of the
moon and rock.

**>** **TIP:** When photographing a combination of sky and water, use a 1-stop ND graduated filter to balance the exposure values of both these elements.

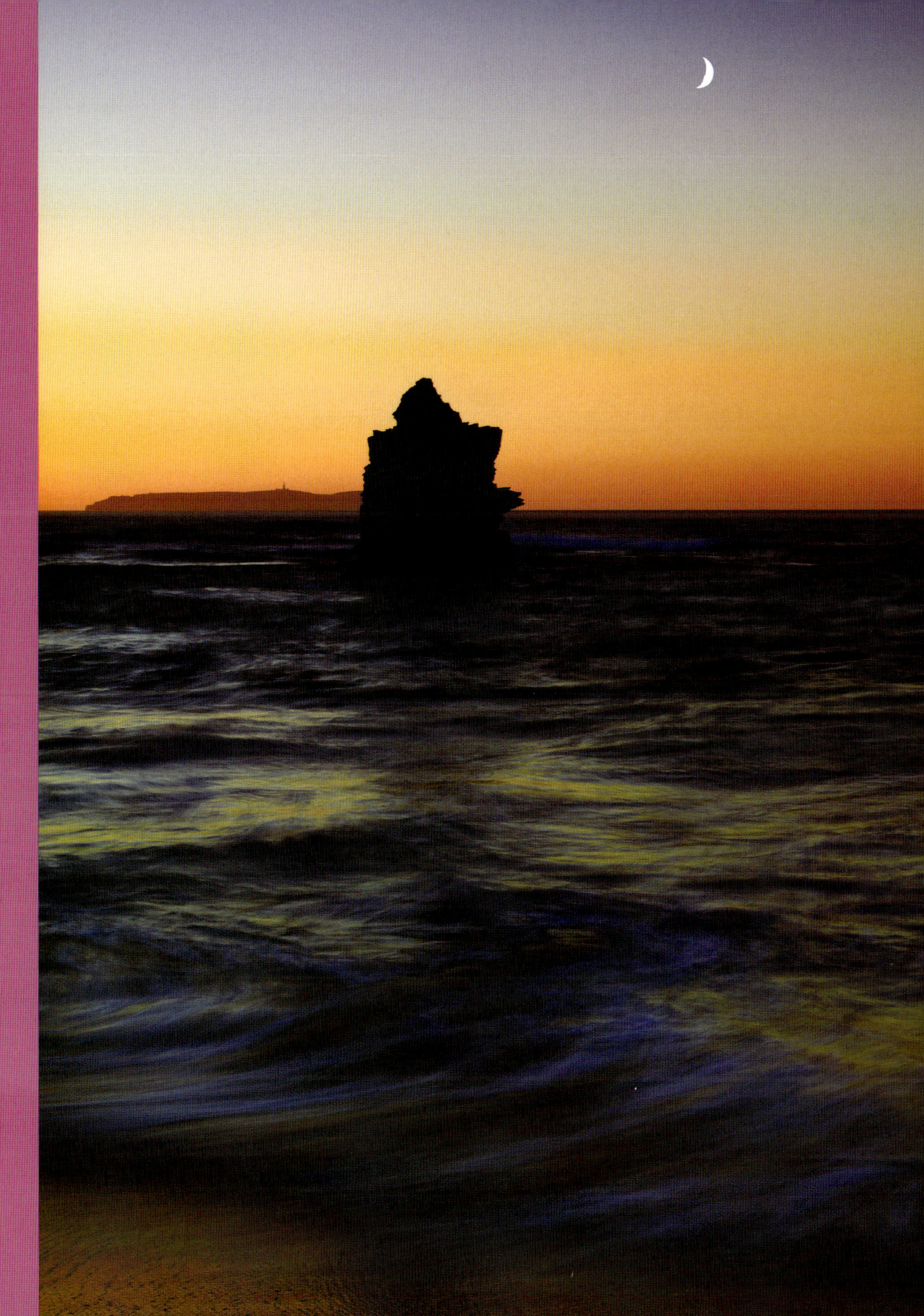

**Peniche, Portugal**

**Camera:** Mamiya 645 AFDII with Mamiya digital back
**Lens:** Mamiya 150mm (telephoto)
**Filter:** 1-stop ND graduated
**Exposure:** 1sec at f/16, ISO 100
**Waiting for the light:** 50 minutes
**Post-processing:** Colour balance adjustment (warming)

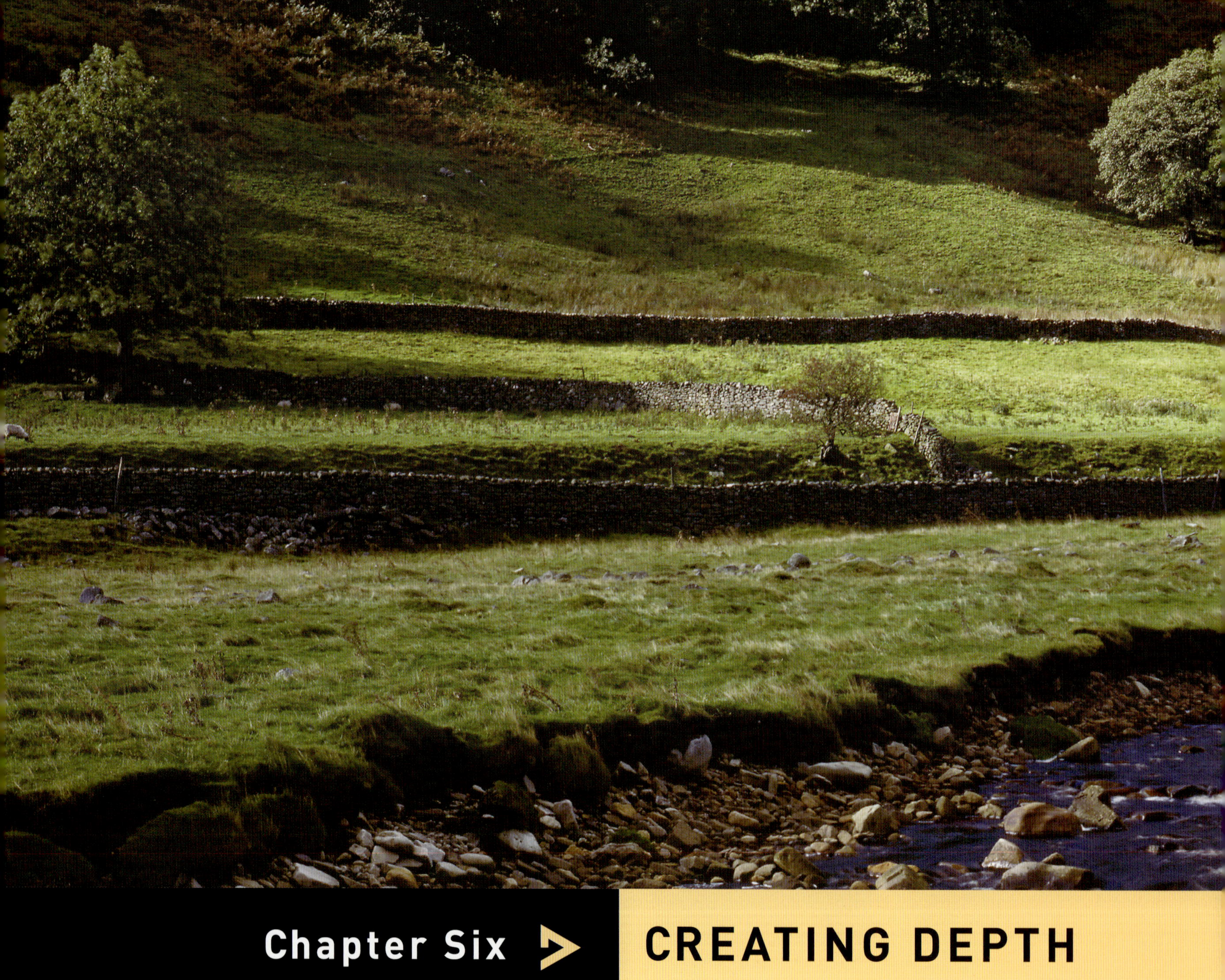

Chapter Six > CREATING DEPTH

The River Swale, The Yorkshire Dales, England

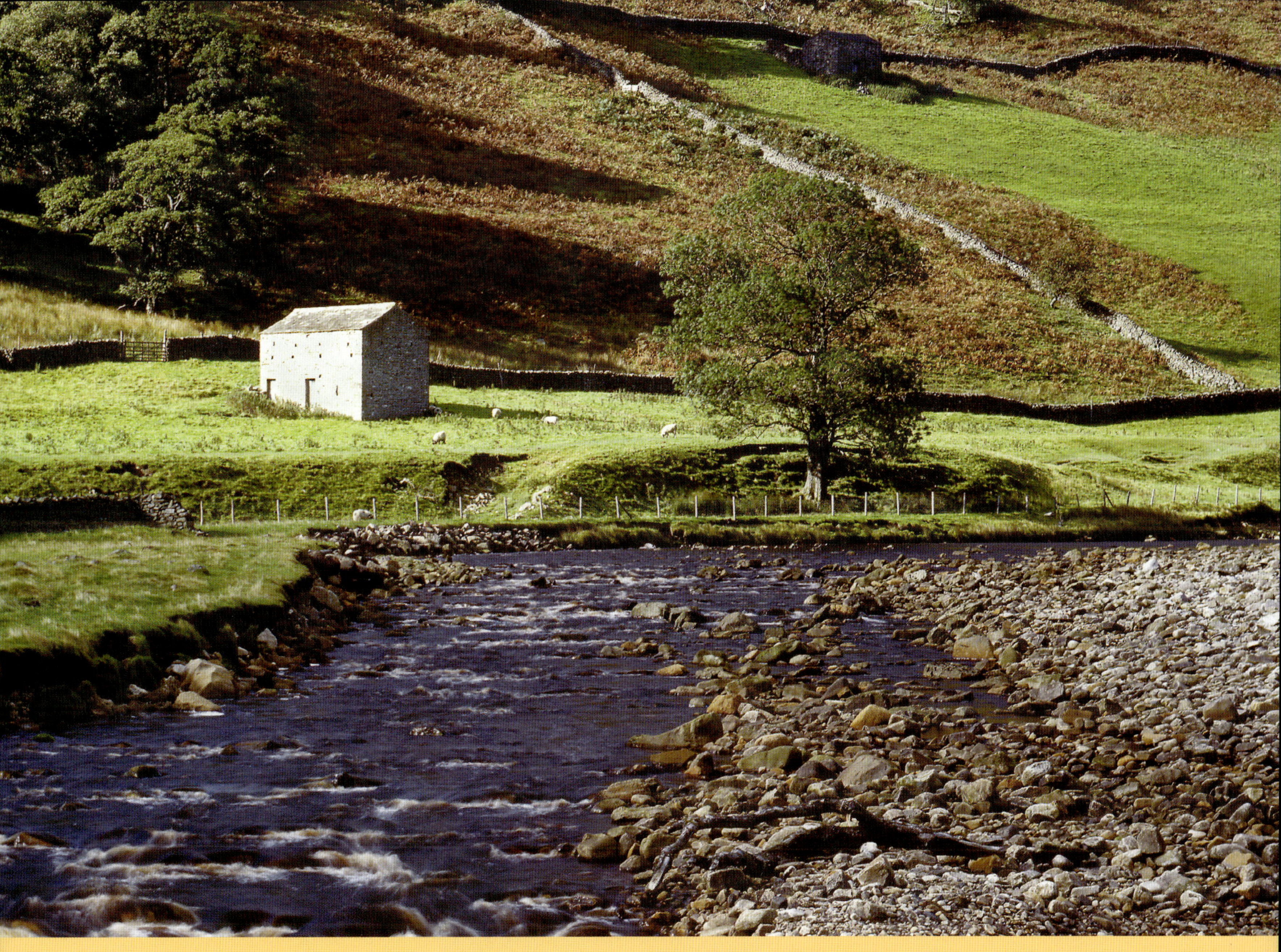

Photography is currently a two-dimensional medium. Although technology is making progress in 3D-imaging, until paper is replaced by holographic or some similar material, the challenge of successfully depicting three-dimensional subjects in just two dimensions remains firmly with the photographer. Depth must be created in a photograph, and this can be a formidable task. With the correct approach, however, striking images can be produced that transcend the restrictions of the flat medium upon which they are displayed. The purpose of this chapter is to explain and demonstrate the correct techniques to employ.

Depth in an image is an illusion. It doesn't exist in the photographic medium and for a landscape view to look convincing an impression of depth must be created and then reproduced onto a flat, two-dimensional surface. This is quite a tall order when you consider that a sweeping view is likely to cover a distance of several miles. So, how do we introduce a sense of depth into a picture?

The most successful technique is to use a wide-angle lens and position the camera close to foreground objects (this is discussed in more detail on the following pages). Using a portrait format will also help to create depth because an upright arrangement encourages the eye to scan an image vertically, travelling from foreground to horizon. To assist in this journey your composition should include visual 'stepping stones' of objects of diminishing size that continue all the way into the distance. This will give something for the eye to latch on to as it travels to the horizon. It is this visual journey, together with the decreasing size of the various elements in a photograph, which creates the illusion of depth. Blind spots, i.e. where the middle ground is obscured by foreground objects, should be avoided because they will interfere with the momentum of the journey and will weaken the composition. To maintain the viewer's attention every part of an image must be accessible and free of obstacles.

Once you have chosen your viewpoint step back and look at it critically. If everything flows from front to back with visual interest across both the length and width of the photograph, then distance is likely to be depicted and you should be able to proceed with confidence. You can then switch your attention to the light and sky and wait for the moment when everything is lit to your satisfaction.

**2-stop (0.6) neutral density graduated filter**

• A 2-stop ND graduated filter was placed at an angle across the sky to reduce its brightness. This enabled both sky and landscape to be correctly exposed.

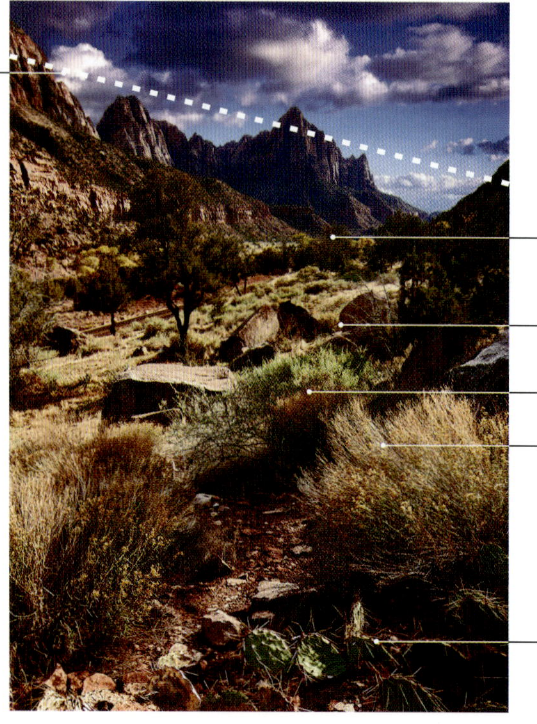

• Objects of diminishing size, from foreground to background, have been used to create an impression of depth.

> **TIP:** Move in close to the foreground and use a low camera position. Filling the lower portion of an image with foreground elements will, on its own, help to convey depth.

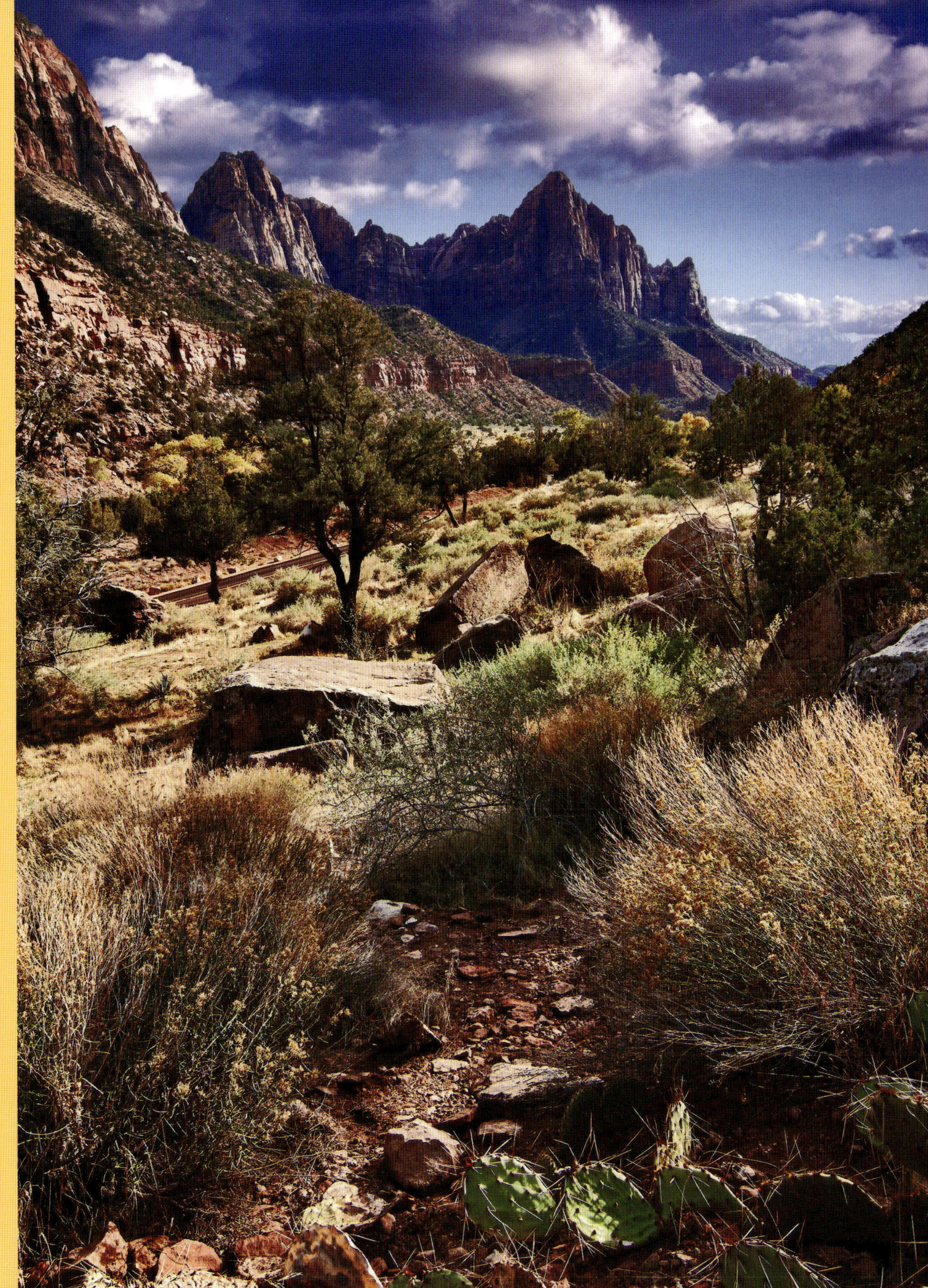

**Zion National Park,
Utah, USA**

**Camera:** Canon EOS 7D
**Lens:** Canon 24–105mm L IS
**Filter:** 2-stop ND graduated
**Exposure:** 1/25sec at f/13,
ISO 100
**Waiting for the light:** 4 hours
**Post-processing:** Suppression
of highlights, colour balance
adjustment

To me, composition is instinctive. Often I choose a camera position with little or no hesitation simply because it feels right. There is no doubt or uncertainty; it is simply a matter of setting up equipment and waiting for the light. This is because of experience gained from many years of photographing a wide variety of landscapes in every type of weather. I don't profess to have been born with a natural talent (and I freely admit that I sometimes still get it wrong!). It is simply the result of trial and error, learning from failure and spending a long time progressing through an often steep and challenging learning curve. All photographers learn in this way because there is no alternative to gaining first-hand experience out in the field. Although there is no fast-track route to success, there are a few techniques you can adopt to speed up the learning process and improve the quality of the images you capture.

One simple step is to place emphasis on foreground features and use them to fill as much as half (or sometimes more) of the picture. This type of composition can transform a photograph and is an easily mastered technique. Decide first on a basic viewpoint and then look for an attractive piece of foreground – don't rush this because the success of the picture will, to a large extent, be determined by its quality. Then set up your camera in a low position close to the nearest foreground object. A common mistake is to place the camera too high. To fill the lower half of the frame a height of no more than 3ft (0.9m) usually gives the best results; anything above this is likely to weaken both the composition and the impression of depth. Because of the close distances involved you will require maximum depth of field and it will therefore be necessary to use a small aperture and focus on the hyperfocal distance. This is discussed in more detail on page 128.

This technique does not suit all subjects and viewpoints, but if you remain aware of the potential benefits of employing a large expanse of foreground then this can only help to improve the overall standard of your photography.



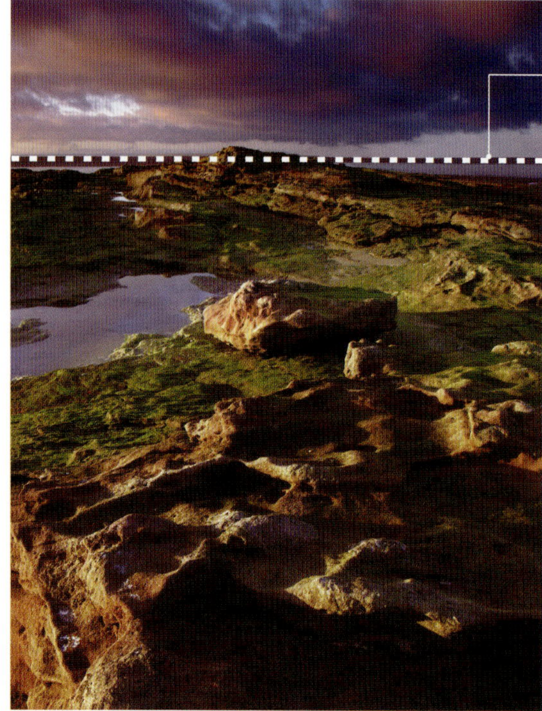

2-stop (0.6) neutral density graduated filter

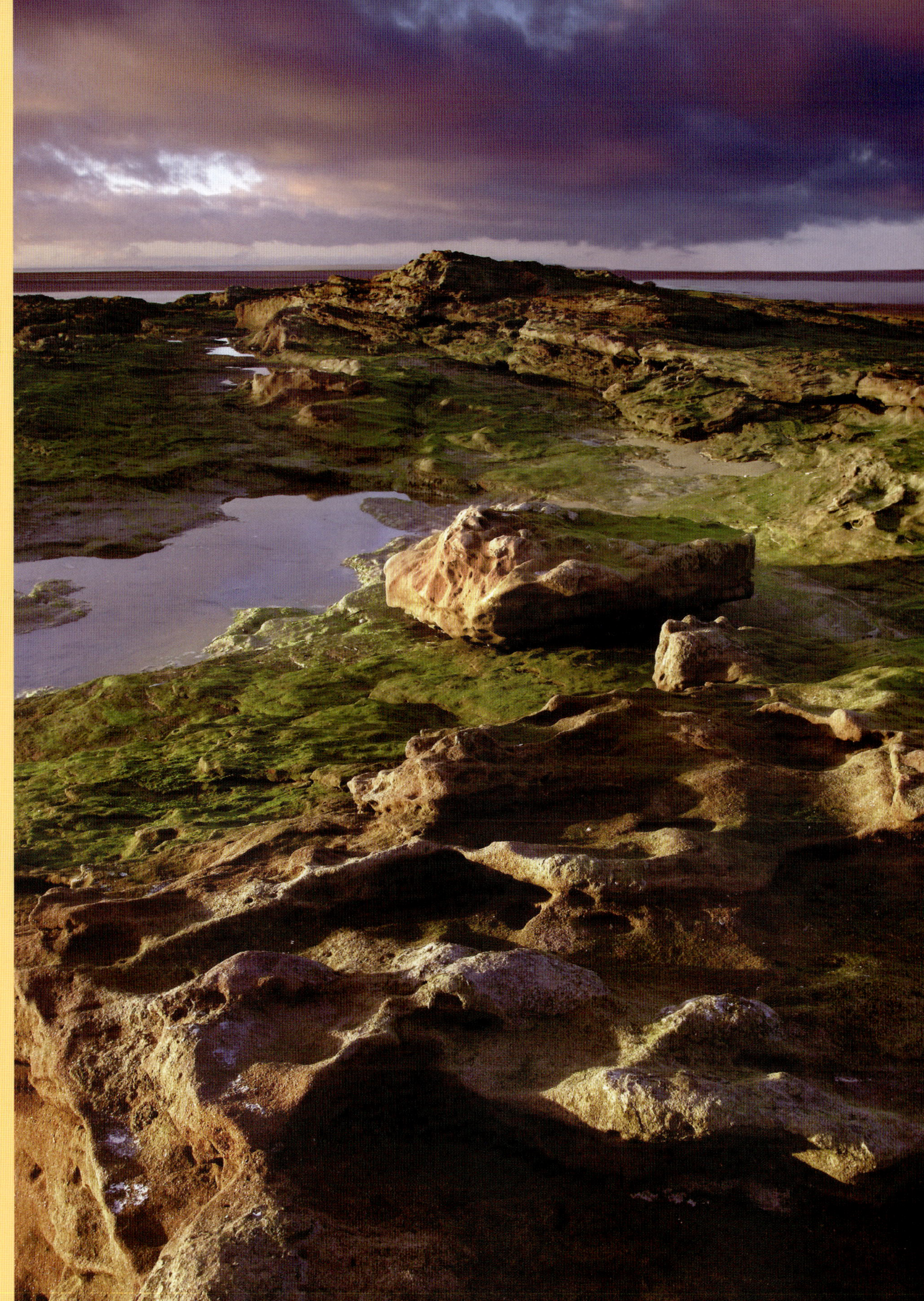

**Hoylake Beach,
The Wirral Peninsula, England**

**Camera:** Mamiya 645 AFDII with
Mamiya digital back
**Lens:** Mamiya 35mm (wide-angle)
**Filter:** 2-stop ND graduated
**Exposure:** 1/2sec at f/22, ISO 100
**Waiting for the light:** 40 minutes
**Post-processing:** Curves and colour
balance adjustment (warming)

Composition, while not in itself technical in nature, requires the application of an underlying sound technique if a photograph is to be flawlessly executed. One essential requirement is accurate focusing, particularly when an image is built around extensive foreground. To ensure that everything is pin sharp, maximum depth of field will be required, and this can only be achieved by using a small aperture and manually focusing on what is known as the hyperfocal distance.

What, you might ask, is hyperfocal distance and how is it calculated? It is simply the closest focusing point beyond which all objects will appear to be acceptably sharp. The position of the focusing point is determined by a combination of the aperture used and the focal length of the lens. Charts are available that show the hyperfocal distances for a wide range of apertures and focal lengths. They are a useful aid but it shouldn't be necessary to refer to them every time you focus your lens, because with just a little practice it is usually possible to estimate the hyperfocal point with reasonable accuracy.

The hyperfocal distance is surprisingly close to the camera. For example, a lens of 28mm focal length fitted to a full-frame 35mm digital SLR with an aperture of f/22 (or its equivalent, a 17mm lens on an APS-C camera with an aperture of f/13*) will give a hyperfocal distance of 3.9ft (1.2m). If the lens is focused on this point then depth of field will extend from half the hyperfocal distance, i.e. 1.95ft (0.6m) all the way to infinity. This, as you can see, is very large so in most cases there is a margin for error when estimating the focus point. I tend to focus slightly beyond this point to ensure that distant objects are sharp because it is not often that sharpness as close as 1.95ft (0.6m) is required. As a guide, focusing somewhere between 4–5ft (1.2–1.5m) should in most situations produce a sharp image from front to back when using a small aperture.

* It is advisable to use apertures no smaller than f/11–f/13 when using a wide-angle or standard lens on an APS-C camera. Diffraction becomes noticeable at smaller apertures and image resolution begins to deteriorate.

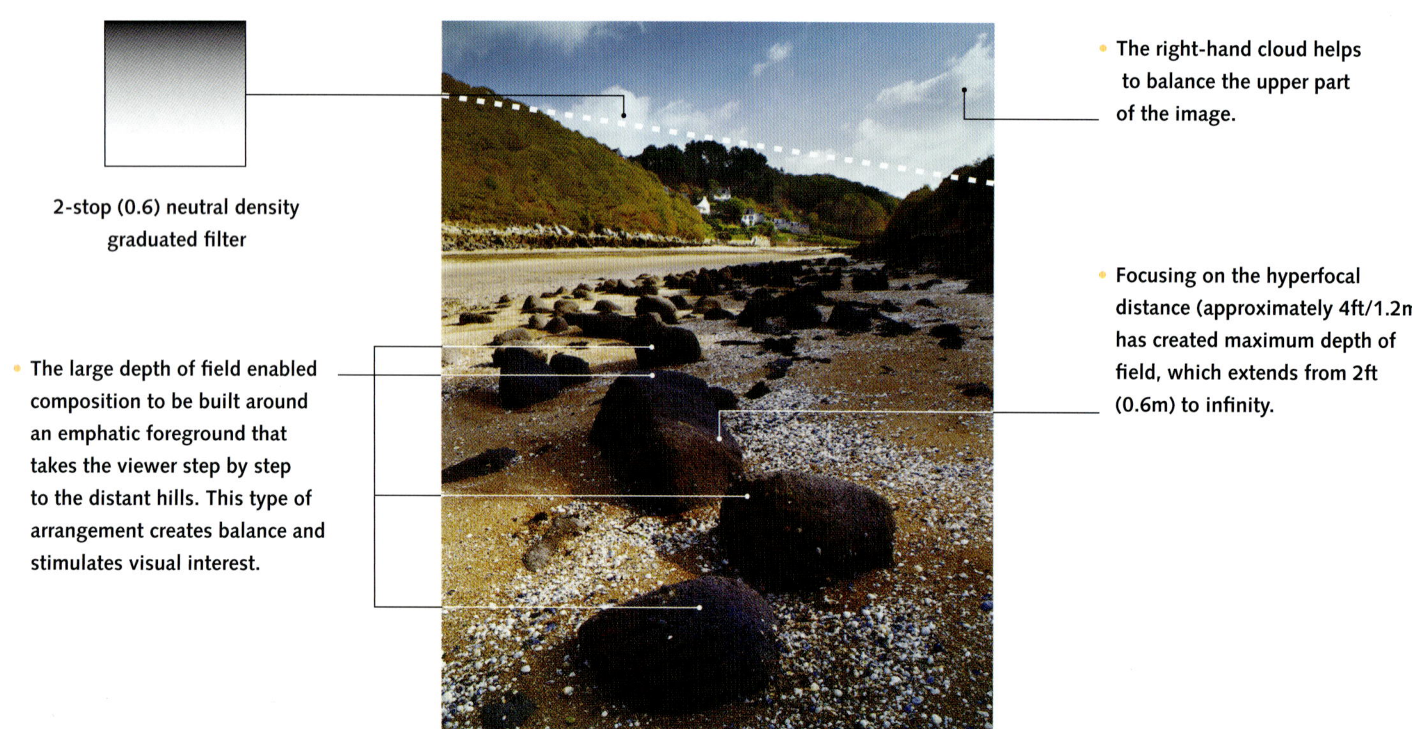

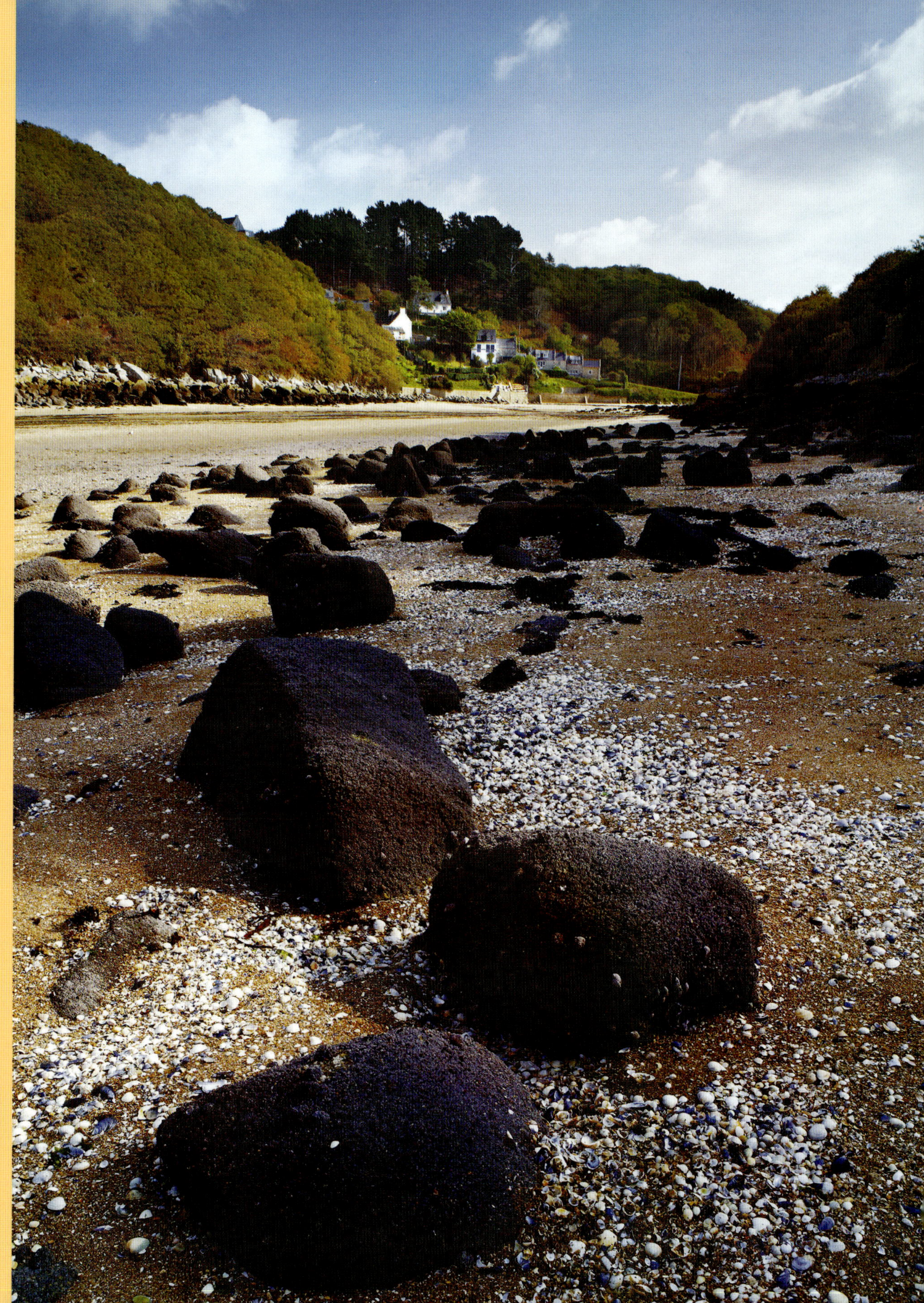

**Le Yaudet, Brittany, France**

**Camera:** Mamiya 645 AFDII with
Mamiya digital back
**Lens:** Mamiya 35mm (wide-angle)
**Filter:** 2-stop ND graduated
**Exposure:** 1/4sec at f/22, ISO 100
**Waiting for the light:** 90 minutes
**Post-processing:** Curves and
colour balance adjustment
(warming)

Loss of depth is inevitable in a photograph. This is hardly surprising as a three-dimensional subject is being depicted in just two dimensions, and the challenge therefore is to minimize the loss and reproduce, as realistically as possible, the scene as it appeared in front of the camera. Using the right composition is an effective means of achieving this.

The inclusion of converging lines that stretch towards the horizon is a powerful aid to enhancing depth, particularly when objects of a diminishing size are also present. To maximize the effect, your camera should be positioned as close as possible to the foreground. A low viewpoint is, as explained earlier in this chapter, preferable because it will help the eye to travel across the landscape and will engage the viewer. This type of composition can be particularly effective when photographing streams and rivers, where the aspect of view looks along the course of the flowing water. To achieve this type of view it will probably be necessary to place your tripod in or close to the middle of the stream, which can sometimes be precarious (if not impossible). Unfortunately, one of the unwritten rules of landscape photography is that the best vantage points are usually the most inaccessible! You might therefore have to compromise or, as I did in the picture opposite, find a shallow stretch of water that doesn't require you to risk life and limb in the making of the image.

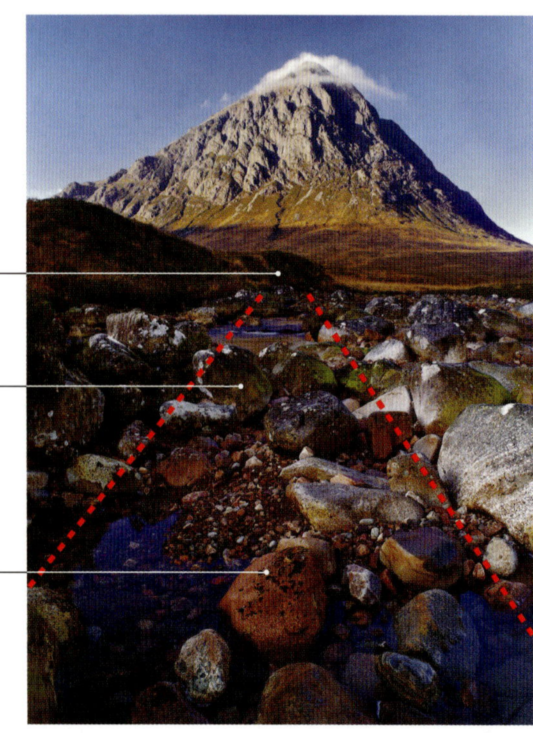

**The viewpoint along the length of the river enables receding stones to be used as a visual pathway towards the distant mountain. This type of arrangement will therefore create the impression of the third dimension. The central position also shows the river narrowing and converging as it travels away from the camera, which also improves the depth in the image.**

> **TIP:** An adaptable and sturdy tripod is essential when taking photographs in water, as is a good-quality tripod head. The ball-and-socket type is very useful, particularly when movement of the tripod legs is compromised by uneven ground.

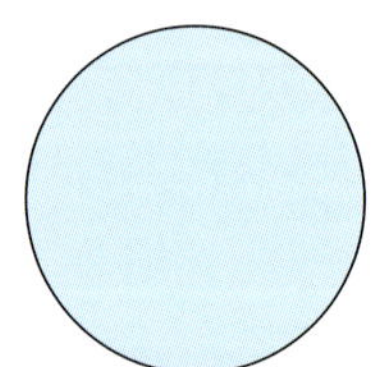

**Polarizer (fully polarized)**

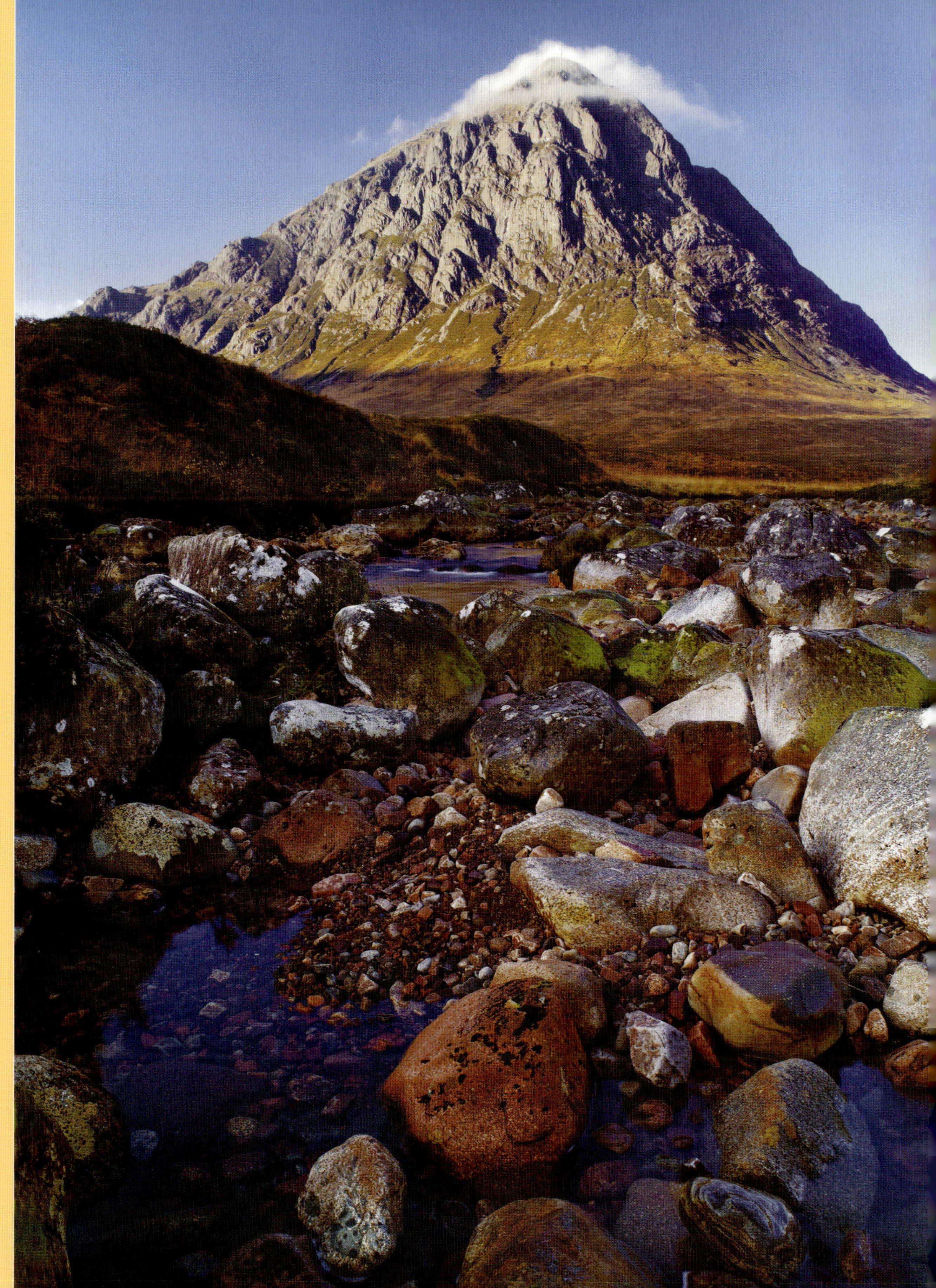

**Buachaillie Etive Mor,
The Highlands, Scotland**

**Camera:** Mamiya 645 AFDII with
Mamiya digital back
**Lens:** Mamiya 35mm (wide-angle)
**Filter:** Polarizer (fully polarized)
**Exposure:** 1/2sec at f/22, ISO 100
**Waiting for the light:** 60 minutes
**Post-processing:** Curves and colour
balance adjustment (warming)

## > CONVERGING LINES  THE LINE OF BEAUTY

*The Analysis of Beauty* is a book written by the eighteenth-century painter William Hogarth, in which he explains his theories of visual beauty. A prominent feature of his theory is the S-shaped curve, which he described as the Line of Beauty. He believed that such lines suggest movement and liveliness and arouse the attention of the viewer. He also believed that they are the basis of all great art and it is perhaps for this reason that curves are present in many of his paintings (often on an almost subliminal level).

The presence of an S-curve is particularly useful in landscape images, because in addition to their aesthetic qualities their converging lines are a very effective means of creating depth. The nature of a curve is in itself magnetic and if it travels away from the camera and tapers off into the distance, it becomes a powerful tool and will carry the viewer along its meandering course. The visual effect can be so strong that curves can easily become the dominant feature, so they have to be used with care. To create a balanced image with visual interest in all areas, other attractive, eye-catching elements should therefore be present.

In the picture opposite it was, initially, the sky that caught my attention. Heading for a lake, which you can see in the distance, I realized that the road I was driving along, which was a series of sharply twisting bends, could be depicted as a depth-enhancing S-curve. This, together with the rugged terrain it traversed and the dramatic sky, could be a compelling combination. I immediately stopped and after a little searching found a viewpoint that included a glimpse of the lake, and quickly made three exposures. No time was wasted, which was fortunate, because minutes later the sky began to close in and the drama was lost. Sadly, the lake remained unphotographed but a Hogarthian Line of Beauty was without doubt a more than adequate substitute.

**> TIP:** To prevent an S-curve dominating your composition, ensure other eye-catching features are present. Here the dramatic sky and distant mountain and lake help to maintain interest beyond the end of the road.

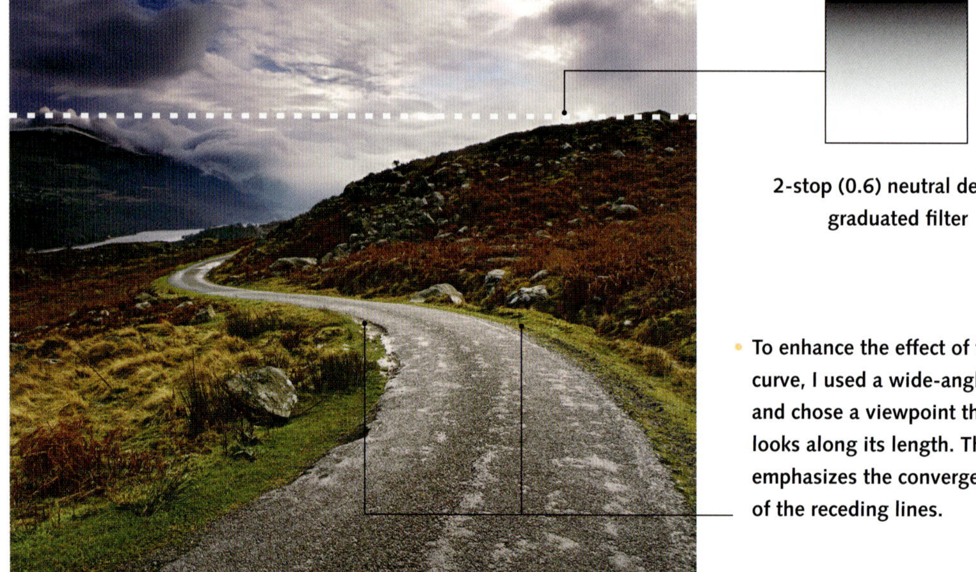

2-stop (0.6) neutral density graduated filter

To enhance the effect of the curve, I used a wide-angle lens and chose a viewpoint that looks along its length. This emphasizes the convergence of the receding lines.

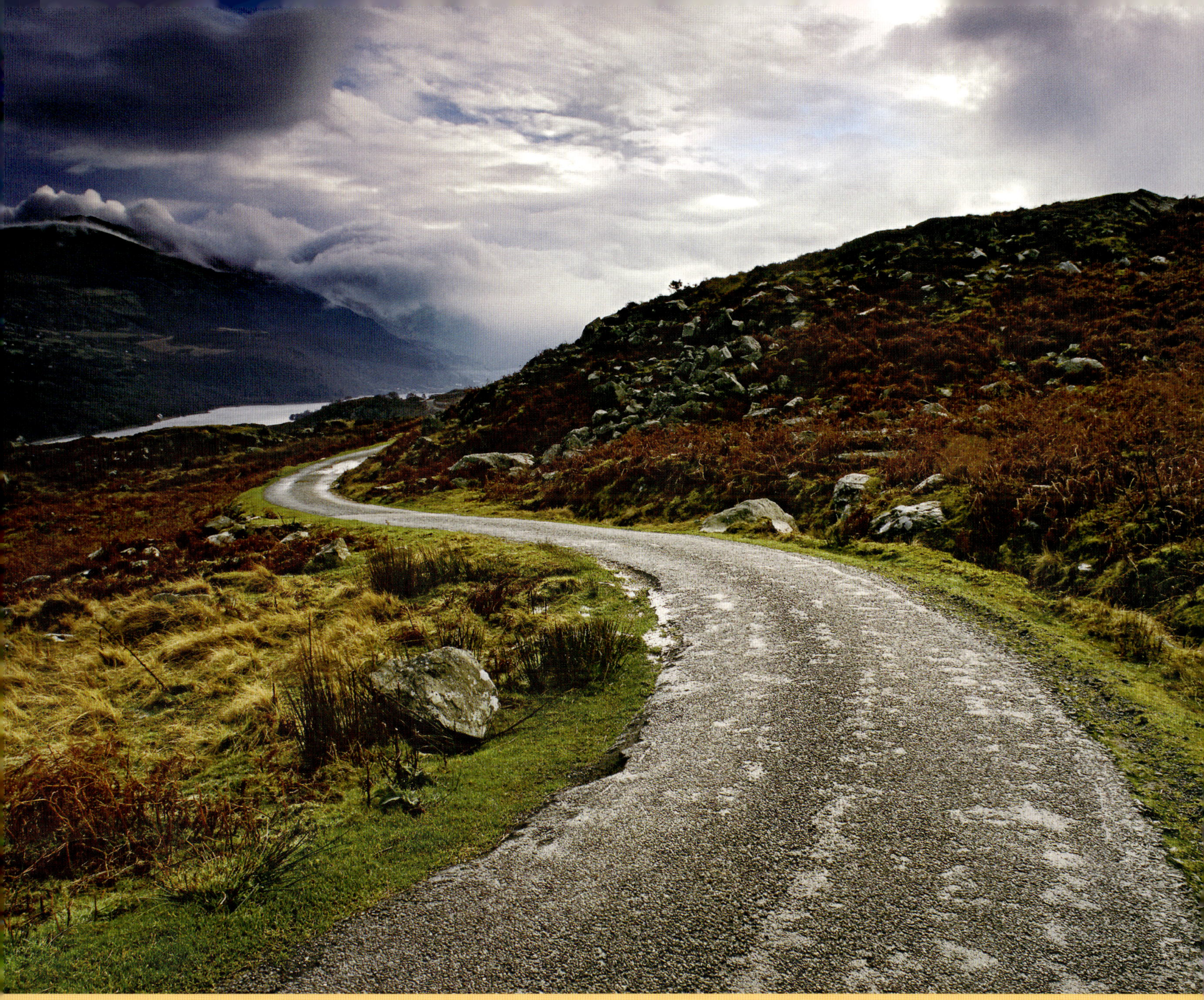

**Near Llanwrst, Snowdonia, Wales**

**Camera:** Mamiya 645 AFDII with Mamiya digital back
**Lens:** Mamiya 35mm (wide-angle)
**Filter:** 2-stop ND graduated
**Exposure:** 1/4sec at f/22, ISO 100
**Waiting for the light:** Immediate
**Post-processing:** Suppression of highlights

Footpaths and narrow lanes are one of the few features in a rural landscape that consist of symmetrically converging lines and they often also have S-bends and curves. They are therefore a perfect foreground, although to make a complete photograph they must of course lead to something interesting. So what do you look for first: the subject or the S-curve?

To avoid missing an opportunity you should in fact seek both. If you find an attractive subject, look at it from every angle and search for an S-shaped foreground that leads the eye to it. Similarly, if you discover a striking curved foreground, attempt to compose the picture in such a way that it leads to something that the viewer can latch on to. Sometimes the solution is obvious and you almost stumble upon an image, but often it requires careful exploration and a lot of searching. There are times when it is a lost cause and, despite your best efforts, the elements stubbornly refuse to fall into place. It can be frustrating but there is no need to feel despondent; I have lost count of the number of times I have seen a perfect 50 per cent of a picture then, despite exploring every possible angle and viewpoint, have sadly failed to find the remaining half. It is a common occurrence and it happens to everybody. You can tell yourself that at least you tried and that is all anybody can do. There is always next time.

2-stop (0.6) neutral density
graduated filter

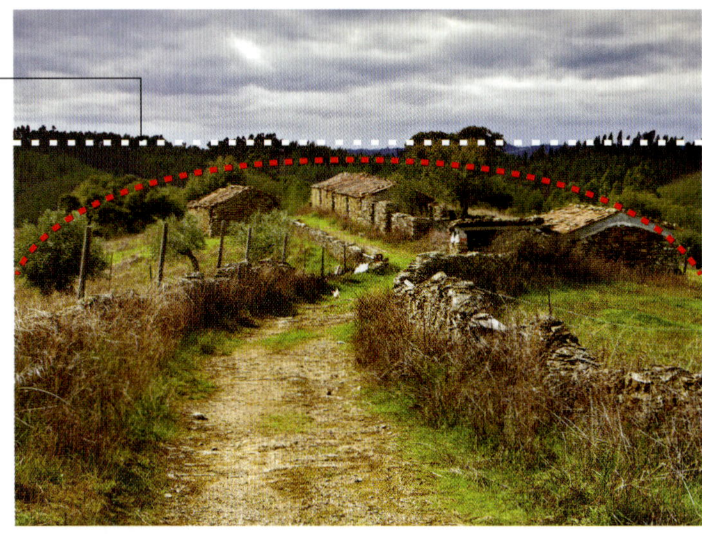

There is a second, less obvious, curve in this composition. The buildings and trees make a horizontal curve which, although the viewer is not consciously aware of its presence, rests easy on the eye and prevents the lane from becoming too dominant.

> **TIP:** Basing the composition of a picture around a number of curves will create images that have strong aesthetic appeal.

The S-shaped lane occupies a large proportion of the image and is rather dominant. It was therefore important that the right balance was found with the remainder of the composition. Dead space had to be avoided and this was achieved by filling the entire width of the picture beyond the lane with the main subject. The group of trees and buildings has a rustic charm that draws the eye towards them and together with the lane makes a complete image.

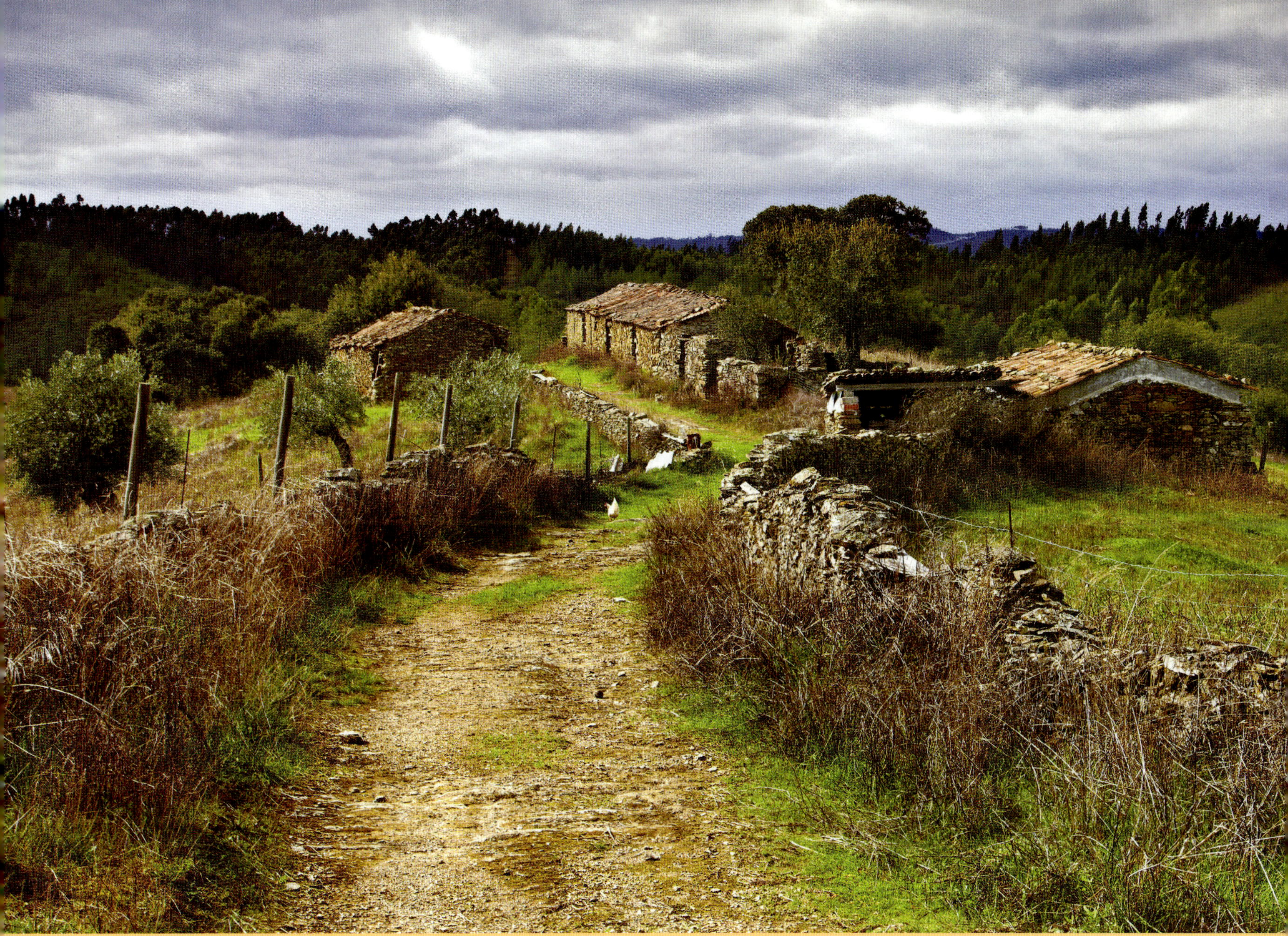

**Silveira, Castelo Branco, Portugal**

**Camera:** Mamiya 645 AFDII with Mamiya digital back
**Lens:** Mamiya 80mm (standard)
**Filter:** 2-stop ND graduated
**Exposure:** 1/30sec at f/22, ISO 100
**Waiting for the light:** 60 minutes
**Post-processing:** Curves adjustment, colour balance adjustment (warming)

There had been a prolonged dry spell in northern Scotland and water levels were unusually low. In some places riverbeds were becoming visible, which is a relatively rare occurrence in the Highlands, but it was an intriguing sight because the newly exposed rocks and boulders created a marvellous opportunity to build images around richly coloured and textured foregrounds. There was no shortage of enticing viewpoints, but the foreground elements were so attractive that there was a real danger they would dominate the picture to such an extent that other features would fail to make their presence felt. Careful composition was therefore going to be necessary if evenly weighted images were to be made.

The presence of at least one strong focal point beyond the foreground was going to be essential if bottom-heavy images were to be avoided, and in this type of situation trees are an absolute blessing. The elevating effect they have on a landscape image cannot be overstated. Just one tree can act as an anchor towards which all other features – and indeed the viewer – will gravitate, and this will bring balance and equilibrium to a photograph.

As soon as I caught a glimpse of the isolated tree standing proudly on the bank of the river Abhainn Shira, it became apparent that even with a large span of foreground there was a good chance that a balanced image would be possible.

One hour later a viewpoint was found and the picture taken, with the glorious rock-strewn riverbed being captured in all its glory. The rain returned the following day and those precious stones were once again consigned to their watery abyss. Who knows how long it will be before they again reveal themselves to another fortunate photographer?

> **TIP:** To prevent an image being dominated by an extensive foreground, build the composition around a strong focal point in the middle distance.

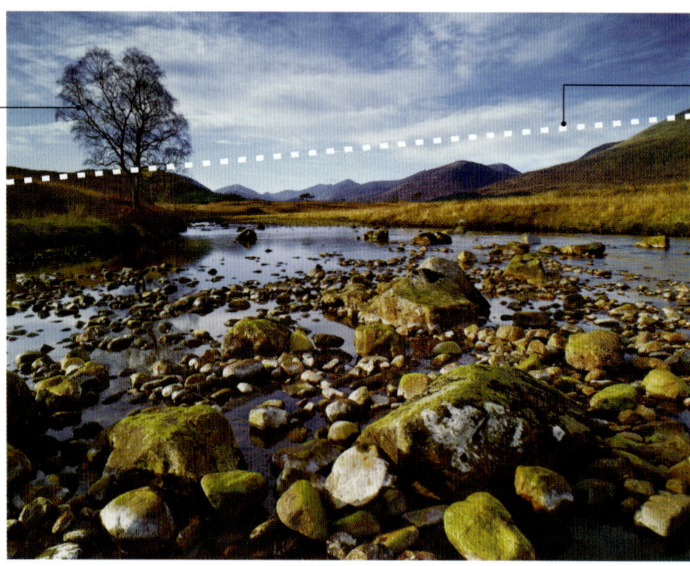

2-stop (0.6) neutral density graduated filter

- A 2-stop ND graduated filter was used to reduce the light value of the sky to that of the landscape and enable both to be correctly exposed.

- The impression of distance is enhanced by the presence of rocks of a diminishing size stretching away from the camera. The effect was strengthened by employing a wide-angle lens with the camera placed close to the ground and foreground rocks.

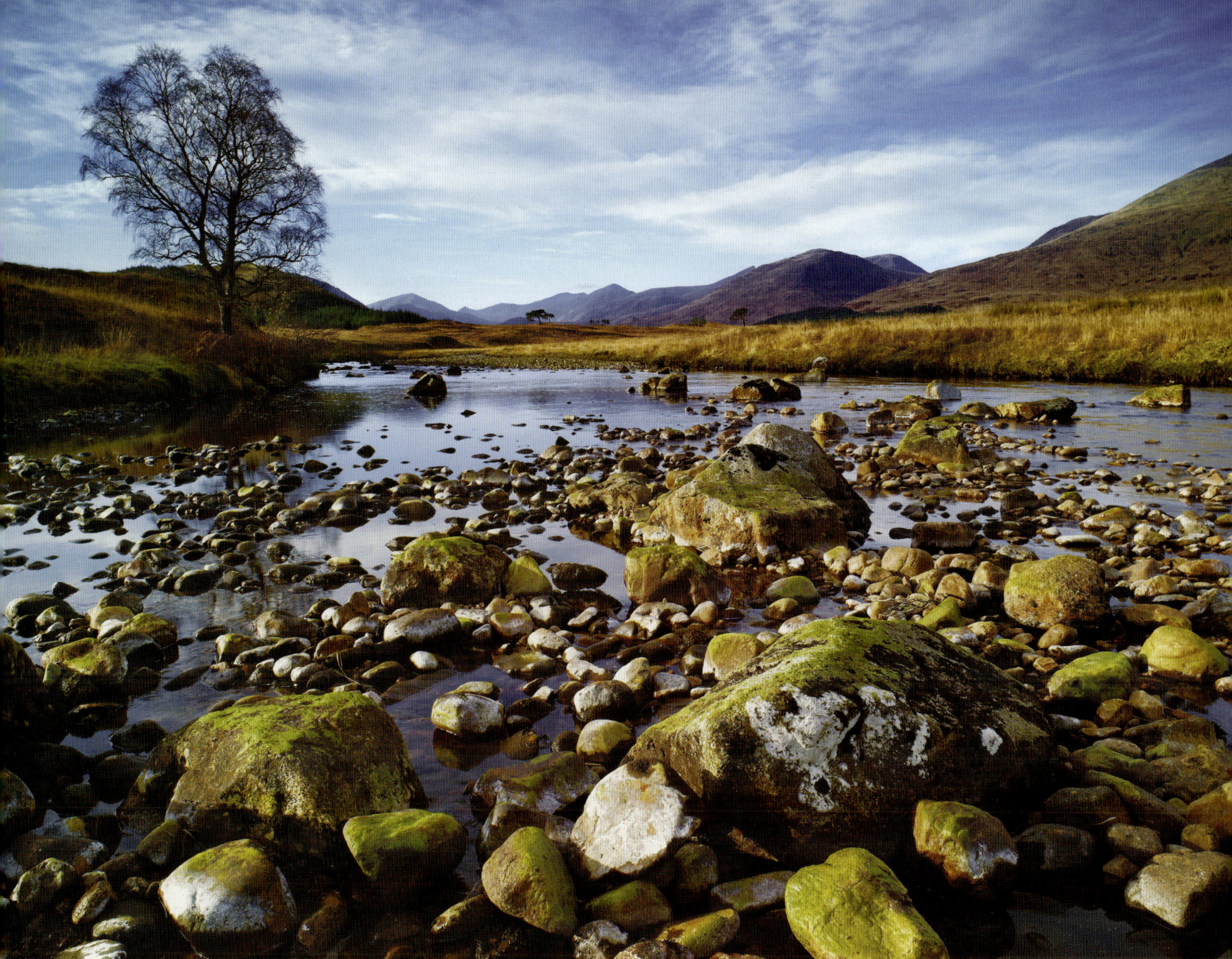

**Abhainn Shira, The Highlands, Scotland**

**Camera:** Mamiya 645 AFDII with Mamiya digital back

**Lens:** Mamiya 35mm (wide-angle)

**Filter:** 2-stop ND graduated

**Exposure:** 1/2sec at f/22, ISO 100

**Waiting for the light:** 45 minutes

**Post-processing:** Curves adjustment and suppression of highlights

There are occasions when contours and graphic lines can act as the main feature in an image. Fortunately depth is not essential in this type of composition, because these elements are most effectively depicted by compressing the landscape in an abstract or semi-abstract arrangement. This can be achieved by using a telephoto lens, as it will reduce apparent distance and bring together foreground and background. The longer the focal length, the greater the effect (which you can observe by zooming in and out across an open view). This flattening of perspective is a useful option but it should be used only when appropriate. You should consider your subject carefully, assess it through your photographer's eye and decide on the best approach. Do you choose an abstract or semi-abstract graphic design, or a more traditional composition? There are no rules or guidelines that apply, so follow your instincts and choose an arrangement that emphasizes the features of your subject that most appeal to you.

In the picture opposite the main attraction is the distinctive pattern of striped bands across the sandstone surface. The only way to depict them adequately was to compress the view and stack together the four quite different sections. To prevent the image from becoming a total abstract (which I felt was the wrong approach on this occasion) it was necessary to include a focal point that provided more information about the nature of the location. The inclusion of a small bush was the answer as it enabled the composition to be built around it, but it is regrettable that there is additional foliage to the left. A focal point should be clear and distinct, but the loose greenery and untidy rock formation surrounding the bush are all a little unsightly. They spoil the image but excluding them wasn't an option. Sometimes a compromise has to be accepted and as a result this photograph is flawed. I think it is still a reasonable portrayal of a characteristic of the Zion Mountains and, even with its imperfections, was worth capturing.

The upper portion of the image is a little unsightly but to exclude it would have weakened the composition. The green bush adds important information about the nature of the location and prevents the picture from becoming a vague abstract arrangement.

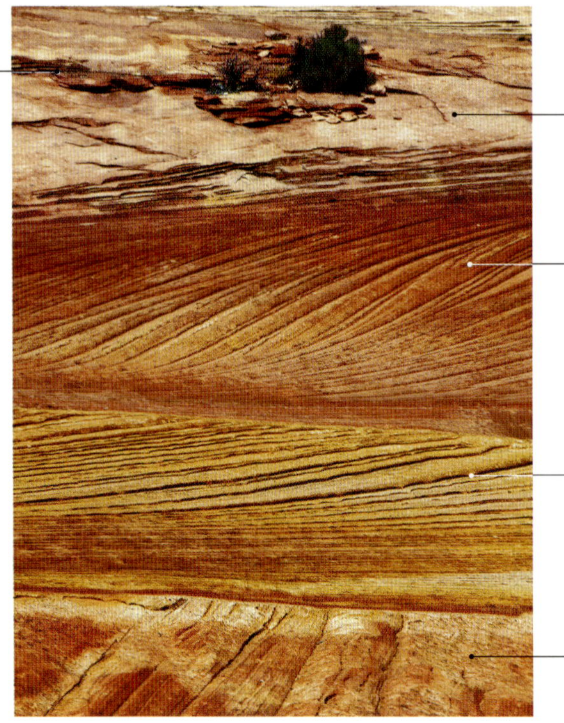

The telephoto lens has compressed distance and, by condensing the patterned bands of rock, has strengthened the graphic nature of the landscape.

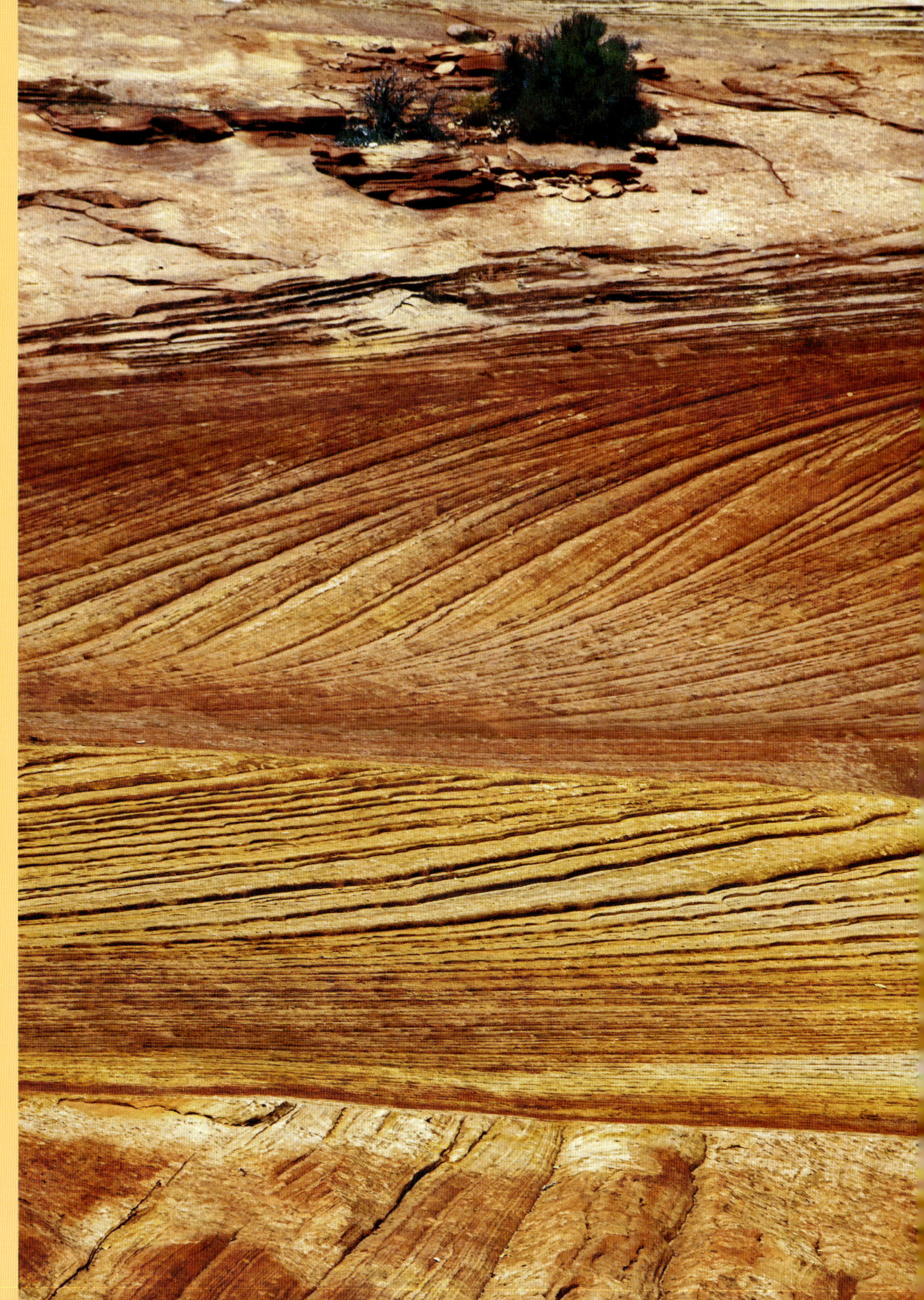

**Zion National Park,
Utah, USA**

**Camera:** Canon EOS 7D
**Lens:** Canon 24–105mm L IS
**Filter:** None
**Exposure:** 1/60sec at f/13, ISO 100
**Waiting for the light:** Immediate
**Post-processing:** None

As my plane landed at Las Vegas airport I was feeling a little jaded, but at the same time exhilarated. It had been a tiring ten-hour flight but it was a small price to pay, because at last the time had come to experience at first hand the glittering attractions I had read so much about. Casinos and gambling are not my particular interests and it was slot canyons, not slot machines, that held my fascination. These uniquely beautiful rock formations are one of the most captivating landscape subjects to be found anywhere in the world. But, magnificent as they are, they can be a challenge to photograph because of their confined space, low light levels and potentially high contrast.

Because of the poor light, shutter speeds of several seconds can sometimes be required, which makes a tripod essential, but the space available to set up bulky equipment is often restricted. A small but adaptable sturdy tripod fitted with a ball-and-socket head is the best option, as is a zoom lens, which is a useful aid to composition and also prevents the need to change lenses. This should be avoided because the interior of a slot canyon can be dusty and exposure of equipment should be minimized as far as possible. You might also have to work fast as the more popular canyons can be crowded and time restrictions sometimes apply. Using a zoom lens will considerably speed up the image-making process.

With the right equipment and a little preparation stunning photographs of a unique type of subject can be captured, and when you see your final images, you might just feel that, unlike the majority of Las Vegas visitors, you have well and truly hit the jackpot!

**The composition has been based on a series of waves and curves of varying tone and colour. In such an arrangement it is not always essential to have a specific focal point, but if one is included it should be positioned in such a way that it does not conflict with the theme of the photograph. Here the apex of the lower rock has been centrally positioned, approximately one third from the top of the picture. This enabled the curved lines to flow around it and allowed all parts of the image to make a contribution.**

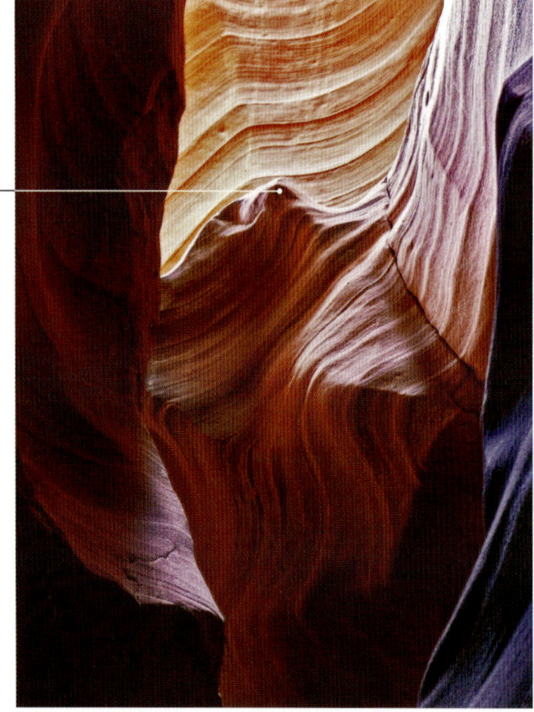

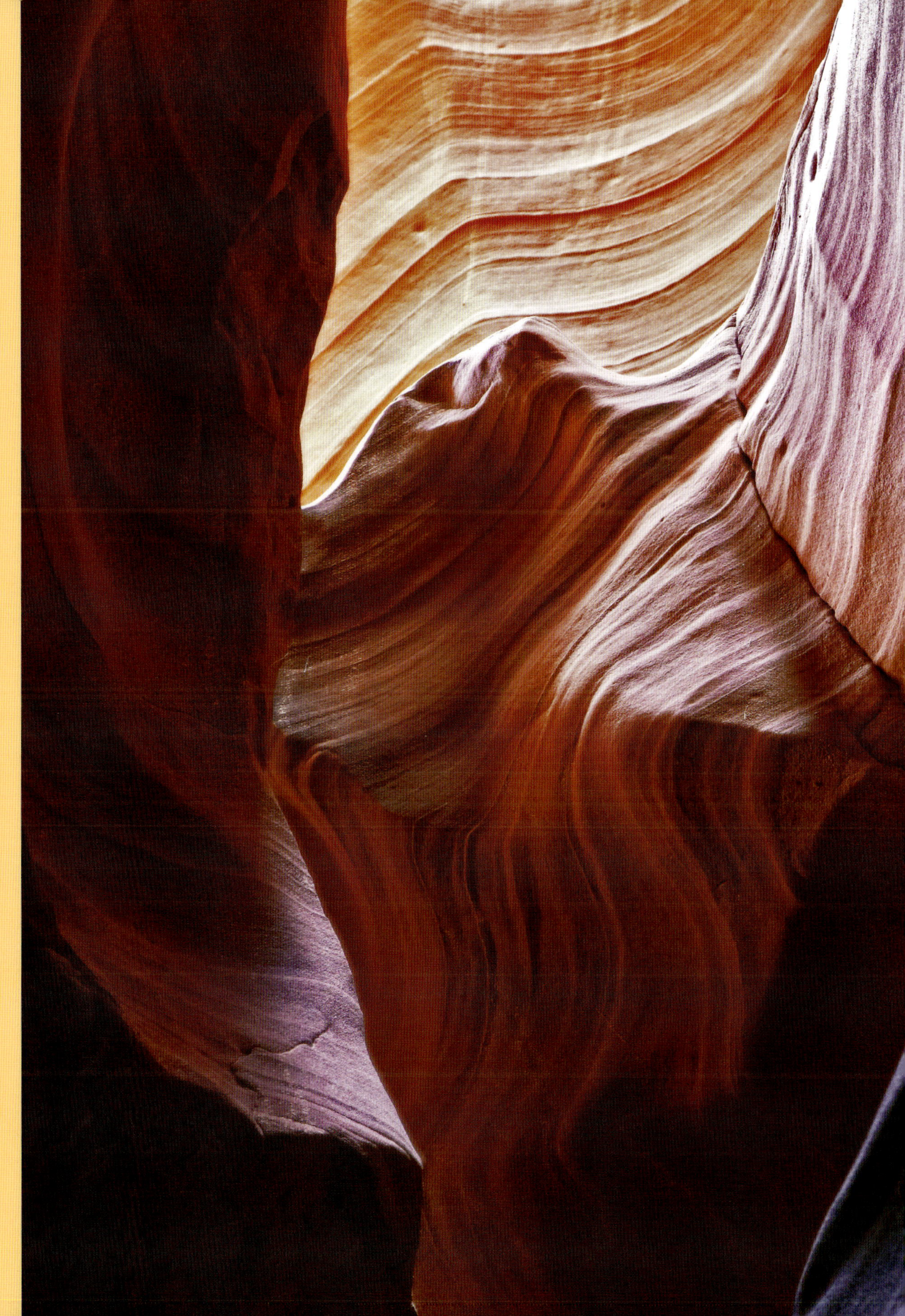

Upper Antelope Canyon,
Arizona, USA

Camera: Canon EOS 7D
Lens: Canon 24–105mm L IS
Filter: None
Exposure: 1sec at f/13, ISO 100
Waiting for the light: Immediate
Post-processing: Curves adjustment,
suppression of highlights

There are occasions when the purpose of a focal point is, in addition to conveying distance and scale, to introduce another element. It might be colour – a single bright red leaf against a green background, for example – or a contrasting shape. In this view across the River Tagus, the tree-clad hills consist almost exclusively of soft edges, circles and curves. The trees, because of the angle of light, are clearly defined and there is a gradual reduction in their size as the hills recede towards the horizon. The scale of the photograph is therefore in little doubt; the buildings make a small contribution in this respect but their main purpose is to introduce another shape. Their straight lines provide a necessary contrast to the roundly textured fabric of the surrounding hills, as without them the landscape would verge on being too repetitive.

In addition to the small houses the reflections on the water and the curved edge of the riverbank also add variety and interest. These are in fact important features and together with the presence of the buildings and the quality of light were the reason the view was captured. It would have been preferable to have had a more centrally positioned curve along the top of the hills, but you can't always have everything you want and the end result is, I think, quite acceptable.

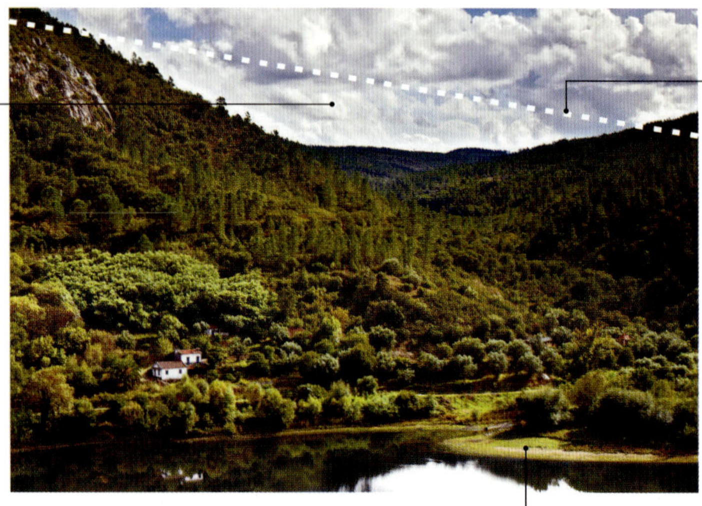

The ND graduated filter has, because of the shape of the hills, darkened only part of the sky. The portion not covered by the filter was therefore darkened in post-processing using a combination of Curves and the Shadows/Highlights tools. Another option would have been to make two exposures, one based on the sky and one on the landscape, and then merge them together.

2-stop (0.6) neutral density graduated filter

The curved outline of the riverbank in the bottom right corner adds weight to this side of the picture. It helps to balance the slope of the hillside on the left and prevents the picture from being one-sided.

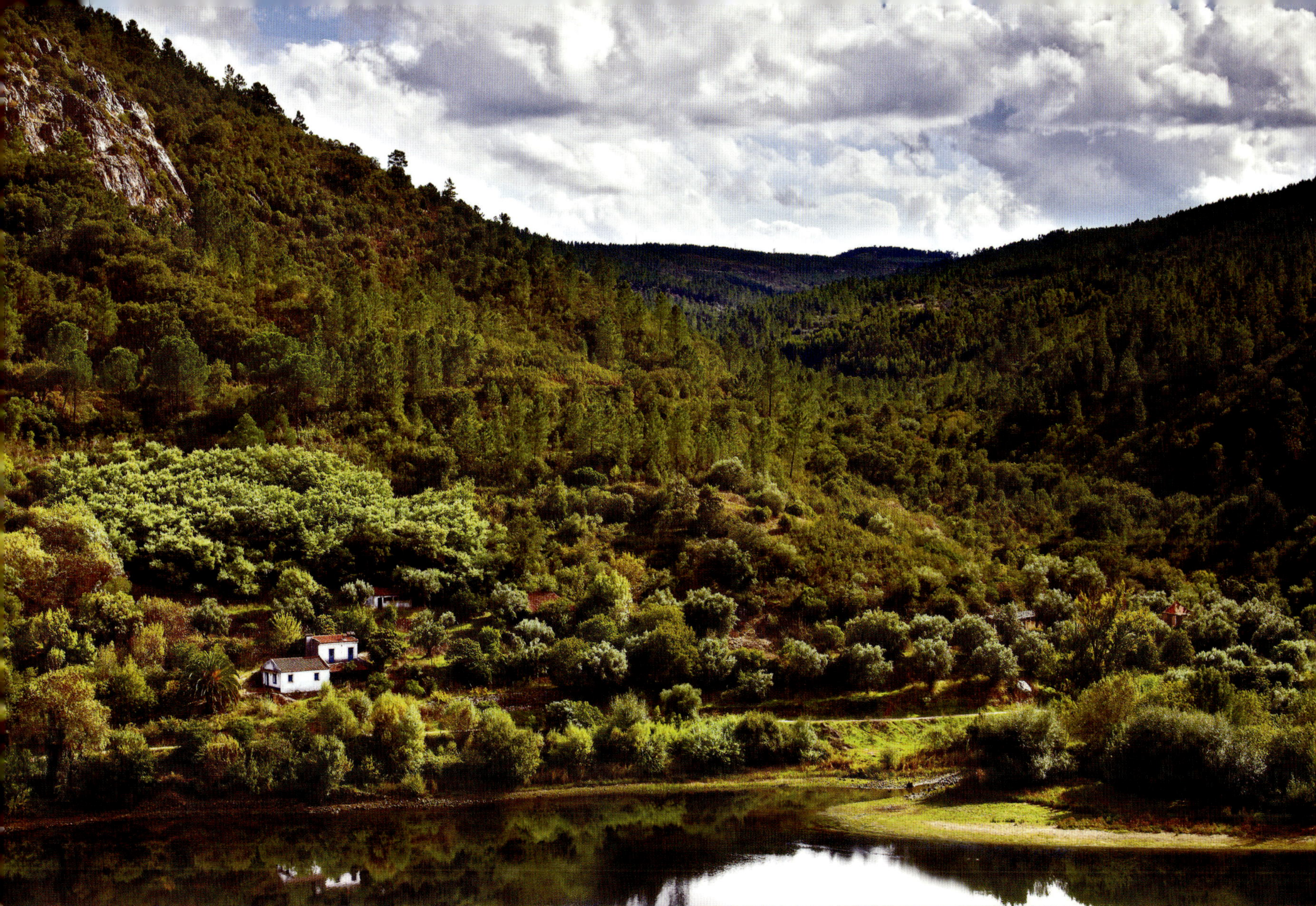

**Rio Tejo, Vila Velha Da Rodao, Portugal**

**Camera:** Mamiya 645 AFDII with Mamiya digital back
**Lens:** Mamiya 80mm (standard)
**Filter:** 2-stop ND graduated
**Exposure:** 1/40sec at f/16, ISO 100
**Waiting for the light:** 90 minutes
**Post-processing:** Curves adjustment, colour balance adjustment

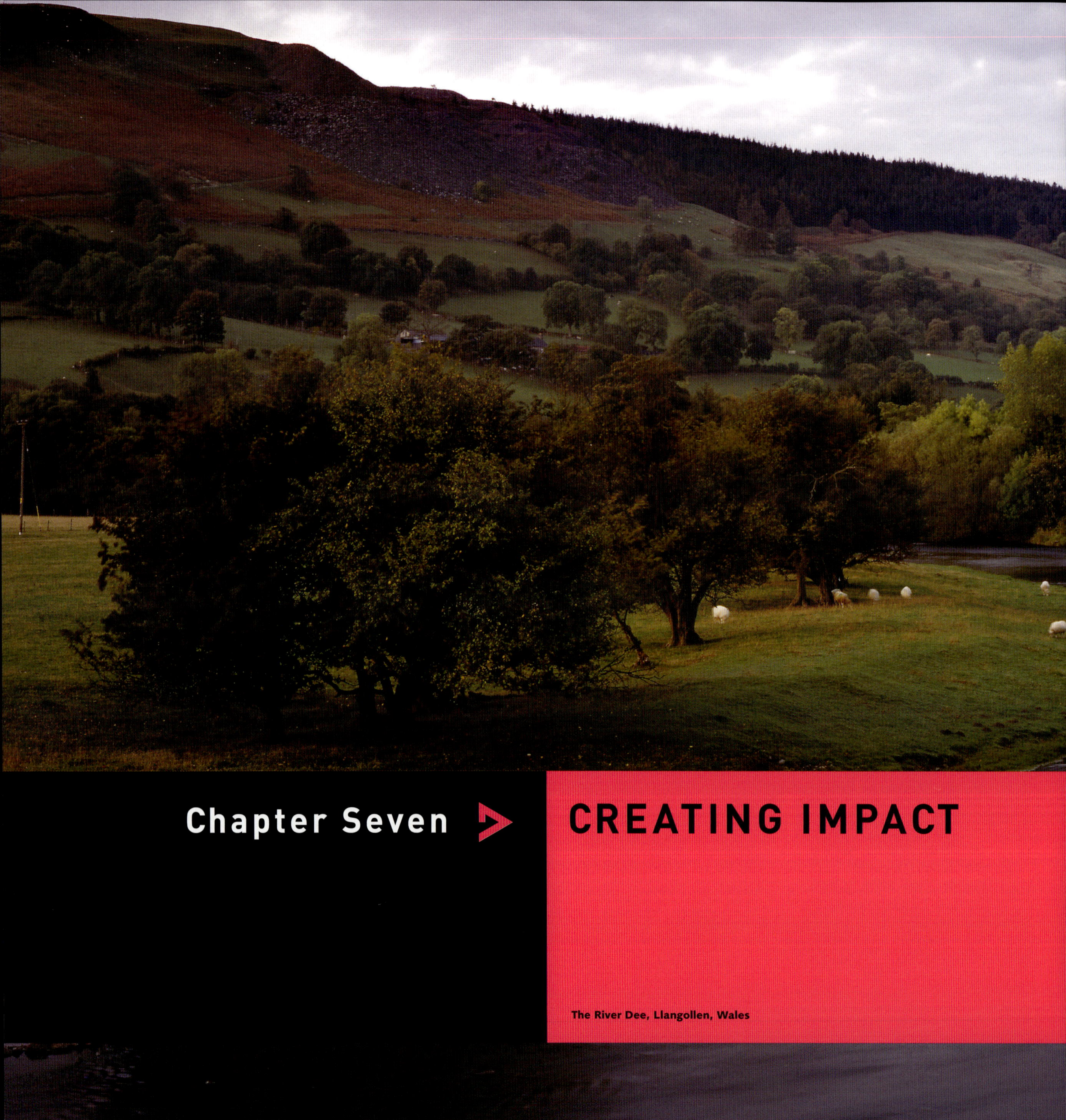

Chapter Seven
CREATING IMPACT
The River Dee, Llangollen, Wales

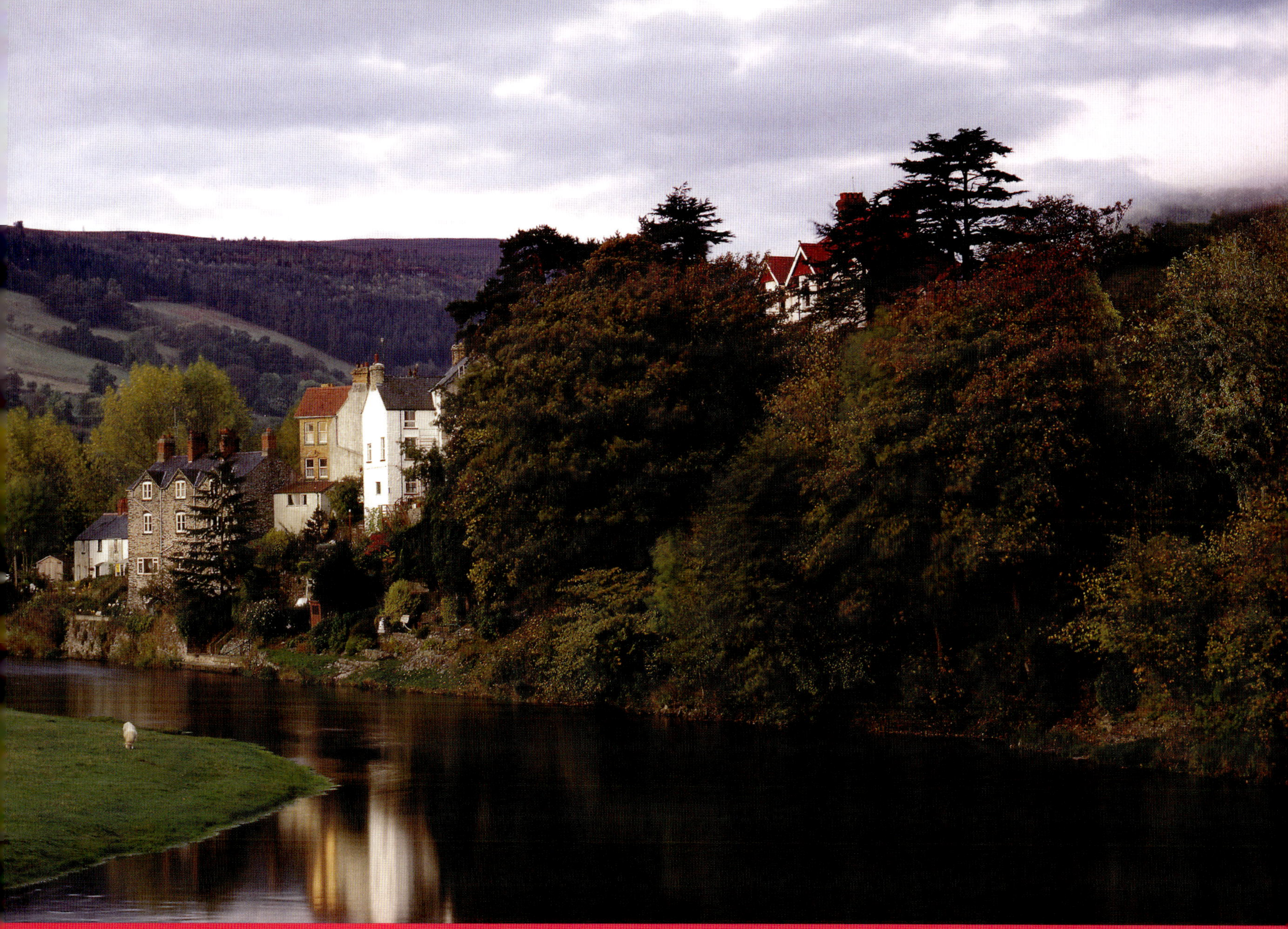

Impact is the key ingredient in any piece of visual art. It is what every artist strives to create each time he or she applies paint to canvas and what every photographer seeks when exposing a sensor or film to light. It is an intangible quality that cannot be categorized, but when present in an image it evokes an immediate emotional response from the viewer. Impact, quite simply, is what sets images apart, and the following chapter explains exactly how to create it and use it to maximum effect in your photography.

Antelope Canyon is in fact two separate canyons. Several miles apart, they are known as Upper and Lower Canyon. The more accessible – and much more heavily visited – is the Upper Canyon, and it is perhaps also the more spectacular. It is the wider of the two and this allows light to penetrate further, which gives the rocks a vibrant luminosity. However, in its own way, the Lower Canyon is just as attractive. Its qualities are more subtle and its lower contrast levels provide opportunities for more intricate compositions.

The other bonus is that there are fewer people and, depending on when you visit, you might well have the canyon to yourself. You can then adopt a more relaxed, considered approach and contemplate your subject without worrying about time (the Upper Canyon is accessible by guided tours only and they tend not to linger) or obstructing other photographers.

The picture opposite was not as obvious as it might appear and it took some time to decide on the arrangement I wanted to capture. Being at the time the sole occupant of the canyon enabled me to devote considerable thought to its planning and composition. Having considered several options I eventually decided to use a long focal length lens as it seemed to tighten the arrangement and knit together the conglomeration of textured surfaces into what hopefully looks to be a unified structure.

Both canyons have been, and continue to be, heavily photographed. The challenge is therefore to create original images that have impact. I hope this is the case with this composition. There can be no guarantee of course, but an attempt was at least made to produce something new, and that is all a photographer can do.

**• The ability of telephoto lenses to compress distance is a very useful tool for creating impact in many different types of subject. By reducing distance between objects a powerful image can emerge that, if viewed in normal perspective, would fail to engage the eye. In this photograph the shortened distance between the front and back has greatly strengthened the visual presence of the background rock formations and has enabled the picture to be viewed as a single abstract arrangement.**

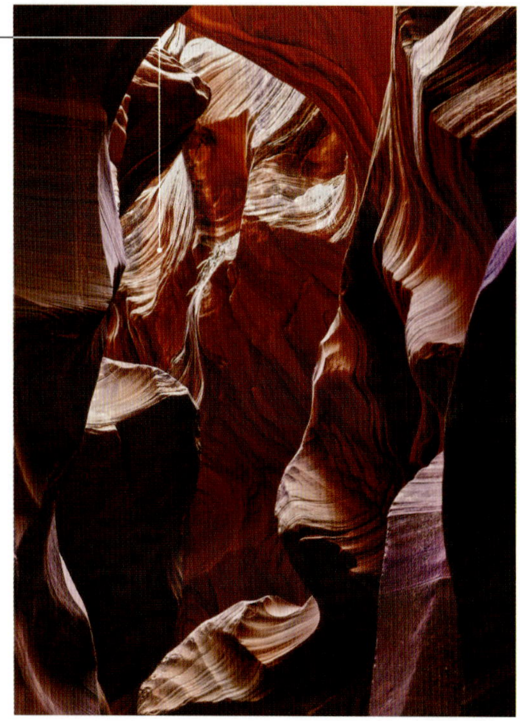

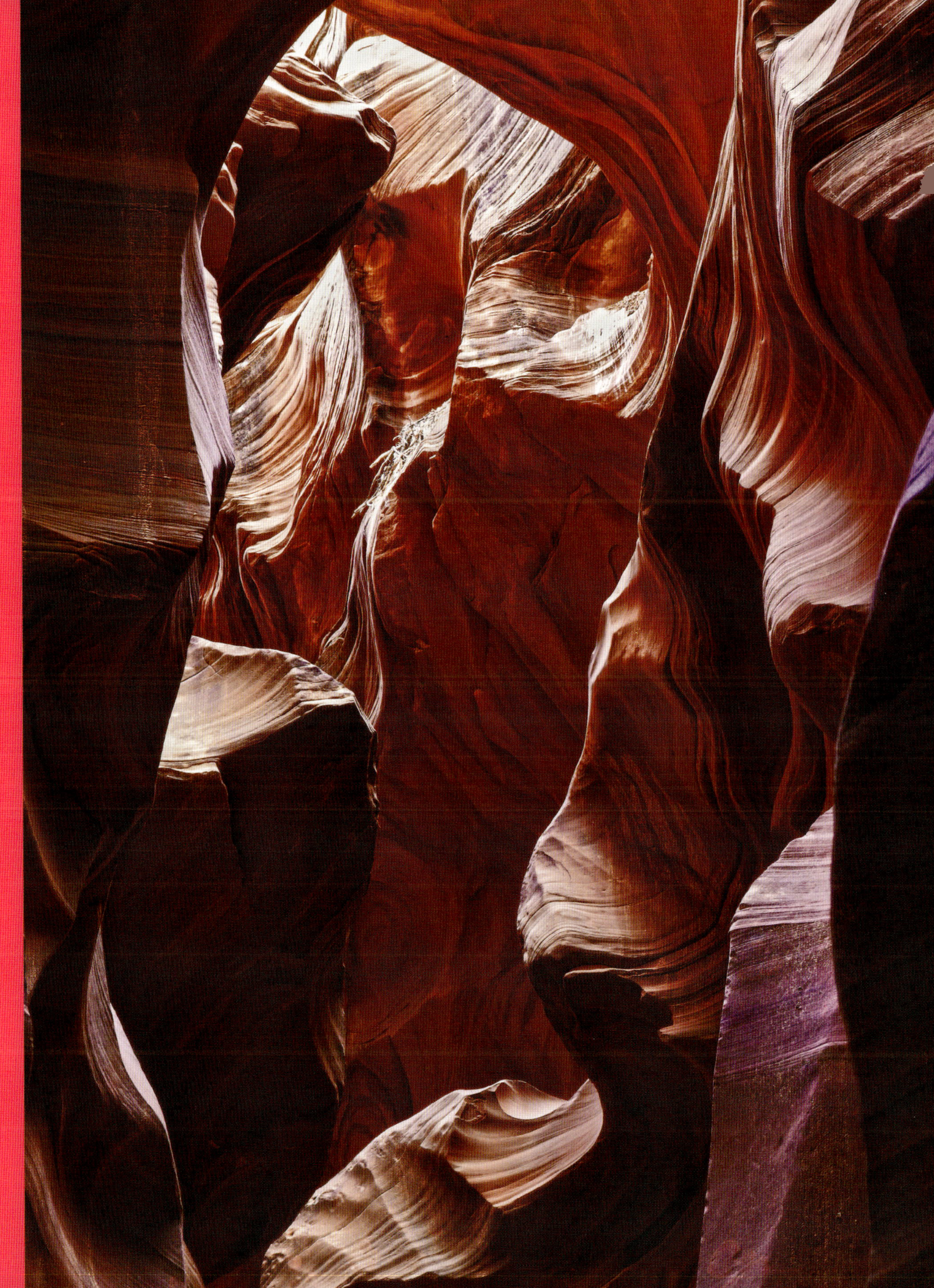

**Lower Antelope Canyon,
Arizona, USA**

**Camera:** Canon EOS 7D
**Lens:** Canon 24–105mm L IS
**Filter:** None
**Exposure:** 5sec at f/13, ISO 100
**Waiting for the light:** Immediate
**Post-processing:** Curves
adjustment, suppression
of highlights

Waterfalls are one of the landscape's most photogenic subjects. They photograph particularly well because, almost uniquely in the natural world, they have an intrinsic ability to convey time. Like the ticking of a clock, flowing water, when captured, shows the passing of time, and if photographed in a particular way the accumulative effect of the passing of time. The combination of moving water and time can be very powerful and can give images great impact, and with the right approach this impact can often be boosted still further.

Depth in a photograph is a sought-after and, generally speaking, beneficial quality, but when a waterfall is the subject this is not always the case. Often it is the flat images that make the stronger impression because space and distance sometimes have no role to play. The attraction of a waterfall is the cascading torrent and the arrangement and connection of the silken movement of water contrasted against the solid, immovable stillness of rock. Flattening the image by photographing the subject from a distance using a telephoto lens can strengthen the composition by linking together all the interconnecting elements. Compressing the picture in this way will also eliminate empty space. You will be able to fill the frame with visual interest and, as a result, the image will gain additional impact and make a lasting impression with viewers.

• The picture was composed in a way that ensured every part of it contains either flowing water or colourful rock. The resulting tight composition adds further impact to a naturally photogenic subject.

> **TIP:** When photographing a waterfall, fit your camera with a telephoto lens to eliminate dead space and pack the image with visual interest.

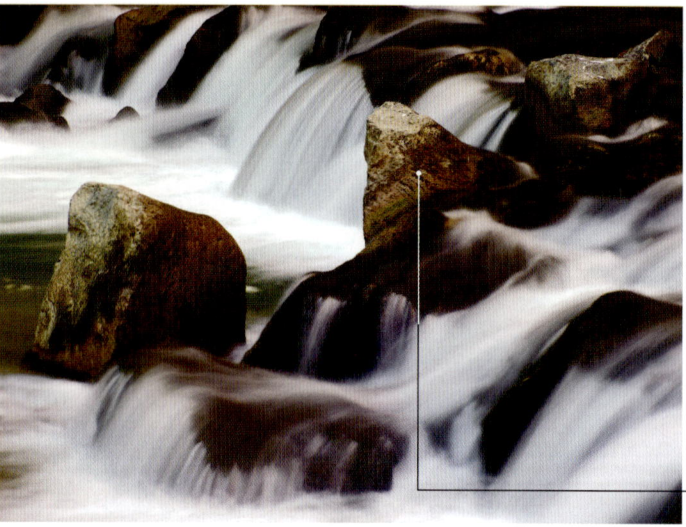

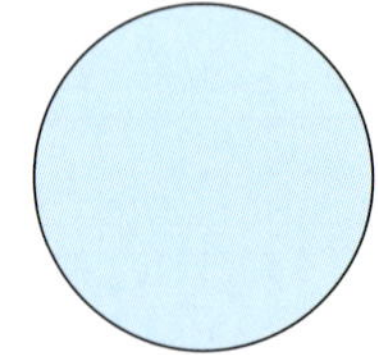

Polarizer (fully polarized)

• A polarizer was employed to reduce reflections on the wet rocks. The filter also enabled a longer exposure to be used, which was necessary in order to blur the water.

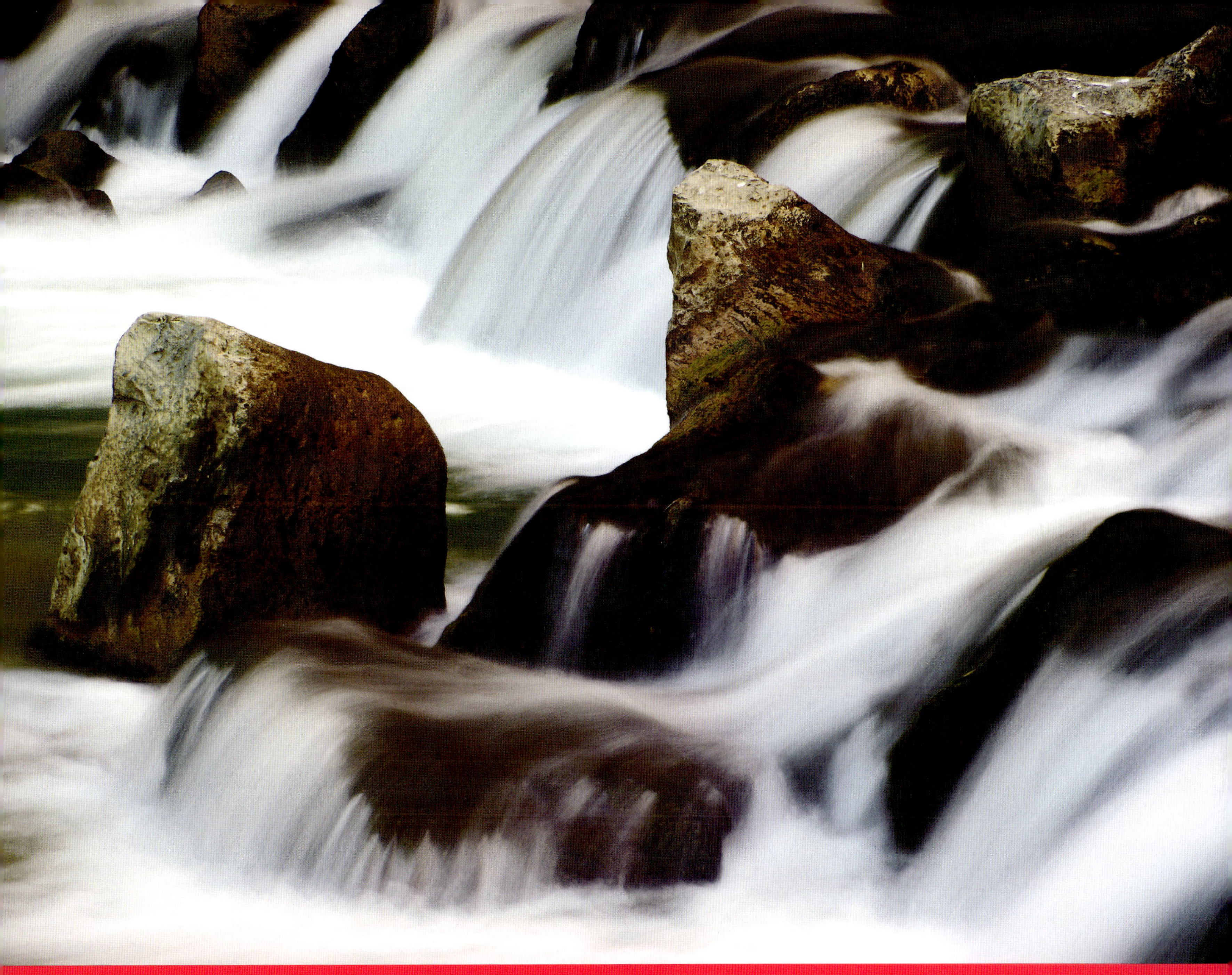


**Zion National Park, Utah, USA**

**Camera:** Canon EOS 7D
**Lens:** Canon 24–105mm L IS
**Filter:** Polarizer (fully polarized)
**Exposure:** 1sec at f/13, ISO 100
**Waiting for the light:** Immediate
**Post-processing:** Curves adjustment, suppression of highlights

This book isn't a guide to flower photography, but this picture of a peony has been included to illustrate an important point concerning impact. The image shows that potential subjects can have hidden depths. There can be more to them than at first glance meets the eye, so any object that interests you should not just be taken at face value.

Whatever it is you are looking at – from a close-up of a flower to a sweeping vista – it should be viewed from all possible angles. Your first composition might not be the only option; there might be a better image, with greater impact, to be captured by simply searching for a different viewpoint. Take, for example, flowers. Like people, they are rarely photographed from the rear but creative image-making is a result of creative thinking. The building blocks of a picture are usually quite basic – colour, subtle tonal variations, texture and intricate shapes. Nature follows no aesthetic rules and these building blocks can appear anywhere, so ignore convention and think creatively. If an object looks better from the rear then photograph it from the rear, or from any other angle or perspective that appeals to you.

It is an inescapable fact that while nature creates the building blocks of images it is you, the photographer, who knits them together to create visual impact. Consider this every time you assess a possible subject and it will be to the benefit of your photography.

> **TIP:** To capture subtle tonal variations use soft, shadowless light. This will prevent delicate hues from being obscured by harsh highlights and shadows.

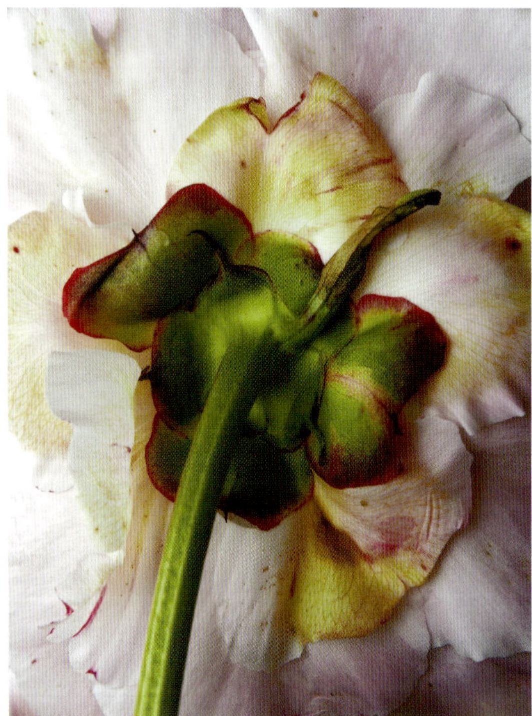

> **TIP:** To maximize impact consider every angle of view and keep an open mind. An original – even unusual – approach might turn out to be the best choice.

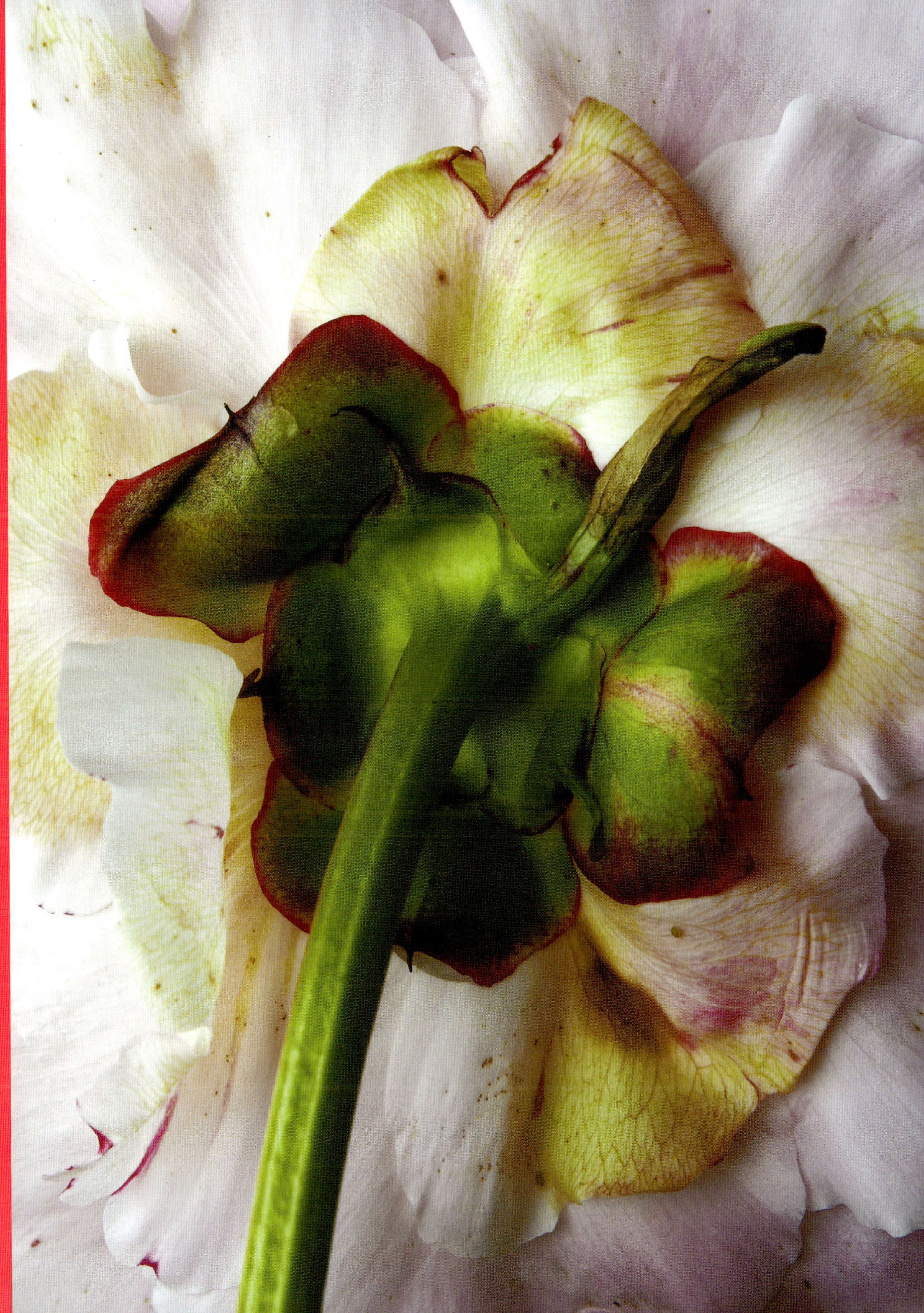


The Wirral Peninsula,
Merseyside, England

Camera: Canon EOS 7D
Lens: Canon 24–105mm L IS
Filter: None
Exposure: 1/15sec at f/13,
ISO 100
Waiting for the light:
Immediate
Post-processing: Colour
balance adjustment (warming),
suppression of highlights

With the exception of sheep and cattle, and possibly other livestock, I very rarely include animals in landscape images. Purity of composition is the objective and this requires the exclusion of unnecessary elements. I have absolutely nothing against animals but sometimes they can be a distraction, hence their rare appearance in my photographs. There are always exceptions, however, and although landscape is my subject I couldn't resist capturing this tableau of unadulterated rustic charm.

Cats, or indeed animals of any description, were far from my thoughts as I explored Riscada, a small, remote and very old village in northern Portugal. It was a surprise then to discover three cats sitting contentedly and quite perfectly arranged on a gloriously dilapidated bench. It was sheer good fortune that not only was I carrying a camera, but also that it was one with an image stabilization lens. There would have been no time to set up a tripod, but even with the ability to hand-hold the camera and capture the shot quickly I fully expected my feline subjects to scatter as I approached them. But no: my luck not only held, it actually increased. The cats not only remained perfectly still, they, as one, looked directly at the camera and held their gaze as I crouched down to focus and compose a picture, all the time pleading with them in a soothing tone, 'Keep looking, keep looking, keep looking' and, with not a hint of movement from any of them, made three rapid exposures. They remained quite still, and there was even time to study the image on the camera's LCD screen and check for any sign of camera shake, which is always a concern with hand-held photographs, even with image stabilization. Everything was sharp and, breathing a sigh of relief, I packed away my equipment and resumed my exploration of the village. Wandering down the alley, I turned and looked back. The cats had disappeared.

> **TIP:** When searching for pictures in towns carry your camera with you, preferably one with image stabilization. You never know what you will discover and an opportunity for a photograph might suddenly, and quite unexpectedly, present itself.

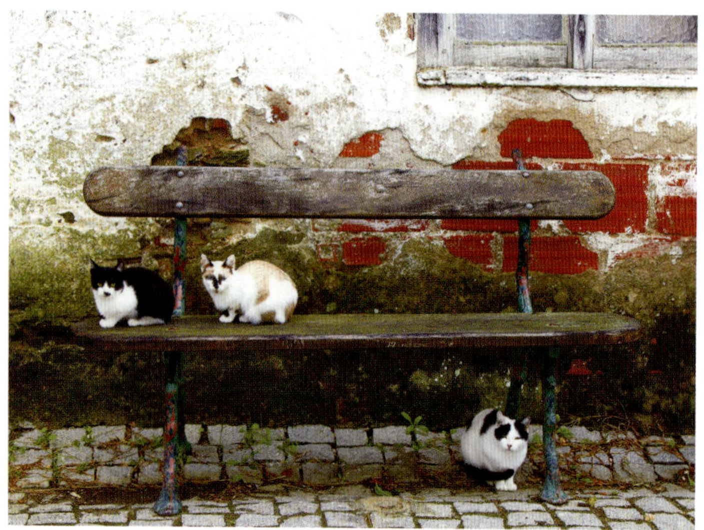

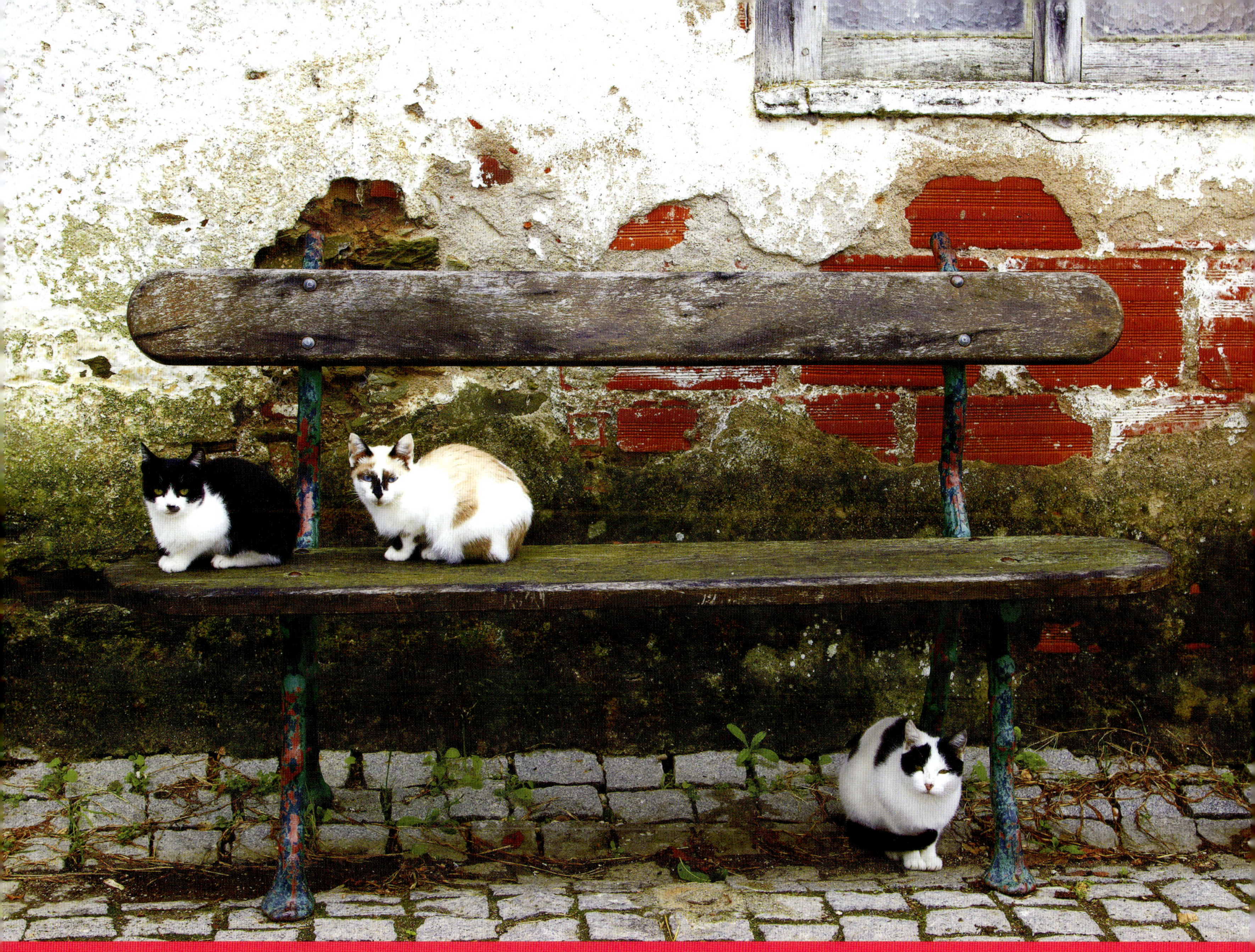

**Riscada, Castelo Branco, Portugal**

**Camera:** Canon EOS 7D
**Lens:** Canon 24–105mm L IS
**Filter:** None
**Exposure:** 1/80sec at f/6.3, ISO 100
**Waiting for the light:** Immediate
**Post-processing:** None

Impact in a photograph is, in many ways, an intangible quality. Composition, colour, light and time all contribute to the end product. Sometimes all four of these elements play an important role, and often it is simply a result of an image being taken at the optimum moment – that magical split second when all the ingredients coalesce to stunning effect. Such occasions are elusive – that is, of course, what makes them so special – but there are a few basic guidelines that, if followed every time you make an image, will give your pictures a noticeable boost.

The first and most fundamental rule is to avoid wasted space. Every pixel should make a contribution, so scrutinize your subject from left to right and top to bottom and compose your photographs in such a way that monotonous areas are excluded. Once you are happy with the arrangement the next consideration is light. Contours, shape and distance should be depicted, or even emphasized, by the light. This can be achieved by using cloud to create a scattered distribution of highlights and shadows. Focal points should if possible be more strongly lit than other parts of the picture as this will help to engage the eye.

The angle of the light and therefore the time of day is important, as it will have a noticeable effect on the appearance and impact on your subject. View your location at different times, in various lighting conditions, to ensure you capture it at the best moment.

Finally, colours should, generally speaking, be strong. However, before you reach for the Saturation tool, take a careful look at your processed image. A general increase in saturation can produce a garish, artificial-looking photograph and might not be necessary, but some colours might be weaker than others. A selective, fine adjustment of a specific colour might therefore be the answer or, if the picture still looks flat, a slight increase in contrast might be required. Your goal is to achieve impact while remaining faithful to the subject's original appearance. A delicate touch is all that is required.

Follow the simple points outlined above and your photography should make a lasting impression with your viewers.

**Polarizer (fully polarized)**

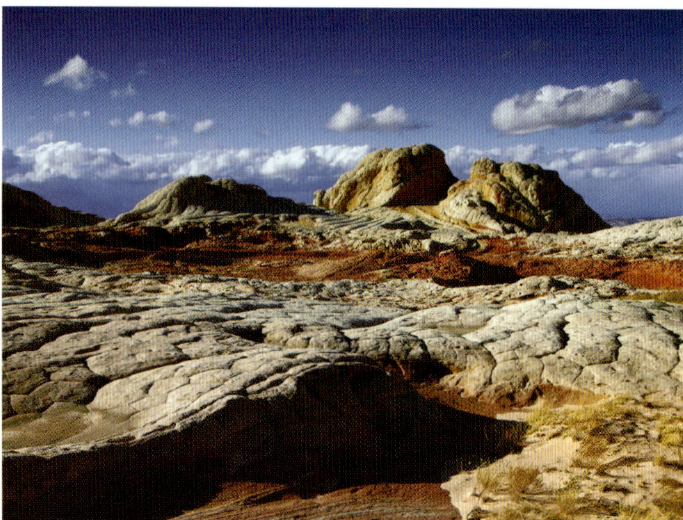

> **TIP:** Use a polarizer to heighten impact of the image by enhancing colour and increasing contrast. The effect of polarization on colour is fairly moderate, but is often sufficient to boost impact without deviating from reality.

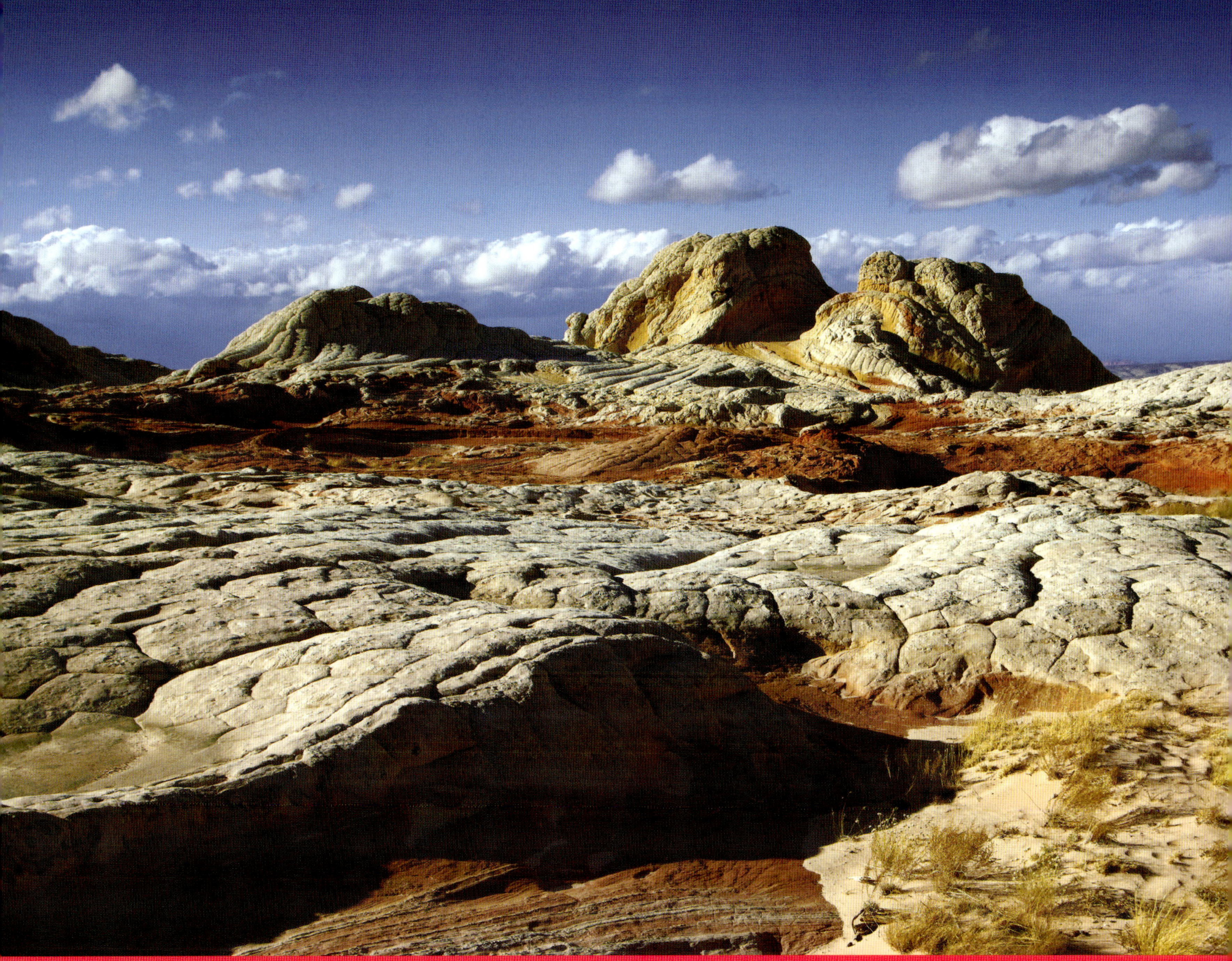

**White Pocket, Arizona, USA**

**Camera:** Mamiya 645 AFDII with Mamiya back
**Lens:** Mamiya 35mm (wide-angle)
**Filter:** Polarizer (fully polarized)
**Exposure:** 1/4sec at f/22, ISO 100
**Waiting for the light:** 60 minutes
**Post-processing:** Selective colour balance adjustment

Llantysilio is one of my favourite locations. I have visited it many times and it is always fascinating to watch the appearance of the landscape change as sunlight and shadow play across its sharply undulating terrain. The elevated position provides a sweeping view of the Clwydian Hills and is the perfect viewpoint from which to observe the powerful effect light has on contoured land. When clouds are scudding across the sky it is possible to capture a series of images in quick succession, from the same position, with no two being identical. This means of course that there is endless opportunity for creative photography.

As part of the learning process I can think of no more effective way to gain experience and an understanding and appreciation of light than spending several hours in this type of place just watching the sky and light. At no other time do you feel such a sense of involvement as photographer, light and landscape combine together, with the role of the photographer being to observe and capture the precise moment when the elements act in harmony to maximum effect.

Light is the key ingredient in the picture opposite. It was essential that the valley was brightly lit, with the foreground area in shadow. I took several versions of this image and although there are patches of cloud on the distant hills this is the one that was most successful. The distribution of the light delineates the contours of the hills very effectively, but the photograph isn't perfect because the group of buildings to the right of centre is in shadow. It should act as a focal point and therefore be brightly lit but sadly this isn't the case. The flaw isn't particularly noticeable but it is a fault, albeit a small one.

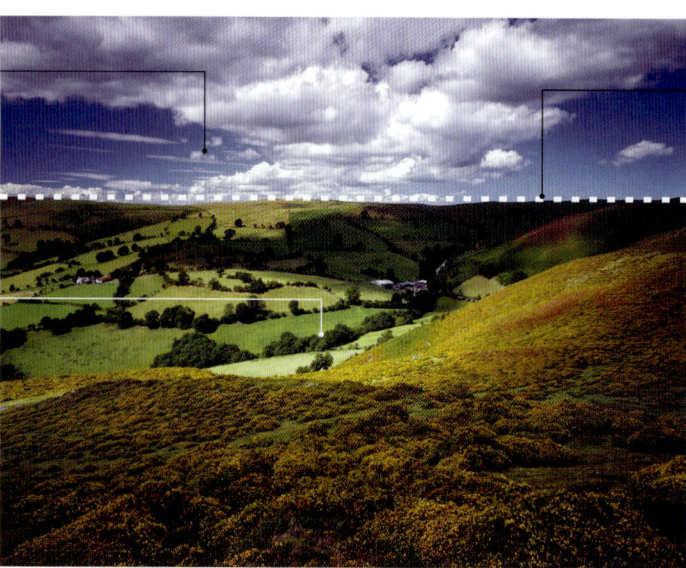

- **The decreasing size of the clouds as they recede towards the horizon helps to create the impression of distance and depth.**

- **The play of light is the critical element. The combination of light and shadow depicts the rise and fall of the hilly terrain while the brightly lit valley draws the eye, which also helps to give the image depth and impact.**

**1-stop (0.3) neutral density graduated filter**

**Polarizer (fully polarized)**

- **A combination of a polarizer and 1-stop ND graduated filter were used to enrich the sky and prevent it from being overexposed. The polarizer has also enhanced colour and contrast in the landscape.**

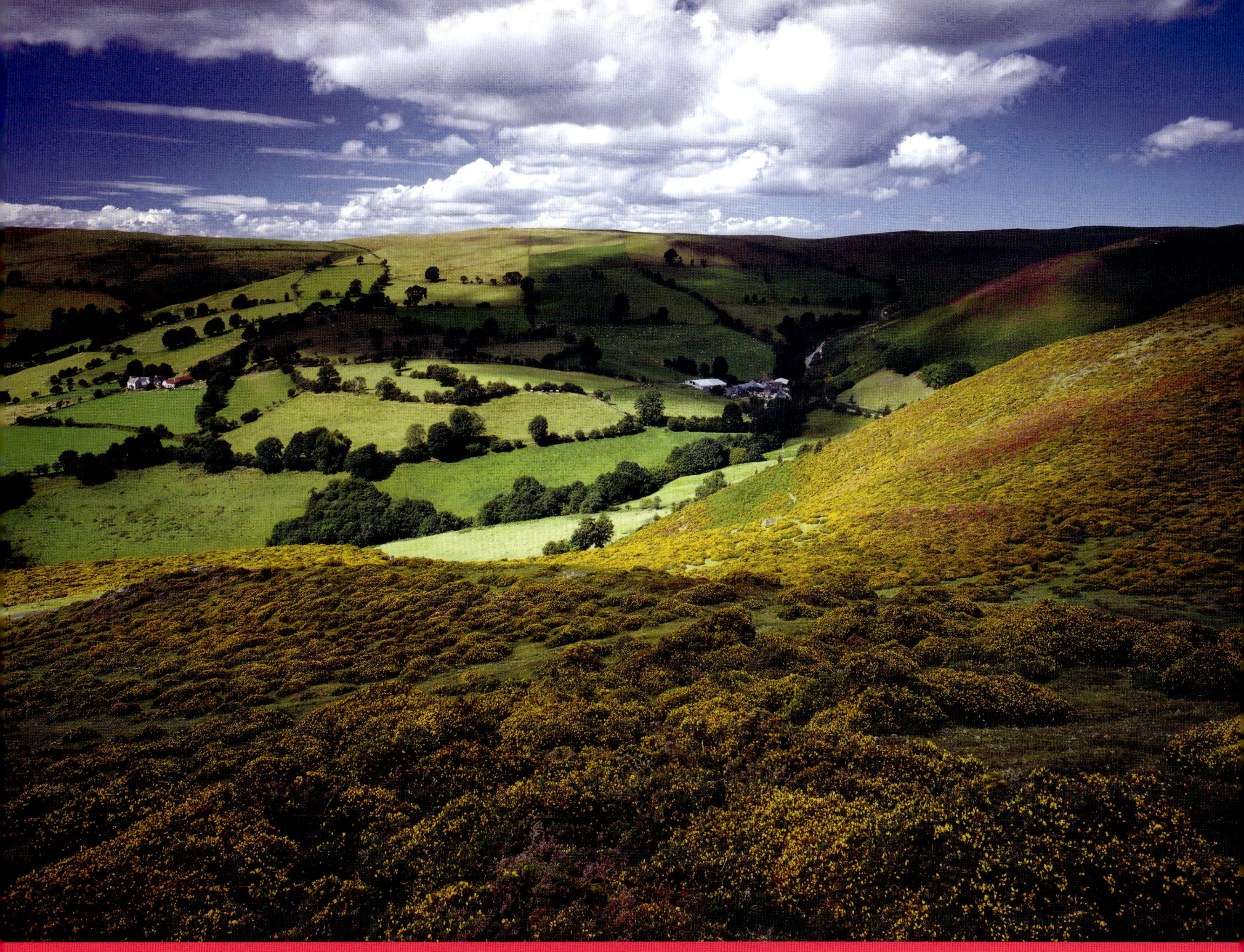

**Llantysilio, Clwyd, Wales**

**Camera:** Mamiya 645 AFDII with Mamiya digital back
**Lens:** Mamiya 35mm (wide-angle)
**Filter:** 1-stop ND graduated, polarizer (fully polarized)
**Exposure:** 1/4sec at f/22, ISO 100
**Waiting for the light:** 2 hours
**Post-processing:** Curves and colour balance adjustment (warming)

The quality of light can have a profound effect on the impact of an image. Your composition might be planned with meticulous care but if the light you use is anything less than perfect it will weaken the appearance of your photograph.

Light is of supreme importance; it is your most powerful tool and can often act as a catalyst and the inspiration for making an image. I have lost count of the number of times when the light has been so captivating I have been catapulted into a frantic search to find a viewpoint that makes the most of the heaven-sent opportunity. By nature, I don't like to waste anything and light is certainly no exception. I will do everything possible to avoid missing the magical moment, but it can be frustrating because where light is concerned we are always working against the clock.

In the picture opposite it was the sight of the spotlit tree that spurred me into action. It was important that a viewpoint and a successful composition were found quickly because the light would have soon been clipping the background mountain. So, as is often the case, it was a race against time. It was fortunate that a winding river was perfectly situated to enable a picture to be built around its flowing waters. With a quick scramble down its bank I was able to position my tripod in the river (this can be precarious!) and use the splashing water as a foreground that leads the eye onto the middle ground and the brightly lit tree. Everything then fell into place quite naturally and there is nothing in this photograph that I would change. It was a rare moment of perfection and there was little to do other than release the shutter. It was one of those unexpected, special moments that makes the pursuit of landscape photography so rewarding and it will remain with me for ever.

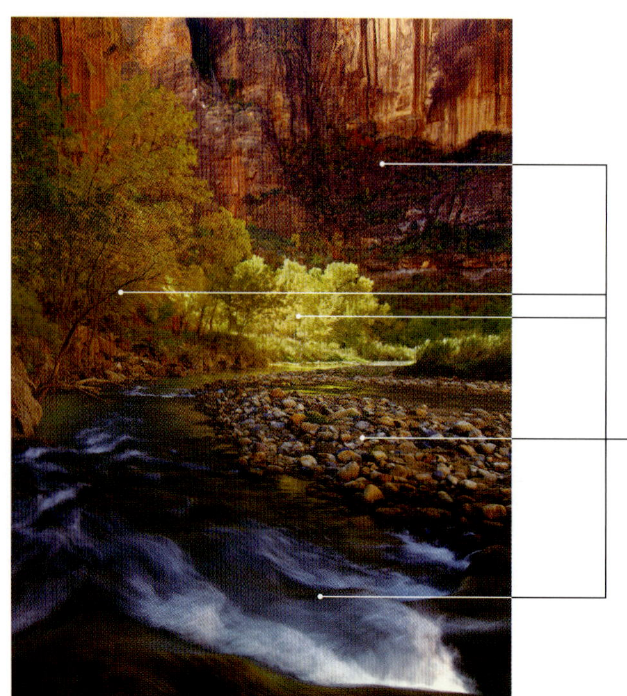

• **The impact in this picture is a result of the splash of sunlight falling only on the single tree. It is also because of the arrangement of the elements and the omission of dead space. Every part of this image – the river, stones, trees and mountain – all make an important contribution and strengthen the visual impact.**

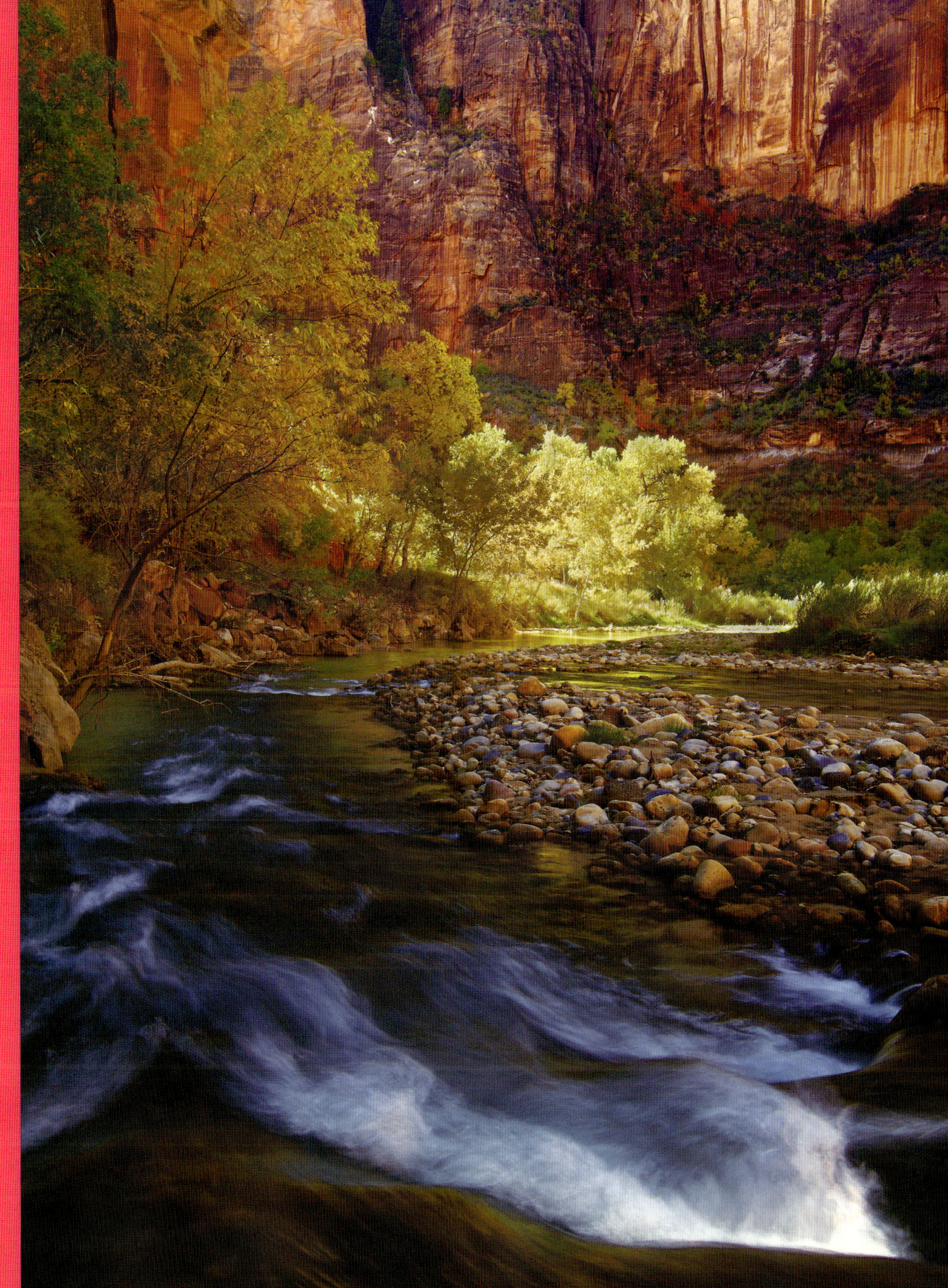

**Zion National Park,
Utah, USA**

**Camera:** Mamiya 645 AFDII
with Mamiya back
**Lens:** Mamiya 35mm
(wide-angle)
**Filter:** None
**Exposure:** 1/2sec at f/22,
ISO 100
**Waiting for the light:** Immediate
**Post-processing:** Curves
adjustment, colour balance
adjustment (warming)

Reflections on still water are a compelling sight and will always add impact. They are a beautiful source of repetition and can form the basis of quite stunning, memorable photographs. They also create balance in a composition, both vertically and horizontally, and are therefore a great aid to image-making.

Where reflections form a large part of a picture it is quite possible that there will be no requirement for foreground because the main subject's reflection can be used to fill the lower half of the composition. This is particularly the case where scattered cloud is present, because the reflected sky can act as the foreground. Having said that, the presence of a small number of supporting features – an obvious example being rocks and boulders in a lake – will help to distinguish between the two halves of the photograph. Success is not dependent upon an absolutely flawless mirror image and in fact this can sometimes weaken a picture. It can be unsettling to view an image and not be certain that you are looking at it the right way up. The presence of just a few small features in the foreground will prevent this uncertainty and will also add visual weight and interest to the lower part of the photograph.

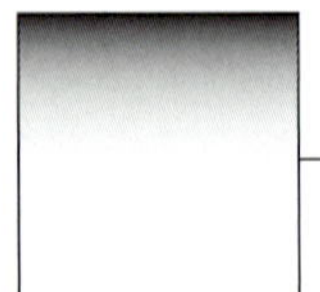

**1-stop (0.3) neutral density graduated filter**

- A combination of a 1-stop ND graduated filter and a half strength polarizer was used to balance the light values of the sky and water and the mountain and its reflection.

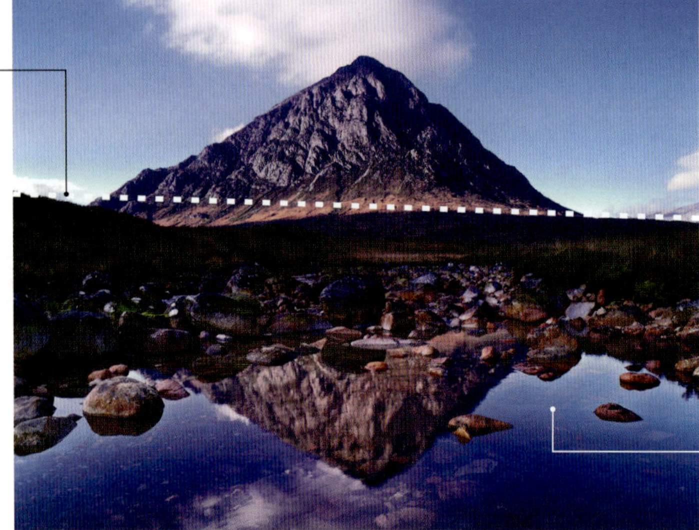

**Polarizer (half polarized)**

- The presence of rocks in the foreground water adds an additional element of interest to the lower portion of the picture.

> **TIP:** Water doesn't need to be perfectly still to create impact. A slightly impaired reflection will often bring an added dimension to an image. A hint of breeze does not, therefore, necessarily mean that a picture will fail.

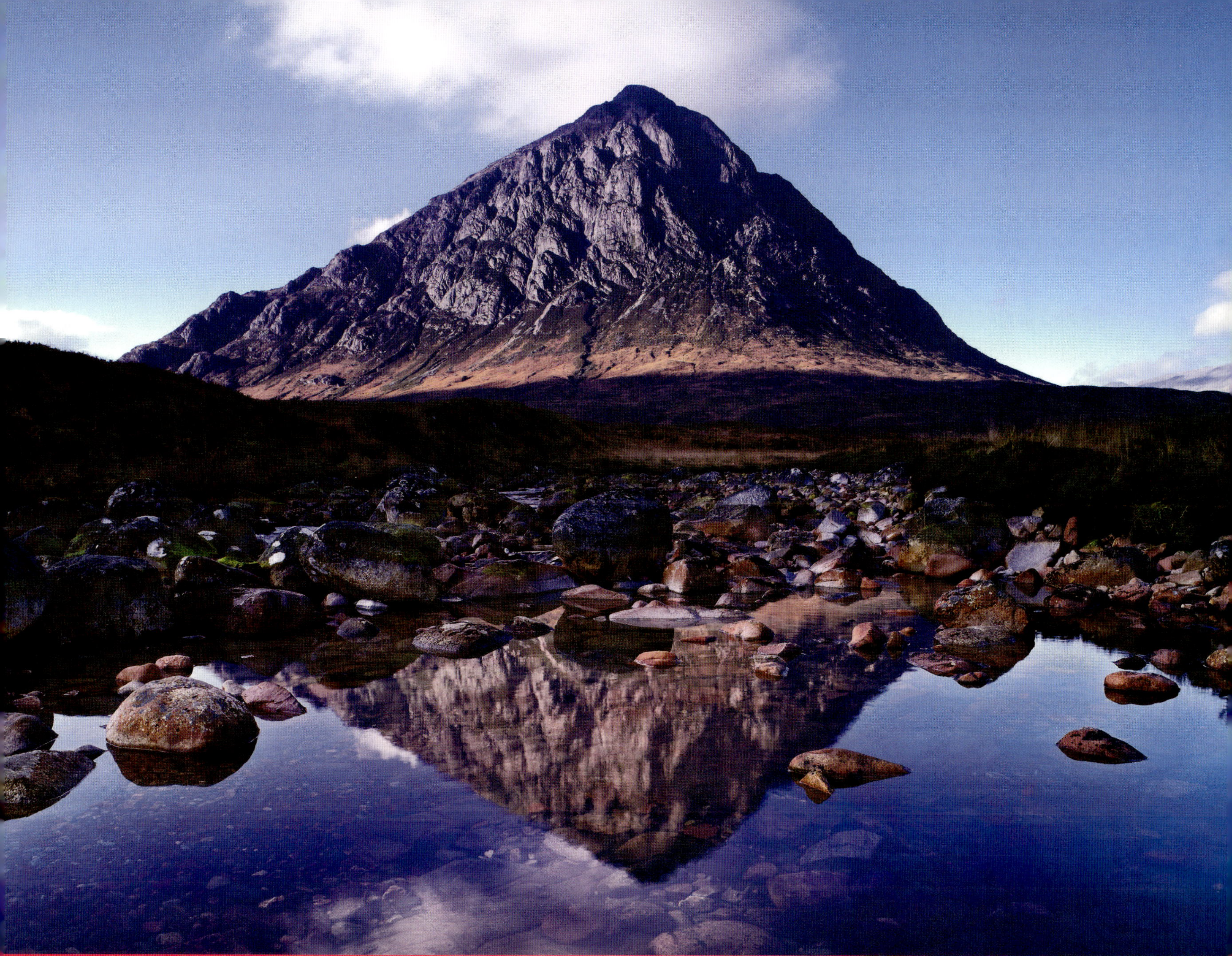

**Buachaillie Etive Mor, The Highlands, Scotland**

**Camera:** Mamiya 645 AFDII with Mamiya digital back
**Lens:** Mamiya 35mm (wide-angle)
**Filter:** 1-stop ND graduated, polarizer (half polarized)
**Exposure:** 1/4sec at f/22, ISO 100
**Waiting for the light:** 5 days
**Post-processing:** Curves and colour balance adjustment (warming)

The film director Woody Allen once said that 80 per cent of success is simply showing up and, while it might have originally been intended as a humorous observation, the principle certainly holds true in the context of landscape photography. To have any chance of succeeding in the attainment of your goals you have to be there, in the right place, waiting and hoping for that perfect moment.

Time and time again you have to show up, just in case the right conditions materialize, and it is the persistent photographer who ultimately is the successful photographer. I was reminded of the Woody Allen quote while making the fifth journey in as many days to the tantalizingly beautiful Loch Nah Achlaise, located in the remote but equally beautiful Rannoch Moor.

It is a rugged, dramatic landscape with weather to match. The climate can be capricious, with wind and rain virtually a constant threat – precisely what you don't want when photographing a lake. If a view of the loch was to be successfully captured it was likely to be a long haul. It was therefore a great relief when day five of what had practically become a vigil dawned bright and calm. After a quick dash to a pre-selected viewpoint it was at long last possible to make several exposures before a breeze began to ruffle the water's surface. Altogether I had been monitoring the weather for ten days when finally the elements all fell into place. It had been a frustrating marathon but that was the price to be paid, because impact doesn't come easily. You have to keep watching and waiting and, of course, showing up.

**> TIP:** The presence of reflections on water will always improve impact. A lake is likely to be at its calmest at, or just after, dawn when there is often little wind.

• A polarizer can sometimes over-darken an image, particularly areas of deep blue. In this photograph the foreground grasses have prevented this and have also added weight and impact to the foreground.

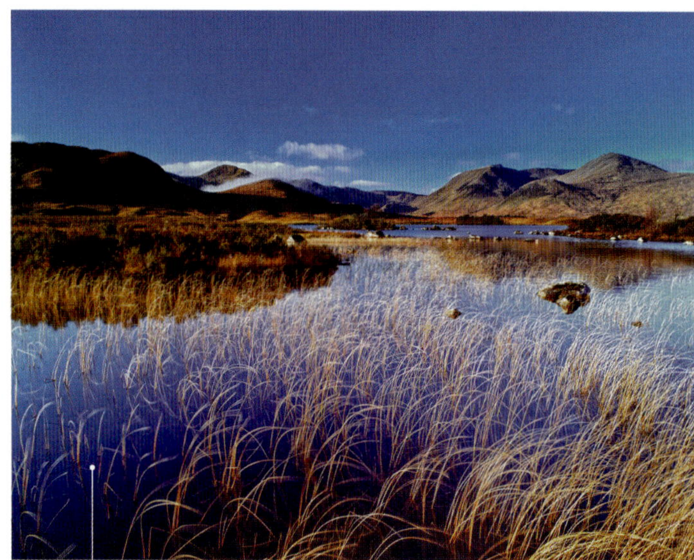

**Polarizer (fully polarized)**

**> TIP:** Use a polarizer to strengthen reflections on a lake's surface. The filter will reduce highlights and improve the clarity of the water. A blue sky's colour will also be enhanced by being polarized.

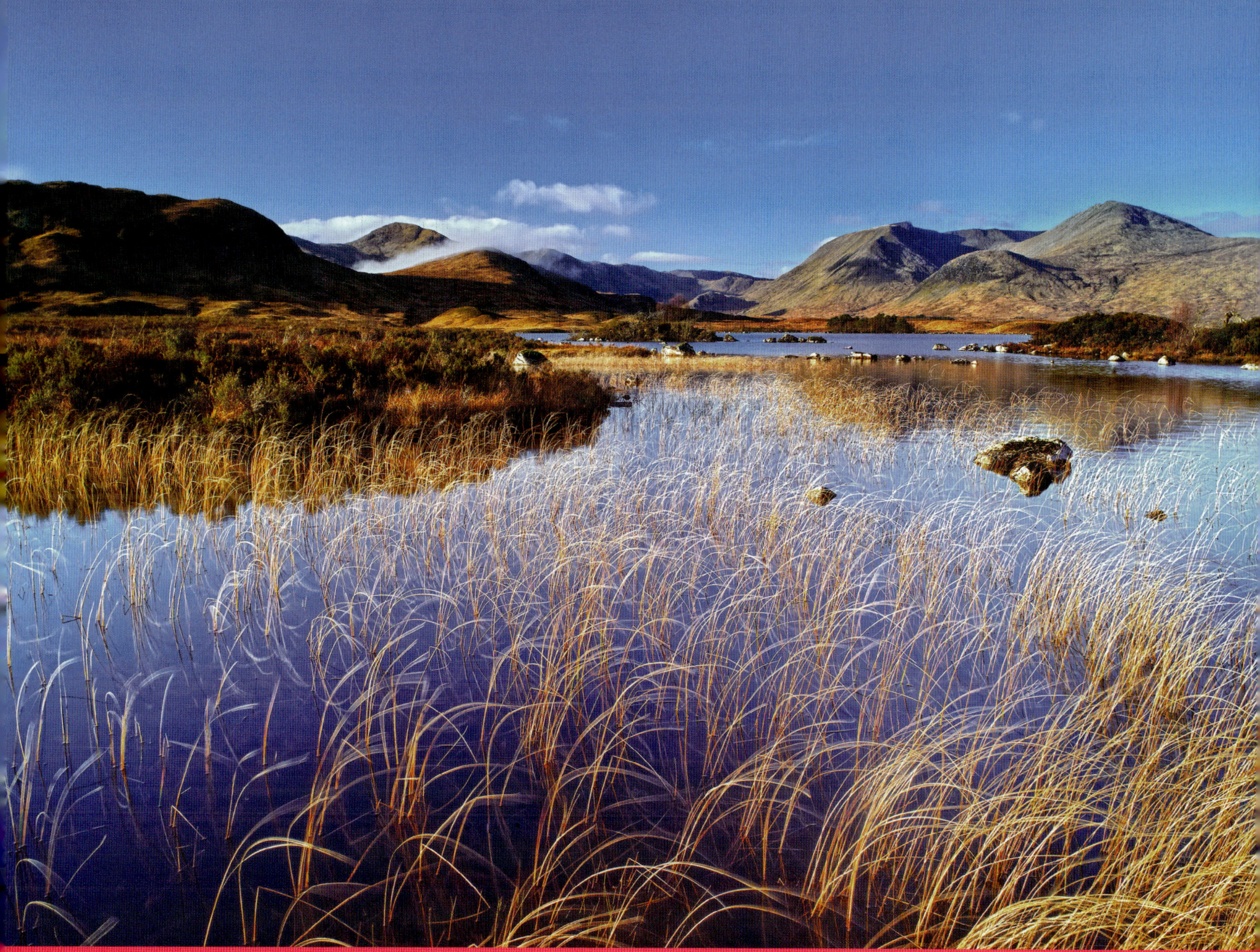

**Loch Nah Achlaise, Rannoch Moor, Scotland**

**Camera:** Mamiya 645 AFDII with Mamiya digital back
**Lens:** Mamiya 35mm (wide-angle)
**Filter:** Polarizer (fully polarized)
**Exposure:** 1/2sec at f/22, ISO 100
**Waiting for the light:** 5 days
**Post-processing:** Curves adjustment

A natural and very effective source of impact is the sky. Indeed, apart from perhaps light itself, the sky is the element most likely to grab a viewer's attention and induce an emotional response. As an impact-creating device it is unequalled, and it therefore pays dividends to remain aware at all times of what is happening above you.

This was certainly the case as two fellow photographers and I were approaching the end of a winter's day in the area around Hadrian's Wall in Northumberland. The weather had been disappointing and our image count for the day was sitting at zero. With the light beginning to fade we were a little downhearted but, peering at the sky for what was likely to be the last time that day, it became apparent that the stubborn blanket of cloud that had ruined our plans was starting to fragment. We drove to an elevated position for a better view and from there could see that the horizon was clear. The cloud was definitely dissipating so there was at least a possibility that the day was going to end on a memorable note. The challenge now was to find a location with an aspect that suited the direction of the light at this late hour.

We had passed a solitary tree in a field a couple of miles back and could see from the map that there was a good chance it could be photographed as a backlit silhouette. Leafless trees make attractive silhouettes so, with the possibility of a sunset now in our thoughts, we dashed back to the field and arrived just as the sky was beginning to reach its peak. With not a second to spare equipment was rapidly set up and several exposures made before the sky faded. It had been a close call and we had been fortunate, but without the continual sky-watching the opportunity would have undoubtedly been missed.

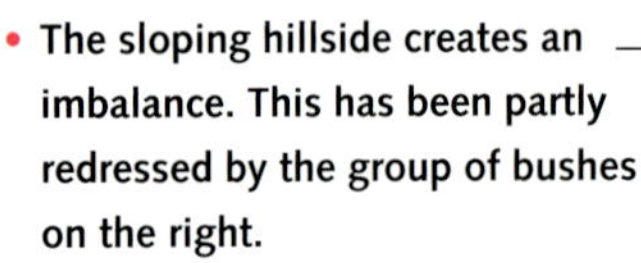

> **TIP:** When you are searching for images think of the sky as well as the landscape. Look up as frequently as you look in any other direction.

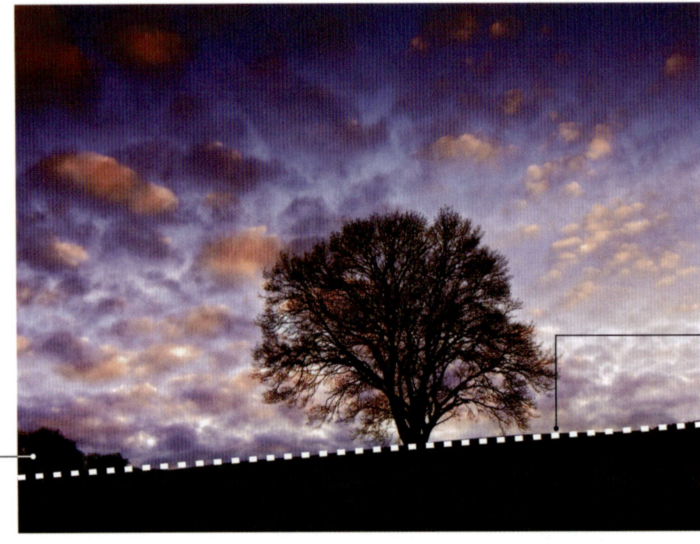

2-stop (0.6) neutral density graduated filter

• The sloping hillside creates an imbalance. This has been partly redressed by the group of bushes on the right.

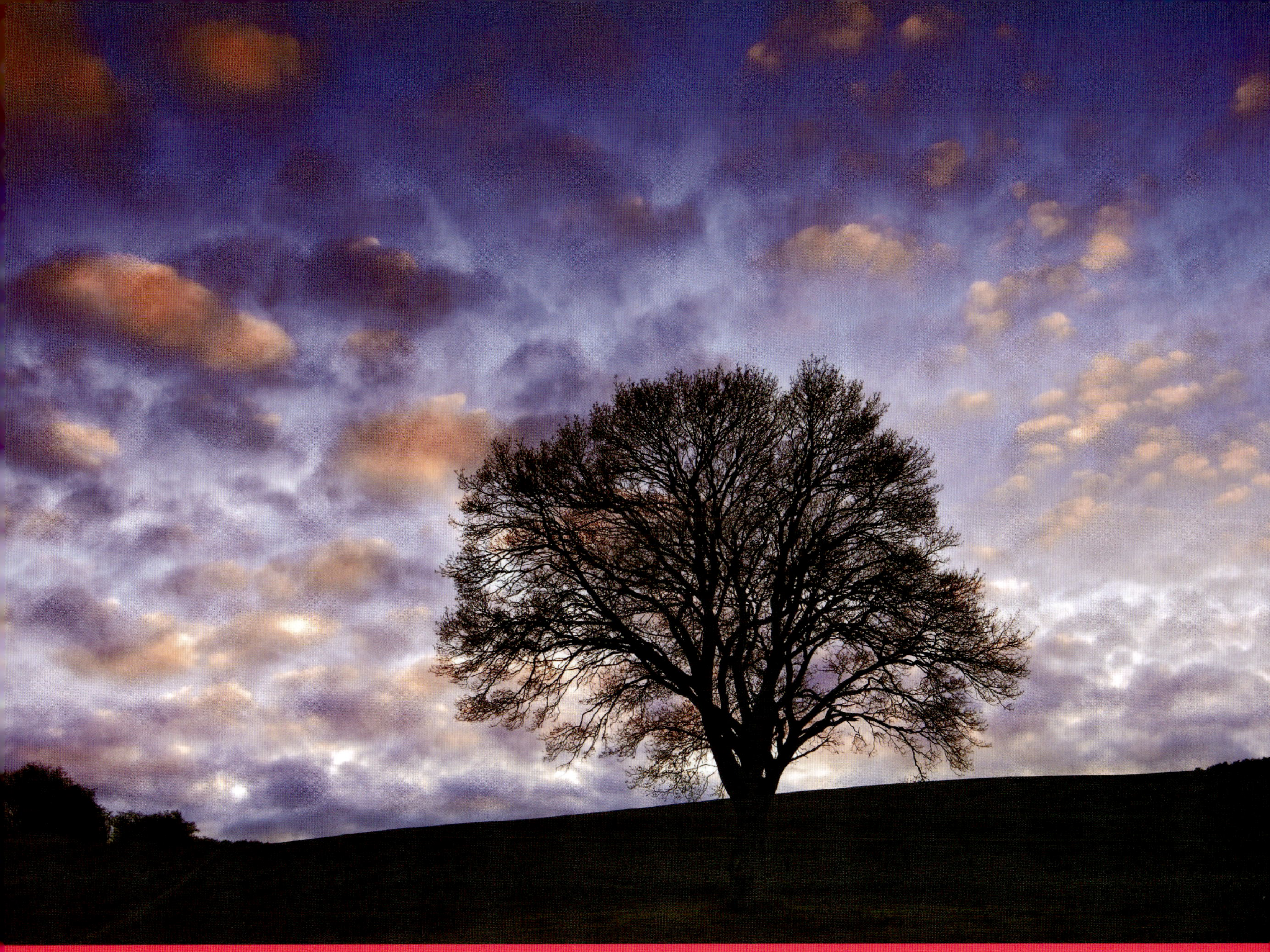

**Near Fourstones, Northumberland, England**

**Camera:** Mamiya 645 AFDII with Mamiya digital back
**Lens:** Mamiya 35mm (wide-angle)
**Filter:** 2-stop ND graduated
**Exposure:** 1sec at f/22, ISO 100
**Waiting for the light:** Immediate
**Post-processing:** Reduction of highlights and colour balance adjustment (warming)

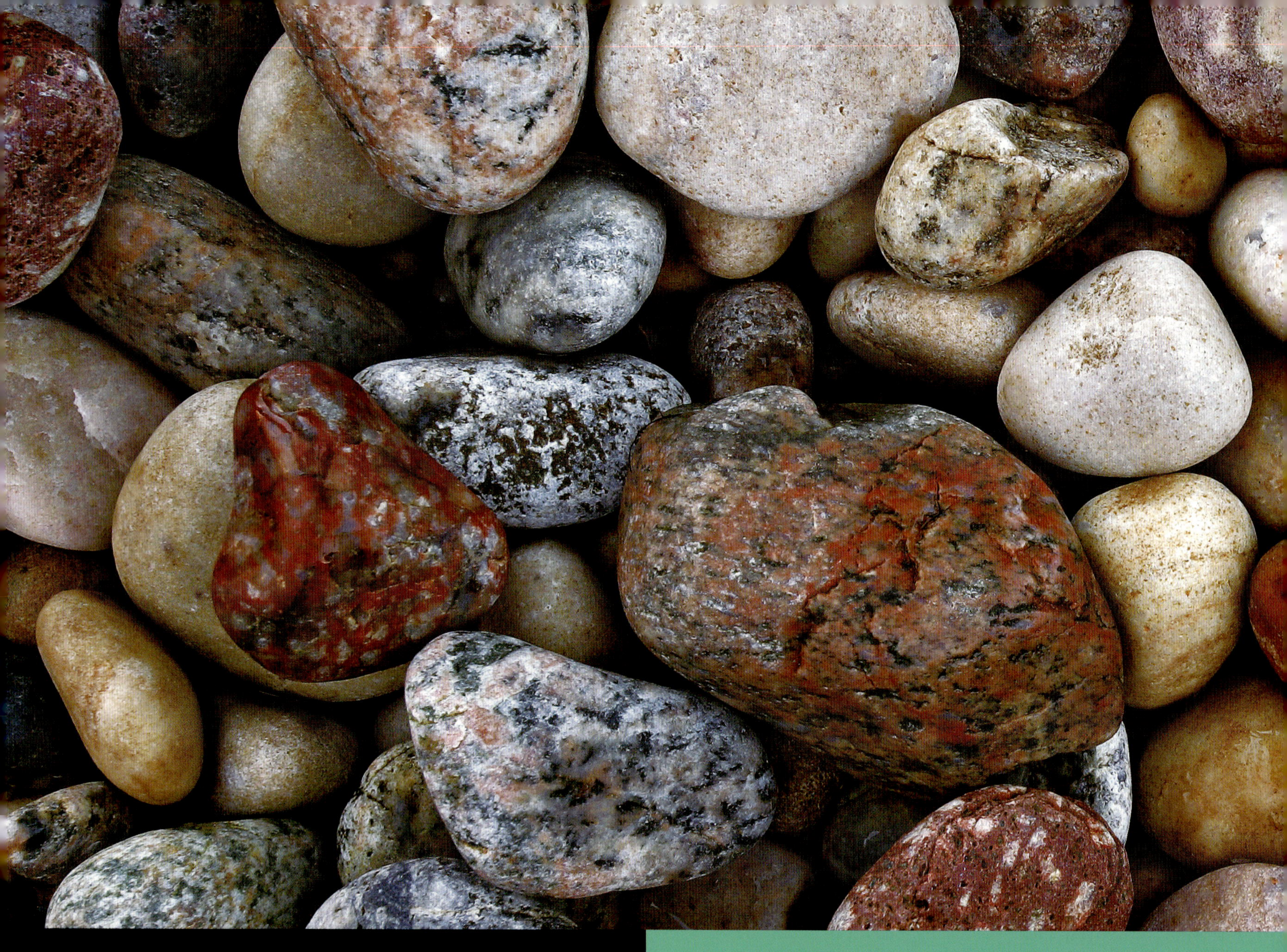


Chapter Eight  ▶  CLOSE-UP IMAGES

Lochinver Bay, Sutherland, Scotland

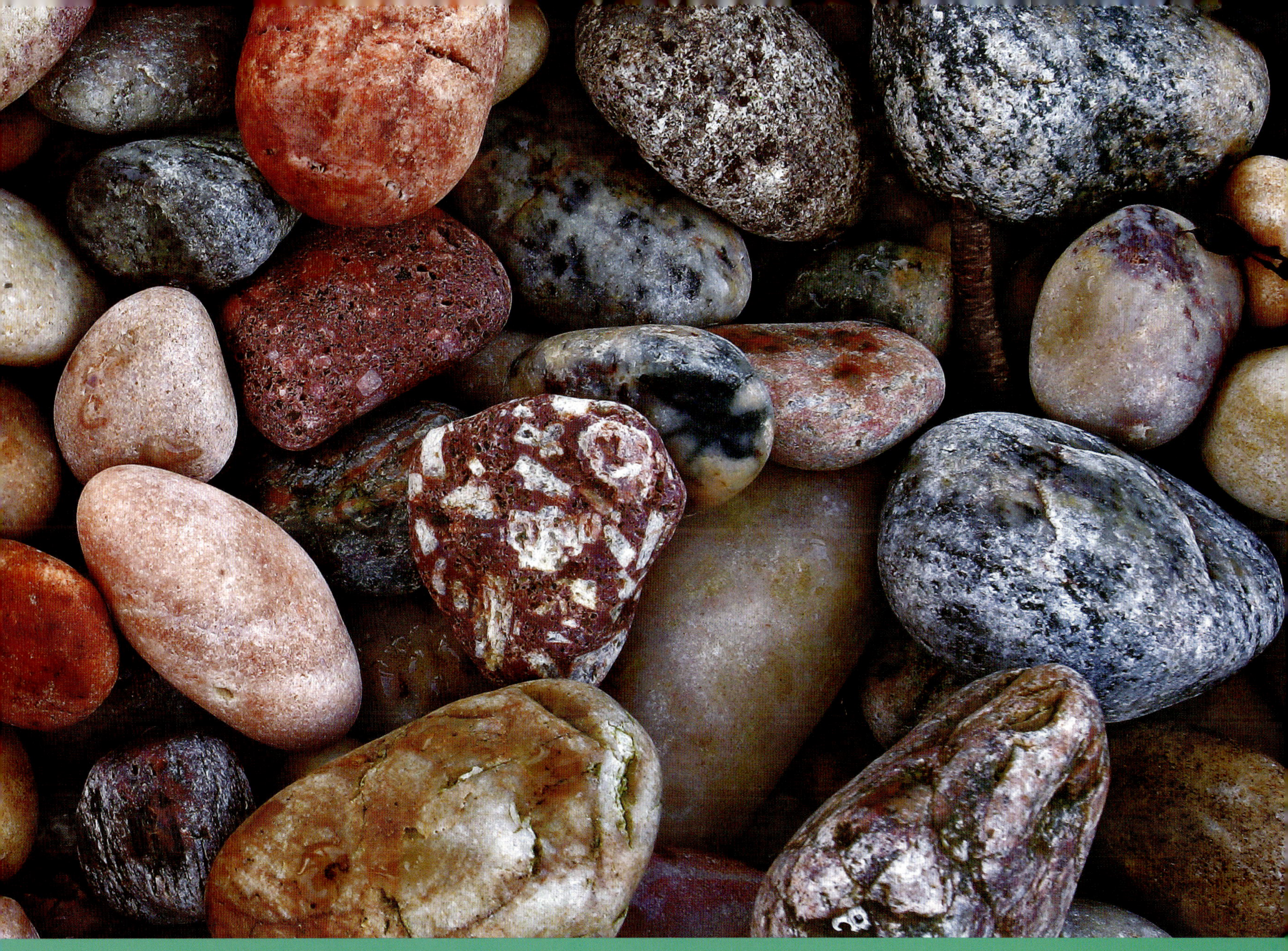

Viewing the natural world in close-up is like stepping into a whole new dimension. Suddenly the building blocks of nature become visible and reveal themselves to be intricate configurations of patterns, colours and textures. From a photographer's perspective this miniature world is another landscape, one that offers endless opportunity for creative and original image-making. Step into this world, observe its intricate beauty and you should be rewarded with many fine and distinctive photographs.

The key to capturing successful close-up images is observation. Potential subjects are everywhere but they must of course be discovered before they can be photographed. It is easy, particularly when you are surrounded by a magnificent landscape, to ignore what at first glance are mundane, everyday objects. However, the medium of photography has a unique and quite magical ability to transform the ordinary into striking pieces of visual art, particularly with small-scale compositions.

When viewed as a photograph the intricate patterns and minute details of colour and texture of what might appear to be unspectacular objects suddenly become apparent. These are features that, when buried in their normal environment, the eye tends to skim over and ignore, but as soon as they are isolated from their surroundings and presented as a piece of art a miraculous transformation takes place and you have before you a distinctive, aesthetically pleasing image.

Look very carefully at all possible subjects, think about the small as well as the large and look at the landscape in terms of patterns, flowing lines and curves. The natural world is, on a small scale, a haven of picture-making opportunities; seek them out and you will be rewarded with many fine photographs.

• **Curved lines always photograph well. In this image both the background and main subject consist of curves and this makes an aesthetically pleasing arrangement. The repetition of the softly curved shapes also strengthens the picture and adds interest to the lower portion.**

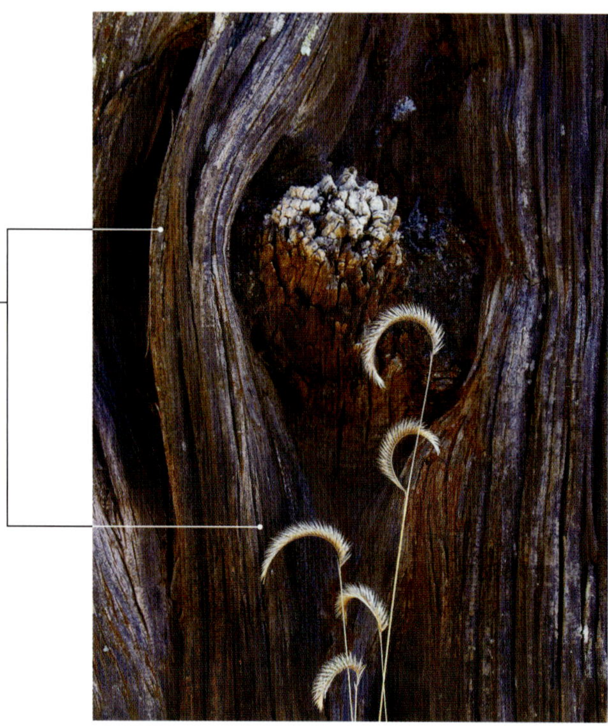

> **TIP:** Look for combinations of an interesting background and a simple, easily discernible subject of a restricted tonal range. Simplicity of colour will then allow the subtleties of shape and pattern to reveal themselves.

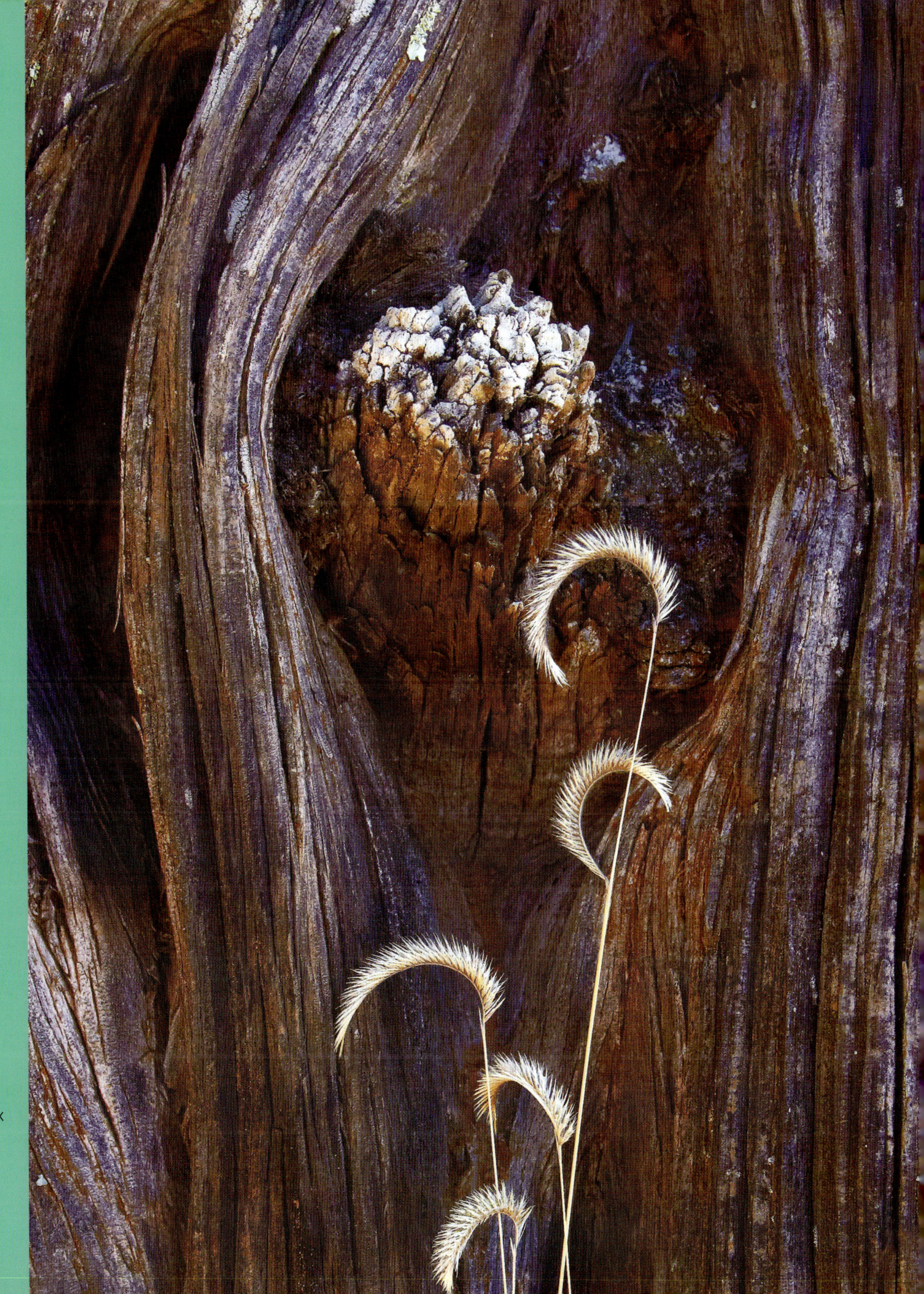

**Near Page, Arizona, USA**

**Camera:** Canon EOS 7D
**Lens:** Tokina 12–24mm AT-X PRO DX
**Filter:** None
**Exposure:** 1/30sec at f/9, ISO 100
**Waiting for the light:** Immediate
**Post-processing:** Curves adjustment

Overnight frost is usually a welcome sight for photographers because it creates many image-making opportunities. From open vistas to close-up subjects, the presence of frost brings an added dimension to the landscape and nowhere is this more apparent than on the delicate surface of winter leaves. A thin coating of ice can bring about a transformation that elevates all types of foliage to enable them to become striking visions of small-scale nature.

It was therefore with a sense of optimistic anticipation that I visited an area of local woodland after heavy overnight frost to search for pictures. But I was also cautious because potential subjects have to be closely scrutinized when being captured close-up, as flaws and blemishes, once photographed, will become painfully obvious and can ruin an image. Over-enthusiasm is likely to lead to disappointment and a feeling that an opportunity was missed. A slow, considered approach should therefore be adopted and a critical appraisal made of the possible subject before you commit to making an exposure.

Having discarded several possibilities I took the picture opposite after an hour of searching and foraging. The decision to make this image was partly influenced by the shaded background as it enabled composition to be built around a central group of more brightly lit, heavily frosted, but colourful leaves. The arrangement works well and the combination of light and shadow has given the photograph a three-dimensional appearance. It is therefore most regrettable that the image suffers from too much depth of field. In large-scale pictures maximum depth of field is usually desirable but this does not always apply to close-up subjects. Here the background, although out of focus, is still too sharp. I should have used a wider aperture and reduced the depth of field. It was a mistake and the image has suffered as a result. It was undoubtedly a wasted opportunity.

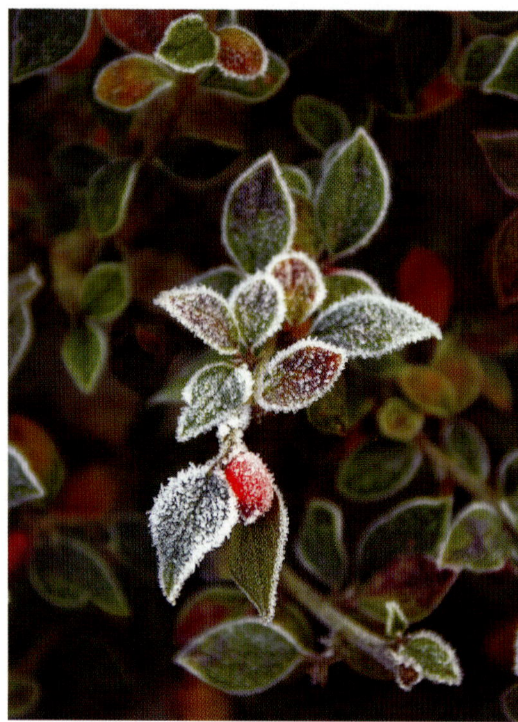

• The contrast between the background and the central group of leaves is the important element. The subdued area encourages the eye to be drawn to the centre of the image. A softer, less clearly defined background, would have also helped in this respect.

> **TIP:** Examine foliage carefully when making close-up images. What seem to be minor blemishes or damage will become starkly apparent once photographed.

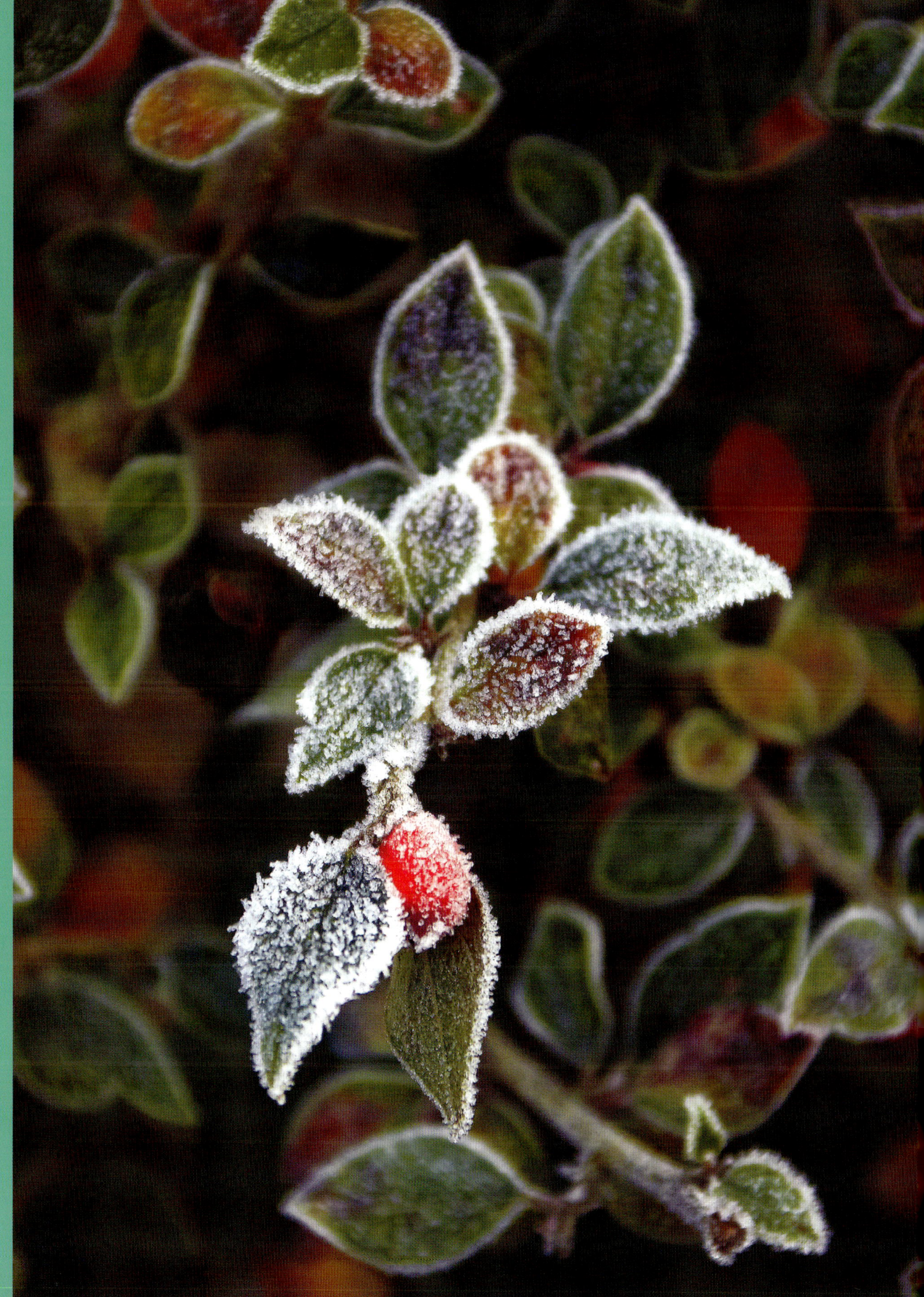


Thurstaston, The Wirral
Peninsula, England

Camera: Canon EOS 7D
Lens: Canon 24–105mm L IS
Filter: None
Exposure: 1/8sec at f/13, ISO 100
Waiting for the light: Immediate
Post-processing: Suppression
of highlights, colour balance
adjustment (warming)

A casual glance at a farm building brought me to an abrupt and unexpected stop along a remote track in the hills above the west coast of Portugal. A warehouse packed to bursting point with enormous pumpkins is an unusual and arresting sight; it was a most compelling spectacle and I simply had to take a closer look. There was no doubt that there was an image to be captured. All I had to do was ask the bemused farmer, who was peering at me from his tractor, for permission. Eventually, after overcoming the language barrier and explaining that, no, I didn't want to buy any produce, I was charitably given free rein of the warehouse.

Resisting the urge to act like a child in a toy shop and run amok through the narrow aisles, I stood back and assessed my subject. Abstract, close-up images were an option and I experimented with a number of small-scale compositions, but the picture that was most appealing – and which ultimately proved to be the most successful – was a wider view of an unbroken expanse of the bountiful pumpkins. This arrangement is a combination of both close-up and distance and was achieved by using an ultra wide-angle lens positioned very close to the subject. This exaggerates depth and creates a strong three-dimensional appearance. Objects close to the camera will look relatively large but their scale will quickly diminish as they recede into the distance. This approach can be very successful when you wish to use repetition of shapes or patterns as an integral part of your composition.

> **TIP:** Use an ultra wide-angle lens to enhance depth and create striking compositions. For added impact, position your camera as close as possible to the subject and use a small aperture to produce maximum depth of field.

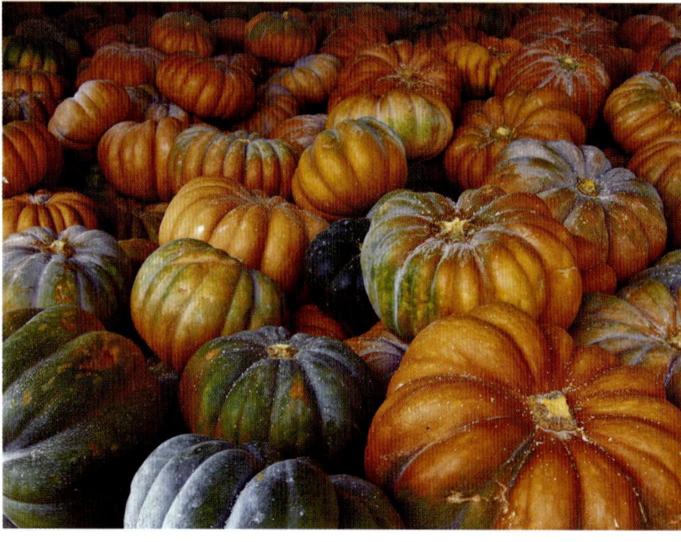

• **This type of picture contains no specific focal points. The eye is drawn to the distance because of the repetition of shapes of progressively diminishing size.**

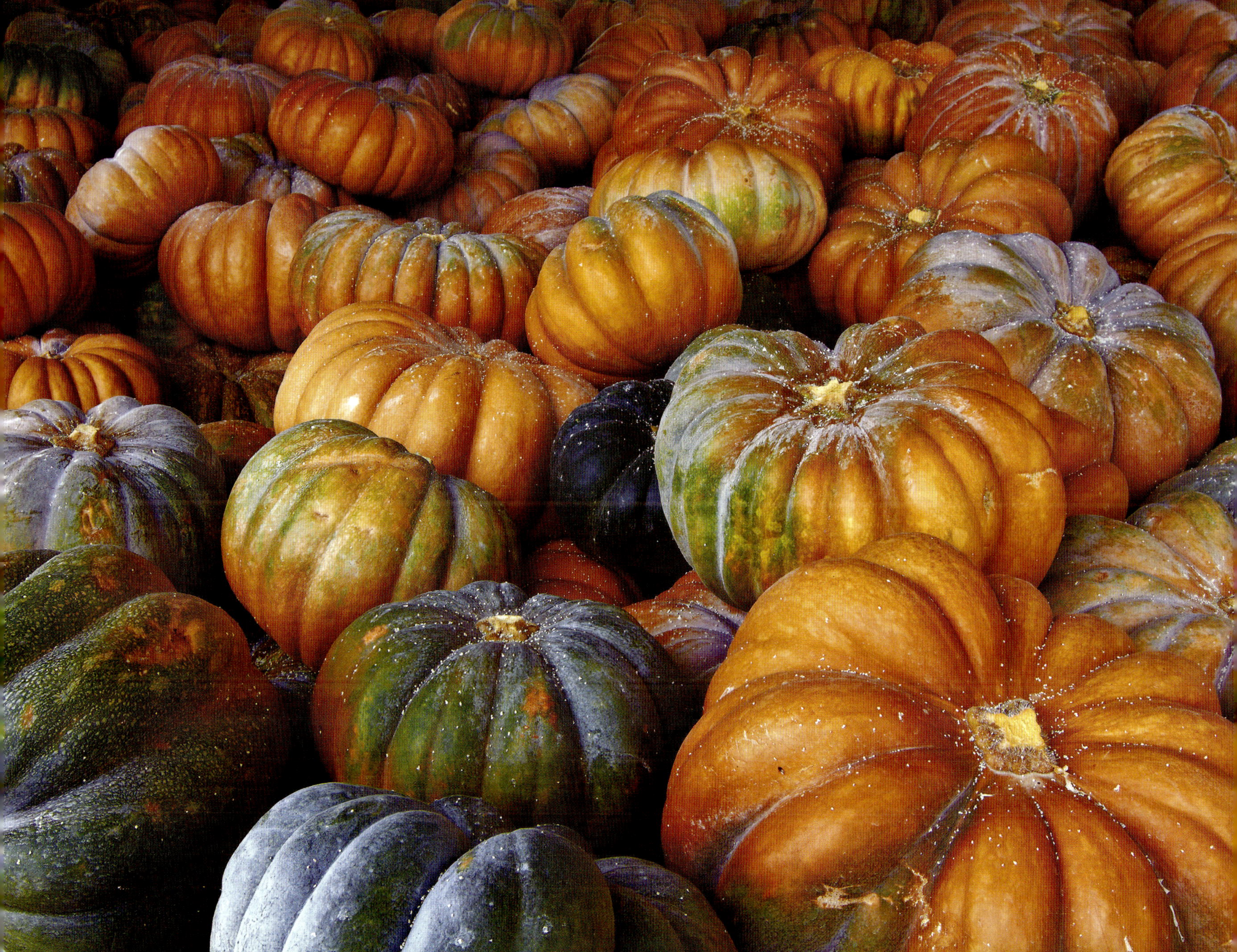

**Near Ferrel, Portugal**

**Camera:** Canon EOS 7D
**Lens:** Tokina 12–24mm AT-X PRO DX
**Filter:** None
**Exposure:** 1/4sec at f/11, ISO 100
**Waiting for the light:** Immediate
**Post-processing:** Curves adjustment, colour balance adjustment

Rivers can be an intriguing and potentially very rewarding source of close-up images. Water flowing over rocks creates what is effectively a series of mini-waterfalls, and these small-scale fusions of stillness and motion are worthy of assiduous scrutiny. Look carefully for combinations of colourful rocks and fast-flowing water. There should be tonal variety throughout the photograph, so large expanses of white water and dark rocks should if possible be avoided. Mid-range tones make the most successful pictures because they hold more visual interest than monotonous areas of white or black. The textured surfaces of weathered rock always make attractive subjects and, taking on the appearance of miniature islands surrounded by fast-flowing water, will act as attractive anchor points that will engage with the viewer.

Once the image has been composed, capturing it is relatively straightforward. Flat light from an overcast sky is preferable as there should be no highlights, other than the splashing water. To blur the water a shutter speed of between 1/2 and 2 seconds will be required. You will therefore need a solid tripod and, as finding a stable position for tripod legs can be difficult in a rocky, fast-flowing river, a zoom lens will be helpful because it will give you some flexibility in your choice of viewpoint. A polarizing filter will also be useful because it will reduce reflections on water-splashed rocks and improve the transparency of clear water, which will enhance tonal variation.

Polarizer (fully polarized)

• **The polarizer has suppressed reflections on the surfaces of the wet rocks and has improved the clarity of the water.**

• **This image was built around the protruding rock at the top of the picture. The use of a portrait format and a long focal length lens has tightened the composition and avoided areas of dead space.**

> **TIP:** Use a telephoto lens to isolate small parts of a river. The long focal length will compress distance and knit together elements in your composition. This will help to reduce static areas of a single tone.

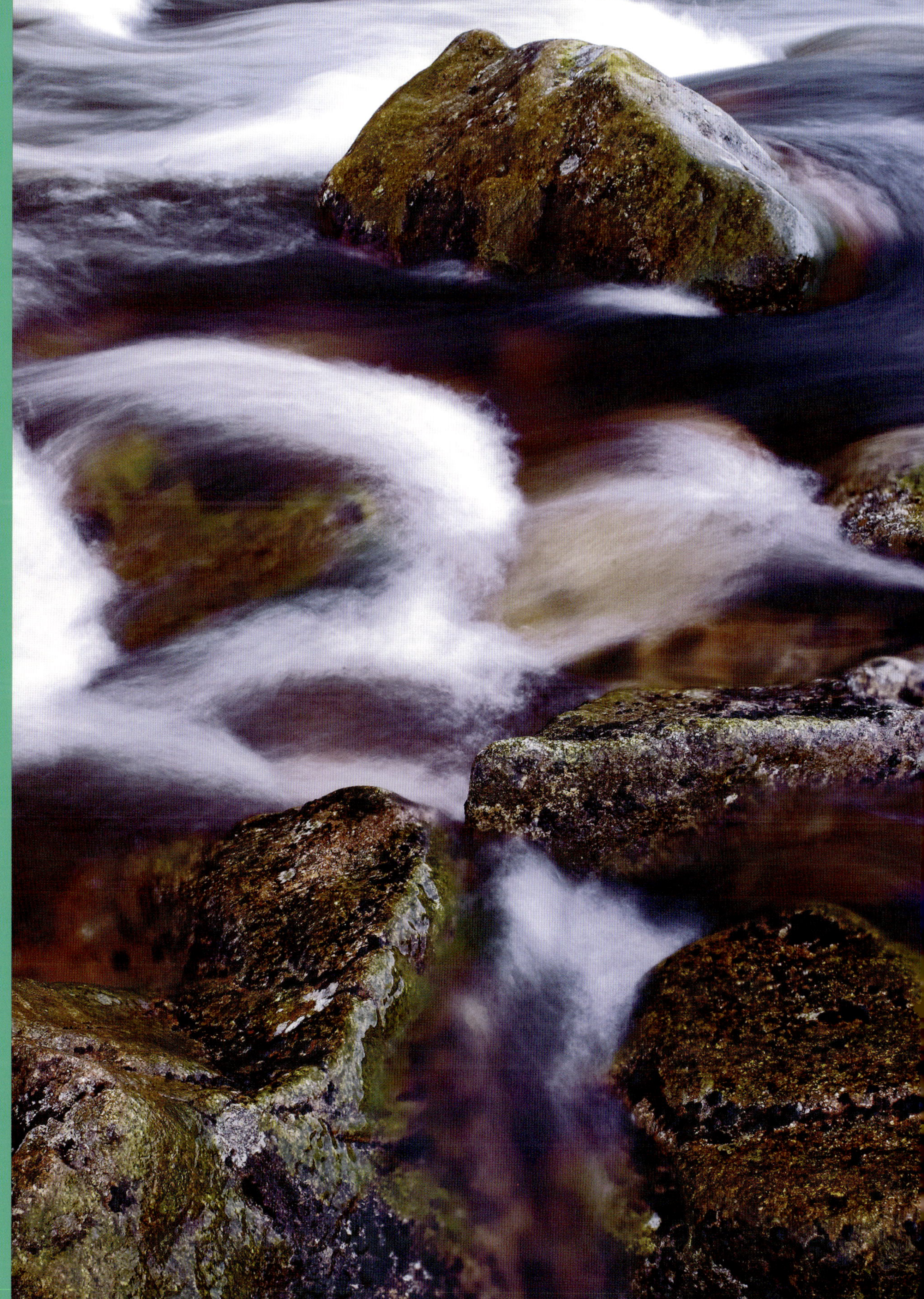

**The River Etive,
Rannoch Moor, Scotland**

**Camera:** Mamiya 645 AFDII
with Mamiya digital back
**Lens:** Mamiya 150mm (telephoto)
**Filter:** Polarizer (fully polarized)
**Exposure:** 1sec at f/22,
ISO 100
**Waiting for the light:** Immediate
**Post-processing:** Colour balance
adjustment (warming)

Leaves and tree bark can be an enticing combination. The contrasting colours of the two elements photograph well together and can give a picture strong visual impact, particularly when the composition is fairly simple. When using colour as a key feature in an image it is, as previously discussed, more effective to use a small number of clearly defined shapes that stand out against the background. Leaves are therefore an excellent subject because their textured, subtly varied surfaces invite close scrutiny and provide repetition of pattern and shape. They can therefore be used as strong points of interest against a more subdued background. In the picture opposite composition has been centred around a single strand of ivy leaves. The curved

shapes of the leaves enable them to fill the image both horizontally and vertically and, because there is just one ivy stem, there is no overlapping of shapes; therefore the outline of every leaf is clearly visible. I felt this was important because the background tree bark is strongly textured and variegated. It is visually demanding and to avoid creating a conglomeration of information, which would have overloaded the viewer, a simple arrangement was essential. The instantly recognizable, clearly defined ivy leaves and the irregularly surfaced bark complement each other and make a complete picture, which I hope portrays the small-scale detail of the character and beauty of a forest interior.

• Curved lines are pleasing to the eye. Composing an image around a curve will encourage the viewer to engage with the photograph and absorb detail.

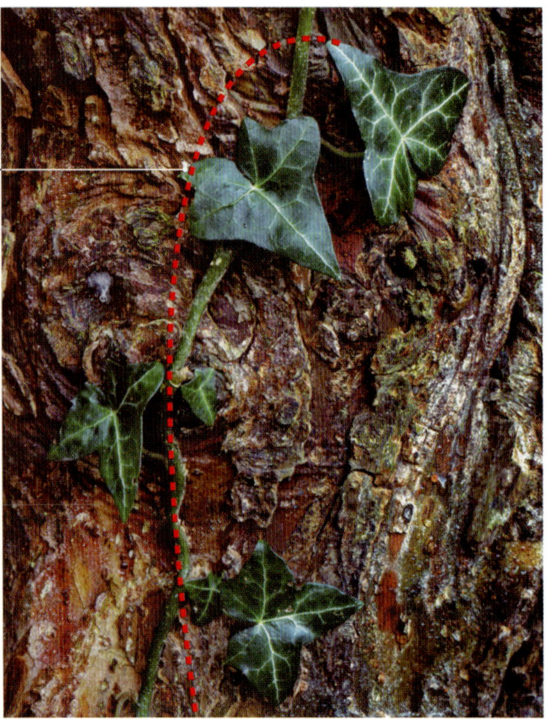

Polarizer (fully polarized)

> **TIP:**  Tree bark is unlikely to be flat so to ensure it is all in sharp focus you will need to use a small aperture. Forest interiors can be dark, so a long exposure will probably be necessary. A rigid tripod should therefore be used.

> **TIP:**  Use a polarizer to reduce reflections from the shiny surfaces of foliage. Even when no moisture is present highlights can dilute colour and contrast. A polarizer will reduce this and increase visual impact.

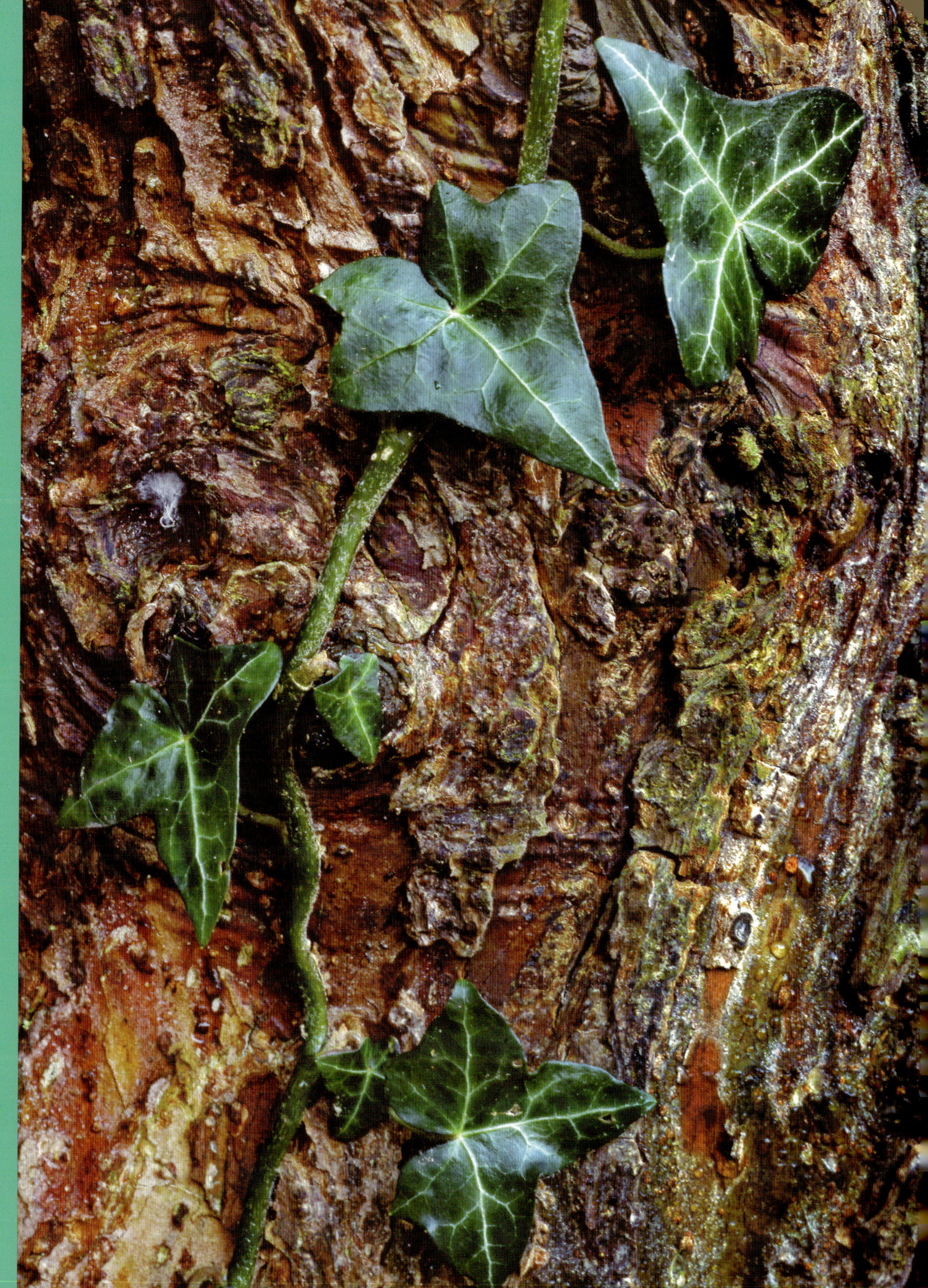

**Phoenicia Wild Forest,
New York State, USA**

**Camera:** Mamiya 645 AFDII with
Mamiya digital back
**Lens:** Mamiya 80mm (standard)
**Filter:** Polarizer (fully polarized)
**Exposure:** 1/2sec at f/22, ISO 100
**Waiting for the light:** Immediate
**Post-processing:** None

Although tree bark is an obvious choice for close-up photography its ubiquity means that you must be particularly discriminating in your selection process. The picture must have a distinctive quality if it is to avoid being seen as 'just another tree'. I have to admit that I no longer actively search for these images because setting out with a tree bark close-up in mind can lead to a second-best photograph simply because it was the best option available at that time. Instead I prefer to maintain an awareness when close to trees and take a closer look only if a piece of bark stands out and is particularly distinctive. Despite the attractions of the surrounding landscape I was drawn to this eroded trunk as a result of its finely varied tonal range and richly textured surface.

This type of subject responds to the camera because the fine details reproduce exceptionally well as photographs. Although close-up images of trees are, essentially, abstract pictures, there is usually no doubt in the viewer's mind about the origin of the photograph. This is sometimes to a picture's benefit because it enables it to be seen in context and the creative role the photographer has played in its making can be instantly recognized. Ubiquitous it might be but tree bark – the right tree bark – can make a fine addition to your portfolio.

> **TIP:** Tree bark and other similarly variegated subjects photograph well as close-up images. For best results composition should be kept simple by excluding background elements. Move in close (a zoom lens is particularly useful for this) or crop the image in post-processing to produce an image that, although varied in colour and texture, is easy to perceive and understand.

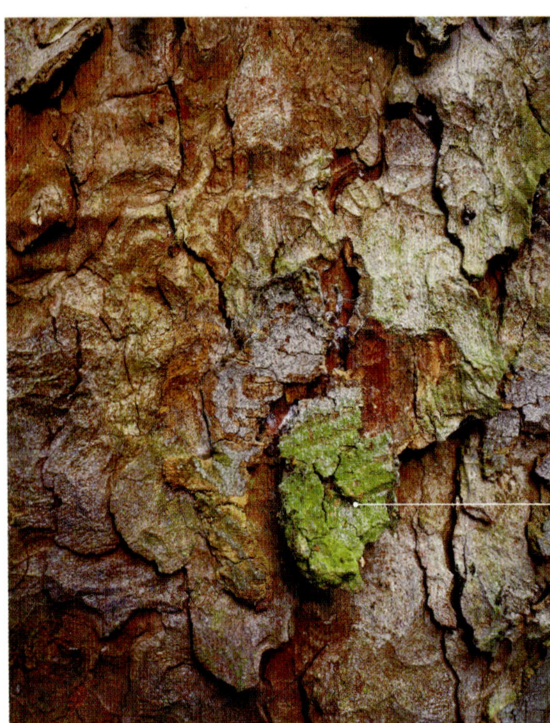

• Focal points are not essential with this type of picture but when they are present they can often create an additional element of interest. Applying the rule of thirds always accentuates the presence of any focal point and here it has been placed approximately two-thirds from the top and one-third from the left. This is a strong position and has enabled the rest of the picture to be composed around it.

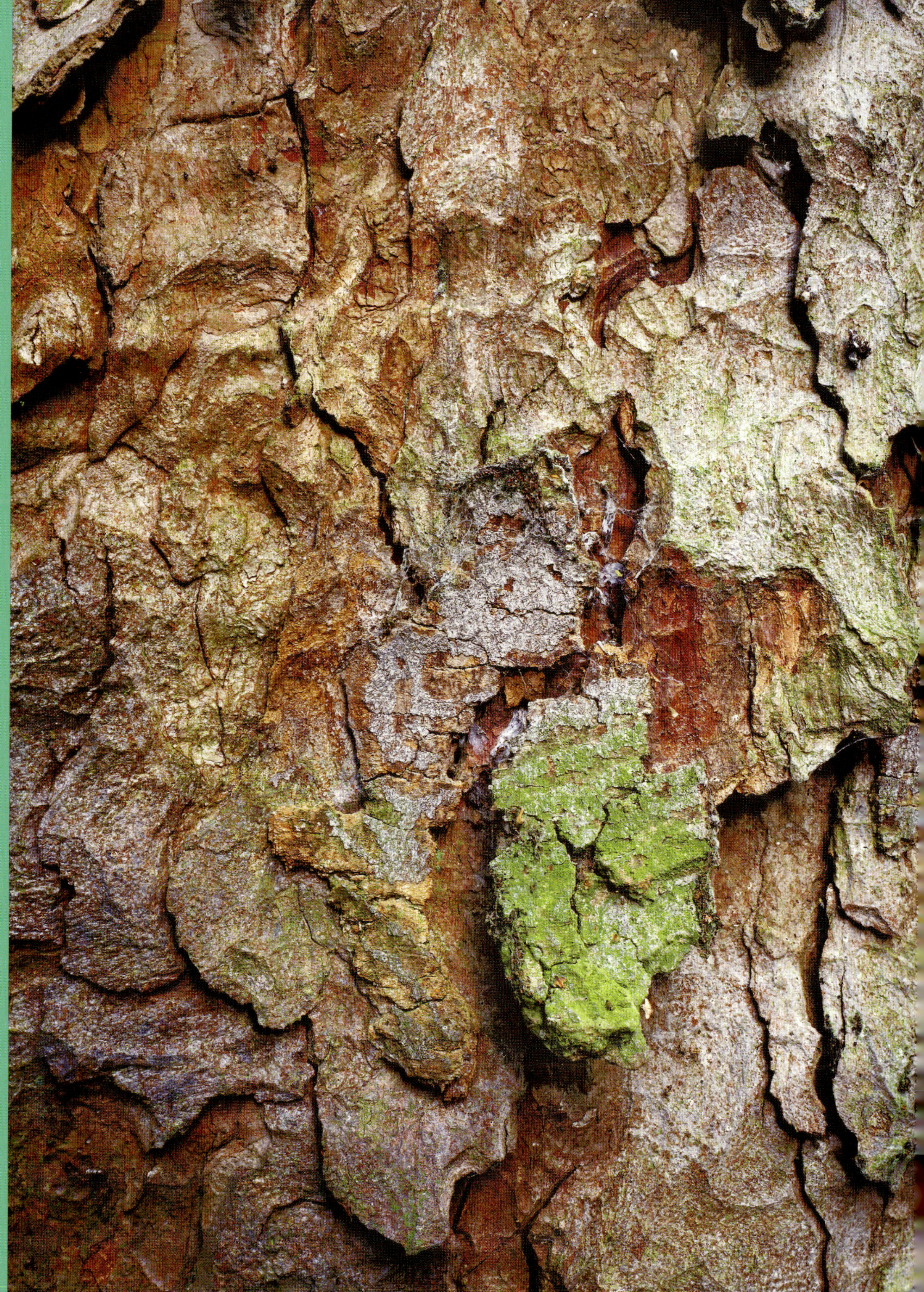


Indian Wilderness,
New York State, USA

Camera: Mamiya 645 AFDII
with Mamiya digital back
Lens: Mamiya 80mm (standard)
Filter: None
Exposure: 2sec at f/22, ISO 100
Waiting for the light: Immediate
Post-processing: None

I recently read a quotation by the painter Pablo Picasso and his wise words struck a chord. He is quoted as saying, 'There is no abstract art. You must always start with something. Afterwards you can remove all traces of reality.' I believe there is truth in this statement because in every landscape there is undoubtedly an abstract image hidden away, buried in reality.

All visual artists start with the same subject matter but, having seen the potential to make a picture, the paths of the painter and the photographer at that point begin to diverge. The painter builds on the opportunity by using reality as a catalyst for inspiration, whereas the photographer, because of the nature of the medium, captures what is actually there, in front of the camera. How reality is recorded is therefore the critical factor in the making of an abstract landscape image.

Choosing precisely the right composition is the key to success. Light is also important – it is for every photograph – but to make distinctive close-up images painstaking attention to detail and an almost microscopic inspection must be made to every part of the picture. My advice is to begin by deciding what you want to include and what to leave out. As a general rule, the simpler the arrangement, the better the photograph. Do not include anything that makes no positive contribution. 'When in doubt, leave it out' is a good rule to apply because in close-up images every pixel must count. There is no room for wasted space, so think carefully about the position and angle of your camera and the focal length of the lens you use. Zoom lenses now make life much easier and enable you to experiment with different compositions and learn by trial and error. Experience gained in this way is invaluable in the development of your photographer's eye.

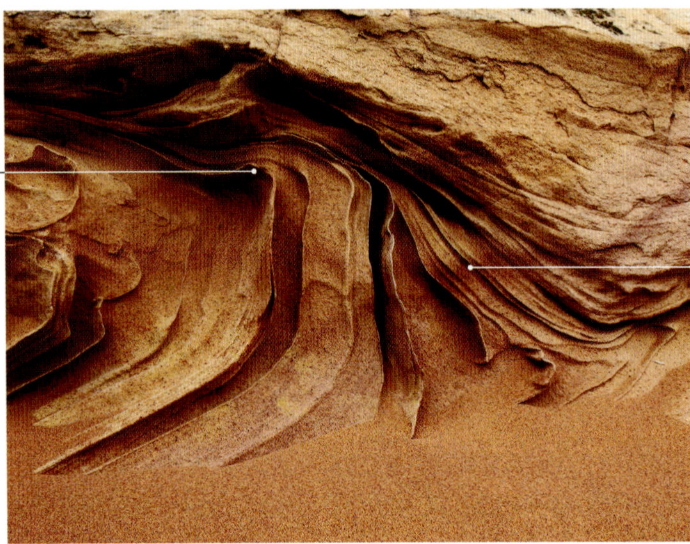

• The intricate detail of the rock face would have been lost in harsh light. I returned two hours after seeing the image to capture it as it fell into shadow. Even with the flat light there is still some soft contrast and this helps to reveal contour lines and shape without overpowering them.

• Composition was centred on a small section of folded rock. The distinct, sharp-edged creases make an interesting and unusual pattern, which is strengthened by being distinct from the surrounding formation.

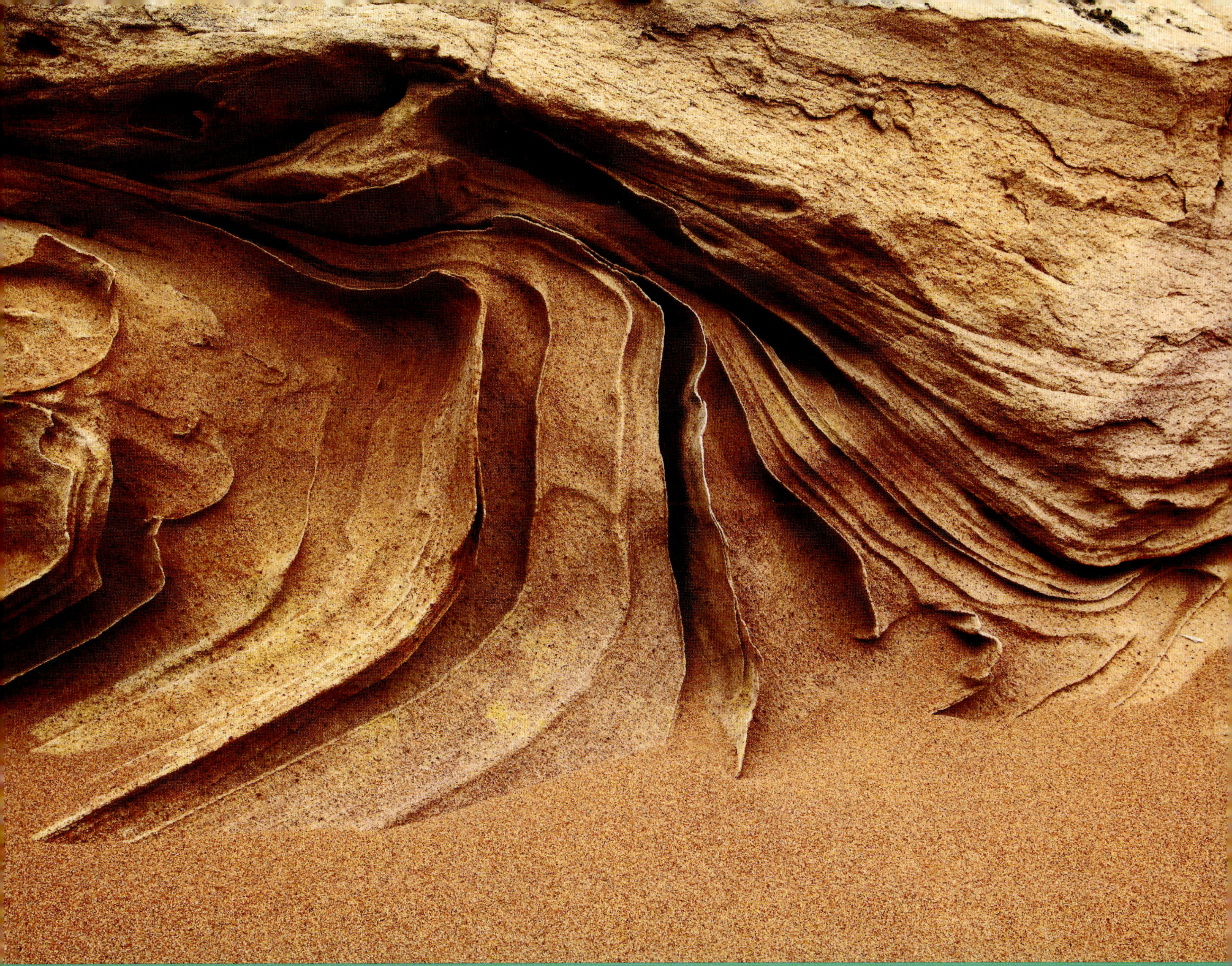

**South Coyote Buttes, Arizona, USA**

**Camera:** Mamiya 645 AFDII with Phase One digital back
**Lens:** Mamiya 35mm (wide-angle)
**Filter:** None
**Exposure:** 1/2sec at f/22, ISO 100
**Waiting for the light:** 2 hours
**Post-processing:** Colour balance adjustment (warming)

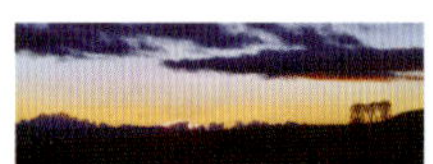

**1 Askrigg Common, The Yorkshire Dales, England**

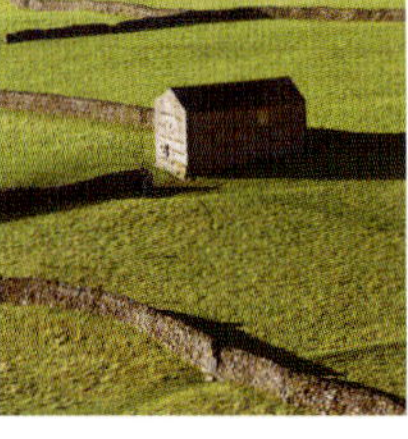

**2 Gunnerside, The Yorkshire Dales, England**

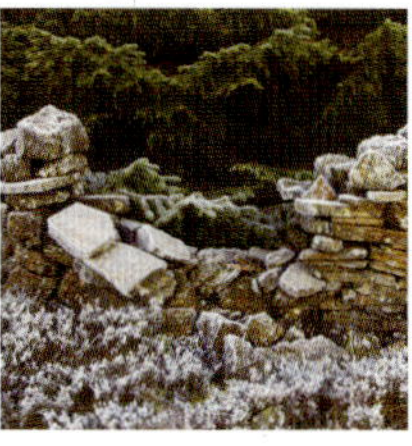

**5 Near Nenthead, Cumbria, England**

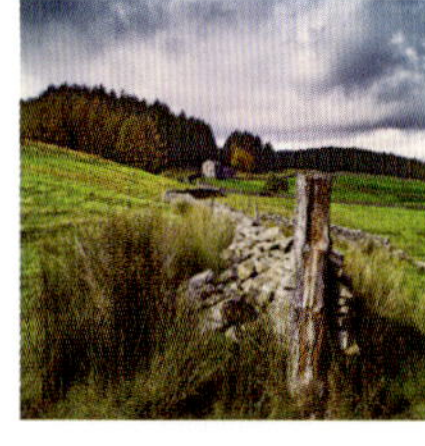

**9 Cotterdale, North Yorkshire, England**

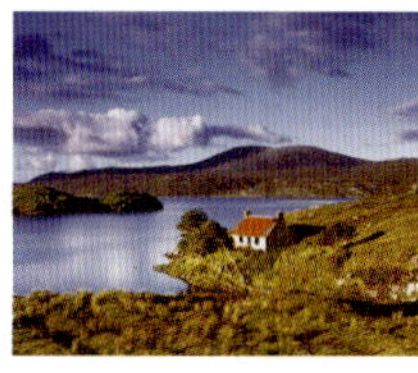

**10 The Isle of Harris, The Western Isles, Scotland**

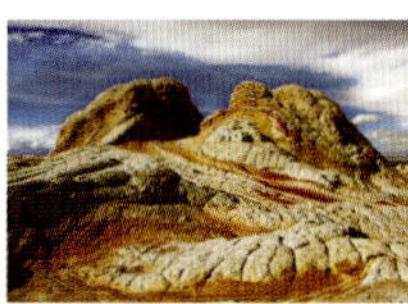

**13 White Pocket, Arizona, USA**

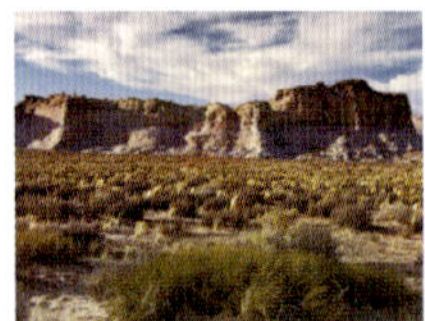

**15 Glen Canyon, Utah, USA**

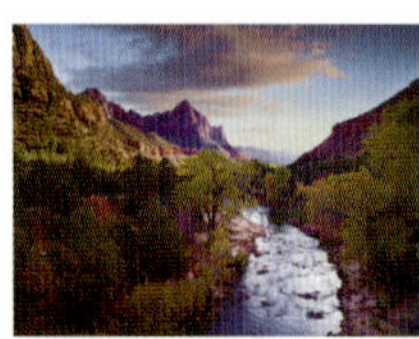

**17 Zion National Park, Utah, USA**

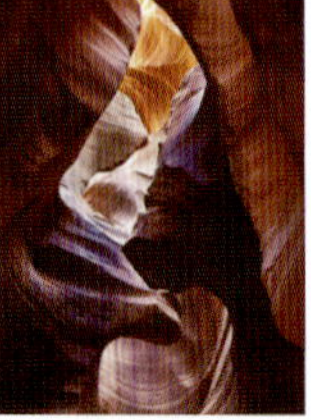

**19 Upper Antelope Canyon, Arizona, USA**

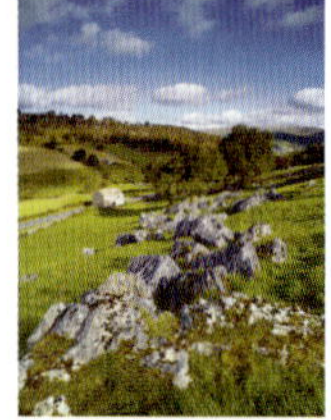

**21 Upper Wharfedale, The Yorkshire Dales, England**

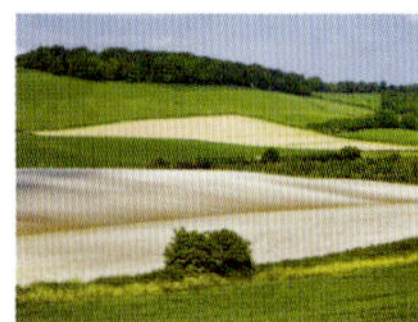

**23 Teglease Down, Hampshire, England**

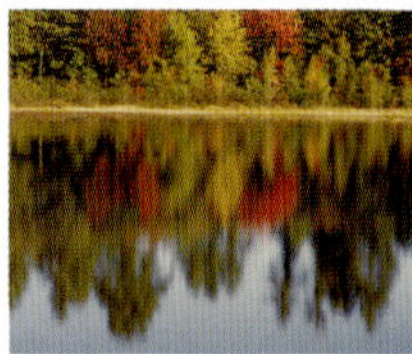

**25 Near Windham, Maine, USA**

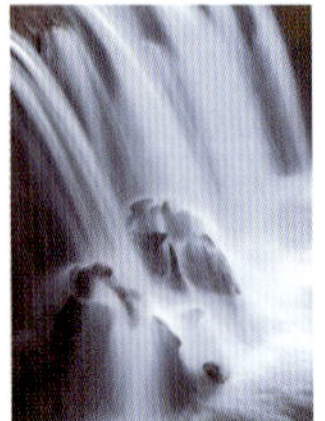

**27 Cenarth Falls, Ceredigion, Wales**

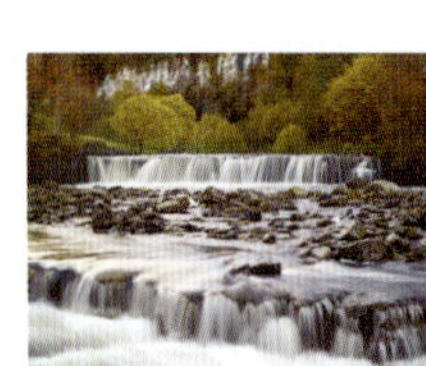

**29 Wain Wath Force, The Yorkshire Dales, England**

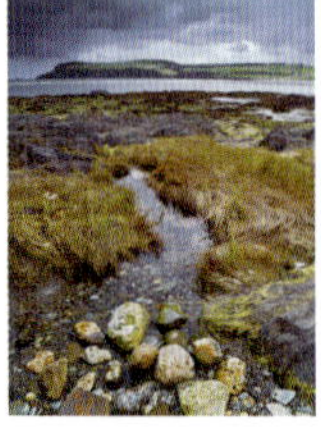

**31 Newport Bay, Pembrokeshire, Wales**

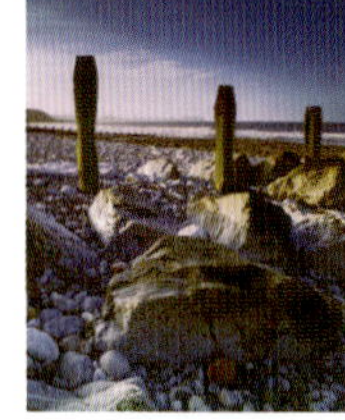

**33 Llandulas, Clwyd, Wales**

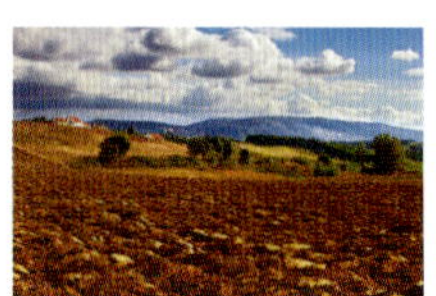

**34 Near Rio Maior, Portugal**

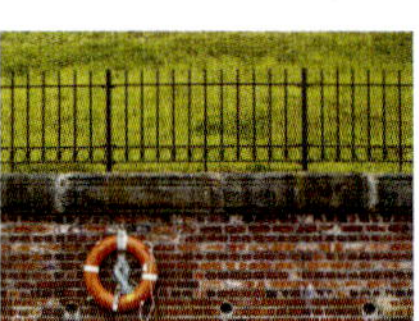

**37 Egremont, Wirral, England**

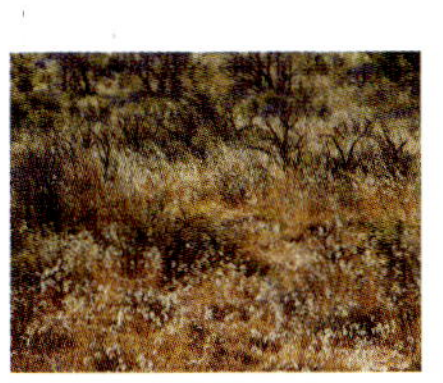

**39 Vermilion Cliffs
Wilderness, Arizona, USA**

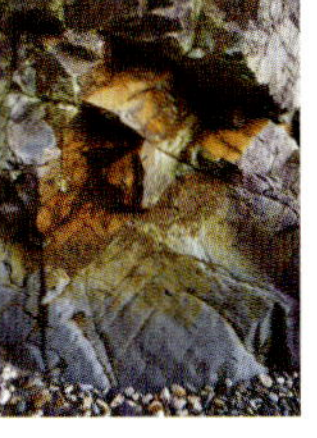

**41 St Brides Bay,
Pembrokeshire, Wales**

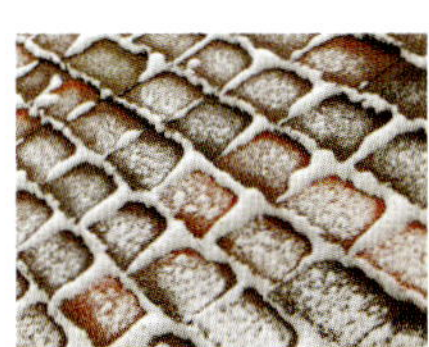

**43 Bala, Snowdonia,
Wales**

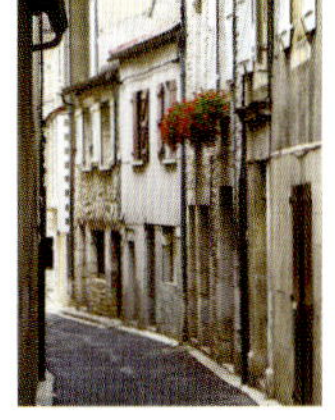

**45 Souillac,
The Dordogne, France**

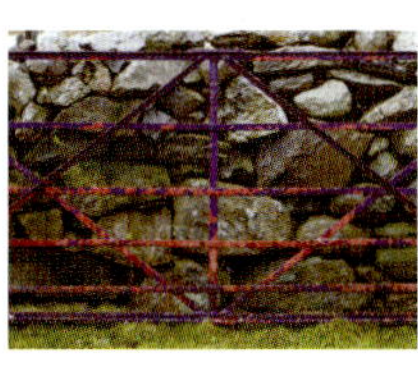

**47 Nant Ffrancon,
Snowdonia, Wales**

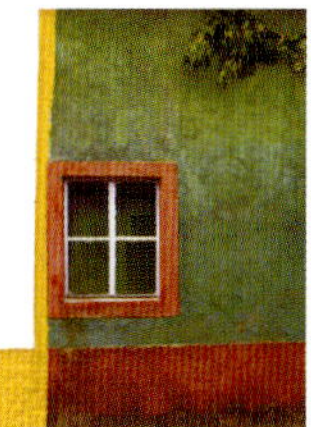

**49 Arneiro, Portugal**

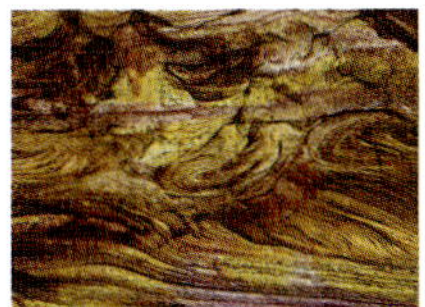

**51 South Coyote Buttes,
Arizona, USA**

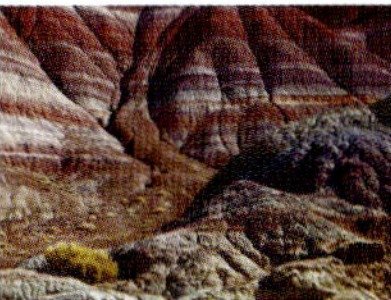

**53 Paria Canyon,
Utah, USA**

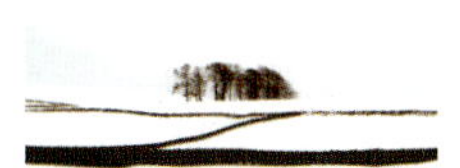

**55 Thornton Rust, The
Yorkshire Dales, England**

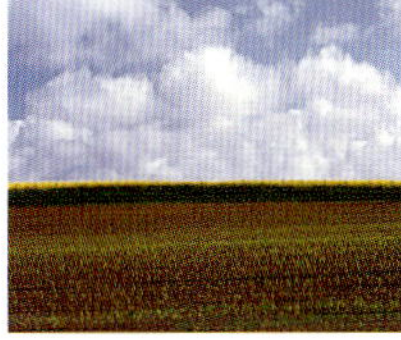

**57 Thurstaston, The
Wirral Peninsula, England**

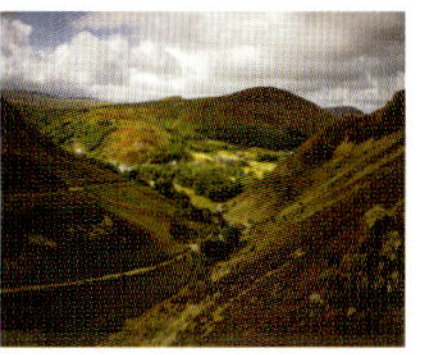

**58 The Sychnant Pass,
Clwyd, Wales**

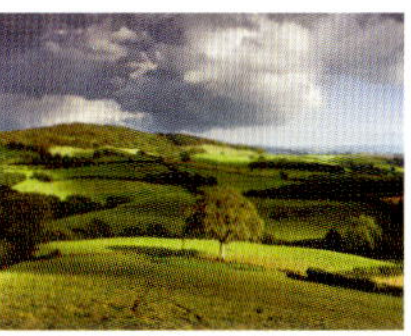

**61 Near Beaminster,
Dorset, England**

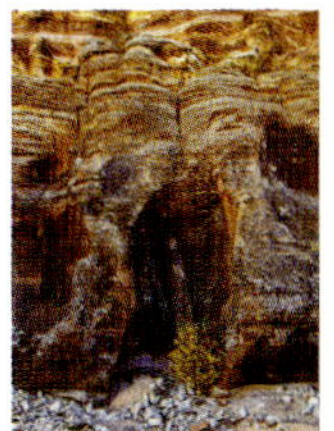

**63 Zion National Park,
Utah, USA**

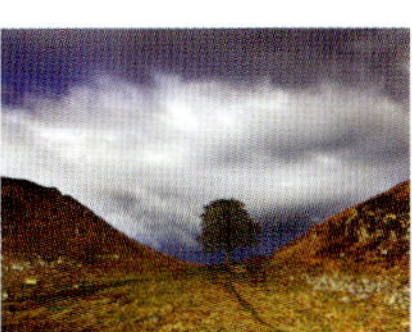

**65 Hadrian's Wall,
Northumberland, England**

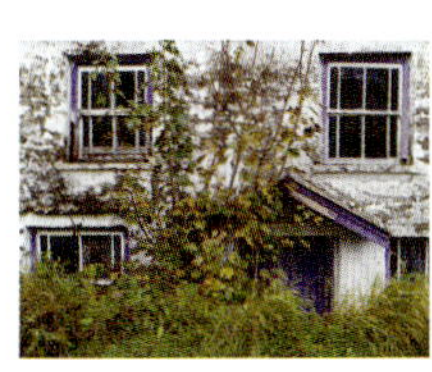

**67 Near Hawes, The
Yorkshire Dales, England**

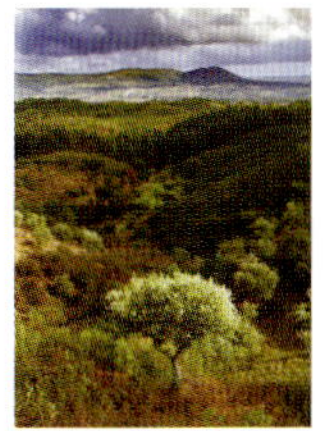

**69 Near Fratel,
Portugal**

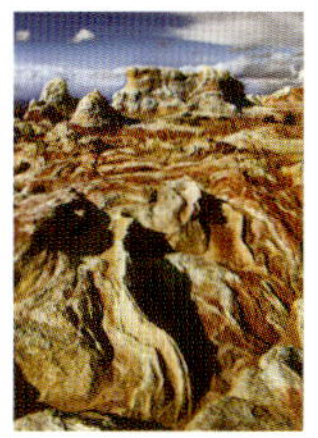

**71 White Pocket,
Arizona, USA**

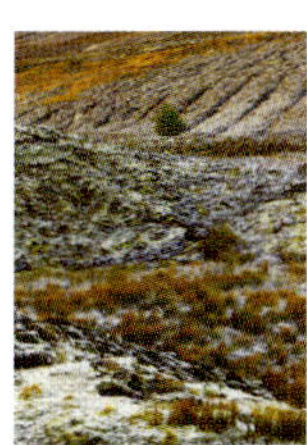

**73 Near Hexham,
Northumberland, England**

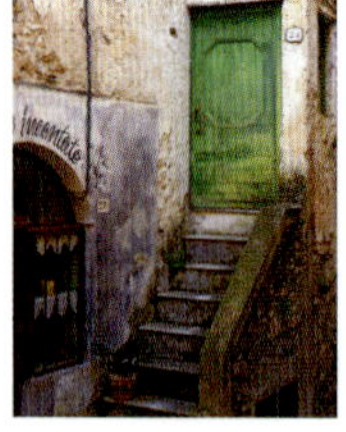

**75 San Biagio,
Imperia, Italy**

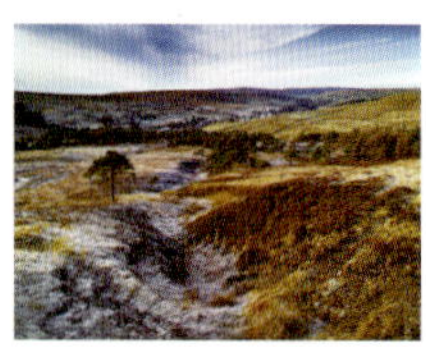

**77 Nenthead, Cumbria,
England**

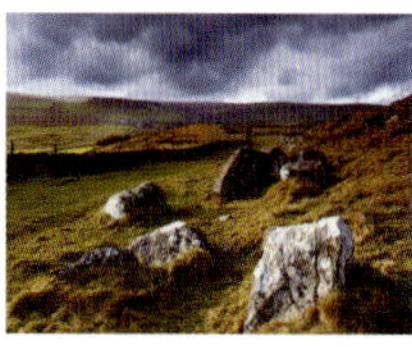

**79 Near Buxton,
Derbyshire, England**

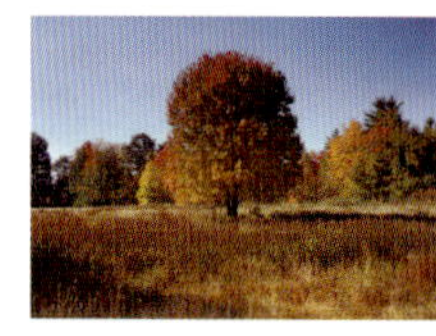

**80 Near South Windham,
Maine, USA**

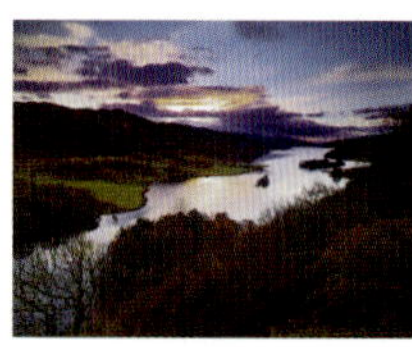

**83 Loch Rannoch,
Perthshire, Scotland**

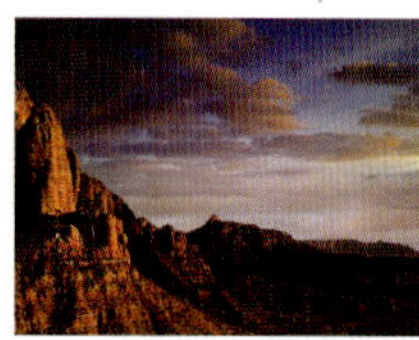

**85 Kolob Mountains,
Utah, USA**

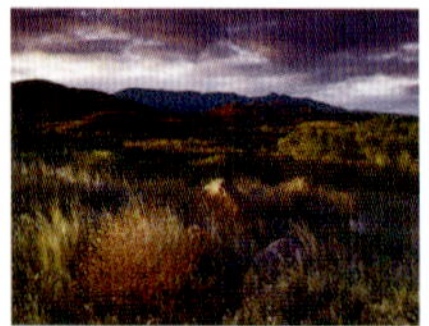

**87 Red Cliffs, Utah, USA**

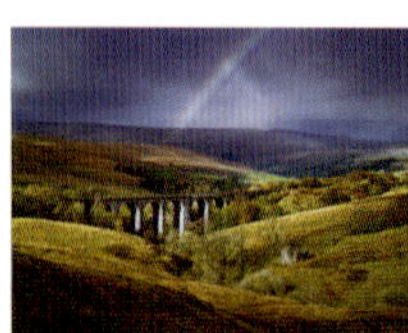

**89 Dent Dale, The
Yorkshire Dales, England**

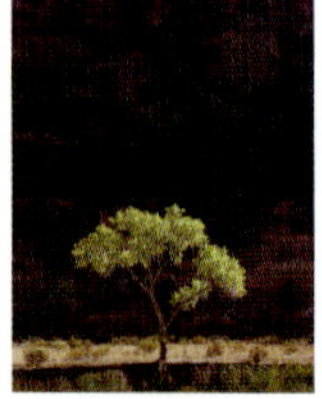

**91 Zion National Park,
Utah, USA**

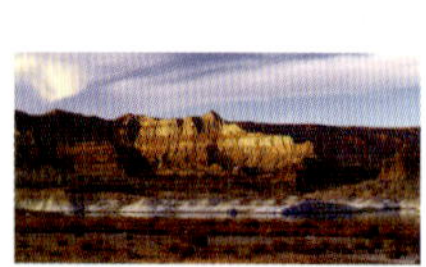

**93 Lake Powell,
Arizona, USA**

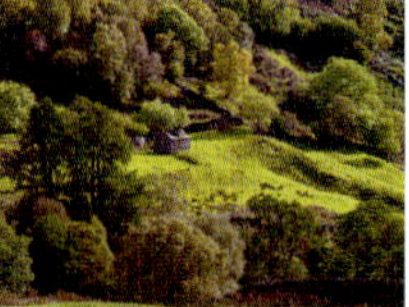

**95 Near Keld, The
Yorkshire Dales, England**

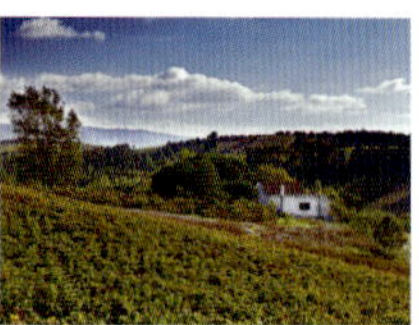

**97 Near Obidos, Portugal**

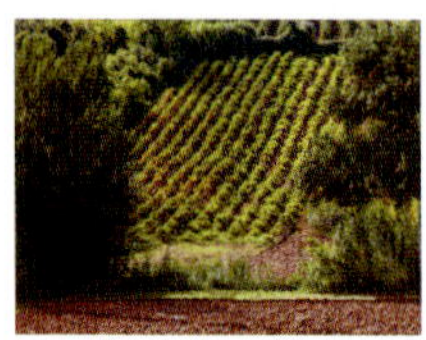

**99 Near Rio Maior,
Portugal**

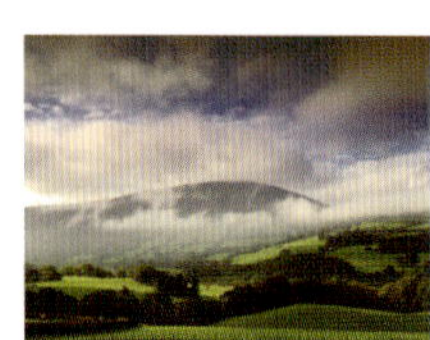

**101 Near Llangynidr, The
Brecon Beacons, Wales**

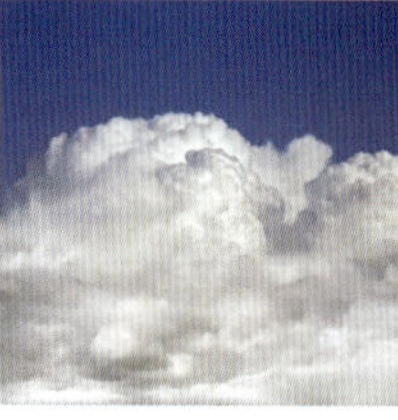

**102 Cloud above the
Brittany Coast, France**

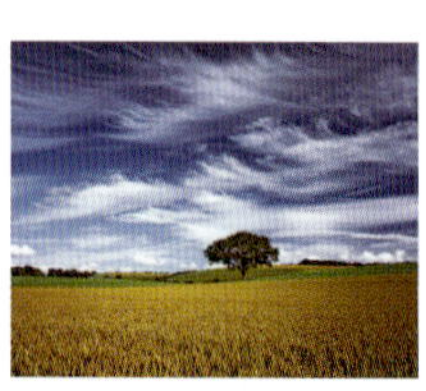

**105 Near Petersfield,
Hampshire, England**

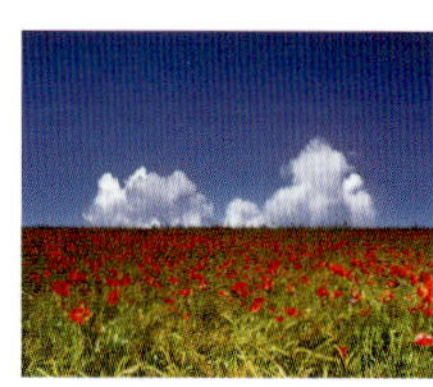

**107 Near East Meon,
Hampshire, England**

**109 Barmouth Bay,
Gwynedd, Wales**

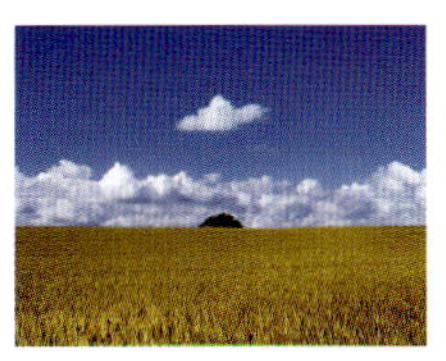

**111 Near Petersfield, Hampshire, England**

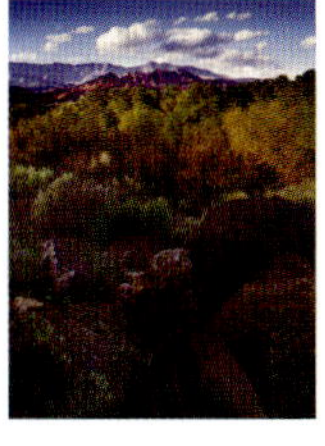

**113 Red Cliffs Reserve, Utah, USA**

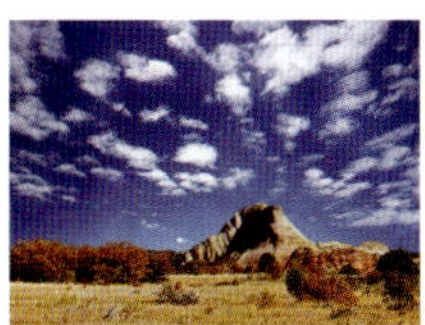

**115 Near Kolob, Utah, USA**

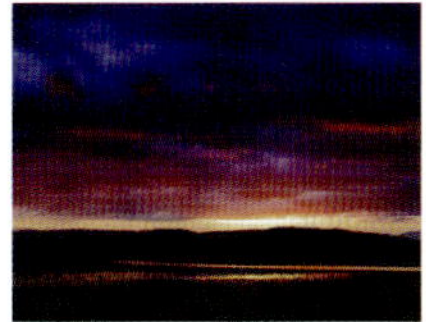

**117 The Dee Estuary, Clwyd, Wales**

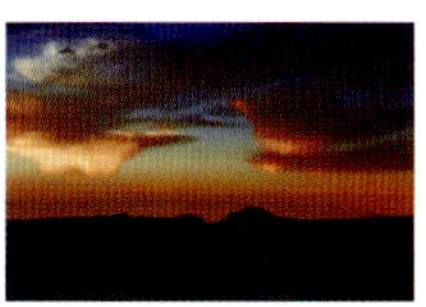

**119 Paria Mountains, Arizona, USA**

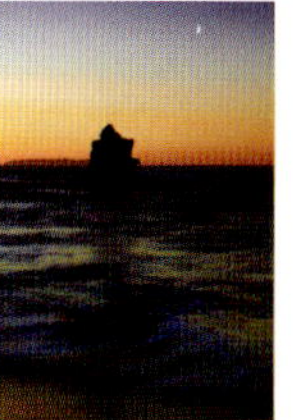

**121 Peniche, Portugal**

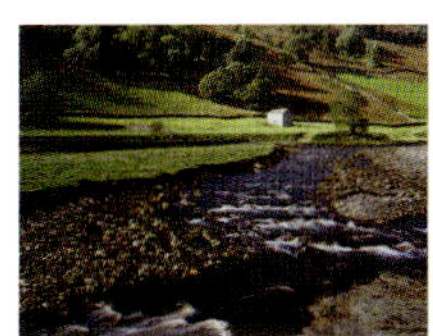

**122 The River Swale, The Yorkshire Dales, England**

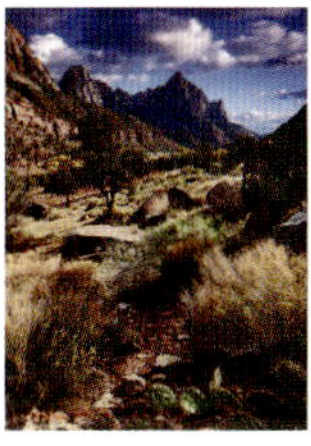

**125 Zion National Park, Utah, USA**

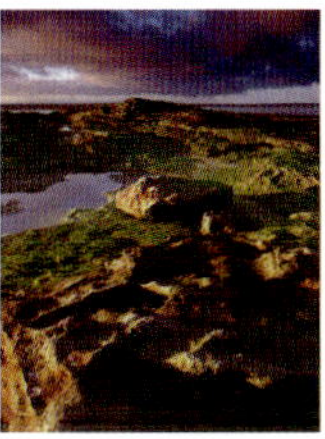

**127 Hoylake Beach, The Wirral Peninsula, England**

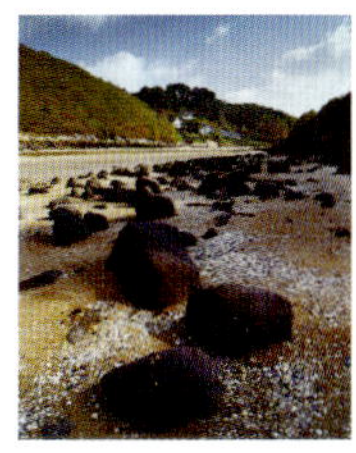

**129 Le Yaudet, Brittany, France**

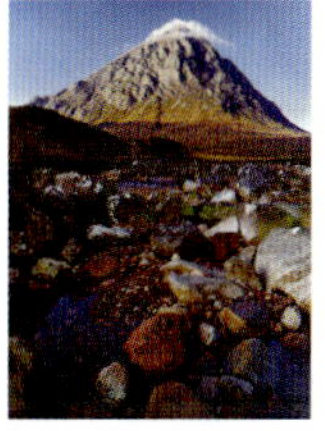

**131 Buachaillie Etive Mor, The Highlands, Scotland**

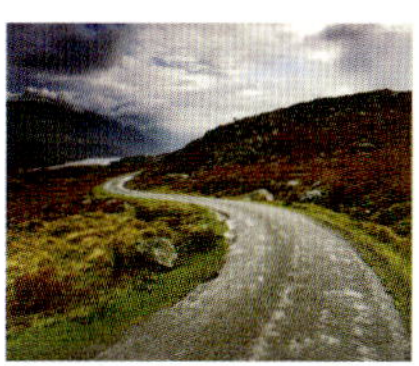

**133 Near Llanwrst, Snowdonia, Wales**

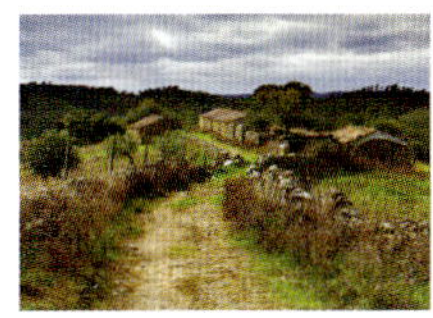

**135 Silveira, Castelo Branco, Portugal**

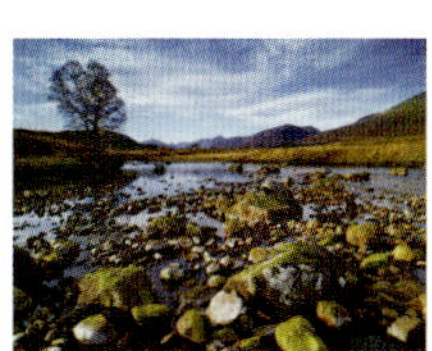

**137 Abhainn Shira, The Highlands, Scotland**

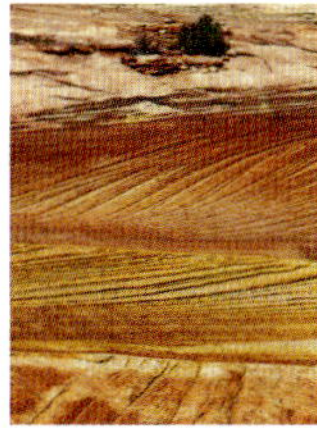

**139 Zion National Park, Utah, USA**

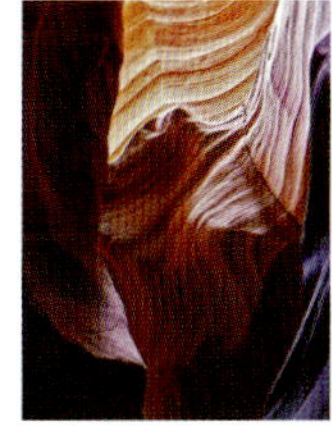

**141 Upper Antelope Canyon, Arizona, USA**

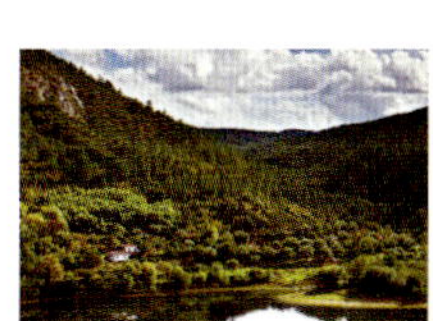

**143 Rio Tejo, Vila Velha Da Rodao, Portugal**

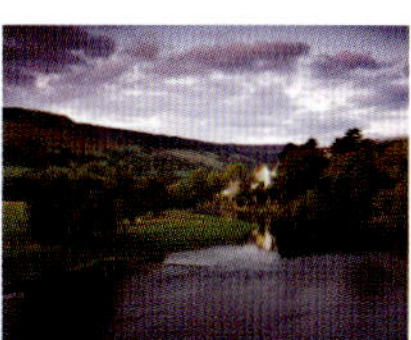

**144 The River Dee, Llangollen, Wales**

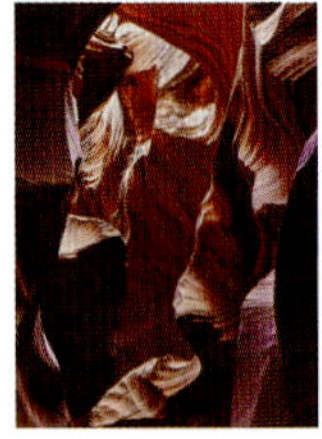

**147 Lower Antelope Canyon, Arizona, USA**

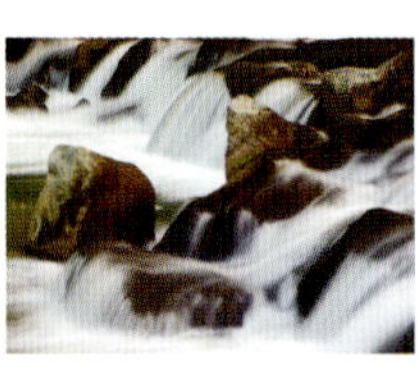

**149 Zion National Park, Utah, USA**

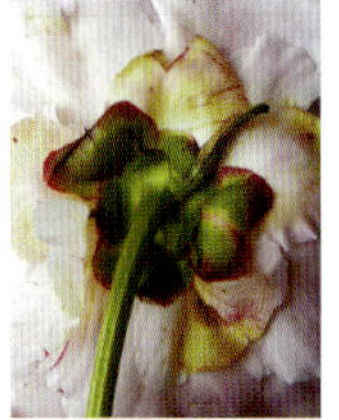

**151 The Wirral Peninsula, Merseyside, England**

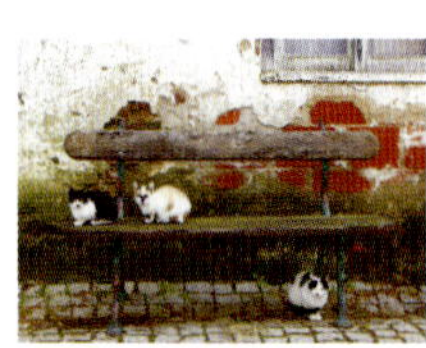

**153 Riscada, Castelo Branco, Portugal**

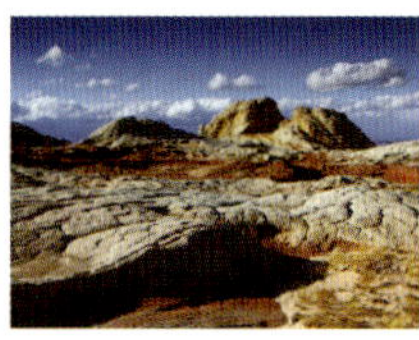

**155 White Pocket, Arizona, USA**

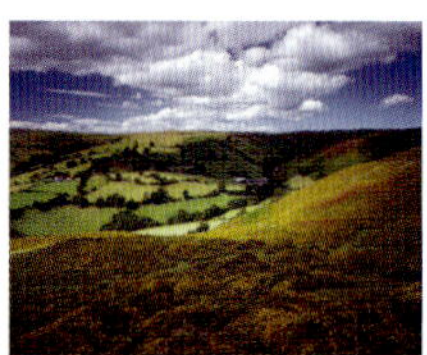

**157 Llantysilio, Clwyd, Wales**

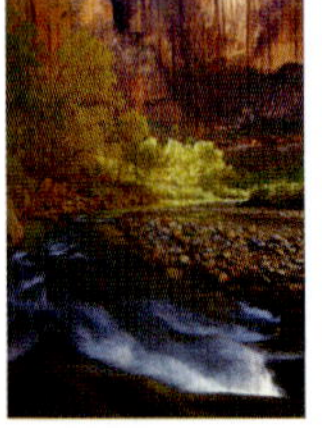

**159 Zion National Park, Utah, USA**

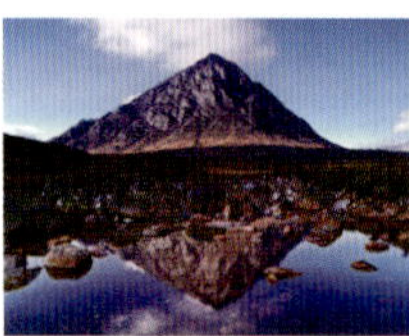

**161 Buachaillie Etive Mor, The Highlands, Scotland**

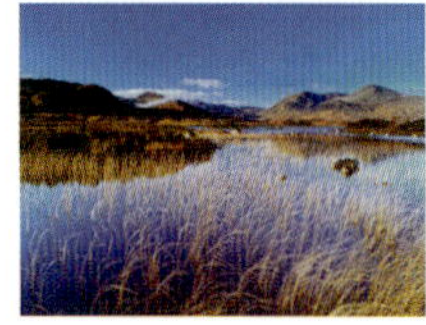

**163 Loch Nah Achlaise, Rannoch Moor, Scotland**

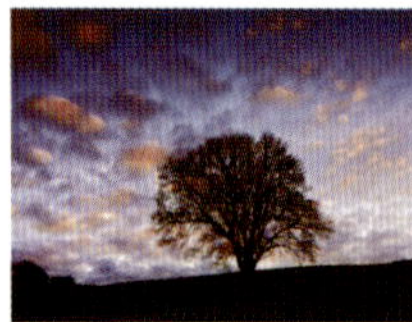

**165 Near Fourstones, Northumberland, England**

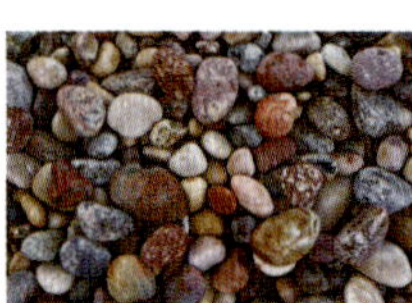

**166 Lochinver Bay, Sutherland, Scotland**

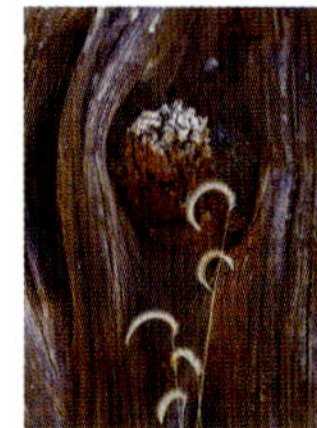

**169 Near Page, Arizona, USA**

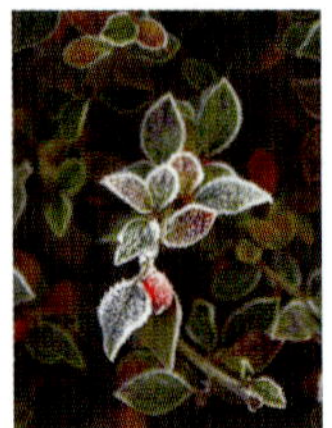

**171 Thurstaston, The Wirral Peninsula, England**

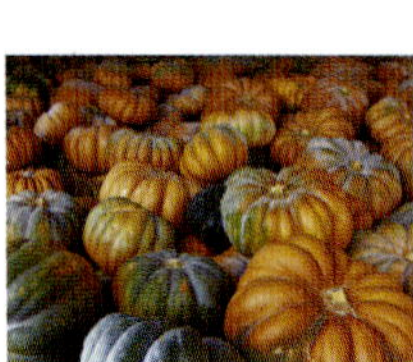

**173 Near Ferrel, Portugal**

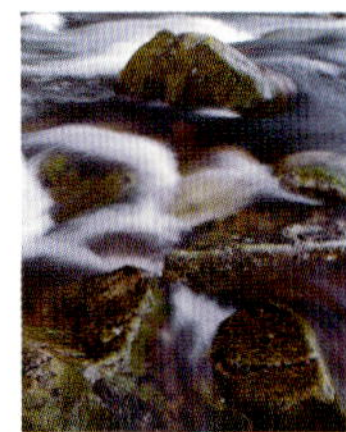

**175 The River Etive, Rannoch Moor, Scotland**

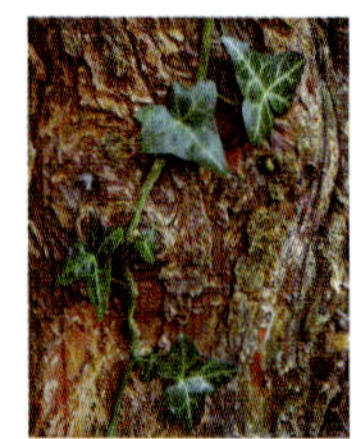

**177 Phoenicia Wild Forest, New York State, USA**

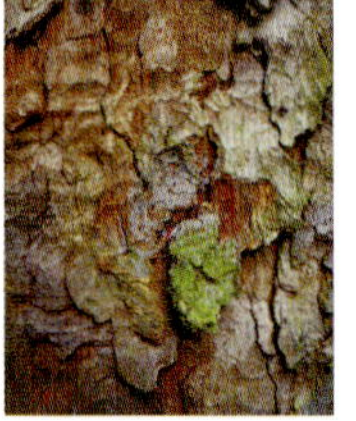

**179 Indian Wilderness, New York State, USA**

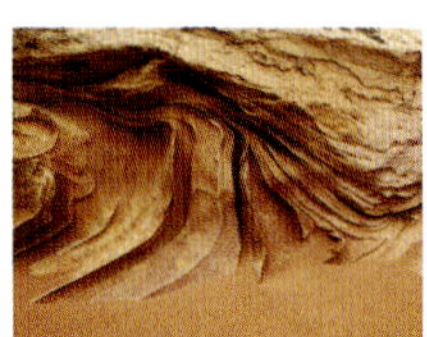

**181 South Coyote Buttes, Arizona, USA**

**Angle of incidence** The angle between the incident light falling on the subject and the reflected light entering the camera lens.

**Angle of view** The angle seen by a given lens. The shorter the focal length, the wider the angle of view. With the subject-to-camera distance, this determines the field of view.

**Aperture** The hole or opening formed by the leaf diaphragm inside the lens through which light passes to expose the film or sensor. The size of the aperture relative to the focal length is denoted by f-numbers (f-stops).

**Aperture priority** Automatic in-camera metering of exposure based on a pre-selected aperture. Exposure is therefore adjusted by the shutter speed.

**Aspect ratio** The ratio of the width to the height of the frame.

**Autoexposure (AE)** The ability of a camera to recommend the correct exposure for a particular scene.

**Autofocus (AF)** An in-camera system for automatically focusing the image.

**Backlighting** Light coming from behind the subject shining towards the camera.

**Bracketing** Making a series of exposures of the same subject at different exposure settings, typically in steps of 1/2- or 1/3-stops.

**Cable release** A flexible cable, used to minimize the risk of camera shake, which is attached to the camera to enable remote release of the shutter.

**Camera Raw** A file format offered by most digital cameras. It records the picture as an unprocessed, uncompressed image. It can be considered the digital equivalent of an unprocessed film negative.

**Centre-weighted metering** Type of metering system that takes the majority of its reading from the centre portion of the frame. Suitable for portraits or scenes where subjects fill the centre of the frame.

**Chromatic aberration** Colour fringing caused by the camera lens not focusing different wavelengths (colours) of light on the same focal plane.

**Colour cast** A variation of the colour of light, which causes a distortion in the colour in a photograph.

**Colour correction filter** A filter that is used to compensate for a colour cast, the most common example being the 81 series of warming filters. *See* Warm filter.

**Colour temperature** The colour of light has a colour temperature. This depends on a number of factors, including its source and the time of day. It is measured on the Kelvin scale: lower temperatures produce warmer colours and vice versa.

**Contrast** The range between the highlight and shadow areas of a negative, print, transparency or digital image. Also refers to the difference in illumination between adjacent areas.

**Converging parallels** The distortion of parallel lines, which appear as converging angled lines. This commonly occurs when a building is photographed with the camera pointing at an upwards angle.

**Cropping** Printing only part of the available image from the negative, transparency or digital image, usually to improve composition.

**Definition** The clarity of an image in terms of both its sharpness and contrast.

**Depth of field (DOF)** The zone of acceptable sharpness in front of and behind the point at which the lens is focused. This zone is controlled by three elements: aperture – the smaller the aperture, the greater the DOF; the camera-to-subject distance – the further away the subject, the greater the DOF; and the focal length of the lens – the shorter the focal length, the longer the DOF.

**Diffraction** A change in the direction and intensity of light as it passes through an aperture. The smaller the aperture, the more noticeable will be the effect.

**Diffuse lighting** Lighting that is low or moderate in contrast, such as the light on an overcast day.

**Digital SLR** (digital single-lens reflex) *See* SLR (single-lens reflex).

**Dynamic range** *See* Tonal range.

**Exposure** The amount of light reaching the film or sensor. This is controlled by a combination of aperture and shutter speed. Alternatively, the act of taking a photograph, as in 'making an exposure'.

**Exposure compensation** A level of adjustment given to autoexposure settings. Generally it is used to compensate for known inadequacies in the way a meter will usually recommend a reading, which may result in underexposure such as snow scenes.

**Exposure latitude** The extent to which exposure can be reduced or increased without causing an unacceptable under- or overexposure of the image.

**Exposure meter** A device, either built into the camera or separate, with a light-sensitive cell used for measuring light levels, used as an aid for selecting the exposure setting.

**Exposure value** A single value given for a measurement of light that indicates an overall value that can be reached by a combination of shutter speed and aperture for a particular ISO setting.

**Field of view** The actual dimensions of the scene that can be captured on film or sensor. This depends on the film/sensor format, the angle of the lens, and the camera-to-subject distance.

**Flare** Non-image-forming light reflected inside a lens or camera in an unwanted manner. It can create multi-coloured circles or loss of contrast and can be reduced by multiple lens coatings, low-dispersion lens elements or a lens hood.

**F-numbers** A series of numbers on the lens aperture ring and/or the camera's LCD panel that indicate the size of the lens aperture relative to its focal length. The higher the number, the smaller the aperture.

**Focal length** The distance between the film or sensor and optical centre of the lens when focused at infinity.

**Frontal lighting** Light shining on the surface of the subject facing the camera.

**Highlights** The brightest part of an image.

**Histogram** A digital graph indicating the light values of an image.

**Hyperfocal distance** The closest distance at which a lens records details sharply when focused at infinity. Focusing on the hyperfocal distance produces maximum depth of field, which extends from half the hyperfocal distance to infinity.

**Image sensor** The digital equivalent of film. The sensor converts an optical image to an electrical charge that is captured and stored.

**Image stabilization** An in-camera feature that compensates for any movement of the camera during exposure.

**Incident light** Light falling on a surface as opposed to light reflected from that surface. An incident light meter measures the light before it reaches the surface. Compare with Reflected light.

**ISO rating** Measures the degree of sensitivity to light of a film or sensor, as determined by the International Standards Organization. As the ISO number doubles, the amount of light required to correctly expose the film/sensor is halved.

**Jpeg** A common file format used by digital cameras. It compresses the image, and over time these images can be affected by a degradation of image quality.

**Large-format** A camera that uses sheet film of 5 x 4in or larger.

**Law of reciprocity** A change in one exposure setting can be compensated for by an equal and opposite change in the other. For example, the exposure setting of 1/60sec at f/11 produces exactly the same exposure value as 1/30sec at f/16. *See* Reciprocity failure.

**LCD** Stands for 'liquid crystal display'. It is used in the display screen included on most digital cameras.

**Medium-format** Refers to cameras using rollfilm (normally 120 or 220 film), or a digital sensor of equivalent size, that measures approximately 2¼in (6cm) wide.

**Megapixel** One million pixels.

**Mid-tones** Parts of an image with tones of an intermediate value; i.e., the tonal values between the highlights and shadows.

**Neutral density (ND) filter** A filter that reduces the brightness of an image without affecting its colour.

**Neutral density graduated (ND grad) filter** A neutral density filter that is graduated to allow different amounts of light to pass through it at different parts. These filters are used to balance naturally occurring bright and dark tones. In landscape photography they are commonly used to balance the exposure values of sky and landscape.

**Noise** Graininess in an image that becomes apparent during long exposures and when using high ISO settings.

**Panoramic camera** A camera with a frame of which the aspect ratio of width to height is greater than 3:2.

**Pixel** Short for 'picture element', this is the basic building block of every digital image.

**Polarizing filter** A filter that absorbs light vibrating in a single plane while transmitting light vibrating in multiple planes. When placed in front of a camera lens, it can eliminate undesirable reflections from a subject such as water, glass or other objects with a shiny surface, except metal. It is also used to saturate colour.

**Prime lens** A lens that has a fixed focal length.

**Raw** *See* Camera Raw.

**Reciprocity failure** At shutter speeds slower than 1sec, the law of reciprocity begins to fail because the sensitivity of film reduces as the length of exposure increases. This affects different films to different extents, but means that the exposure will need to be increased slightly to compensate.

**Reflected light** Light reflected from the surface of a subject. The type of light that is measured by through-the-lens meters and handheld reflected light meters such as spot meters.

**Resolution** The amount of detail in an image. The higher the resolution, the larger the potential maximum size of the printed image.

**Shutter** A mechanism that can be opened and closed to control the length of exposure.

**Shutter release** The button or lever on a camera that causes the shutter to open.

**Shutter speed** The length of time light is allowed to pass through the open shutter of the camera. Together, the aperture and shutter speed determine the exposure.

**Sidelighting** Light shining across the subject, illuminating one side of it. The preferred light of most photographers, it gives shape, depth and texture to a landscape, particularly when the sun is low in the sky.

**SLR** (single-lens reflex) A type of camera that allows you to see the view through the camera's lens as you look in the viewfinder.

**Soft focus filter** A filter used to soften an image by introducing spherical aberration, it is not the same as out-of-focus; a sharp image is necessary in order for the effect to succeed.

**Spot meter** An exposure meter that measures a small, precise area. It enables a number of exposure readings to be taken of different parts of a subject and therefore provides a very accurate method of metering.

**Standard lens** A lens with a focal length approximately equal to the diagonal measurement of the film format. It produces an image approximately equivalent to that seen by the human eye, and equates to the following focal lengths: 35mm for digital APS-C cameras, 50mm for 35mm film or digital cameras, 80mm for 645, 90mm for 67, and 150mm for 5 x 4in cameras.

**Telephoto lens** A lens with a long length and narrow angle of view. When used at a long distance from the subject, a telephoto lens can help create the impression of compressed distance, with subjects appearing to be closer to the camera than they actually are.

**Through-the-lens (TTL) metering** A meter built into a camera that determines exposure for the scene by reading light that passes through the lens during picture taking.

**Tiff** Stands for 'tagged image file format'. It is a common image format supported by most types of photo-editing software.

**Tonal range** The range between the darkest and lightest areas of an image.

**UV filter** A filter that reduces UV interference in the final image. This is particularly useful for reducing haze in landscape photographs.

**Vignetting** The cropping or darkening of corners of an image. This can be caused by a lens hood, filter holder or the lens itself. Many lenses do vignette, but to a minor extent. This can be more of a problem with zoom lenses rather than prime lenses.

**Warm filter** A filter designed to bring a warm tone to an image to compensate for a blue cast, which can sometimes be present in daylight, particularly with an overcast sky. The filters are known as the 81 series, 81A being the weakest and 81E the strongest.

**White balance** A function of a digital camera that allows the correct colour balance to be recorded for any given lighting situation.

**Wide-angle lens** A lens with a short focal length and a wide-angle of view.

**Zoom lens** A lens with a focal length that can be varied.

## ABOUT THE AUTHOR

Peter Watson is a self-taught landscape photographer who has been photographing the landscape since the 1970s. He is based in England and travels extensively throughout Britain, Europe and the USA. His work is published internationally and is widely used in many forms of advertising and media.

Born in Wallasey, England, Peter's photographic career started in his teenage years when he photographed and produced his own black-and-white prints in an improvised darkroom. They were sold in a local gallery, and this early success encouraged Peter to pursue a career as a photographer. He studied art and graphic design and in 1993 obtained a diploma in photography from the New York Institute of Photography.

Before becoming a full-time professional landscape photographer, Peter worked in advertising and commercial photography. As well as continuing to practise photography, he teaches workshops and produces practical photography books and articles. He has previously written six books: *Seasons of Landscape*, *Reading the Landscape*, *Capturing the Light*, *Light in the Landscape – a Photographer's Year*, *A Field Guide to Landscape Photography* and *Views Across the Landscape*.

## EQUIPMENT USED

Below is a list of the equipment used in the making of the photographs in this book:

**Cameras**
Canon EOS 7D
Mamiya 645 AFDII with Mamiya ZD and Phase One digital backs
Mamiya RB67

**Lenses**
Canon 24–105mm L IS
Canon EF 300mm IS USM
Mamiya 35mm, 80mm, 150mm, 210mm, 250mm, 300mm
Tokina 12–24mm AT-X PRO DX

**Filters**
Lee ND hard graduated from 0.3 to 0.75, circular polarizer and Lee filter holder system. (Graduated filters are available with hard and soft graduation. Hard-grad filters have a more abrupt transition from dark to light. I prefer this, although soft filters might be preferable with small sensors, particularly when using small apertures.)

**Tripods**
Benbo Mini Trekker
Uni-Loc Major 2300 and 1600
Velbon Ultra Rexi L

**Ball and socket heads**
Manfrotto 054 with quick-release plate
Uni-Loc with quick-release plate

**Viewfinder**
Linhof Multifocus

**A**

abstract images 22, 36, 42, 50, 180
Analysis of Beauty, The (Hogarth) 132
angle of light 14, 70, 92, 94, 142
angle of view 72, 74, 150, 187
angles, softening 66
animals 152
aperture 128, 170, 172, 187
autumn 24

**B**

backlighting 32, 94, 96, 98, 187
balance
    light and shadow 60, 64
    mountains 12, 62, 129
    rule of thirds 76, 78, 178
    skies 64, 112, 129
    symmetry 66
ball and socket heads 130, 140
bark 176, 178
beaches 40
blind spots 60, 124
bracketing 187

**C**

cameras types 189
canyons 18, 146
caves 18–19
close-up images 166–181
clouds 106, 110, 112, 114, 129
coastal locations 30–33, 40, 120
colour see also tonal variations
    blocks 44, 48, 106
    close-up images 168, 174, 176
    enhancing 154
    forms and shapes 36, 38
    limiting 44, 66, 168
    shadow 32
compression 72, 138, 146, 174
contours 22, 60, 68, 138

converging lines 30, 74, 130, 132, 134
countryside 20–23, 60, 110
cropping 187
curves
    close-up images 168, 176
    coastal locations 30
    contrasting with 142
    multiple 134
    S-shaped 132, 134
Curves tools 16

**D**

darkening skies 16, 22, 96
dawn 32, 108, 116, 118, 162
dead spaces 60, 134, 148, 174
definition 187
depth 20, 38, 68, 122–143
depth of field 128, 170, 172, 187
diffuse lighting 187
diminishing size 124, 136, 172
dusk 32, 108, 116, 118, 120, 164

**E**

equipment 189
exposure 98, 100, 120, 178, 187

**F**

far distance 20, 32
filters 189
flat light 28, 30, 74, 174, 180
focal length 72, 74, 174, 187
focal points
    animals 152
    balance 60
    caves 18
    diminishing size of 124, 136, 172
    middle distance 136
    mountains and wilderness 12
    non-specific 172
    rolling landscape 22
    scale 52
    spotlighting 90

foliage 170
foregrounds
    adding depth 68, 124, 126, 128
    mountains and wilderness 12
    reflections 160
    viewpoints 70
forests 24–25
forms 36
frontal lighting 187
frost 170

**G**

gallery 182–186
glossary 187–189
graphic lines 56, 138

**H**

Highlights see Shadows/Highlights tools
Hogarth, William: Analysis of Beauty, The 132
hyperfocal distance 128

**I**

image compression 72, 138, 146, 174
images, seeing 34–57
image sharpness 128
image stabilization 74, 152
impact, creating 144–165

**L**

landscape selection 10–33
Lasso tools 82, 96
lenses 189
lens flare 82
light see also dawn; dusk; sunlight
    angle of 14, 70, 92, 94, 142
    backlighting 32, 94, 96, 98, 187
    balance 60, 64
    coastal locations 32–33
    colour 154
    contours 22, 68
    flat 28, 30, 74, 174, 180
    and location 156
    quality of 82
    and shadow 80–101
    spotlighting 90, 92, 158
    tonal variations 28, 32, 98, 118, 150
lines
    close-up images 168, 176
    converging 30, 74, 130, 132, 134
    graphic 56, 138
    softening 66
    vertical 44
low-angled light 92
low viewpoints 124, 126

**M**

man-made structures 42
maps, planning with 20, 88
merging images 18, 100
middle distance 14, 20, 76, 136
minimalism 54, 56
moon 108
mountains 12–19, 52, 84

**N**

neutral density (ND) graduated filters
    role of 100
    skies 20, 30, 98, 108, 118

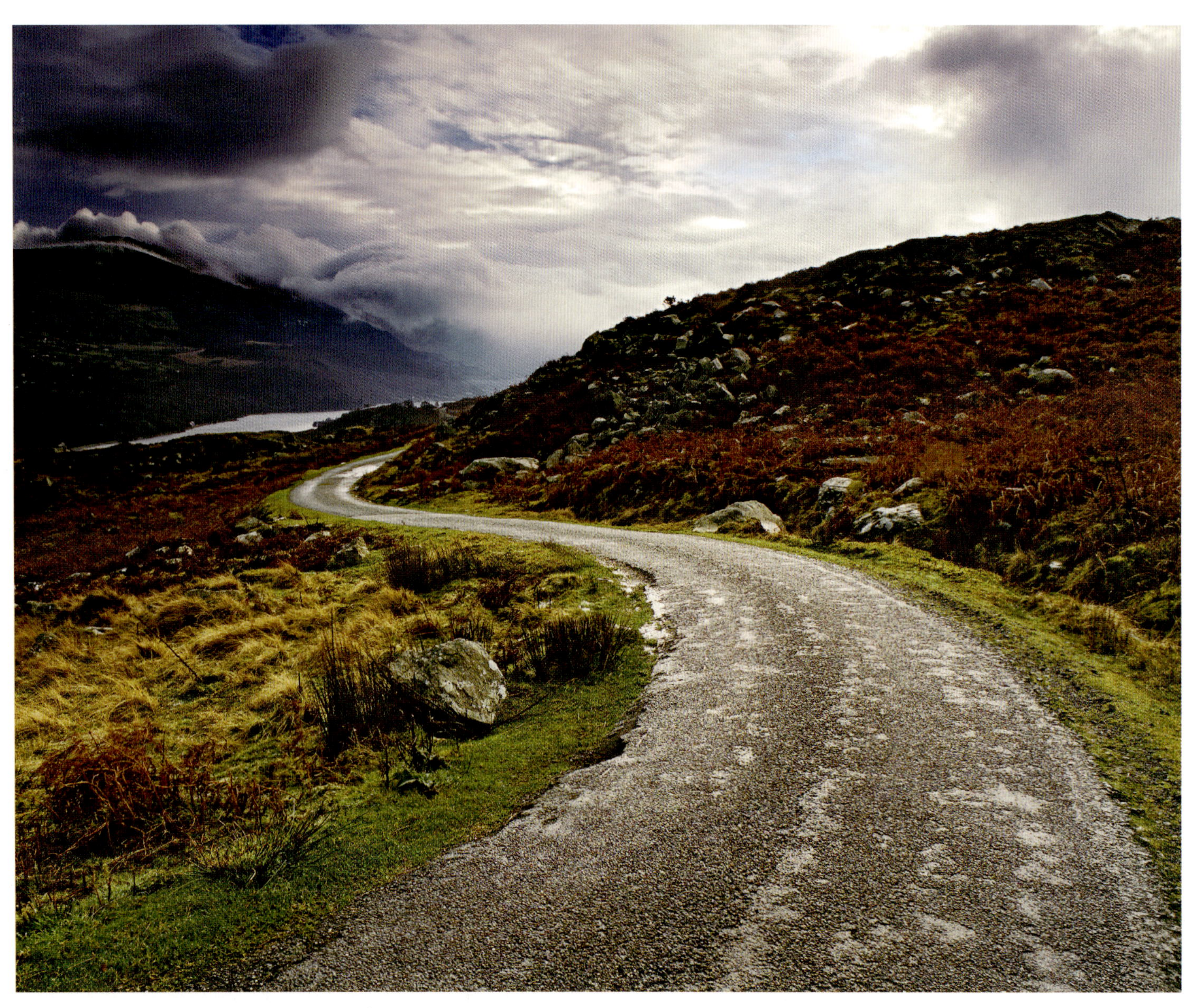

To order a book, or request a catalogue, contact:
**Ammonite Press**
AE Publications Ltd, 166 High Street, Lewes,
East Sussex, BN7 1XU, United Kingdom
Tel: +44 (0)1273 488006
www.ammonitepress.com